Self and Cinema

A TRANSFORMALIST PERSPECTIVE

BEVERLE HOUSTON & MARSHA KINDER

REDGRAVE PUBLISHING COMPANY   Pleasantville, NY 10570

O 3650

PN
1995
.H68

In Memory of Lou Stone

CONTENTS

Introduction

A Transformalist Perspective

The way to deal with the problem of "subjectivity," that shocking business of being preoccupied with the tiny individual who is at the same time caught up in such an explosion of terrible and marvellous possibilities, is to see him as a microcosm and in this way to break through the personal, the subjective, making the personal general, as indeed life always does, transforming a private experience . . . into something much larger: growing up is after all only the understanding that one's unique and incredible experience is what everyone shares.

Doris Lessing, "Introduction," *The Golden Notebook*

The way OUT is the way IN.

William Burroughs, *Naked Lunch*

Transformalism is a method of criticism that explores the ways in which artistic and cultural conventions are transformed in the context of individual works, creating a unique combination of the new and the familiar. Rooted in formalism and phenomenology, it attempts to integrate three sets of polarities: (1) the tension between centripetal meanings that are created within the individual work and centrifugal meanings deriving from and influencing other works and the outside world; (2) the tension between the subjective experience of the artist and audience and the objective existence of the artifact and the society that produced it; (3) the relationship between the individual text and the structural systems and codes of meanings it expresses. All three bi-polarities center on the relations between the one and the many, the individual and the community, the self and the other.

Transformalism assumes that a film is like a human being. Each is individual in its arrangement of characteristics and the dynamics of its behavior. The combination of qualities is complex, and no two are exactly alike. Yet, at the same time, films are members of the same species or medium with certain shared basic qualities. The enrichment of transformalist criticism, like the development of self-realization for the individual, depends on the expansion of one's ability to see, understand, and respond to as many different kinds of films as possible. In *Self and Cinema*, we explore self-realization as theme in the films, as process for the filmmakers, as a key issue implicit within current theoretical frameworks, and as development for ourselves as critics. We share Northrop Frye's assumption that:

> There is always a sense in which criticism is a form of autobiography.[1]

Like any art, films invite collaboration with their viewers, who bring their own experience to the work and discover their own potentialities in the process. It is our aim to enrich that collaboration, both intellectually and emotionally.

Transformalism is based on six key assumptions:

1) *The primacy of practical criticism*

The first responsibility of transformalism is to explore the autonomous universe of the film. We assume that each text will reveal certain foregrounded elements of the medium's potentialities, developed into significant patterns through repetition and consistency. The deeper one goes into the analysis of one film, the closer one gets to the archetypes and structural systems at the center of art and the human mind.

Transformalism does not subordinate the individual text to any theoretical framework because it assumes that practical criticism, more than any other kind, is likely to discover the authentic innovations that break through the conceptual structures of the culture and indicate new directions for criticism. This approach assumes that radical innovation comes, not only from rational adherence to or manipulation of known structures, but also, and perhaps more likely, from subversive forces, whether conscious or unconscious, that take over the creative process. Thus, the unpredictable individual transformation may advance the medium or the possibilities for humanity. Though shaped by the social, political, and economic forces of the culture, the individual artist is capable of transcending cultural limits through imaginative power.

Transformalist criticism remains open to what is new and advanced in any particular transformation. If a critical system becomes closed, it discourages experimentation and finds truly radical works to be self-indulgent, decadent, dangerous, chaotic, or simply not-art. The history of literary criticism offers many such examples, for instance, the eighteenth-century response to Shakespeare. The close-minded critics condemned his plays for violating Aristotelian rules of classical tragedy, and even the more flexible open ones argued that, although the plays reflected Shakespeare's natural genius, they would have been far better had they conformed to the rules. But a critical genius like Samuel Johnson finally realized that there was something wrong with the rules rather than with the plays. Similar prescriptions still operate in film criticism, such as the arguments for the superiority of depth focus over montage and realism over stylization, or the limited notion of "pure cinema" that some would impose on all filmmakers. Transformalism rejects such prescriptions, and acknowledges that in all media, individual works put pressure on criticism to develop new formulations.

2) *The necessity for multiple conceptual frameworks*

Transformalism assumes that the critical enterprise can be expanded by transforming and integrating multiple conceptual frameworks into a holistic methodology. This expansion was pioneered by Northrop Frye in *Anatomy of Criticism*, which is one reason we quote him so frequently throughout our book and have chosen his archetypal approach as the framework for one of our chapters. Yet, any critical system must remain open-ended, leaving room for the unknown; we expect future criticism to be enriched by what is yet unthought, unwritten, unvisualized. Flexible and generative as *Anatomy* may be, it still presents a closed system, which is implicit in the choice of a series of circles as the basic model. Recently, in reflecting on the *Anatomy*, Frye speaks to this issue:

> My work since then has assumed the shape of what Professor Jerome Bruner would call a spiral curriculum, circling around the same issues, though trying to keep them open-ended.[2]

Transformalism turns to other conceptual frameworks precisely for the discovery of new issues.

As transformalists, we assume that the foregrounded stylistic and thematic patterns of a work reveal the central issues with which it is concerned, and that a concept and a work of art may be unified in exploring the same questions about human life. Sometimes this similarity is obscured because the arts and sciences use different media and modes of discourse. Recognizing these differences, we seek the underlying similarities between art and theory and feel free to draw upon any concept or method from any discipline that will illuminate the foregrounded issues. Yet, we do not use them in their "pure" form, but as Frye suggests, in a special way:

> Structuralism, hermeneutics, phenomenalism, cultural anthro-pology, and the philosophy of language have, as I think, made a rather disappointing contribution so far to the understanding of literature, however relevant the context for it they have set up. . . they interpenetrate my critical work but keep their own context in their own discipline. For a contemporary critic interested in Freud or Wittgenstein or Lévi-Strauss, such writers, like Medi-eval angels, do not travel through space from another subject; they manifest themselves from within the subject.[3]

Though we always seek precision, we often adapt the theories we use to our transformalist goals and to the particular works we examine. However, we recognize that such an approach must rely on the refinement of theories and methods being carried out by other scholars and critics.

While the world is willing to grant that use of a variety of styles may express growth in an artist, it suspects a critic who uses a similar approach of being weak, indecisive, or uncommitted, preferring its critics to remain firmly fixed in one stance. But we would argue that this is counterproductive because it tends to narrow the range of art to which one can respond. To observe that a film focusing on individual consciousness fails to examine class structures may be valid; to show what a thing is not can be part of the process of explaining what it is. Such an observation may also reveal limitations in the film's development of its subject. However, to devote whole books and essays to these "sins of omission" is to deny experience as it is and to change the subject—from exploration of film to scrutiny of economic structures. Feminism is the particular perspective that we find most compelling. Thus we explore this issue in most of our criticism. But to "discover" and focus solely on the fact that *El Topo* or *Zardoz* is a sexist film will not take us very far in understanding the selection and arrangement of elements that make these films unique. Films like *Persona, Sweet Movie, Red Desert,* and *Une Femme*

Douce, on the other hand, invite detailed exploration of female identity, which lies at their center. Exclusive attention to any one of these perspectives obviously limits the depth, breadth, and precision of analysis and interpretation. Yet in striving for consistency or elegance, such theoretical systems as semiotics, psychoanalysis, auteurism, Marxism, or Feminism are sometimes necessarily exclusive. While each could broaden the understanding of any individual work, as self-contained structures of thought, each pursues only a single kind of truth. While these systems are important in aesthetic theory, especially as correctives for the narrow formalism of previous decades, they have also tended to obscure the experience and analysis of individual films, and in some cases to dehumanize the critical enterprise.

We do not offer a handbook of critical theories and methods because our procedure is to adapt the ones that can best help in translating into critical language whatever lies at the center of the movie in its own terms. This variety of resources seems particularly necessary for the twentieth-century critic who is faced with the additional problem of expressing a sensibility dominated by fragmentation and relativity. In *The Genesis of a Painting: Picasso's Guernica*, Rudolf Arnheim argues that the unresolved configuration of divergent forces, which he finds in Picasso's work, may be the most characteristic pattern of unity in our time.[4] Acknowledgment of these multiple truths may help us understand the dominance of the ironic mode in the twentieth century. It's as if the artist dare not rely upon a single stance but must incorporate a variety of tones and forms to express a flexibility that is survival-adaptive. Just as we no longer have pure tragedy or comedy, we no longer encounter the conventional hero or heroine who gains strength from an unswerving commitment to a single vision or set of values. Instead, we find mixed forms, mixed media, self-reflexive, anti-genre, and absurdist works, and at the center a protean figure who must constantly transform experience to avoid being overwhelmed and to expand his or her own capacities as an individual. Throughout *Self and Cinema*, we engage this cultural concern by developing a flexible critical repertoire that can deal with these divergent forces and discover value in a wide variety of works.

3) *The value of discovering and creating meaning*

The central goal of transformalist criticism is to locate, explicate, and construct the meaning of individual works, not just to describe the surface, as in the aesthetics of Sontag and Robbe-Grillet, and not just to show how meaning is created, as in structuralism. We recognize and accept that meaning or interpretation is to some extent a construct rather than a pure discovery, and therefore is to some extent subjective. We assume that any work will yield multiple meanings, depending on variables like the analytic point of view, the experience and state of mind of the analyst, the context in which the work of art is displayed, the effect of time on connotations of language and image, and the unpredictable insight. Therefore, we attend not only to "historical" or "intentional" meaning, but to "anachronistic" or contemporary interpretations as well, where we show relations among works and phenomena that did not exist at the time of their creation. But all communication involves the problem of signs that must be decoded and recoded by individuals to create meaning. Hence, as a goal of criticism, interpretation seems closely tied to the central function of all communication.

The subjectivity of this process is somewhat controlled by certain procedures and assumptions adapted from formalism. When the foregrounded patterns of a film are found, they form the basis of an hypothesis about the film's meaning. In order to be valid, these hypotheses must account for a great number of the film's characteristics, which must be cited and analyzed in concrete detail. Two values emerge from this process: thoroughness and verifiability; others can see the arguments and evidence clearly and check them against their own perceptions. Frye develops a similar position in relation to his system:

> The vision has an objective pole: it is based on a study of literary genres and conventions and on certain elements in Western cultural history. The order of words is there, and it is no good trying to write it off as a hallucination of my own. . . . But of course my version of that vision also has a subjective pole: it is a model only, colored by my preference and limited by my ignorance. Others will have different visions, and as they continue to put them forth the objective reality will emerge more clearly.[5]

4) *The inevitability of evaluation*

Unlike Frye's approach, transformalism emphasizes evaluation, which is implicit in the choice of works and the amount of time spent on them as well as in what aspects of a work are chosen for analysis. It incorporates a broad conception of evaluation, which functions on three levels:

a) How well does the work fulfill its own implicit goals within its own terms?
b) How effectively does it expand the possibilities of the medium?
c) On a broader cultural level, how does the work expand possibilities for the individual and society?

These three criteria interphase. While transformalism may tend to favor works that are experimental in form, it discriminates among them. For example, while a film like *Zardoz* may use a transformational structure to comment on the medium, its implicit goals are quite limited in their cultural implications, particularly in contrast with films developing similar structures and issues, like *El Topo* and *2001: A Space Odyssey*.

5) *The necessity of attending to the emotive qualities of the work*

Like evaluation, emotive response troubles most theoreticians. Transformalism not only accepts its omnipresence, but assumes that it will enrich critical writing, especially through systematic efforts to bring it to conscious clarity. We take into account the emotive powers of an individual work of art in three ways:

a) by attending introspectively to our own responses on a phenomenological level.
b) by observing the external signs of affective behavior in the larger audience.
c) by tracing these responses back to specific elements in the text that evoked them.

In its close scrutiny of the work, formalism has been attacked for draining the life out of art. While this charge is sometimes valid, it is not a necessary effect of transformalism. We believe that emotional response is the raw material of criticism and leads us directly back to the film to discover the specific qualities that aroused it. As in human interaction, the first necessary information is perception of the other with as little distortion as possible; we must try to hear the authentic voice, see the actual body before translating this experience into another vocabulary, medium, or set of categories, which inevitably causes changes in perception and emotion. Thus, we must attend to the surface and the specific context in order to capture the affective power of any element in a work of art.

6) *The value of evocative, detailed description of the film's surface*

As in art, the meaning of criticism is shaped by both form and content. Hence, a writer's choice of language expresses critical assumptions about the nature of art. Our use of evocative, detailed description implies that we value highly the emotive quality of the film and consider the phenomenology of the filmviewing experience to be essential to meaning. In choosing such a style, we hope to balance reductive tendencies of criticism that is designed to advance theory. This choice shows respect for the artist's individuality and strengthens the critic's role in the collaborative process by more fully revealing the consciousness in which the images develop their range of meaning. The analogy between critic and artist is even more fruitful in cinema than in literature, for the film critic uses a different medium from that of the art being described. Like novelists, film critics must stretch the possibilities of language to re-create the multisensory experience that is their subject. Perhaps that helps to explain why novelists-turned-critics like James Agee and Graham Greene and phenomenologically oriented critics like Susan Sontag and Raymond Durgnat have thus far been most successful in pursuing this goal. Just as it adapts conceptual frameworks, transformalism also attempts to use the creative power of language like these artists/critics.

Self and Cinema is a book of practical criticism—six long essays offering detailed discussion of fourteen films. Each chapter draws upon a different theoretical framework. In Chapter 1, we bring together depth psychology, specifically the personality and dream interpretation theories of Freud and Jung, and the films of Ingmar Bergman, focusing on *Persona* and *The Ritual*. Bergman's work particularly invites scrutiny of his entire canon from a psychological perspective because he is a very personal director who describes his films as dreams, who sees the unconscious as the prime source of his creativity, and who uses art as psychic exorcism. On one level, all his films are about himself and his role as an artist, and all of his characters represent aspects of his personality. He uses art as a means of fending off madness and discovering meaning in the face of inevitable death.

In Chapter 2, we draw upon Marxism and Feminism—particularly the writings of Frederic Jameson, Wilhelm Reich, and current Feminist theory—to explore the relationship between sex and politics, the individual and society, in three explicitly political films:

Godard's *Weekend*, Wertmuller's *Seven Beauties*, and Makavejev's *Sweet Movie*. In each one, we demystify the sexual and political implications of the form and content, and analyze the means of production and the audience response.

In Chapter 3, we bring together the psychological writings of B. F. Skinner and R. D. Laing (particularly *Beyond Freedom and Dignity* and *The Politics of Experience*) and Antonioni's *Red Desert* and Bresson's *Une Femme Douce*, all of which focus on the gap between experience and behavior. Both films center on an alienated woman whose experience is not perceptible to those around her. We demonstrate how the structure, visual techniques, sound, and point of view express the contrast between the self and the view of it held by others. We show how Skinner's and Laing's radically different views of self-realization lead to opposing interpretations of the relationships between the individual and society within the films.

In Chapter 4, we discuss two films dealing with the theme of individuals trapped in time and in the highly civilized world of patterned experience—Resnais' and Robbe-Grillet's *Last Year at Marienbad* and Buñuel's *Exterminating Angel*. Within the baffling surfaces and intricate structures of both films, escape is possible only through acknowledging the subjective nature of experience. We draw upon phenomenology, particularly the criticism of Alain Robbe-Grillet and Jean Paul Sartre, which is concerned with the relationship between subjective consciousness and objective phenomena. From this perspective, art is seen as the one kind of experience in which an object (the work of art) functions like a subjective consciousness, guiding the perceptions of the viewer who re-creates it. The phenomenological perspective enables us to see the special ways both films draw their audiences into the collaborative process.

In Chapter 5, we explore the quest for survival and self-realization in Jodorowsky's *El Topo*, Kubrick's *2001: A Space Odyssey*, and Boorman's *Zardoz*, using Northrop Frye's archetypal approach articulated in *The Anatomy of Criticism*. Archetypal analysis enables us to discover the special nature of the filmmakers' achievements: the absorption and transformation of a large body of mythic material into a unique, allusive work that presents an individual's journey as symbolic of the development of the species. It also helps us to identify a new genre—the transformational journey—in which breaking through the genre barrier is a formal expression of breaking through ego boundaries.

In Chapter 6, we use Claude Lévi-Strauss's method of structuralist analysis to find the deep structure in the four films directed by Nicolas Roeg: *Performance, Walkabout, Don't Look Now,* and *The Man Who Fell to Earth.* Adapting Christian Metz's "Grand Syntagmatique" and the structuralist methodology used by Roland Barthes in *S/Z,* we do a semiological analysis of the intersecting codes within *The Man Who Fell to Earth* and a summary of the same codes in *Walkabout.* Structuralism and cinesemiology are concerned, not with explicating meaning, but with describing the process by which humans assign meaning. Since all of Roeg's films center on an encounter between two cultures, which perceive and express meaning in quite different ways, and since they employ a highly unconventional narrative and visual style, forcing the audience to perceive in new ways, the application of this particular conceptual framework to the films of this auteur is particularly illuminating.

The fourteen films we have selected have several elements in common. Dramatic features from the sixties and early seventies, all of them focus on self-realization or its failure, developed in terms of the individual's relationship with the community. They are all concerned with survival—its cost and its value. They present a search for meaning within the dismal context of a fragmented and corrupt civilization. Many confront violence and death, especially suicide, which is seen as a serious option in the modern situation. They all present a complex, mysterious surface, which seems to emphasize the disguised, frustrating, or chaotic nature of the experiences they embody, and to draw the audience into the search for meaning. They are all experimental or innovative in form, developing complex visual imagery and non-linear structures, as if breaking new ground for a means of survival. Not surprisingly, then, all of the films were made outside of the United States and beyond the formulaic constraints that dominate Hollywood. In this country, many of them have been misunderstood or attacked; their values are not so readily accessible to audiences whose expectations have been shaped by more conventional movies. In fact, the films we have selected contrast ordinary reality and expanded vision, inviting us to move beyond the known. They offer the innovative imagination as one means of survival in the confusion and entropy of our planetary crisis. In Frye's terms:

> The question therefore resolves itself into the question of the
> relation of ordinary life, which begins at birth and ends with
> death and is lived in the ordinary categories of linear time and

extended space, to the other possible perspectives on that life which our various creative powers reveal . . . the distinguishing of the ordinary waking consciousness of external reality from the creative and transforming aspects of the mind.[6]

The conceptual frameworks we have adapted are among those that have had the greatest impact on contemporary criticism. Many of them are psychological in emphasis. Explicitly or implicitly, they all present a view of how the human mind works, and what is necessary for survival and growth. The chapters have been organized to reflect the ways in which these frameworks deal with the polarity between the self and other. Chapter 1 shows "the way in" through depth psychology, which finds progress in the expansion of individual personality. While drawing on the structuralist implications of Freudian and Jungian theories, we retain the focus on self by applying this method to the works of a narcissistic *auteur* obsessed with self scrutiny. Chapter 2 moves to the opposite extreme, "the way out," through Marxism and Feminism, which focus on changing social structures. Yet we choose Frederic Jameson as our primary model of Marxist criticism because he has attempted to reconcile his ideological position with phenomenology; the films under analysis all demand attention to the phenomenological surface since they redefine the meaning of any audio or visual image by the highly textured context in which it appears. The rest of the book mediates between the two poles of inward and outward movement. In Chapter 3, we perform the mediation between Skinnerian psychology that tries to modify external behavior and Laingian existential psychology that seeks to validate inner experience. We support Laing rather than Skinner because he defends the uniqueness of the self and thus is better equipped to illuminate the mysterious heroines and humanistic values of the films. In Chapter 4, the mediation is built into the phenomenological framework, which sees all experience as having both an objective and subjective dimension. In an attempt to demonstrate the range of this perspective, we focus on films that portray dehumanized persons trapped within social conventions and draw on a Marxist like Sartre and a surrealist/anarchist like Buñuel as well as a pure formal phenomenologist like Robbe-Grillet. In Chapter 5, Frye's archetypal criticism offers another form of mediation, this time between the one and the many, the unique artifact and the body of conventions it transforms. We apply this system to films analogously concerned with the relationship between the self and the species. In Chapter 6 we conclude with a structuralist analysis of the *langue* of an *auteur*—Nicolas Roeg—whose primary myth explores the ethnographic situation of an individual encountering an alien culture. In assuming that the structures of the human mind are ever the same, structuralism and semiology offer the most baroque form of mediation:

> This universal grammar is the source of all universals and it gives definition even to man himself. Not only all languages but all signifying systems obey the same grammar. It is universal not only because it informs all the languages of the universe, but because it coincides with the structure of the universe itself.[7]

At this particular time, structuralism/semiology is exerting the greatest influence on film theory, and has already absorbed important elements of formalism and the work of proto-structuralists like Frye, who were using similar procedures.[8] Under pressure from exponents of other conceptual frameworks, it is also attempting to integrate the concerns of Marxism, phenomenology, and psychoanalysis into its search for codes of signification. This integrative range is one of the reasons that the structuralist/semiological approach has generated the longest chapter in the book, is used in a somewhat purer form than any of the others, and is reflected in the organization of the book as a whole. As with the other frameworks, we adapt structuralism/semiology to our transformalist assumptions and to the primary goals of this particular book—the search for expanded visions of survival for the self and the culture.

The greatest obstacle in adapting structuralism to our goals is the fact that one of its main effects has been the destruction of the concept of the self. Jonathan Culler describes the process very clearly:

> The need to postulate distinctions and rules operating at an unconscious level in order to explain facts about social and cultural objects has been one of the major axioms that structuralists have derived from linguistics. And it is precisely this axiom that leads to what some regard as the most significant consequence of structuralism: its rejection of the notion of the "subject." A whole tradition of discourse about man has taken the self as a conscious subject. . . . But once the conscious subject is deprived of its role as source of meaning—once meaning is explained in terms of conventional systems which may escape the grasp of the conscious subject—the self can no longer be identified with consciousness. It is "dissolved" as its functions are taken up by a variety of interpersonal systems that operate through it. The human sciences, which begin by making man an object of knowledge, find, as their work advances, that "man" disappears under structural analysis.[9]

In its integrative function, structuralism has absorbed this tendency from other non-linguistic theoretical systems such as Marxism, which already de-emphasized the role of individual choice; this process has made it possible for Louis Althusser to attempt to reconcile Marxism and structuralism by emphasizing pure theory and totally denying intentionality. Although Freud's depth psychology helped define and strengthen the conception of the self, it has been adapted by structuralists like Jacques Lacan, who discard the concept of the ego and develop instead Freud's arguments for unconscious structures controlling human behavior, which undermines the illusion of personal freedom. Jung's personality theory could easily be subjected to a similar process of adaptation, whereby the personal dimension of the self could be omitted, leaving only the collective unconscious and persona as the source of human instinct and the controlling mechanisms of human behavior.

In *The Order of Things*, Michel Foucault puts this integrative process in an historical perspective. He argues that man is only an invention of the last two centuries—an invention that was launched by Descartes, with his famous dictum, "I think; therefore I am," and which has been kept alive by phenomenologists. It will disappear as soon as knowledge finds a new form. He assures us that the destruction is being promoted by the human sciences—particularly by psychoanalysis through its charting of the unconscious, and by ethnography through its structural analysis of social conventions. We might add that Skinnerian behaviorist psychology, particularly as articulated in *Beyond Freedom and Dignity*, provides more supporting evidence for Foucault's thesis. The great irony, of course, is that two of the greatest individual geniuses of our time have struck the hardest blows against the self—Freud unconsciously, and Lévi-Strauss with full intentionality. The latter expresses his case most powerfully and uniquely in *Tristes Tropiques*, which paradoxically is his most personal, autobiographical work.

> Yet I exist. Not, of course, as an individual, since in this respect, I am merely the stake—a stake perpetually at risk—in the struggle between another society, made up of several thousand million nerve cells lodged in the anthill of my skull, and my body, which serves as its robot. Neither psychology, nor metaphysics nor art can provide us with a refuge. They are myths, now open to internal investigation by a new kind of sociology which will emerge one day and will deal no more gently with them than traditional sociology does. The self is not only hateful: there is no place for it between *us* and *nothing*. And if, in the last resort, I

opt for *us*, even though it is no more than a semblance, the
reason is that, unless I destroy myself—an act which could
obliterate the conditions of the option—I have only one possible
choice between this semblance and nothing. I only have to
choose for the choice itself to signify my unreserved acceptance
of the human condition; in thus freeing myself from an
intellectual pride, the futility of which I can gauge by the futility
of its object, I also agree to subordinate its claims to the objective
demands of the emancipation of the many, to whom the
possibility of such a choice is still denied.[10]

In this book, while trying to benefit from the illuminations of these
theories about the workings of the human mind, we are still
interested in preserving the notion of the self and its corollary
emphasis on practical criticism. As Culler points out,

Structuralism effects an important reversal of perspective, granting precedence to the task of formulating a comprehensive
theory of literary discourse and assigning a secondary place to
the interpretation of individual texts.[11]

Yet, both Culler and Barthes grant that an individual text, or the
works of an individual artist, can function as a *langue*. In order to
retain the greatest possible freedom for both the artist and the
audience in creating and responding to art, we have treated individual
texts as coherent systems and have developed a form of analysis that is
rooted in phenomenology, which we have made the focus of the
central chapter. Throughout the entire book, we apply to individual
texts what Culler defines as a "structuralist attention":

A desire to isolate codes, to name the various languages with and
among which the text plays, to go beyond manifest content to a
series of forms, and then to make these forms, or oppositions or
modes of signification, the burden of the text.[12]

In all of these chapters we are exploring various answers to the
dilemma raised by Lévi-Strauss—how to preserve the self without
sacrificing the many or plunging the whole human enterprise into
nothingness. We believe the best answers come from the avant-garde
in both art and theory. We agree with Fredric Jameson that the
reconciliation of the self and the other, so crucial at this moment of
history, demands a critical freedom:

It is not too much to say that the concept of freedom thus permits
us to transcend one of the most fundamental contradictions in
modern existence: that between the outside and the inside,
between public and private, work and leisure, the sociological

and the psychological, between my being-for-others and my being-for-myself, between the political and the poetic, objectivity and subjectivity, the collection and the solitary—between society and the monad. It is an opposition which the confrontation between Marx and Freud dramatizes emblematically; and the persistence of this attempted confrontation (Reich, the Surrealist, Sartre, left-wing Structuralism, not to speak of Marcuse himself) underlines the urgency with which modern man seeks to overcome his double life, his dispersed and fragmentary existence.[13]

Like the post-structuralist theorists associated with the journal *Tel Quel*, our criticism favors radical experimentation. We resist closed systems, even when the possible transformations are vast. The only kind of theoretical ideal we would be willing to accept in evaluating specific works would be one that included all the infinite possibilities— past, present, and future—of the medium and of the organism, such as Julia Kristeva's geno-text. But since this model can never be defined because it contains the unknown and since the unknown is brought into existence by individual works, we prefer to focus on practical criticism, and by implication, on the transformational power of the self.

Notes

1. Northrop Frye, "Expanding Eyes," *Critical Inquiry*, II, 2 (Winter, 1975), p. 203.

2. Frye, p. 200.

3. Frye, pp. 204-205.

4. Rudolf Arnheim, *The Genesis of a Painting: Picasso's Guernica* (Berkeley and Los Angeles: University of California Press, 1962), p. 8.

5. Frye, pp. 213-214.

6. Frye, pp. 211-212.

7. Tzvetan Todorov, *Grammaire du Decameron* (The Hague: Mouton, 1969), p. 15.

8. "When I published *Anatomy of Criticism* ... I had never heard the word 'structuralism': I realized only that structure was a central concern of criticism." (Frye, pp. 199-200.)

9. Jonathan Culler, *Structuralist Poetics: Structuralism, Linguistics, and the Study of Literature* (New York: Cornell University Press, 1975), p. 28.

10. Claude Lévi-Strauss, *Tristes Tropiques* (New York: Atheneum, 1974), pp. 472-473.

11. Culler, p. 118.

12. Culler, p. 259.

13. Fredric Jameson, *Marxism and Form: Twentieth-Century Dialectical Theories of Literature* (Princeton: Princeton University Press, 1971), p. 85.

1

Self Exploration and Survival in *Persona* and *The Ritual:* The Way In

> *Film-making is for me a necessity of nature, a need comparable to hunger and thirst.... I threw myself into my medium with all the dammed-up hunger of my childhood and for twenty years, in a sort of rage, I have communicated dreams, sensual experiences, fantasies, outbursts of madness, neurosis, the convulsions of faith, and downright lies. My hunger has been continuously renewed.*
>
> Ingmar Bergman, "The Snakeskin"

Ingmar Bergman uses filmmaking as a process of self-exploration—a form of personal exorcism through which he purges himself of the demons and fears that haunt him. In his films he constantly seeks some form of meaning, which may help him survive in the face of inevitable death. The solutions he explores are all traditional—religion, love, work, and art. Although each is found wanting, he clings to them because that's all there is. In the later films, dating from *Winter Light* (1963) when Bergman says he ceased believing in God, religion no longer provides adequate consolation, but love and work persist. Art receives particular emphasis because it is Bergman's own work and his films are autobiographical. In this way, his filmmaking is therapeutic.

> I, too, have felt suicidal.... But it is the creative work that saves us. I have always been at work and you can't commit suicide when you are shooting a picture or directing a play. It can't be done.... At 6 o'clock you have to get up and go into the studio or the theater. Immediately you are involved in all sorts of

problems. . . . Then suddenly you think, "Good heavens, this
morning I intended to commit suicide. It's ridiculous."[1]

The personal nature of his quest demands the same themes,
situations, and characters in film after film. This persistence gives his
work the quality of recurring dreams, suggesting that this material is
highly charged for Bergman and has not yet been satisfactorily
resolved. More than any other filmmaker, he explicitly sees his films
as dreams, coming from and appealing directly to the unconscious.

> All my pictures are dreams. If the audience suddenly . . . meet in
> their minds my dreams and feel that they are close to their
> dreams, that's the best communication of all in art. . . . The
> dream is never intellectual, but when you have dreamt it, . . . it
> can give you a new light on your inner landscape, it can give you
> a new way of handling your life.[2]

In this chapter, Bergman's dream films and depth psychology,
especially the personality and dream theories of Freud and Jung,
come together in their focus on the unconscious as a source of
creativity, a guide to interpreting new levels of meaning in experience
and behavior, and an important reservoir of energy for the survival of
the individual and the species. Though painfully and sometimes
prophetically aware of the destructive elements of society, Bergman
and the psychologists whose theories we will use all turn inward as
the primary means of effecting significant change. Though familiar
with and influenced by both Freud and Jung, Bergman has not
followed either theory systematically. Instead, he has turned to one or
the other whenever it has best served his own inner needs. We would
like to make a parallel use of particular elements of the theories that
will be most illuminating in dealing with Bergman's work, focusing
particularly on *Persona* (1966) and *The Ritual* (1969). We have
chosen these particular films for three reasons: 1) they illustrate most
powerfully Bergman's unique dream style; 2) they represent the
symbolic condensation of certain important thematic lines in his
canon; 3) the characters can be clearly seen as components of a single
personality engaged in a struggle for survival.

Bergman's conception of his own creative process involves a
number of polarities, all concerned with the relationship between the
way in and the way out: 1) the spontaneous emergence of images from
the irrational unconscious and the conscious selection and control of
external forms; 2) the centripetal nature of the medium which
depends on artifice and deception, and the centrifugal representation

of external reality, which paradoxically reflects an inner truth; 3) the isolation of the artist whose work involves narcissistic self analysis, and the communal demands of the medium in which his troupe of artists and his audience must participate.

Spontaneity and Control

The living center of Bergman's creativity is his ability to receive and embody concrete images from his unconscious.

> A film for me begins with something very vague . . . split-second impressions that disappear as quickly as they come. . . . Most of all, it is a brightly colored thread sticking out of the dark sack of the unconscious. If I begin to wind up this thread, and do it carefully, a complete film will emerge.[3]

He speaks particularly of certain films that emerge slowly into concrete representations, which undergo dreamlike transformations.

> They remain in a shadowy zone; if I want to find them, I have to follow them there. . . Faces that are turned aside begin to speak, the streets are strange, a few, scattered people glance out through window-panes, an eye glistens at dusk or changes into a carbuncle and then bursts with a noise of breaking crystal.[4]

The characters, settings, events, and objects in his films are all projections of his inner life, expressing the conflicts of his own dreams and personality development. Though it is sometimes dangerous to make this kind of assertion about an artist, both Bergman's films and his repeated statements support this connection.

> All the characters in my dreams—or if you want to call it my pictures—are parts of my mind.[5]

Yet once these images come to consciousness, he must "transform these dreams into shadows," involving him in the rigorous discipline of his craft.

> The chopping up of a tragedy into five hundred small pieces . . . and finally the putting back together of these pieces so that they constitute again a unity. . . . It is the idiocy of fabricating a tapeworm 8,000 feet long.[6]

Just as Freud saw "secondary revision" serving the moral function of censorship, Bergman invests this part of the creative process with a morality rooted in the Protestant work ethic of his upbringing.

> That strict middle-class home gave me a wall to pound on, something to sharpen myself against. At the same time they taught me a number of values—efficiency, punctuality, a sense of financial responsibility which may be "bourgeois" but are nevertheless important to the artist. They are part of the process of setting oneself severe standards. Today as a film-maker I am conscientious, hard-working and extremely careful; my films involve good craftsmanship, and my pride is the pride of a good craftsman.[7]

Bergman acknowledges the importance of both creative forces by internalizing them into a personal struggle between a hypercritical Superego and a narcissistic Id who loves to play with his own images. But the moral lines are not firm. Both the childish genius and the parental critic can be demonic.

> The devil was an early acquaintance, and in the child's mind there was a need to personify him. This is where my magic lantern came in. . . . Red Riding Hood and the Wolf, and all the others. And the wolf was the Devil . . . with a tail and a gaping red mouth . . . a picture of wickedness and temptation on the flowered wall of the nursery.[8]

> You must look at your own work very coldly and clearly; you must be a devil to yourself in the screening room.[9]

Bergman dramatizes this "bitter combat" between the two forces in many films. In the comedy *All These Women* (1964), a pompous critic, maliciously motivated by his own artistic ambitions, destroys a great musician by stealing his women and threatening to write a bad critical biography. In *The Ritual* (1969), the balance of power is reversed. A bureaucratic official threatens a troupe of actors with censorship and penalties (uncannily foreshadowing Bergman's own troubles with the Swedish tax authorities). Ultimately he is drawn into their performance, which allows the actors to kill him off. This conflict takes a variety of forms in other films: the respectable townspeople vs. the animalistic circus troupe in *Naked Night* (1953); the parasitical patrons vs. the paranoid painter in *Hour of the Wolf* (1968); the skeptical scientist vs. the visionary magician in *The Magician* (1958); the examiner/critic vs. the self-deceiving dreamer in *Wild Strawberries* (1957); the cynical squire vs. the idealistic knight, the religious flagellants vs. the visionary players in *The Seventh Seal* (1957). As this wide variety of characters suggests, the critic/artist polarity becomes a broader conflict between the forces of reason and passion.

This struggle between reason and passion also lies at the center of Mozart's *Magic Flute*, a work which must have imprinted Bergman as a child and which has provided the deep structure for many of his films. When he filmed the opera in 1975, he framed the stage performance with close-ups of the audience's reactions—particularly those of a young girl whose emotional responses are carefully scrutinized by the camera as if drawing our attention to the process of imprinting. In the extremely nihilistic *Hour of the Wolf*, Mozart's opera is presented as an inset puppet show that sharply contrasts with the framing narrative that adapts it. *The Magic Flute* is used as the supreme example of a work of art that successfully maintains the delicate balance between passion and reason, spontaneity and control, madness and genius; Bergman's story is about an artist who loses control of his art and life as he plunges into insanity. The painter Johann Borg is also compared with Tamino, whose rational harmony is upset by his passionate pursuit of the beautiful, elusive Princess Pamina, whom Bergman transforms into the demonic Veronica Vogler. Mozart's comical bird-catcher Papageno, whose magical powers are positive though uncontrolled, is similarly metamorphosed into the manipulative, ghoulish puppeteer who stages the opera and later directs Johann in his final encounter with Veronica; in the hallucination at the end of the film, he literally changes before our eyes into a murderous bird of prey. Unlike Tamino and Mozart, Johann and Bergman are totally subdued by the forces of passion and anarchy that dominate this film.

Mozart's basic myth is reworked once again, this time with comic irony, in *The Petrified Prince*, an unpublished screenplay by Bergman that has not yet been filmed. The plot sounds like a pornographic fairy tale about a mute, paralyzed, effeminate prince named Samson, who is in thrall to his whorish queen mother, who repeatedly rapes him. Finally goaded into rebellion against his phallic mother, he unsuccessfully tries to commit matricide. Threatened with castration by a newly arrived father figure, Samson runs away with a young mother/whore to establish his own neurotic nuclear family. Despite the heavy Freudian overlay, the story explicitly evokes a comparison with Mozart's opera. The turbulent queen says her son is "like a sonata by Mozart"; nevertheless, the young mother/whore (her replacement) turns to a Beethoven symphony to restore Samson's powers. In Bergman's fairy tale, the passionate Queen of Night is not offset by the calm, holy, reasonable Sarastro; God and the King are dead. But the other minor characters who help or hinder the young prince in his quest for manhood and meaning have their historical counterparts. The natural birdman Papageno is replaced by a romantically disheveled Beethoven. The lustful, satanic Moor, who betrays Sarastro and becomes allied with the dark queen, is replaced by Napoleon, who, after a "homeric fuck," restores the Devouring Dowager to the throne. *The Magic Flute* ends with the queen and her forces of darkness fleeing into the void, the young prince and princess reconciling Eros and Logos, and the old king resigning, confident that pure love will bring wisdom. Bergman's ending is not so optimistic. The passionate queen and the lustful tyrant retain the power and the pleasure, the only things besides death that have "tangible reality." While *love* is only a word spoken ritualistically to subdue fear, the prince is at last free to use it, and the young couple ventures off to face the unknown. *The Petrified Prince* offers a bizarre Oedipal resolution in which full-tilt acting out of lust brings about the proper pairings and performances; from a Jungian perspective, it also presents an energetic rite of passage successfully accomplished by the complete triumph of Eros over Logos.

While Freud and Jung associate Logos and reason with masculinity and Eros and passion with femininity, Bergman eventually transcends this sexist identification. He sees women as embodying the full range of human potentialities and uses them throughout his canon to develop both sides of the conflict. In the earlier films that focus on the fear of death, the protagonists are male—the knight in *Seventh Seal* and the doctor in *Wild Strawberries*. Though both men do achieve true community and love in a moment of sensual experience, it is only after a lifetime quest for meaning through religion or rationality. Thus these films try to confront death through Logos—an intellectual search for strength or wisdom. In *Cries and Whispers*, however, he tries to confront the fear of death in experiential terms—the *feeling* that is "never put into words."[10] His choice of a female protagonist is archetypally compatible with his turning toward Eros; although also limited, love, imagination, and community now provide greater solace in confronting isolation and death.

The range of Bergman's female protagonists increases throughout his canon. In fact, he has developed a personal genre that traces a psychic journey of self-exploration made by two women, one a controlled artist and the other a sensuous, childlike creature who seems more emotionally needy and desperate; these two women move back and forth between fusion and alienation as they face death and despair. At the root of this genre is Bergman's desire to understand the cold mother who rejected him when he was a needy, contact-seeking child and to somehow fuse himself with her. The two women thus represent two conflicting aspects of his own psyche.

The chief components of this genre first appear in *Prison* (1949), the first film that Bergman both wrote and directed and which contains the seeds of all his later works. Inside the frame that is dominated by male artists, one of the story lines presents a contemporary vision of hell: a vulnerable young prostitute is forced by her fiance (who also doubles as her pimp) and by her older sister, who is cold, cruel and authoritarian, to give up her child, which they murder. The loss of the baby is the subject of a recurring nightmare that haunts the mother and helps drive her to suicide.

The first film totally dominated by this two-women motif is significantly called *Dreams* (1955). This low-mimetic melodrama focuses on a mature photographer and a childlike model who go to another city on business where they become involved with contrasting relationships with two men, who are both exposed as weaklings. While the independent photographer threatens to draw her lover away from his dependent wife and children, the young model acts as a surrogate daughter for her older lover, who has incestuous yearnings.

The next version is *The Silence* (1963), which departs from realism and becomes increasingly symbolic. As in *Prison,* the two women are sisters, which perhaps makes it easier to see them as two sides of a single personality. The older sister is a translator, rational but extremely intense. The younger has a pathetic son who yearns for more loving contact with his mother. Largely ignoring him, she desperately seeks erotic adventures with strangers and struggles against her dying sister whom she hates. Thus the primary emotional conflict is between the two women rather than with the men they encounter. In fact, there are no important men in the film—only a child, an old man who works in the hotel, a waiter who grunts rather than speaks, and a group of transvestite dwarves. The struggle takes place in an unidentified alien city that is plagued by war, which is symbolically related to the personal combat between the two women.

In *Persona* (1966), the older woman is an actress who has withdrawn into silence, abandoning her artistic career, her husband,

and her pathetic young son; the younger woman is a passionate nurse who recounts an erotic experience with strangers, which led to an abortion, and who reaches out emotionally to the actress. The two women go to a deserted island where their identities merge and separate and where they move fluidly between fantasy and reality. Men are abandoned in the film; they are alluded to in conversations but appear only in hallucinations and in the dreamlike frame.

Cries and Whispers (1973) splinters the personality into four female figures and combines the basic situations from *The Silence* and *Persona*. Attended by her two sisters and a maid whom she has befriended, Agnes (like Ester in *The Silence*) is the older sister painfully dying of cancer, this time of the womb rather than the throat. Ester and Agnes are both independent single women engaged in artistic activities. Marie, Agnes' youngest sister, is like Anna in *The Silence;* indifferent to her husband and children and involved only in the beauty and pleasure of her own body, she responds to her sister's imminent death by turning to eroticism. Karin, the older sister, is similar to Elisabet Vogler in *Persona*. Married to a man who is repulsive to her physically and mentally, she acts in a highly controlled manner, masking her anguish and desperation. Anna, the servant, like Alma the nurse in *Persona*, is devoted to the artistic woman she serves. Having lost her own child, Anna is eager to adopt the role of loving mother. Despising each other for the different aspects of personality they embody, the three women come together with Agnes only because the artist among them is dying. As aspects of a single self, the women fear and loathe the death they are awaiting, which is horrifyingly their own.

The parts of the self and the polarities of reason and passion are reintegrated in Marianne, the lawyer in *Scenes from a Marriage* (1974) and in Jenny, the psychiatrist in *Face to Face* (1976)—who is an elaboration on the character of the female psychiatrist in *Persona*. Marianne must find her way out of a relationship with her husband, who gets in touch with his limitations as she is finding her strengths. Jenny receives help through her suicide attempt and nervous breakdown, not from her cold husband, but from a homosexual colleague; when he leaves her, she survives independently. These women are not artists, but highly competent professionals who overestimate the power of reason. Both must get in contact with their irrational side. *Scenes from a Marriage* focuses on the growth resulting from this contact, while *Face to Face* centers on the breakdown. Jenny's creative abilities are expressed only through dreams, which dominate the film and which repeat the same motifs and images from the prostitute's recurring nightmare in *Prison*. Jenny's submerged passions are also revealed in two other minor characters—a young psychotic patient and her hostile young daughter, who feels rejected by her mother. Although Jenny identifies with both of these characters, she gets in touch with her own irrational nature primarily through isolation, nightmares, and a return to childhood. Her descent into madness nevertheless leads to emotional growth, which parallels Bergman's own artistic development as he explores this dream genre.

In *Autumn Sonata* (1978) the women are quite literally a cold artistic mother and her childlike daughter, who has been emotionally crippled by her neglected childhood. Following the death of her lover, the mother comes to visit her daughter and her minister/husband, the observer who narrates the encounter between the two women. One suspects that Bergman identifies with all three characters—the detached male who tells the story, the monstrous artist who can express feelings only through art but not in human relationships, and the dependent child whose life is devoted to making contact with the cold, rejecting mother through bitter accusations, loving forgiveness, or total identification. Although she once had a loving nature, the daughter has now grown incapable of love like her mother; the only exception was the love she felt for her son, who was drowned at the age of four. There is little hope for either woman, for despite their painful confrontations, they both return to their sheltering personae of the self-pitying martyr and the selfish star.

Truth vs. Deception

For Bergman, the film medium is paradoxical. On the one hand, because of its multi-sensory nature, it has the power to capture and express emotional truth more fully than any other medium. On the other hand, it is based on the powers of illusion, which necessarily involve the filmmaker in deception. Bergman feels that film can "bring in other previously unknown worlds, realities beyond realities"[11] because it reaches directly from the unconscious of the artist to that of the audience.

> With music and film you can talk to the subconscious of the human being ... the soul—without going through the intellect.

> You sit in a dark room and you have this bright square before
> you.... Of course it goes right in you, right into your emotional
> mind.[12]

Unlike music, film is composed of light, an archetypal image for
transcendental truth.

> I am working with an instrument so refined that with it, it would
> be possible for us to illuminate the human soul with an
> infinitely more vivid light, to unmask it even more brutally and
> to annex to our field of knowledge new domains of reality.[13]

Bergman frequently uses light as a means of exposing cruelty.

> It is the strong, unmoving sunlight that is always most
> frightening. My cruellest dreams are flooded with unbearable
> sunlight.[14]

This description brings to mind the overexposed light in the opening
dream sequence of *Naked Night* where the humiliated clown carries
his naked wife in the blazing sun; the harshly lit nightmare in *Hour
of the Wolf* where Johan murders a boy; and the bright exterior scenes
and white garments that only provide an outer cover for the anguish
at the center of *Cries and Whispers*.

Whether Bergman intends it to reveal beauty or pain, the light
must be perceived by a human eye, which can be deceived. Bergman
has always seen himself as a magician, relying on and craftily
manipulating this vulnerability.

> In reality, I am creating illusion; for the cinema would not exist
> but for an imperfection of the human eye, namely its inability to
> perceive separately a series of images which follow each other
> rapidly and which are essentially identical. I have calculated that
> if I see a film that lasts an hour, I am in fact plunged for twenty
> minutes in total darkness. In making film, therefore, I am
> making myself guilty of a fraud; I am using a device designed to
> take advantage of a physical imperfection of man.... I am, then,
> either a deceiver or—when the audience is aware of the fraud—
> an illusionist. I am able to mystify, and I have at my disposal the
> most precious and the most astounding magical device that has
> ever, since history began, been put into the hands of a juggler.[15]

This recognition creates for Bergman an "insoluble moral conflict."
In order to tell "the truth about the condition of man," he must
always wear a mask; displacement of identity through personae is
essential to personal and aesthetic self-realization.

This paradox is a recurring theme through the canon, and is central in *Persona*, where an actress retreats into silence and madness in order to avoid the deceptive masks of her life and art. Other films present a troupe or artists who can be seen as either charlatans or true visionaries. In *The Seventh Seal*, though the performers are only minor characters, they are the only survivors. Their success and their identification with the holy family affirms that the illusionists are on the true path. Although the moral status of the troupe is more ambiguous in *The Magician* and *The Ritual*, their struggles with truth and deception form the central issue of the films. In *The Magician*, the leader of the Magnetic Health Theater tries to reduce the Royal Counselor on Medicine to madness by feigning death and provoking "terrible visions;" finally, his masterful illusions succeed in driving his supposed murderer to suicide. *The Ritual* is fully concentrated on one basic event—a troupe of players uses an illusionary performance to frighten their critical censor to death.

In technique as well as theme, Bergman increasingly recognizes that realism will not serve him. Using his medium like a dreamer, he heightens significance through "condensation" of symbolic imagery.

> I have reduced reality and I have combined realities exactly as they are combined in dreams.[16]

Through his artistic development, the line between reality and dreams tends to dissolve. In early films like *Illicit Interlude* (1951), *Naked Night* (1953), *Dreams, Wild Strawberries*, and *Seventh Seal*, the episodes involving visions, dreams, memories, and the super-natural are clearly distinguishable from the "real" events around them. The later films—*Through a Glass Darkly* (1961), *Winter Light* (1963), *The Silence, Persona, Hour of the Wolf* (1969), *Shame* (1969), *The Ritual, The Passion of Anna* (1970), *Cries and Whispers, Face to Face*, and *The Serpent's Egg* (1977)—may frequently allude to contemporary political events, but they move more fluidly through various modes of reality. In *Through a Glass Darkly*, it is already difficult to distinguish hallucinations from external events.

> The horrifying—the real dream—is always when you dream it very realistic. It is only a small turning of the screw into unreality. . . . In the middle of the picture *Through a Glass Darkly* when Karin stands at the seaside and says three times, "Here comes the rain," that's the exact feeling of dreams, and then everything turns over. You stop watching from the outside and become part of the madness inside.[17]

The ambiguity increases in *Hour of the Wolf.*

> Suddenly about a year ago while making *Hour of the Wolf* I
> discovered that all my pictures were dreams. Of course I
> understood that some of my films were dreams, that part of them
> were dreams. . . . But that *all* my pictures were dreams was a new
> discovery to me.[18]

Although Anna's dream in *The Passion of Anna* is set off from the
rest of the film by being in black and white rather than color, its
images, themes, and tone are drawn directly from *Shame.* The film
opens with the husband recounting a dream in which he escapes into
a happy vision of the past and sees the present wartime reality as
merely a nightmare; it ends with the wife telling him a dream, in
which she escapes into a more hopeful future. In *Shame* dreams are
not only a means of personal escape for the individual, but a form of
communal entrapment. The wife laments:

> Sometimes everything seems like a long strange dream. It's not
> my dream, it's someone else's, that I'm forced to take part in.
> Nothing is properly real. It's all made up. What do you think
> will happen when the person who has dreamed us wakes up and
> is ashamed of his dream?

The shameful dreamer may be the politicians who caused the war,
the gods who created the world, or the artists who made the film.
Recognizable sequences of dream and hallucination occur in *Face to
Face*, but the reality status of others, like the rape scene, is totally
ambiguous. In *Persona*, it is almost impossible to tell the mode of
reality of any individual sequence. Bergman continues to present
entire works as highly condensed and intensified anagogic nightmares in *The Silence, The Ritual, Cries and Whispers,* and *The
Serpent's Egg*—where the horrors of the individual dreamer reflect
the horrors of the larger social vision.

The autonomous nature of the dream reaches a high state of
refinement in *Cries and Whispers.* With an unprecedented sparseness
of dialogue, Bergman relies very heavily on concrete representability,
for the first time using color with the specific symbolic goals and
richness of his black and white films. The beauty and harmony
manifest in the visual surface displace the horror latent in the highly
condensed psychological situation. The drama takes place in a
house, a common dream environment for expressing one's life space.
In describing its red rooms as the inside of the soul, Bergman is

actually drawing a metaphor from the internal tissues of the body, reinforcing even further the interior nature of the action.

> All our interiors are red, of various shades. Don't ask me why it must be so, because I don't know. I have puzzled over this myself, and each explanation has seemed more comical than the last. The bluntest but also the most valid is probably that the whole thing is something internal and that ever since my childhood I have pictured the inside of the soul as a moist membrane in shades of red.[19]

On the Jungian subjective plane, all of the environments and characters can be seen as parts of Bergman himself. The male figures with their cynicism, despair, weakness, and tyranny are all embodiments of the Shadow, whose negative characteristics are repressed from the Ego. The women comprise the Anima, who becomes increasingly important in Bergman's later films. On the Freudian objective plane, the characters represent primary figures in the nuclear family, who are associated with earlier Bergman films and with his personal history. As always, the dreamer identifies with the child, who in this film is dead or dying. The parent figures are evaluated according to what support and comfort they provide in helping Agnes meet death. The "fathers" are all weak or absent, diminished men as they are in all of Bergman's later films. The doctor is cynical (as in *The Magician*); the priest is disillusioned (as in *Winter Light*); the husbands are weak or tyrranical (as in *Shame*); and the Divine Father is dead. Despite the limitations of the "mothers," they are central to the experience, both in the present and in memory. Maria is the selfish, narcissistic mother (like Anna in *The Silence*); Karin is the cold, cruel mother (like Elisabeth in *Persona*); Anna is the humble, all-accepting mother (like Alma in *Hour of the Wolf*). The real mother, present only in Agnes' memory, is a far more complex figure, combining beauty, gentleness, aloofness, playful cruelty, and vulnerability. One suspects she is closest to Bergman's own mother, especially since she appears in a number of films—e. g., *Wild Strawberries* and *Smiles of a Summer Night*. The infantile wish at the center of this dream film is that the child escape the cries of pain and death, and return to an idyllic environment where play, love, and harmony are nurtured by the intimate whispers of an ideal family. Yet this wish can be fulfilled only through art and illusion.

Whatever his moral qualms about artistic deception, as Bergman moves through his canon, he becomes increasingly the masterful illusionist. Many of his works comment self-reflexively on the artistic process, openly acknowledging the artifice. In the early films this is frequently expressed through inset theatrical performances as in *The Devil's Wanton* (1948), *To Joy* (1950), *The Seventh Seal, Illicit Interlude, Naked Night* and *The Magician*. Occasionally the performances are linked specifically to the film medium, as in *Prison*, which includes an inset film (which he was to use again in *Persona*); *Illicit Interlude*, which contains a strange animated sequence drawn on a phonograph record by two young lovers, foreshadowing the tragic end of their romance; *Dreams*, which opens with photographs being developed in a darkroom; and *The Magician*, which traces cinema to its roots in the magic lantern. In later films, dramatic illusion is more frequently broken by specific allusions to the cinematic medium: an inset film in *The Silence*, a television interview in *Shame*, and candid interviews of the actors in *The Passion of Anna*. Many of the later films include such sequences in the important opening position: an allusive montage in *Persona*, an interview in *Hour of the Wolf*, and an examination of photographs through a magnifying lens in *The Ritual*. As if to emphasize the paradox of cinema's ability to document external reality through artifice, Bergman accentuates the self-reflexiveness in those very films that portray the grimmest vision of the outside world. Thus, he tells the truth both centripetally and centrifugally.

Individual Artist vs. the Troupe

Acknowledging both Freud and Jung, Bergman sees artistic creativity as having the double potentiality for greater individualism as well as communal identity. In the contemporary world, both goals involve danger as well as value. Subjectivity in Bergman's cinema has come to mean, not simply a personal style, but the shape and substance of self-realization. Yet, as he is fully aware, this can lead to a painful alienation:

> Today the individual has become the highest form and the greatest bane of artistic creation. The smallest wound or pain of the ego is examined under a microscope as if it were of eternal importance. The artist considers his isolation, his subjectivity, his individualism almost holy. . . . The individualists stare into each other's eyes and yet deny the existence of each other.[20]

As Bergman has become increasingly innovative with his medium, especially since *The Silence,* this problem has intensified.

> Any experimentation necessarily involves a great risk, for it always keeps the public at a distance, and keeping the public at a distance can lead to sterility and to isolation in an ivory tower.[21]

In fact, critics have accused him of self indulgence and obscurantism. Much as he may desire a broad communication, attempts to satisfy demands and complaints from the outside may be destructive.

> The act of creation has, under the effect of causes that are as much interior as they are exterior and economic, become an exacting duty. Failure, criticism, coldness on the part of the public today cause more sensitive wounds. . . . I wanted to try to explain to you why . . . we become fools and allow ourselves to be annihilated by colorless and vile compromises.[22]

Throughout Bergman's canon, this conflict between self and other is expressed in a double focus, frequently within the same film—the individual artist with great powers, and a troupe of performers whose cooperative work is necessary for a powerful communal identity. Sometimes we encounter an individual artist whose selfish preoccupation with his own creativity alienates him from his family. Through his personal power, he takes over their identities and drives them to madness or despair. In *To Joy,* a concert musician almost destroys his wife and child because he cannot accept the truth about the limitations of his talent. In *Through a Glass Darkly,* a novelist pushes his children to incest and madness through a desire for greatness based on fear of the void. *All These Women* presents a comical version, featuring a virtuoso cellist, whose face is withheld even from the audience but whose music we constantly hear, as he lords it over a harem of several women. His First Lady has become so indoctrinated with his self-importance that, when he compromises to please a critic, she shoots him. In *Persona,* an actress abandons her husband and child in order to purify her life and art. Moreover, her cold silence torments the nurse who tries to restore her. The painter in *Hour of the Wolf* undermines the sanity of his pregnant wife, as his psychic demons invade her consciousness. Finally, he tries to kill her and himself. In *Shame,* under the pressures of war, a weak musician betrays and murders in order to survive. Although his wife is repelled by his actions, she reluctantly follows him; Bergman

seriously questions whether survival is worth such a "vile com-
promise." In *The Passion of Anna,* a cynical architect loves to
capture people in photographs, particularly in huge close-ups
(perhaps suggesting that he is an ironic parody of Bergman). His
own easy success and contemptuous attitude toward the world lead
his wife to infidelity and despair. The lone artist is seen more
positively in *Illicit Interlude,* where a ballerina's dedication to
dancing prevents her from making a total commitment to any love
relationship, yet it enables her to go on living after the death of her
first lover. In a key sequence, she is told the "naked truth" by her
Director, who is masked as a magician: "You're afraid to live or to
die. . . . You're a dancer, that's your purpose, stick to that." The
virtuoso pianist follows the same advice in *Autumn Sonata,* even
though it helps destroy her husband and two daughters. Yet she
claims that she really had no choice, for art was the only means
through which she could express her feelings. Without it, she is
totally cold and empty. While in these two films, art is a means of
personal survival for the artist, its sustaining value for the community
is emphasized in *Cries and Whispers.* The humblest of all Bergman's
artists, Agnes, the painter, is a source of spiritual and emotional
support for her family, friends, and congregation. Turning her
energies to others, she has perhaps weakened her own art. Though
she is the one who is dying, her words and images provide the richest
moments of harmony in the film. In the end, her diary speaks for
Bergman as well as for Agnes.

> I still go on painting, sculpting, writing, playing. In the old
> days, I used to imagine that my creative efforts brought me into
> contact with the outside world, that I left my loneliness.
> Nowadays, I know that this isn't so at all. In the end, all my
> so-called artistic expression is only a desperate protest against
> death. Despite this, I keep on.[23]

In several other films, this problem is reworked by making the
artist belong to a group of players, which functions like a family.
Though led by a powerful visionary, the group depends on its
communal identity for survival. In *Naked Night, Seventh Seal, The
Magician, The Ritual,* and *The Serpent's Egg,* the group struggles to
stay together despite hostile forces from without and conflicts from
within. In all five films, the outside threat comes primarily from the
levelling, conforming jealousy or power-madness of the bourgeoisie.
In *Serpent's Egg,* the conflict between the disbanded troupe of Jewish

circus performers and the outside community becomes horrifyingly demonic; two members are killed by a group of insanely nationalistic scientists doing hideous secret "experiments." Abel, the one artist who does escape, might suggest a parallel with Bergman himself, who had recently "escaped" Swedish tax litigation. In *The Silence*, the group of artists is reduced to a grotesque troupe of transvestite dwarves, who comfort and amuse the lonely little boy with whom Bergman identifies.

The Passion of Anna exhibits Bergman's greater conscious awareness of his double concern through a self-reflexive strategy. Speaking as narrator, Bergman is the overseeing artist/director who breaks the dramatic illusion by transforming the characters into a group of actor/artists who comment on the roles they are playing.

By working with a repertory company, Bergman lives out the central role of the visionary leader, guiding his troupe toward a meaningful unity. The players provide communal support for his craft. They also externalize the fragments of his psyche—genius, critic, magician, scientist, craftsman, child, parent, idealist, cynic, performer, observer, victim, tyrant, male, female. As they act out these parts of his personality, Bergman expects his players to draw on their own inner resources.

> All of the characters . . . are parts of my mind, but when the actors take over I want them to make it their property, to create out of their minds and make it their property.[24]

His unique relationship with his actors, many of whom have also worked with him on the stage, extends to the entire company— cameramen, editors, and other technicians. In order to work successfully, Bergman needs the security of being surrounded by friendly vibrations: "First I must create an atmosphere of tenderness."[25] Before a film, he gathers his troupe together to explore the pace and atmosphere; he prefers working indoors because when striving for a difficult scene, "we have to be very tight together."[26] In satisfying the demands of the self and other, Bergman draws strength from the collaborative nature of the film medium, which so many other directors see as an obstacle to personal expressiveness.

Perhaps more than those of any other director, Bergman's films are woven together like the rich dream life of an individual. The externalization of self through fluidly changing identities results in centripetal repetition of names and faces throughout the canon. Bergman assigns the name *Vogler* to the mute illusionist in *The*

Magician, the seductive demon in *Hour of the Wolf*, and the silent actress in *Persona*, all characters who illuminate each other. All three have an almost magical power over others that can be both inspiring and destructive. Meaning "bird catcher," Vogler evokes Papageno from Mozart's *Magic Flute*, which has obviously had such a great influence on Bergman. The first name of the Vogler figure in *The Magician* is Albert Emanuel, which links him with two other characters who also belong to a troupe of players: Albert Emanuel Sebastian Fisher (also known as "Bird"), who is the demonic actor in *The Ritual;* and Albert, the circus leader, in *Naked Night.* Throughout the canon, there is a procession of repeated first names—such as Alma, Mary, Anna, Andreas, Johan, Eva, Karin, and Elisabet—which are interwoven with recurring surnames with complex effects. *Vergerus* (one on the verge, one who bends) is the family name of professional establishment figures whose supreme rationality is undermined by their own extreme resistance to and curiosity about passion and insanity: the skeptical scientist who is terrified by wizardry in *The Magician;* two cuckolded husbands—the cynical architect in *The Passion of Anna* and the reasonable doctor in *The Touch;* and the evil doctor who drives human guinea pigs mad in *The Serpent's Egg.* In both *The Passion of Anna* and *The Ritual, Winkelman* (man in a corner) is the name of a character who is trapped in an impossible, humiliating situation and must resort to violence to escape. Bergman calls attention to this symbolic use of names at the end of *The Passion of Anna* when he visually moves in on Max von Sydow whose image gradually blurs and disintegrates as the narrator (Bergman) observes: "This time he was called Andreas Winkelman." This remark identifies him as another version, not only of Anna's first husband Andreas and of the Christ archetype, but also of the many trapped creatures who populate Bergman's cinematic dreams.

The pattern of interweaving is most complex with Mary and Anne. In the early films, Mary is an innocent character, linked with nurturing and the life force. Mia, the holy mother in *The Seventh Seal,* and Marie, the successful artist in *Illicit Interlude,* survive while others around them perish. In the later films, Mary becomes weak and unholy as she turns to sensuality and destruction: Maria, the selfish, seductive sister in *Cries and Whispers;* and Maria, the obsessively sexual psychotic patient in *Face to Face.* With the Annas a similar polarity exists, but the pattern is reversed. In the early films, she is sensual and destructive: Anne is the bareback rider in *Naked*

Night whose infidelity leads to the public humiliation of her lover; the title character in *The Passion of Anna* brings out violence in others through her possessive anger, and causes the death of her husband and child. In later films, Anna is more the passive victim, who must find the strength to cope with the death of others: the servant in *Cries and Whispers* who is resigned to the loss of her own child, and who tries to help her mistress face death; and the daughter in *Face to Face* who feels rejected by her suicidal mother. The two Mariannes reintegrate these polarities into characters who are successful in breaking old patterns to free themselves and others for new growth. In *Wild Strawberries*, the daughter-in-law fights to have her baby and to save her Marriage by breaking the pattern of cold destructiveness in which her husband is trapped; it is also she who helps her father-in-law make authentic contact before he dies. In *Scenes from a Marriage*, the divorced lawyer is able to free herself of conditioning for the conventional female role: she gets in touch with her sexuality and, through new experiences, is able to expand her relationship with her ex-husband.

A similar pattern of interwoven repetition occurs with faces in Bergman's films; it is more complex still because it involves not only characters, but the actors and actresses who play them. Their faces can be associated with similar or contrasting roles, enriching the films with allusions or ironic variations. In *The Magician* and *The Ritual*, which both deal with the same basic situation, Ingrid Thulin plays the female member of the troupe who is married to the leader; Gunnar Bjornstrand plays the man of science who is hostile to the artists in *The Magician* (a role related to his performance as the cynical squire in *The Seventh Seal*), while in *The Ritual* he is the leader of the troupe. *The Ritual* is also linked to *Naked Night* by the performance of Anders Ek, who plays a childlike member of the troupe in both films. In the former he is associated with fire and is master at humiliating others while in the latter he is Frost, the "icy" clown who is a prime object of humiliation. Ek plays a priest in *Seventh Seal* and *Cries and Whispers;* in the former, he is a zealous, self-flagellating believer, while in the latter, he is disillusioned with equal intensity. Liv Ullmann plays Vogler in *Persona* while Bibi Andersson is Alma; in *Hour of the Wolf* Ullmann becomes Alma and Ingrid Thulin is Vogler. In both *Hour of the Wolf* and *The Passion of Anna* Max von Sydow plays the vulnerable, selfish role of the poor guest who is pitted against his rich and cynically destructive host, Erland Josephson. While Bibi Andersson plays the unfaithful wife in both *The Passion of Anna* and *The Touch*, she is called Eva Vergérus in the former and Karin Vergérus in the latter; Max von Sydow plays the lover Andreas Winkelmann in one film and the cuckolded husband Andreas Vergérus in the other.

Perhaps the best known of Bergman's male players in his early films is Max von Sydow, whose extraordinary face—with its range from slack-jawed weakness to craggy strength—appears like a recurring phantom in film after film, linking together the parts he plays like threads from the unconscious. The strong idealism of the Knight in *The Seventh Seal* is undermined in the role of the father in *The Virgin Spring*. The visionary powers of the artist in *The Magician* lead to madness in *Hour of the Wolf*. He plays the weak husband in several films, developing the role through impotence in *Through a Glass Darkly*, suicide in *Winter Light*, cruelty and violence in *Shame* and *The Passion of Anna*, and passivity in *The Touch*. So accustomed is the audience to von Sydow's central importance and intensity in Bergman's movies that when he appears in the small role of humble gas station attendant in *Wild Strawberries*, he is greeted with surprised murmurs or even laughter. The many masks worn by players like von Sydow emphasize Bergman's assumption that the individual is composed of many selves.

In the later films, with their greater focus on women in the central roles, Liv Ullman emerges as the pivotal character. Visually, she is as versatile as the parts of Bergman's psyche. A plain and somewhat shapeless woman in *Hour of the Wolf*, *Shame*, and *Autumn Sonata*, she becomes a reasonably attractive and realistic modern woman in *The Passion of Anna*, *Scenes from a Marriage*, and *Face to Face*. In *Scenes from a Marriage*, we watch her transformation to greater beauty and sensuality. In *Persona*, she conveys a powerful glamour; in *Cries and Whispers*, a poisonously seductive beauty; in *Serpent's Egg*, the purposely ill-suited cabaret costume cannot suppress her beauty, which gives a poignant ambiguity to the grotesque disguise. Above all, it is her face to which Bergman has devoted so much loving scrutiny. In close-up after close-up, we are amazed by her range of expressiveness. In *Persona*, where she is not allowed to speak, her face is highly articulate, subtly communicating from moment to moment the slightest emotional change and nuance. Her roles move between the extremes of passivity in *Hour of the Wolf* to the powerful dominance of *Persona*. Above all, she is always convincing, as though she believes in her role, and is persuasive in justifying her point of view, even as the selfish sister in *Cries and Whispers*, the self-deceiver in *The Passion of Anna,* and the slack-mouthed, whining daughter in *Autumn Sonata.* Like Bergman, she is apparently able to locate all these aspects of herself, and find the means to display them to the world. Her role in *Face to Face* is the most demanding, for it calls for the expression of her full range in a single brilliant performance.

Despite the intricate interweaving of faces, names, situations, and themes throughout Bergman's dreamworld, the later films tend to reduce the earlier, more diffuse and conventional plots to primary configurations: there are fewer characters; the tone is consistently dark and ominous; the psychic intensity is unrelieved by comic sub-plots; the structure moves inward toward a greater psychological penetration; situations are primordial, involving incest, madness, and death. Drawing on the personality and dream theories of Freud and Jung, we will examine in depth two films that exhibit this condensation of Bergman's self-analysis: *Persona* and *The Ritual.*

Persona (1966)

The power of *Persona* lies in its stylistic richness and emotional resonance; its plot is minimal. An actress named Elisabeth Vogler has had a breakdown in the middle of a performance of *Electra.* Silent ever since, she leaves her husband and child and is hospitalized. A woman psychiatrist offers her beach house as a retreat, where Elisabeth goes to recuperate with her nurse Alma. At first, Alma enjoys talking about herself, but eventually grows resentful of Elisabeth's silence. A conflict builds, finally erupting into violence. Their identities seem to merge and fragment. In the end, they pack their things, and we see Alma leave on a bus.

In analyzing the relationship between an author and his characters, Freud observes:

> It has struck me that in many of what are known as "psychological" novels only one person—once again the hero—is described from within. The author sits inside his mind, as it were, and looks at the other characters from outside. The psychological novel in general no doubt owes its special nature to the inclination of the modern writer to split up his ego, by self-observation, into many part-egos, and, in consequence, to personify the conflicting currents of his own mental life in several heroes.[27]

Alma and Elisabeth embody two aspects of Bergman striving for wholeness within his personality. These characters grew out of a photograph that provided the germinal image for the film—Bibi Andersson and Liv Ullmann, wearing large hats, comparing their hands—which he saw just after his close friend Andersson had introduced him to Ullmann for the first time. Alma represents his passionate, demanding side, and Elisabeth is the cold, analytical artist. Alma accuses Elisabeth of stealing her emotions and gestures to use them as artistic material for her role as actress, a charge that his leading ladies may have levelled at Bergman.

> I always thought that great artists had this tremendous feeling of sympathy for people. That . . . they created out of sympathy with people, from a need to help them. . . . You've used me . . . and now you don't need me anymore you're throwing me away.[28]

Highly self-critical like Bergman, Elisabeth tries to avoid all deception, even the creative illusion essential to her artistry. She withdraws into silence, unable to integrate her life and art as Bergman does successfully in making this film. When interpreted on the "subjective plane," the other characters in *Persona* can also be seen as parts of Bergman's psyche. Clad in the white coat of authority, the psychiatrist who brings the two women together represents an even more public aspect of Bergman's directorial role. She identifies with Elisabeth, granting her permission to remain fragmented: "Keep playing this part until you've lost interest in it. When you've played it to the end, you can drop it as you drop your other parts." (The story of the psychiatrist and her identification with her female patient is told later in *Face to Face*.) Elisabeth's abandoned child, vulnerable and demanding, and her weak, needy husband also embody aspects of Bergman: his unfulfilled self and his potentiality for cowardice and cruelty—"the secret pain of my life." We have encountered these figures throughout his canon.

Bergman embodies his psyche, not only in his characters, as Freud suggested, but also in a number of self-reflexive techniques. The narrator of the psychological novel is transformed into a less explicit but equally powerful presence. Bergman makes his omniscience known through the brief emergence of a narrator who moves us from the hospital to the beach house; in the self conscious, exploratory camera work; and in a complex outer frame of abstract images.

Bergman has described the opening montage as a "visual poem" of images that came into his mind while he was in the hospital writing the screenplay. He was suffering from vertigo, and he pretended to himself that he was a boy who had died.

> I wanted to make a poem of the atmosphere in which *Persona*
> grew . . . the whole atmosphere was one of death, and I felt like
> that little boy. I was lying there, half dead, and suddenly I started
> to think of two faces, two intermingled faces, and that was the
> beginning, the place where it started.[29]

He originally intended to call the film *Kinematography*, and indeed many of the images are preoccupied with filmmaking: the arc lamps of the projector, film passing through the reels, leader countdown, old footage of cartoons and slapstick, a blank white screen, tachistoscopic images during the titles. These images force us to acknowledge Bergman and his creative process, which lie behind the film.

As in dreams, many of the concrete images in the montage are highly condensed, drawing their power from their association with Bergman's filmic past (and future) and with cultural archetypes, creating a reservoir of images and moods for the audience to draw upon during the rest of the film. The frightening image of death, displaced through farcical humor, is actual footage from an inset film in *Prison*, his first important work as an auteur. The huge spider evokes Karin's mad vision in *Through a Glass Darkly* where she sees God as a spider, a predatory demander like the husband and child in *Persona*. The images of martyrdom and sacrifice (a wooly animal being slaughtered, a spike being driven through a human hand) are reminiscent of *The Seventh Seal* and *The Virgin Spring*, preparing us for the emphasis on pain and cruelty to follow, and anticipating the animal murders in *The Passion of Anna*. A powerful series of images begins as we see a huge close-up of an old man's profile that looks like an abstract landscape, then an old woman's face shot from an odd angle, next the slight body of a child, and finally a dangling hand. The bodies are all covered with sheets and appear to be lying on slabs in a morgue. Suddenly the phone rings, bringing contact from outside like the radio, television, and letters that intrude upon Elisabeth's withdrawal. The old woman opens her eyes, the child rises from his slab, and we are shocked to discover they are not dead. These images evoke the scene from *The Silence* where the same boy pulls the sheet off the body of his dying aunt, who, surprisingly, is still alive. They also anticipate one of the most terrifying scenes in *Hour of the Wolf*—the long hallucination where Johan draws a sheet off Veronica Vogler's naked body as she lies on a slab, mocking him, her deathly pallor drawing him into a frenzied eroticism. These images of the living dead will also enrich our future understanding of Elisabeth's willful minimizing and simplifying of experience—her refusal to respond to the demands of others. When Alma leaves the

room after examining Elisabeth's face as she sleeps, Elisabeth opens
her eyes as if she had been aware of Alma's presence all along,
reminding us of the old woman whose eyes suddenly open, suggesting
she was feigning death. The inverted image of this old woman
anticipates later shots of both Alma and Elisabeth. We see Alma in
this position just before she hallucinates the presence of Elisabeth's
husband; and in the final sequence we se an inverted image of
Elisabeth in a viewfinder. The chiming clock reminds us of passing
time and inevitable death, as it does in so many Bergman films—
particularly *Wild Strawberries* and *Cries and Whispers*. The sound of
dripping water anticipates the painful scene where Alma reads
Elisabeth's letter.

The richest image from the opening montage is that of the boy. As
he moves restlessly on the slab, putting on his glasses to read, he is
associated with the later shots of Alma, short-haired and boyish, as
she tosses and turns in her narrow bed. Like Johan in the opening
scene of *The Silence*, the boy is reading Lermontov's *A Hero of Our
Time*. He reaches out his open hand toward a blurred image (the first
time we see the merging of Elisabeth's and Alma's faces), as if to make
contact. Hand imagery runs throughout Bergman's films, a source of
contact, communication, violence, and control. In the montage, we
have already seen a quick shot of small hands moving after an
animated cartoon, a hand gutting a sacrificial lamb, a twitching
hand impaled upon a spike, and the dangling hand of a corpselike
body. These seeking hands, particularly the child's, provide rich
associations for later shots in which Elisabeth's husband reaches out
for her, and Alma's hand makes a threatening and demanding
gesture. In light of the entire film, we are tempted to assume that the
boy is Elisabeth's son—the child she hoped would be stillborn. But
since we see him only in the opening and closing montages (*The
Silence*, too, is framed by images of the same boy), he takes on a more
symbolic significance, his vulnerability and suffering linked to that
of the child in the photograph of the Warsaw ghetto (also holding up
his hands) and to other young victims in earlier Bergman films: the
boys whose brains are dashed out in *The Virgin Spring* and *Hour of
the Wolf*, and the love-starved child (also played by Jörgen Linström)
in *The Silence*. The boy is central to Bergman's identity as an artist.
As Freud has suggested, the uncontrolled energy of child's play is
transformed into the creative power of the mature artist. At the end of
the screenplay of *Persona* (though not the film), the psychiatrist

offers a final diagnosis of what was wrong with Elisabeth: "Personally I would say you have to be fairly infantile to cope with being an artist in an age like ours" (p. 99). Bergman explicitly locates the child at the center of his imaginative power: "A contact-seeking child, beset by fantasies, I was quickly transformed into a hurt, cunning and suspicious daydreamer."[30]

The Jungian concept of personality development (psychosynthesis) is more useful than Freud's in understanding the relationship between the two major characters in *Persona*, perhaps because Bergman was reading Jung when he made the film. In fact, the title alludes directly to both an important component in Jung's personality theory—the collective part of the conscious self that handles the relations between the individual and the outside world, creating a mask to meet the expectations of others and fulfill the roles defined by society—and an ancient word for the identities assumed by players in dramatic performance. It is precisely the Persona, which Elisabeth has consciously rejected because, as the psychiatrist explains, she has seen "the abyss between what you are for others and what you are for yourself" and experiences "the burning need to be unmasked" (p. 41). Alma struggles to maintain the Persona as inner forces press to break through. Alma asks Elisabeth:

> Is it so *important* not to lie, always to tell the truth . . . always to have the right tone of voice? . . . Can you even live without . . . talking nonsense, excusing yourself, lying, evading things? I know you have stopped talking because you're tired of all your parts, all the parts you could play perfectly. But isn't it better to let yourself be silly and sloppy and lying . . . let yourself be what you are? (pp. 79-80)

As the Ego in the Freudian system tries to strengthen itself through integration of its various parts, so the Self of the Jungian system struggles to reduce the gap of inauthenticity between the Persona and the private Self.

We can also see Alma and Elisabeth as Shadow figures for each other—archetypal doubles of the same sex who represent either a psychic force that is missing from the personality, or the dark side that is repressed from the Ego because it is potentially damaging to the Self. For Elisabeth, Alma is a Shadow representing deception, hysteria, and dependency. Alma fears Elisabeth as Shadow, for she, too, is "poisonous, bad, cold, rotten" (p. 89). Yet, identification gives Alma special insight into Elisabeth.

> You're *playing* healthy. And you do it so well that everyone
> believes you. Everyone except me. Because I know just how
> rotten you are (p. 80).

Their Shadow relationship reaches its full mythic intensity in a
vampirish ritual where Alma forces Elisabeth to suck her blood.
It is Alma who seeks identification with Elisabeth, not the reverse.
She is the one who insists they look alike.

> That evening when I had been to see your film, I stood in front of
> the mirror and thought "We're quite alike." (Laughs) Don't get
> me wrong. You are much more beautiful. But in some way we're
> alike. I think I could turn myself into you. If I really tried. I mean
> inside. Don't you think so? And you wouldn't have any
> difficulty, of course, turning into me. (pp. 57-59)

On the island, she even begins to dress like Elisabeth. Alma desires
the very characteristics that Elisabeth has rejected; now neither side of
the personality provides them. Specifically, she needs Elisabeth's
sexuality and performing powers. Clean-cut with boyish, short hair,
Alma is unsure of her feminine identity. Having had an abortion and
a painful love affair ("I remember it all as absolute agony" in which
"I was never quite real to him" [pp. 49-50]), she is moved by Elisabeth
to explore various aspects of her own sexuality. Her identification
with Elisabeth ("I've always wanted a sister") enables her to
confess that she does not love her fiance. Elisabeth also evokes an
erotic response which leads Alma to tell her the story of a beach orgy
with two young boys and another girl. Elisabeth seems to be fully
developed as a woman. A beautiful, long-haired, glamorous star, she
is also wife and mother. Although Alma yearns for these outward
signs of femininity embodied in Elisabeth's Persona, Alma is
actually the one who is emotional and dependent—characteristics
frequently associated in our sexist culture with the female—in
contrast to Elisabeth's "masculine" coldness, objectivity, and
willfulness.

Alma's desire for identification is transformed into sexual desire
for Elisabeth, which is expressed primarily in two wish-fulfillment
fantasies. In the first, Alma imagines that Elisabeth visits her bed;
they embrace sweetly while Alma leans her head against Elisabeth
who strokes her hair. They look directly into the camera as if in a
mirror; the camera holds on this portrait, etching it in our memory to
be recalled when this image is repeated later in the film. The second
fantasy is triggered by Alma's reenactment of the bedroom visit; this

time it is she who goes to Elisabeth, gazing on her while she sleeps. Suddenly we hear a man's voice calling, "Elisabeth!" As Alma moves toward the hallucination, Elisabeth follows behind her like a shadow. Elisabeth's husband speaks to Alma as if *she* were his wife. Endorsing the substitution, Elisabeth takes Alma's hand and places it on his face. At first we think he may be blind, but when he removes his dark glasses, he focuses on Alma's face and embraces her. When they make love, Alma tells him what she imagines he wants to hear: "I live for your tenderness . . . you're a wonderful lover, darling. You know that, my love" (pp. 87-88). This sexual fantasy brings Alma several rewards. She is actually making sexual contact with Elisabeth without acknowledging the homosexual dimension; she also receives gratification from the husband, who is a stranger like the young boys in the beach orgy. Finally, for once she is superior to Elisabeth, for she is loving and tender. But then suddenly, after the lovemaking, Alma switches from sexual identification with Elisabeth's Persona to an adoption of the dark void of Elisabeth's private Self, crying:

> Give me something to stupefy my senses, or beat me to death, kill me . . . it's all counterfeit, a lie. Just leave me alone, I'm poisonous, bad, cold, rotten. (p. 89)

Alma also seeks the performing powers that the Ego has lost through Elisabeth's withdrawal. When Alma is first assigned to Elisabeth's case, her remarks reveal her insecurity.

> For a moment I thought I ought to refuse the job. . . . Perhaps Mrs. Vogler should have a nurse who's older and more experienced, who knows more about life. I mean, I might not be able to manage her. . . . Mentally. . . . If Mrs. Vogler's not moving is the result of a conscious decision, which it must be since she is perfectly healthy . . . then it's a decision that shows mental strength. I think whoever is going to look after her will need a lot of spiritual strength. I just don't know if I'm up to it. (pp. 26-27)

Even in the story of the beach orgy, Alma was the passive watcher, drawn in by the other woman. But since Elisabeth refuses to speak, Alma is allowed to assume the more dominant role of the performer:

> A lot of people have said I'm a good listener . . . you're the first person who's ever listened to me. . . . I hope it doesn't bore you. It's so nice to talk. (pp. 50-51)

Yet she is unable to sustain the role of performer on her own.

resorting to the manipulative tactics of the underdog, moving from submissive begging and self-recrimination to bitter accusations. After pleading with Elisabeth to make a sacrifice and say one word, she turns on her in anger, snapping: "I know you'd say no. . . . You're a Devil, an absolute devil. People like you ought to be shot" (pp. 74-75). Then she begs Elisabeth to forgive her emotional outburst, confessing:

> I suppose I was a bit flattered too, a great actress like you taking an interest in me. I think I almost hoped you would have some use for what I told you. . . . It's sheer exhibitionism. (p. 81)

A few moments later she screams in fury:

> No, you don't want to forgive me. You won't forgive me. You're proud, aren't you? You won't stoop to my level, because you don't have to. I'm not going—I'm not going to! (p. 81)

Her passionate anger leads her to adopt the actress' role by verbalizing Elisabeth's refusal: "I'm not going to!" as if they were role-playing in a psycho-drama.

One of the reasons Alma turns to Elisabeth is that her own personality is comprised of contradictory parts that do not make a unified whole. In describing her ambivalent feelings about the orgy, the subsequent lovemaking with her fiance Karl-Henrik ("It's never been so good between us, before or since" [p. 56]) and the abortion, that followed, Alma says with confusion:

> It doesn't fit, nothing hangs together. . . . Can you be quite different people, all next to each other, at the same time? And then what happens to everything you believe in? (p. 57)

Clinging to the Persona of nurse or passive helper, she is baffled by her own sexuality and aggression. The casual cruelty of Elisabeth's coolly detached letter triggers in Alma an unexpected violence. Elisabeth writes of Alma:

> Alma is good, a real diversion. . . . She is rather attached to me, actually a little in love, in an unconscious and charming way. It's extremely amusing to study her. . . . I encourage her to talk, it's very educational. . . . I have her confidence and she tells me her troubles large and small. As you see, I am grabbing all I can get and as long as she doesn't notice it won't matter. (pp. 64-65)

After reading this letter, Alma deliberately plants a piece of broken glass where Elisabeth is sure to step on it, and waits with visible malice.

Whether acting out the Shadow or Persona relationship, Alma and Elisabeth function as contrasting parts of a single self. This very difference accounts for the intensity of both Alma's yearning and her hatred.

The pattern of separation and fusion between the two women controls the structure of the film. In almost every scene there is an alternation between fragmentation and merging that is reinforced by the visual composition and the editing. The film moves back and forth between two basic editing styles: montage sequences made up of several brief cuts that stress fragmentation; and scenes linked by dissolves, fades, and gradual lighting changes, which obscure time, creating the impression of a single flowing experience.

The opening montage is extremely fragmented, yet it ends with an image that fuses the two women. In the hospital they are separated by their roles as nurse and patient, but as soon as they reach the island, they dress alike. Although Elisabeth's silence distinguishes her from the talkative Alma, the recitation of the orgy begins to unite them and leads to Alma's statements about their physical similarity. In the imagined visit to Alma's bedroom which follows, the two women are united visually. The latter incident again begins to separate them into user and victim—the one who studies and the one who feels— leading to the first violent act of alienation with the broken glass. At the end of this scene, Alma pulls back the drapes and looks out the window; then we cut to Elisabeth standing outside and then back to Alma inside. The women occupy neither the same space nor the same frame. This separation is strongly underscored by a break in the film, the ultimate destruction of fusion and continuous motion. After the break, the violence continues as Alma threatens to throw boiling water at Elisabeth. They fuse in the next scene during the husband's visit.

This merging is most fully developed in the story of motherhood, which ends with their faces totally integrated for the first time. With complete certainty, Alma describes why Elisabeth got pregnant, and her later feelings of revulsion and rejection toward her son. The sequence begins with a close-up of Elisabeth's hands piecing together the torn photo of her child. Laying her hands on Elisabeth's, Alma invites her to talk about her son, saying: "Tell me about it. (pause) All right, *I* will then." Not only is she aware of all the circumstances of Elisabeth's pregnancy, she also knows that Elisabeth was accused of lacking motherliness by someone at a party that Alma, as a separate individual, could not have attended. Although Alma may be projecting her own fears onto Elisabeth, we are more likely to think she possesses this detailed knowledge because they are parts of the same personality. When Alma first tells the story, the static camera sits behind her, looking at Elisabeth's face. At various points in the narrative, this image dissolves suddenly to a larger close-up, revealing with greater clarity her pained response and confirming the truth of Alma's description. At the end of the chronicle, we hear a loud, discordant sound and the camera returns to a shot of Alma laying her hands on top of Elisabeth's; interpreting this circularity as an emotional denouement, we feel that this conversation has concluded. But instead, the camera reverses position, sitting behind Elisabeth to watch Alma's face as Bergman offers a bold, ritualistic retelling of the story, including the same series of dissolves into larger close-ups. Again the visuals affirm that Alma, too, has these secret feelings. She is on the point of marrying someone she doesn't love, having a child, preparing to go through the very motions from which Elisabeth has withdrawn. Alma's Persona tries to deny the identification:

> I don't feel like you, I don't think like you, I'm not you, I'm only trying to help you, I'm Sister Alma. I'm not Elisabeth Vogler. It's you who are Elisabeth Vogler. I would very much like to have—I love—I haven't— (p. 97)

But as she speaks, the visuals reaffirm the identification. In the final close-up, Elisabeth's features appear on the right side of Alma's face, condensing the two women into a single image. The camera holds on this disturbing shot, which gradually fades into white nothingness. Both visually and verbally, this sequence reveals not only the identity of the two women as part of a single self, but also the central emotional void in the total organism. Both of them experience a profound coldness, explaining Elisabeth's withdrawal as well as Alma's desperate need.

In the next sequence, the two women are once again very distant, as Alma reappears in her nurse's uniform and the camera intercuts between shots of their separate profiles. While Elisabeth remains calm and silent, Alma expresses her frustration, reaching out as if to scratch Elisabeth's face, and pounding on the table:

I'll never be like you. I change the whole time. . . . You'll never reach me. (p. 92)

But this confrontation once more leads back into fusion. As we see Elisabeth's lips moving, we hear another voice speaking disjointed but significant gibberish, suggesting the madness that might tumble out of Elisabeth if she were to speak:

> Perhaps a form of trespass, a shade of despair. Or the other, counselling, and it all gathers. No, not inwards. It ought to, but that's where I am. Yes, then you could cry, or cut up your leg. The colours, the sudden swing, the incomprehensible disgust at pain and then all the many words. I, me, we, us, no, what is it, where is closest, where can I get a grip? The failure that never happened when it should, but which came unexpectedly at other times and without warning. No, no, now it's another sort of light, which cuts and cuts, no one can protect themselves. (pp. 92-93)

They perform an ancient ritual of fusion where Alma scratches her own arm and Elisabeth sucks the blood. It is not clear whether Alma is pressing Elisabeth's head down or trying to pull it away. Is the ritual violent, or sexual, or both? As if overwhelmed by the intensity of this act, Alma strikes Elisabeth again and again until the image fades, this time into black nothingness.

The blackness gradually fades into a huge close-up of Alma's face, introducing a scene that gives verbal expression to the void of the empty screen that Bergman has used as a significant transition throughout the film. Alma enters what appears to be the hospital room, raises Elisabeth's head, and begins a dialogue:

> ALMA: Try to listen, please. Can't you hear what I'm saying?
> Try to answer now. Nothing, nothing, no, nothing.
> ELISABETH: Nothing. (pp. 97-98)

Alma has previously gotten Elisabeth to speak only through violence: she says "Ouch" when she steps on the piece of broken glass and "No, stop it" when Alma threatens her with boiling water. The fact that Elisabeth now speaks without being threatened makes us question the mode of reality of the hospital scene. Is it a flash back or forward, or is it Alma's fantasy variation on the bloodsucking ritual? In this scene, the contact is soothing rather than hostile and the merging is verbal. The dialogue implies a transformation since earlier, when

Alma had read to Elisabeth of despair, Elisabeth had nodded her assent while Alma expressed disagreement. ("All this anxiety we bear with us, our disappointed dreams, the inexplicable cruelty, our terror at the thought of extinction, . . . have slowly crystallized out our hope of heavenly salvation. The great shout of our faith and doubt against the darkness and silence is the most terrifying evidence of our forlornness," [p. 47]) It is ambiguous who is influencing whom; while Alma succeeds in getting Elisabeth to echo her "Nothing," the word only confirms Elisabeth's negation of life.

The final departure scene, though highly ambiguous, seems to suggest a failure of integration between the components of the Self. The visuals are fragmentary, comprised mainly of discontinuous cuts of Elisabeth and Alma (still in uniform) preparing to leave the beach house. In the midst of packing, Alma looks into a mirror and sees herself leaning on Elisabeth who strokes her hair, the same image we saw at the end of the fantasy in which Elisabeth visits her bedroom Perhaps this suggests that Alma has incorporated her Shadow. But her longing for closeness is undercut by a return to other images from early in the film. As Alma leaves the house and walks past the strange sculpture of a woman with her head thrust back unnaturally (perhaps like an actress declaiming), the film suddenly cuts to the image of Elisabeth as Electra at the moment when she ceased to speak. Then we get only the barest glimpse of Bergman and Sven Nykvist, his cinematographer, standing beside a camera, in whose viewfinder we see an inverted image of Elisabeth, a film-making reference that returns us to the opening montage. Then we cut to a longshot of Alma boarding a bus, a public conveyance, which Jung interprets as a vehicle of social norms. These final images seem to imply that the Self can no longer deal with its inner needs; the two women return to their Personae as nurse and actress. Either they are going back to what they were before their encounter, or Alma (whom we actually see) has in some way absorbed Elisabeth (who is no longer visible in the present). If this incorporation has taken place, we suspect it is destructive, for the deathlike pose of Elisabeth in the viewfinder and the contorted sculpture are both associated with the pained expression of Elisabeth's Electra. All three images are artistic renderings, suggesting that Bergman is considering possible fates for Elisabeth, particularly in the scene where director, cameraman, and viewfinder explicitly reveal the process of cinematic choice. Whereas in the screenplay the psychiatrist informs us that "early in December Elisabeth Vogler returned to her home and to the theatre, both of which welcomed her with open arms" (p. 99), in the film. Bergman makes a precise interpretation impossible. In any case, a tone of futility and circularity pervades the conclusion. After the bus drives off with Alma, the camera moves in to a close-up of the gravel, an abstract shot that might have come from the opening montage. Then we actually do return to the opening with a shot of the boy, still reaching out to the hazy image of the woman's face, gradually going out of focus. Suddenly the film breaks, spinning through the reels, and we return to the arc lights, the very first image of the movie—the ultimate fragmentation and the end of the illusion.

Persona is characterized by shifting modes of reality, which express Bergman's vision of the fluid boundary between self and other, between inner and outer experience. This is powerfully expressed in the structural relationship betwen the film's outer frame and inner psychological drama. The framing montage sequences emphasize Bergman's creative consciousness as opposed to the fictional consciousness of his characters, and remind the audience of the external reality of the theater, limiting their subjective identification with the charcters. The recurring image of the child reaching out to the blurred face of the woman also deals with Ego boundary; every human being first gains awareness of his own identity through the painful separation from his mother.

When the film moves inward from the frame to the psychological encounter between Alma and Elisabeth, Bergman emphasizes the shifting modes of reality through his transitions. The first frame of the hospital sequence begins with abstract light and shadow. Near the bottom of the grey screen a dark line appears; gradually a door fades into definition and walls become visible. The door opens and Alma, in uniform, walks in, defining the space as a hospital room. The next transition inward to the more private world of the seashore is accomplished by a narrator (Bergman) who, like the conventional intrusive author in fiction, jars us with a reminder that a story is being told; he is never heard from again.

Bergman also introduces other media to obscure further the boundary between inner and outer reality. We hear voices that seem to come from the radio but, like auditory hallucinations, could also be the unspoken words of Elisabeth's or Alma's mind. First in the hospital the radio dialogue seems to express Elisabeth's guilt toward her family:

All I want is your forgiveness. Forgive me so that I can breathe

again—and live again. (Elisabeth laughs until the tears come to
her eyes.) What do you know of mercy, what do you know of a
mother's suffering, the bleeding pains of a woman? (Elisabeth
again breaks into laughter.) Oh God, God, somewhere out there
in the darkness that surrounds us all. Look in mercy upon me.
Thou who are love. (p. 29)

Later at the beach house, as Alma awakens from a bad dream, she
turns on the radio, which seems to speak from the depths of her mind:

Don't speak, don't listen, cannot comprehend—What means are
we—us to persuade—to listen. Practically—excluded. These
continuous calls upon—. (p. 82)

The television footage of rioting and immolation in Viet Nam and
the photograph of the Warsaw ghetto, though introduced through
the artifice of media, actually document the violence of real events. As
Elisabeth cowers in a darkened corner, the unreal half-light from the
TV creates an atmosphere of nightmare, making it easier for
Elisabeth to internalize the chaotic horror. Since the Ego defines
itself partly in the image of external reality, it is inevitable that public
violence will foster violence within the individual psyche. These
images force us to see the psychological struggle between Elisabeth
and Alma in the context of war and genocide. (This connection
between private and public warfare, with media as liaison between
the two, is developed more fully in *Shame*.)

Bergman's films imply that it is impossible for anyone to recount
events in the external world without distorting them through a
subjective filter—another means by which the individual incorporates
the outside world. This process is demonstrated in the inset story of
the beach orgy told by Alma, where instead of resorting to a
conventional flashback, Bergman focuses his camera on the teller
and listener, suggesting that what is really important is how this
storytelling process affects the relationship between them. Despite
the lack of sexual images that would have been present in a flashback,
the scene is highly erotic because that is the motive and effect of
Alma's present experience. We watch Elisabeth's face growing larger,
as she is turned on and greedy for more lurid details. This focus on
present emotional reality is even stronger in the scene where Alma
tells the story of Elisabeth's motherhood. Both stories have an
emotional truth that neither woman can deny. It is this kind of truth
that informs Bergman's use of the medium and which, paradoxically,
must be achieved through fictionality and artifice.

After Alma tells about the beach orgy, the distinction between inner and outer reality becomes increasingly irrelevant in several important scenes that have the quality of hallucination. In the very next scene, when Alma is exhausted from reliving her story, a voice whispers: "You'd better get off to bed, otherwise you'll fall asleep at the table" (p. 59). We cannot tell whether these words are spoken by Elisabeth or thought by Alma, and the ambiguity is increased when Alma sits up and says: "Yes, I'll go to bed now. Otherwise I'm sure to fall asleep at the table" (p. 59). The blurring of distinction between inner and outer reality is developed visually in the next scene, where Elisabeth visits Alma's bed. The gray light of the bedroom, the filmy gauze curtains, the white mist, the distant foghorn, Elisabeth's sheer white nightgown, and the gliding movements of the women all create the feeling of a dream. This quality is emphasized by contrast with the scene that follows. Abruptly we cut to a brightly lit long shot of the beach. In the extreme foreground, Elisabeth pops her head into the bottom of the frame and takes a picture, as if of the audience, startling us with this form of direct address, and shattering the illusionary tone of the previous scene. Alma asks: "Did you talk to me last night? Were you in my room last night?" (pp. 62-63). Elisabeth shakes her head no.

Then comes one of the most jarring shifts in reality. Between the two most violent events of their interaction—the broken glass and the boiling water—the film suddenly breaks and burns and we return to some of the images of the opening montage. As the focus blurs, we see a ghost-like figure and movements that freeze and resume. When the focus sharpens, our recognition of Elisabeth is underscored by a loud, discordant tone. This shocking interlude imposes an aesthetic distance on the audience at a moment of extreme psychological intensity when they are likely to be deeply involved with the two women. It can be seen as an escape for both audience and characters, an emotional withdrawal triggered by Alma's committing an act so repugnant to her Persona as helper and guide. It is also analogous to Elisabeth's suddenly stopping in the middle of her performance as Electra, withdrawing from her tragic role and retreating into nervous laughter and fearful silence.

The next hallucination scene of the husband's visit further obscures the mode of reality because it does not use the same techniques as the earlier bedroom fantasy. Basically darker, in sharper contrast, and without the mist and soft grey light, this sequence gains its illusionary quality from the spatial arrangement of the three people, which reflects Alma's mixed desires in creating this fantasy. Early in the sequence, as the husband talks to Alma, Elisabeth stands behind her listening like a shadow in the background; frequently her forehead and eyes are cut off at the top of the frame, perhaps suggesting the part of Elisabeth that Alma wants to censor. Then we cut to a strange shot reversing their positions. A huge close-up of Elisabeth's face looms in the extreme foreground, while the couple embraces in the background. The strange proportions of this special-effects shot imply that these people could not be occupying the same real space, heightening the effect of subjective distortion.

The film does not return to the world of objective reality, as after the previous hallucinations. All the scenes that follow move in and out of fantasy even when they contain some of the elements that previously signalled realism. In the motherhood story, the objectivity of Alma's reportage is undermined by the repetition. In the next scene, Alma's uniform implies a return to the public Persona, but the mysterious stream of consciousness (which may or may not be Elisabeth's) and the blood ritual move us back to subjective reality. Although the hospital scene takes place in what was formerly a realistic setting, the dislocation in time and the fact that Elisabeth speaks heighten the ambiguity. The last scene is concerned with practical reality—the two women closing down the house; but the cuts to the statue, the Electra flashback, and the viewfinder shot once more return to artifice.

The power of Persona as mask is developed through the facial close-ups, which dominate the visuals of the film. Bergman sees the human face as one of the medium's most important resources.

> The approach to the human face is without doubt the hallmark and the distinguishing quality of the film. . . . The close-up, if objectively composed, perfectly directed and played, is the most forcible means at the disposal of the film director.[31]

In the scene where Elisabeth closely examines the photograph of the Warsaw ghetto, the camera moves from face to face as if each might reveal the experiences that lie behind it. In the early hospital scene as Alma walks out the door into empty brightness, the film cuts to a close-up of Elisabeth's mask-like face as she lies quietly in her bed, listening to Bach. Both face and camera remain motionless; the image darkens with extreme slowness, leading us to expect a fade-out. Instead, she turns her head slightly, breathes deeply, puts her hands up to her face, and the film cuts abruptly to Alma tossing restlessly in her bed. These visuals accentuate Elisabeth's alienation, even from Alma whom we glimpse before and after this long take. Their fusion is developed through brilliant composition in the scene before Alma tells about the beach orgy. As the two women move closer together while talking, Alma's profile passes in front of Elisabeth's face, and the camera holds a moment, emphasizing the illusion of a Self composed of Alma's head and Elisabeth's body.

In Bergman's dreamlike vision, clear distinctions are futile or impossible: objective reality merges with fantasy; characters become parts of the same personality and then split again; conscious artifice helps to express emotional truth: one film absorbs and is absorbed by the entire Bergman canon.

The Ritual (1969)

The power of *The Ritual* resides in the intense visual condensation and the extraordinary range of primordial emotions developed in the conflict between Bergman's troupe of players and their critic/judge. The film is concerned with three players—Hans Winkelmann (Gunnar Bjornstrand), his wife Thea (Ingrid Thulin), and her lover Sebastian Fisher (Anders Ek). Their act (called "Les Riens," [nothing]) has been charged with obscenity and is being investigated by a Court of Appeals Judge, Dr. Abramsson (Erik Hell). After each player is interrogated separately by Dr. Abramsson, the troupe performs privately in the judge's office, and their "number" frightens him to death. A narrator informs us that "A doctor who was summoned said Dr. Abramsson died of a heart attack. The three artists were later sentenced in connection with the mimed number named The Ritual. They paid their fines, and at the end of the summer, went away on a holiday. They never returned to this country."

As in *Persona*, the main characters seem to function as aspects of a single self, but their relationship more closely follows Freud than Jung. The judge represents the Superego and the troupe of players embodies the Id and Ego, which, in Freud's early theory, are part of the same structure and draw on the same energy source.[32] The critical judge, Dr. Abramsson, is cut off from the players, of whom he says: "I don't understand what drives you. I don't understand your relations." The judge is a work addict who strives for surface respectability, trying to cover his low class origins and animal nature with obsequious manners. Despite the sadistic pleasure afforded him by his powerful role in the investigation, he claims that he is incapable of aggression. Frequently he fears that others are laughing at him. Subject to feelings of guilt and inferiority himself, he tries to arouse those feelings in others. Tormented by memories of his childhood fears, he enjoys acting out the parental role with the players. As Sebastian accuses him: "You would like to pull our pants down and smack our bottoms."

Hans is the highly organized Ego who is subject to the pressures of the outside world (he makes the business arrangements for their act), of the Superego (he tries to placate the judge), and of the interior Id (he tries to maintain discipline and control over the other two "maniacs" in the troupe). Freud describes the "dependence of the ego upon the id as well as upon the superego, and . . . its impotence and apprehensiveness towards both, and also the superiority which it maintains so arduously."[33] Hans is aware of this relationship; he tries to make Thea and Sebastian dependent on him, though he knows that they are the source of the group's creative energy. He confesses to the Superego/judge:

> The really great artists can't be hurt. I'm not one of them. I've one great terror—of being alone. I'm dependent on them. . . . I try to make myself indispensable to them.

Freud describes the deviousness of the Ego in maintaining this illusion:

> From a dynamic point of view it is weak . . . and we are not entirely ignorant of the methods—one might almost call them "tricks"—by means of which it draws further amounts of energy from the id.[34]

As the Ego, Hans also identifies with the Superego in striving for respectability and seeing duty as a valid concept. In one scene, he carefully wipes a spot from his clothing, a gesture that identifies him with the excessive cleanliness of the judge.

Thea and Sebastian represent the erotic and aggressive forces of the Id respectively. In contrast to the down-to-earth Hans, they are associated with fire, air, and water. Sebastian, the bird, is like the phoenix that arises from the flames of self-immolation. Easily moved by hatred and other passions, he confesses his pleasure in having repeatedly stabbed his best friend, though he loved him and now misses him. He feels no guilt or remorse because he believes that he is his own god. This releases Sebastian from any social or moral obligation and gives him what the judge calls "a terrible freedom."

Thea, the erotic female flower, is open, moist, and receptive. She is described as a flowing stream who is threatened by the islands she encounters. She embodies many paradoxes: ecstasy and suffering, tragedy and hilarity, certainty and doubt, Virgin Mary and the circus whore. Her hypersensitivity and desire to please others are the source of her weakness; her fluidity allows the men to shape her according to their wishes. Sebastian tells her that she needs four men—"One to support you, one to love you, one to amuse you, and one to look after your soul." In this film she has three and they have her. Hans clearly distinguishes himself from the interior Id figures because he, like the judge, recognizes the true nature of their "terrible freedom":

> I'm worried about you and Sebastian tearing each other to pieces. I'll never be like you. I don't want to be. You can commit any infamy! Nothing touches you! You're both monsters!

Each of the characters makes a speech that explicitly comments on his identity as part of a single self. Thea, whose character is most lacking in boundaries, quotes her psychiatrist who told her: "You're not substance, you're movement—you flow into others and others flow into you." In describing the troupe to the judge, Hans says: "We're so involved in each other, I can't say whose idea that act was, we have so much in common . . . we've become a single working body." At one point, Dr. Abramsson confuses Hans and Sebastian; he envies their unity: "Such a trinity must be wonderful," and finally admits, "Perhaps I wanted to take part in it." The actors are also able to adopt Abramsson's role; Sebastian says to Hans: "We're always having scenes in which we're both audience and actors."

The only other character in the film is a priest, played by Bergman himself. As Dr. Abramsson's confessor, he is identified with the judge, yet his black hood links him as well with the hooded players who in the final ritual draw a confession from Abramsson and frighten him to death. By playing the role of the mute priest, Bergman strengthens the symbolic identification of the four characters as parts of his own psyche.

We see these four characters paired in every possible combination, dramatizing the sado-masochistic power struggles among various aspects of the Self. Although each part of the personality is capable of both dominance and vulnerability, the individual contexts reveal a pattern that defines which part plays what role with whom. It is easy for Dr. Abramsson to control and humiliate Hans, who must mediate between him and the interior Id figures. The judge is two hours late for an interview. Although the nervous tapping of his keys and the tiny twitch around his mouth reveal Hans' anger, he masks these feelings with an ingratiating humility. To show that they are both responsible citizens, Hans begins by telling the judge that, in case they are found guilty, he has already deposited a sum in the bank to cover the fine. Hans offers the judge a cigarette, though Abramsson has made no similar hospitable gesture. The judge asks questions designed to humiliate—"Why don't you visit your children?" "Are Fisher and your wife sleeping together?" Instead of responding with scorn or anger, Hans willingly accepts his suppliant role: "I've learned everything there is to know about humiliation . . . there's something in me that invites it." We see this quality manifested throughout this scene, particularly as he urges the judge not to interview his wife: "So you won't cancel the interview—not even if I beg you on my knees." In mentioning his wife's weakness to the judge, he actually invites her humiliation. The judge responds at first with false sympathy, turning off the tape-recorder and trapping Hans into offering him a bribe, which he then refuses with scornful virtue. When he coldly dismisses him with, "I've nothing more to say," Hans obsequiously replies: "I'm grateful for your magnanimity." He gives the judge another opportunity to reject him when he extends his hand and is totally ignored. Although in this scene the judge has completely dominated Hans, before the ritualistic murder at the end, Hans forces him to share in the humiliation: "You yourself must have known this weakness, a sensual longing for humiliation." This shifting power struggle between Hans and the judge sounds very much like Freud's description of the conflict between the Ego and the Superego when the personality is suffering from melancholia; in fact, Freud seems to provide a plot summary for the entire film.

> His super-ego becomes over-severe, abuses, humiliates and ill-treats his unfortunate ego, threatens it with the severest punishments, reproaches it for long forgotten actions . . . and behaves as though it had spent the whole interval in amassing complaints. . . . The superego has the ego at its mercy. . . . It is a very remarkable experience to observe morality . . . functioning as a periodical phenomenon. For after a certain number of months the whole moral fuss is at an end, the critical voice of the super-ego is silent, the ego is reinstated, and enjoys once more all the rights of man until the next attack. . . . The ego . . . triumphs, as though the superego had lost all its power or had become merged with the ego.[35]

Since the interior parts of the Id are not subject to the pressures of the Superego, Dr. Abramsson is unable to control Thea and Sebastian. Although he tries to dominate them, they have the power to bring out in him the lust and cruelty that he attempts to deny. Hence his encounters with both of them are marked by shifting power dynamics. In the interview with Sebastian, the actor first adopts the role of the whining underdog, complaining about his aching bones and diarrhea, asking for a drink to sustain him, and implicitly pleading for mercy. Trying to take advantage of his weakness, the judge asks questions to arouse his guilt. He first pries into the murder of his friend:

> JUDGE: Has it tormented you since?
> SEBASTIAN: Do you mean, do I miss him? Of course I miss him. I loved him.
> JUDGE: No pangs of conscience?
> SEBASTIAN: No (angrily).

The judge persists with questions about his children, whom Sebastian has "never bothered to count." But, then, without warning, Sebastian suddenly bursts into a passionate attack against the supercilious judge:

> How absurd you are with your self-esteem . . . you don't even keep yourself clean . . . under your after-shave I can smell the rank stench of fat. There's a ring of filth on your collar, your nails are black. I despise you. . . . You'd like to hobnob with three famous artists, to see your face in the newspaper. . . . I want a judge on my own level.

Trying to maintain his rationality and regain control by asserting the superiority of his humanistic ethics, Dr. Abramsson calmly replies:

> I regret you find my body repulsive. I do sweat profusely. I have seen specialists. . . . But that I'm dirty—no, I can't agree. No man washes himself more than I do. You say I am low class. That's a flexible concept. I had a good upbringing. . . . I've done my best not to embarrass you. . . . Your little outburst is forgiven and forgotten. You may leave now . . . you'lll have no more problems.

Realizing that this generosity is a devious maneuver to regain the power, Sebastian counters with greater violence. Moving forward aggressively, he calls the judge an animal and (like Alma in *Persona*) goes right for the judge's center: "You're rotten to the core. People

like you haven't the right to live." Totally shaken, the judge begins to
sweat profusely and humbles himself before Sebastian's aggression,
sinking into despair.

> I'm incapable of aggressiveness, I feel utterly powerless, I've no
> relations . . . nothing to live for.

As a means of supposedly calming the terrified judge, Sebastian
describes one of their numbers from the show in which a man, who is
overcome by hunger and emptiness, eats everyone around him—"his
wife, a shop assistant, two children, and a tough old granny." He
even eats a fillet from God's rump. Then he goes to the police station
where he reveals his empty interior. As if dumbfounded by this
sacrilegious story that parodies communion and by his own failure to
arouse Sebastian's guilty conscience, Dr. Abramsson poses one last
question: "Your religion?" Sebastian's reply explains why he has
been able to gain power over the Superego:

> I have none. I'm my own god. I supply my own angels and
> demons. . . . No one's ever going to frighten me again.

In the interview with Thea, Dr. Abramsson is at first very polite
and reassuring, beginning with simple banal questions, compli-
menting her on her appearance, offering her brandy. When he leaves
the room for a few moments, she panics. As if anticipating her
reaction, as soon as he returns, he stands behind her and strokes her
hair. Thea responds defensively; she begins to stammer and hands
him a written statement explaining her sensitivity ("the normal
pressure of my dress, for instance, can make me crazy with pain") and
the changes in her name and appearance ("My hair is dyed and I
hardly know my name . . . my mouth is my own but it changed shapes
when I got my new teeth"). He responds to her claims of martyrdom
("I play the saint and martyr, that's why I call myself Thea. Once a
redness appeared on my hand, but it didn't bleed. I play at being the
Virgin Mary") by attacking her aggressively, as if aware that her mask
will crumble, exposing her desperate eroticism.

> Sometimes you stammer, sometimes not. Where is your stammer
> now? Are you trying to make a fool of me? Where's the truth?
> You don't use your real name. What is this poetic profusion?
> Why all this acting? All these theatrics? But I glimpse your real
> nature behind it.

As he discovers her real name, he leans over her and presses her for the truth: "Your age, you lousy circus whore!" She begins to writhe and moan, pushing him away but shrieking, "Can't you kiss me?" When she panics under verbal pressure, she relies on her body. Is he raping her or is she seducing him? The action that follows is dominated by confusion and contradiction: she shouts, "Please stop!" but pulls off her underpants cooperatively; as she becomes more hysterical, he slaps her sadistically (as Sebastian later slaps him) and says: "It was your own fault, you made me furious." The sound of Hans pounding on the door adds to the tension. When Hans breaks in, Thea has an epileptic fit, the judge says defensively, "How the hell was I to know she wasn't acting . . . the bluff is over . . . I've tried being friendly and failed." The judge's main defense is to pretend that he has been the victim of play-acting by Hans and Thea, and hence is not responsible for his behavior. As Hans comforts Thea during her seizure, the judge says with self-conscious authority, "The play is over," and calls the police. Yet we are aware of the hypocrisy of Abramsson's behavior, for in trying to arouse and manipulate her eroticism, he has exposed his own lust and cruelty. Yet later in the final ritual scene, when he is again confronted with Thea's sexuality and Sebastian's aggression, he is indeed the victim of their play-acting. When Sebastian teases him with a knife and repeatedly strikes him in the face, the judge first tries to assert his moral superiority: "You have struck me and humiliated yourself. Perhaps you feel repulsion and desire." Yet these are the feelings he himself experienced in his earlier encounters with Thea and Sebastian.

Each of the players had tried to destroy the judge in his individual encounter—Sebastian through a verbal and physical assault, Thea by engaging him sexually, and Hans by outdoing him in humility and obsequiousness. Yet, each failed in his solo attempt, particularly the Ego: the judge drives Sebastian into an insane rage, Thea into an epileptic fit, and Hans into a bribery attempt. Freud suggests that the Ego can act from strength only when it is not isolated.

> If an actual disjunction of the two has come about, then the weakness of this ego becomes evident. If, however, the ego remains one with the id and indistinguishable from it, then it is its strength that is apparent.[36]

By reuniting as a trinity and performing a group ritual, the three players succeed in making the judge acknowledge his own evil.

Finally he breaks down and admits "even in my profession there's an element of cruelty . . . to make judgments . . . the lust of cruelty, you artists must know!" In identifying with the forces of the Id, the Superego is destroyed.

Although the responsible Hans is easily intimidated by the authoritarian judge and susceptible to the powers of the interior Id figures, he sometimes plays a dominant fatherly role. The scene in the dressing room begins with Thea drunk and weeping. She combines the roles of clown, child, and manipulator in a complex interchange of power with Hans. Frightened by her forthcoming interview with Dr. Abramsson, Thea invites Hans to play the role of the protective father. He promises to take her to an inn with lovely food and pleasant walks. But even within this relationship Thea can easily wound him by displaying her willfulness and sexual power as she demands that they take Sebastian along and urges Hans to keep him in the act. She justifies this request by telling Hans that Sebastian can't be without her, "He wants me in his bed every night." Trying to disarm him by anticipating his anger, she asks him whether he still loves her. Hans tries to regain the power by expressing his own weakness, telling her he is tired, which implies he may abandon her. Freud suggests that "when the ego struggles against an instinctual force in the id, it merely needs to give a signal of distress to attain its purpose through the aid of the all but omnipotent pleasure principle."[37] Afraid that she will lose the safety and indulgence provided by Hans, Thea responds by attacking Sebastian and acknowledging her dependence on the Ego.

> I think he's going out of his mind. . . . I'm afraid of him. . . . If I didn't have you, I'd kill myself.

Hans coldly replies, "No, you'd have someone else." Thea insists on her need, which unexpectedly arouses anger from Hans.

> THEA: You're my only security.
> HANS: Isn't it better to have insecurity with small artificial islands of security. . . . I'm tired of you, I'm tired of Sebastian, I'm tired of you and Sebastian. I'm tired of touring around with two maniacs . . . we're meaningless, disgusting, absurd . . . people don't need us any more. . . . You're lazy and sloppy and not worth one tenth of the money you earn. After the contract's over, you can go to hell.

Pleased with regaining power through his attack, Hans begins to hum, pours himself a drink, and then quietly says:

> Yet, I love you. Can you grasp that? In spite of everything, I love you. I feel sorry for you. I'd do anything to save you trouble.

His declaration of love only softens Thea for the next attack:

> We've reached the limit. It's humiliating and unworthy. I've had enough. You haven't understood a thing I've said.

Then muttering like Henny Penny, "The world's falling apart," Thea mocks him with: "Poor Hans, poor bad conscience, kiss, kiss, kiss." Hans reminds her of the service he performs for himself and the others:

> HANS: I cling to my sanity.
> THEA: So do I. I cling to you, I won't desert us. (coyly) Have I gotten ugly?

Rejecting Thea's assertion of the sexual tie, Hans sinks into greater despair:

> HANS: God, how tired I am, let me out of this prison. I'd like to sleep late.
> THEA: You woke at five with a black bird on your chest.
> HANS: No, I don't want to die.
> THEA: We cannot talk to each other . . . our words don't fit . . . utter lack of communication

Weeping and snivelling on Hans's shoulder in a return to her childlike role inspired by real fear of the forthcoming interview, Thea shifts the mode of the conversation and Hans resumes the supportive role of the Ego:

> THEA: He's horrible.
> HANS: He's only doing his job.
> THEA: You don't believe that.

Because Hans is less susceptible to Sebastian's aggressiveness than to Thea's sexuality, his power is much more stable in the bar scene with Sebastian. Although Sebastian makes Hans wait almost as long as the judge had, his tardiness demonstrates not his superiority and power, but his irresponsibility in coping with his obligations. As Freud points out:

> The ego is an organized entity, whereas the id is not; in fact, the ego is the organized part of the id.[38]

Hans's role as efficient businessman is emphasized by his making

notes and checking items off a list; he forces Sebastian to operate
within this incongenial mode by making statements like: "I can't go
on lending you money indefinitely . . . (showing him an accounting)
credit on the left, debit on the right. . . . " Sebastian plays the role of
the irresponsible child, motivated entirely by his desire to reduce the
tension of this unpleasant scene and fulfill his immediate needs. For
a little cash in hand, he readily signs a new contract, despite his
earlier determination to leave the act. Once Hans has established his
financial control as a source of power, he very subtly shifts the
conversation to the realm of sexuality while pretending that he is still
talking about money. Because he knows that responsibility frightens
Sebastian, he cleverly begins with a question that couples him and
Thea: "What are you and Thea going to do . . . Thea could start
stripping. . . . " Then he makes his real power play, using the same
strategy that worked in the dressing room with Thea.

> HANS: Who's to pay Thea's hotel bill? We must be clear as to
> who is managing her affairs.
> SEBASTIAN: You're her husband.
> HANS: Exactly. . . . Will you tell her that tactfully? She's under
> the delusion that she's handling her own expenses.

Having rationally demonstrated his control over both Sebastian and
Thea, he checks off the last item on his list and prepares to enjoy his
conquest by assuming a fatherly, almost therapeutic manner:

> HANS: How do you feel?
> SEBASTIAN: Goddamn awful.

This change in mode invites Sebastian to seek fatherly advice, but on
the subject of how to bring on an orgasm in the woman they share.
Hans explains graphically the manual procedures that he hit on out
of "sheer desperation." Despite their rivalry for Thea and despite
Hans's manipulative behavior in this scene, the two men now
cooperate as Hans gives Sebastian good advice. As Freud emphasizes,
"it would be quite unjustifiable to conceive of the ego and the id as if
they were two opposing camps."[39] Like Thea, Sebastian now asks
questions designed to gain reassurance:

> SEBASTIAN: Do you hate me?
> HANS: Far from it . . . but I liked you far better before you started
> drinking and getting careless. I admired you . . . you had
> something special, an inner light. . . .
> SEBASTIAN: And Thea and I are putting that light out.
> HANS: I'm expecting the agent at 5:00.

As Hans responds to this poignant admission of self doubt by bringing the conversation back to business, he demonstrates the Ego's power to control the emotional forces of the Id's interior.

The bedroom scene between Thea and Sebastian demonstrates the most fluid exchange of power between two childish equals, who display hostility and affection while playing a petulant game of "Can you top this?" She announces she hates him, and he accuses her of having bad breath. She complains that he can't satisfy her sexually, that he always wants her with him, and that he's unfaithful. Sebastian is not taken in, and says "I don't believe in your jealousy. it's just bad temper." When someone knocks at the door, Sebastian thinks it's Hans, and Thea gets her revenge by accusing him of having a bad conscience. After Sebastian tells about a dream in which he comically rejects both mother and school, Thea tells one of hers in a delivery that makes it sound as if she invented it to get back at Sebastian: she must choose between an old horse and a young horse. Unfortunately, she chooses the young one who climbed into the cart and "kept talking about love and art" while she was forced to do the pulling. As Thea blocks her face with a mirror, Sebastian begins a poem that identifies and elevates his own qualities: "I'm half bird, half man . . . bird head, human heart." Midway through the poem, she puts the mirror between them and takes over the recitation, using the poem to identify herself: "the membrane . . . of never satisfied longing." Then Sebastian begins a parallel dialogue about Thea the "gorgeous woman flower . . . Mother Earth's own sister" as he tries to pull her pants down, and she holds the mirror in front of her crotch. As if to deny him the satisfaction of defining her, she quotes a psychiatrist who told her: "You're not substance, you're movement. . . . Islands in a river are signs of approaching death. One day the stream is choked by the islands. . . ." As if to deny the glamour of this self vision, Sebastian responds with a parody: "An old producer once said of actors . . . The miracle is always the same. Lillies shoot up from the arseholes of corpses." In defeat and despair, Thea cries: "God have mercy on me, save my soul before it perishes from emptiness." Becoming more demonic in the silence that follows her plea, Sebastian toys with a book of matches, his face registering sensuous anticipation of the triumphant gesture that has occurred to him. Very deliberately, he applies the lighted match to the sheets and whistles contentedly as the flames leap up around him. The camera is now occupied exclusively with Sebastian in profile and front view, ignoring Thea who has been magnificently upstaged by this performance. This gesture has also expanded the film's potentialities by transforming the mode of reality. As Sebastian sits enjoying his self-immolation, we know that in this film we can expect anything.

These four characters, who represent different parts of the personality, all share certain qualities common to the organism. Enjoying a highly developed taste for sado-masochism, they are all demons (who mistreat their own children) and childlike victims themselves. Dr. Abramsson is controlled by childhood fears and sensual memories of humiliation. Thea and Sebastian are like crazy children who must be taken care of by Hans, and Sebastian imagines himself living on a stony island with the sound of a child crying. Thea and Hans have institutionalized their idiot child, and both Hans and Sebastian are more than willing to let the lawyers take care of their offspring from former marriages. They all share the fear of dying and of being alone and, finally, as each character reveals, the whole personality is sick with emptiness and despair.

The dreamlike quality of *The Ritual* lies primarily in its sparseness or condensation, which helps to develop the emotional intensity and symbolic identity of persons and situations. Swiss citizens out of convenience, the players have come from Poland and are on their way to Holland and the Far East, but we are never told the location of the present action. Characters and settings are minimal, with little centrifugal extension to external reality. The stark black and white photography is essential; it is almost impossible to imagine this film in color. Simplified and abstract environments set off the whole film as a ritual action, and are particularly effective on television, the medium for which it was originally made. Most of the rooms are small, cramped, and windowless. Only in the opening scene in the office do we see a window, but it is barred and the camera does not allow us to look at the world outside. The walls are completely bare in the office, in the hotel room and in the bar; characters frequently move slowly into the frame against these backdrops as if preparing to pose for institutional photographs. The usual noise and movement of a bar are reduced to a fragment of the bartender's hand as he sets drinks before Sebastian and Hans; the hotel room contains nothing but a bed and chair; the shallow stage space of the confessional has only a screen and a statue of the Virgin. This extreme simplification strongly emphasizes the few details of setting that do appear in the film: in huge close-ups, telephone and tape recorder become mechanical substitutes for real communication; in the dressing room the circus poster of a bear being led by a beautiful woman illuminates the relationship between Thea and Hans; the enormous shot of the

Union match box ironically invites us to ponder its symbolic significance. The monotone quality of the lighting reduces the realistic contrast in a given setting and instead emphasizes the discreet, autonomous identity of scenes. The opening, for example, is characterized by a soft dark gray, while the second scene in the bedroom is lit with thin, white brightness in which shadows are almost completely eliminated. The symbolic condensation is enhanced by the static camera which, like the audience at a drama, sees the characters only as they move into its narrow field of vision, implying that they have no extraneous life.

As in *Persona*, the film's imagery is dominated by the facial close-up, which has a double function. As Bergman has said, the face can reveal the depths of human experience; yet ironically, faces are frequently hidden or distorted, stressing the limitations of human perception and knowledge. Both functions are suggested by the very first close-up of Abramsson's eye, distorted as he looks through a magnifying glass at the photos of the players. This implies that the judge is going to investigate the lives of these characters through a lens, magnifying selected events and isolating each individual for observation, as Bergman will isolate the pairs, simplify the images, and emphasize the close-up. At one point, the judge raises his lens and looks directly at the camera as if to imply that Bergman, the other observer, is watching the audience, who are *his* subjects of investigation— linking them to the major characters in the film. In this way we, too, play the double role of subject and audience. Nor do we get a true picture of Abramsson because his face is distorted by the lens he wears in his role as the "devil" critic. Yet when he interviews Sebastian, a huge shot of Abramsson's face as he wipes off the sweat truthfully reveals the intense humiliation and fear that lie beneath his surface respectability. In the scene where Sebastian sets the bed on fire, the series of close-ups from various angles cannot reveal his motives for this bizarre action.

The treatment of the human face is also one of the important ways in which the no-exit quality of the film is imposed on the audience experientially. Characters are trapped in masks and personae like Sebastian and his dark glasses, their self-realization frozen behind immobility and deception. In the opening scene, Thea and Sebastian stand behind a barred window, their faces revealing their first experience of entrapment and their desire to murder the judge. In scene two, Thea deliberately blocks her face with a mirror as she plays empty sexual games with Sebastian, who tugs at his face as if it were a rubber mask; in the confessional scene, a hood and a latticed screen block and distort the two faces; Thea's clown make-up—one of her many disguises—ironically substitutes her true grotesquery for the outward beauty of her appearance; in the very next scene, she offers the judge her mask-like beauty in an unsuccessful effort to disguise her "true nature." In the same scene, her vulnerability and frustration are expressed through a close-up where the judge, his back to the camera, looms in the foreground as he partially blocks the face of Thea, who is backed against the wall by his accusations. Bergman denies us the freedom of full perception, as the judge denies escape to Thea. The ironic use of close-up and distortion, the starkness of setting, and the regimented structure all manifest non-discursively the fragmented, trapped, and desperate quality of the characters, with whom we have been identified in the film's opening shot.

These condensation techniques are combined with special power in the final ritual scene, which has many connections with earlier sequences and functions as a microcosm of the whole. Like the opening, in which we were informed that it was Sunday, this scene locates us even more specifically in time—it is "Wednesday, August 9." Dr. Abramsson is reporting to his tape recorder a second encounter with Sebastian that alleviates the humiliation he suffered in the first (we are not sure, however, if the second interview really took place). We learn that the judge has invited the players to put on a private performance and that the troupe has requested that no one else be present. Thus, in contrast to the previous scenes, both factions have participated in setting up the conditions. Reversing the power relationship in the interview with Hans, the troupe, dressed in dark hoods like the priest in the confessional, arrives late. Just as in the opening, the troupe is in the foreground, exchanging pleasantries; the power relationships seem neutral. Whereas in the first scene, the judge had stood over them while they sat passively on the couch, now they surround him ominously as he sits powerless in his chair, signalling that the first stage of the ritual has begun. Like a Black Mass, it incorporates primitive elements into a parody of Christian ceremony, mocking the cannibalism and violence implicit in the wine-drinking sacrament; it is a funeral rite for the judge, preparing him for the death that it effects. Sebastian initiates the action by brandishing a knife, which he then uses to slash open a bladder full of dark liquid that flows into a bowl. As Hans begins to describe their number, they remove their black robes to reveal their costumes— Thea plays a bare breasted goddess; Hans and Sebastian wear enormous menacing phallusses and don their bird masks. Hans stands behind the seated judge (as Abramsson had stood over the humiliated Hans in their previous encounter) and places his hands over his ears, assigning the judge his role; "The audience's voice is hushed." Thea begins to beat the drum. All of these preliminary actions succeed in reducing the judge to a state of whining terror. As if aware of the spectre of death, the judge begins to confess, initiating the second stage of the ritual.

> Let me say something. My father wanted me to be a lawyer, but I had no talent. . . . I behaved badly and ask for forgiveness. . . . I've always been afraid. My first memories are of fear. I'm a victim of stupid phobias. How can I give you the key to myself? Why do you smile? Am I ridiculous? It was a mistake to arrange this performance.

As if purged by this confession, Abramsson shifts mode:

> No more fear. It's you who decide. I am your obedient onlooker. You never had a more grateful audience.

As in their earlier encounter, Sebastian responds to this self-abasement with greater hostility, slapping him repeatedly in the face. Regaining his composure through humor ("Has the performance begun, or is the orchestra tuning up?"), the judge resumes his confession:

> I've lived a number of days and nights—known joy, sorrow, disappointment, tears . . . it's all here (pointing to his face).

He concludes with a command for the performance (or third stage) to begin. A close-up of Hans's face dominates the foreground, while Sebastian and Thea stand directly behind him; together they seem to form a trinity—"one single body" with four arms, like a Hindu god. While Hans chants, the others perform the actions. "Just before dawn, the wind sweeps across the water. Then dawn comes." As Hans raises the bowl toward the sun, they begin to hum and Thea puts on the god's mask. Stretching his arms behind him, Sebastian grasps Thea's forearms and lifts her slowly upward as Hans recites:

> At the same time I raise the bowl above my head. . . . Now the light is on the face, which is reflected in blood . . . now I drink the mirrored image from the bowl.

As Hans drinks her image, Thea slowly sinks down behind Sebastian and the three parts of the Id briefly form one body. Then Hans, the

Ego, moves forward and says, "Briefly, this is our number," and the judge cries out passionately, "I understand." The camera cuts to a tight close-up of his face; gasping with his head thrown back, he sinks into death as Hans delivers the last line of the recitation: "Now Dr. Abramsson is dead."

This ending suggests a series of correspondences among the literal ritual in the film, the Christian communion it imitates, and the psychological struggle among parts of the Self it symbolizes. In the performance, the "divine image" is drunk to reunify the troupe; in the Christian sacrament, the body and blood of Christ are consumed to renew the soul. But unlike the divine images, the Superego cannot be consumed and born again; drawn in by the power of Id and Ego, it is defeated and destroyed, but *they* are nourished by this cannibalism. In a world with no God, the internal psychological drama replaces religion.

> I'm still convinced there is no God anymore—that God is dead. .
> . . But it is a part of the human being—a room in his mind that is
> holy. . . .[40]

Thus throughout his canon, Bergman continues an almost theological exploration of the forces of the Id. They are both creative and destructive, but without being in touch with them, it is impossible to survive primordial conflict.

The ritual movement of the symbolic drama is intensified by the structure. The film is divided into nine scenes, each numbered and labeled according to its setting, each introduced and concluded by discordant music (practically the only music in the film). The opening ("Scene 1: An Office") and closing (Scene 9: An Office") bring all four characters together, enclosing the film in a circular trap. The other three scenes that take place in "an office" reveal the judge interviewing each member of the troupe individually. These meetings alternate with scenes in a hotel room, a confessional, a dressing room, and a bar—all intimate settings for the pairings of the characters in every possible combination. An individual character is never alone in a scene. Dr. Abramsson comes the closest, for in the confessional the priest is silent, almost as cold and lifeless as the statue of the Virgin, both suggesting the sterility of the Church in coping with man's alienation and despair. This contrived, fragmented structure repeatedly breaks the dramatic illusion and works in tension with the fluidity of the characters' interactions. We do not know how much time elapses between sequences. Like the islands in the river, these discreet scenes either provide something secure to cling to or threaten to choke the stream to death. Bergman's device of the highly conventional scene markers (like his undermining of the facial close-up) indicates an ironic attitude toward aesthetic structures, a means of control which limits potential self-realization through innovation and freedom.

The highly patterned structure with its repetition and variation implies that the film, like the players' final performance, satisfies a "sudden urge to carry out a rite . . . a ritual game, an incantation, a formula . . . a sensual longing for humiliation." By elevating psychological games to the level of archetypes, Bergman forces us to see their connection with institutional rituals within our culture. The deep structures of the mind are like those of society. The elaborate procedures of the law (the judge claims the investigation is a "mere formality" but insists: "Our laws may be antiquated, but they must be enforced. . . . I must stick to the rules") and the prayers, sacraments and ceremonies all embody this analogy. If members of a society can't express their individual energies, if the power of people like Dr. Abramsson is too great, then the struggle between passion and reason is out of balance. People must find a release. This is the function of traditional religion. Although all four characters deny the existence of God, they call out to him out of their despair, as if going through the motions of an habitual action or repeating a conventional phrase that no longer has any meaning. As the judge tells the priest: "I don't want to confess, but I must speak with someone . . . you know that non-believers often pray, it relieves the anguish." Without traditional religion, rituals may culminate in murder. Under the eye of a corrupt bureaucracy, desperate and alienated individuals perform acts of inexplicable violence and participate, willy nilly, in wars among nations. Ritual is a means of imposing order, however empty, on spiritual anarchy, a way of creating a "frail ring of human warmth," a troupe of players who help to keep each other alive.

Like the final ritual, each discreet scene functions as a microcosm of the entire film, making it more like a dream. The symbolic condensation extends beyond the boundaries of *The Ritual*, as each scene alludes to earlier films or anticipates future works.

The first scene looks forward to *The Passion of Anna,* in which an architect is obsessed with his files of photographs and enjoys humiliating the subjects of the pictures. Like Abramsson, Bergman interrogates his actors about the roles they are playing. The bedroom scene between Sebastian and Thea parallels a scene in *The Silence* where Anna (the boy's mother) makes love with the waiter. Both sexual encounters are set in hotel rooms in strange towns; both environments are rendered highly abstract and symbolic, partly through the extreme lighting—very bright in *The Ritual,* and very dark in *The Silence;* both end with a break in the mode of reality that suggests a connection with war and death—Anna looks out the window at an ominous tank rumbling by in the deserted street below, and Sebastian suddenly immolates himself like the priests and others protesting the Viet Nam war (an image that also appears in *Persona*). The scene also evokes the two erotic encounters in *Naked Night* between Anne, the vulnerable young "circus whore" who lives with the middle-aged leader of the troupe, and Frans, a demonic young actor who seduces her. In these scenes, as in the sequence from *The Ritual,* Bergman relies heavily on mirrors and has the lovers play reversible sado-masochistic games in which he accuses her of smelling bad and she attacks his sexual prowess. The sado-masochistic encounter between Sebastian and the judge is reminiscent of the meeting between Johan and the school teacher as they walk along the high plateau in *Hour of the Wolf.* Both involve unstable artists who defy the control of an authoritative figure by erupting into sudden physical violence. The fluid shifts of power between these characters are continued later in both films—the dinner party in *Hour of the Wolf,* and the final performance in *The Ritual.* The confessional scene is almost identical to the one in *Seventh Seal* where the despairing knight, whose faith has been undermined as death approaches, tries to reduce his anguish by confessing. The screen conceals not the comfort of religion, but the black-hooded figure of Death, who is dressed exactly like the mute priest in *The Ritual.* In both films, this encounter with Death foreshadows their fate. The basic situation in the encounter between Hans and Abramsson is similar to that of the dream sequence in *Wild Strawberries.* The competent, rational, but unimaginative doctor is asked humiliating questions by a bourgeois investigator who makes vague accusations. The doctor's timid response parallels Hans's obsequiousness. The dressing room scene condenses two sequences from *Naked Night* in which Anne, the young mistress, begs the circus leader not to leave her. Many of the same lines are actually used in the scene from *The Ritual.* In the earlier film, it is the fear of abandonment that leads the woman to be unfaithful. Too frightened to commit suicide, her betrayed lover deals with his humiliation by shooting the caged circus bear, who has been his alter-ego throughout the film. In *The Ritual*, the picture of a woman leading a bear alludes directly to *Naked Night*. In both films the man and the woman are sick of each other and try to escape, but they are "stuck in hell," united by their struggle against outside forces. Thea's clown make-up in this scene also evokes Frost, who like the bear is an alter-ego for the circus leader. Out of love for his wife Alma, the "circus whore" who trains the bear, Frost tries to hide her nakedness; together the couple experiences an intense humiliation. Despite the extreme differences in tone, the confused rape scene in *The Ritual* is linked to the one in *The Virgin Spring* not only through the painful brutality of both, but also through the desire for revenge, which provides the climatic scene in both films. It is also related to the incestuous scene in *Through a Glass Darkly* where the madness of the woman finds expression through ambiguous sexual invitation, and to the rape scene in *Face to Face*, which may be an hallucination and where the victim later admits she wanted to be raped. The barroom scene between Hans and Sebastian recalls the conversation between Jan and the mayor in *Shame*, where the husband and lover discuss the protection and economic control of the woman they share. A similar situation also occurs in *Through a Glass Darkly* where the father and husband discuss each other's inadequacies in dealing with the insane Karin. The final enactment of the ritual evokes *The Magician*. The troupe is commanded to perform before the town by the scientist who doubts their power; the performance ultimately leads to the death of an innocent bystander, and the scientist is forced to acknowledge the terror aroused in him. Just as the troupe has begun to disintegrate under the condemnation of the townspeople, they are commanded to perform before the king and, like the players who go on a holiday at the end of *The Ritual*, the troupe leaves joyously, turning its back on the confinement and violence in the town.

All of these parallels enrich the symbolic power of *The Ritual*, which, like *Persona*, condenses so many of the themes, situations, and images that provide the unique characteristics of Bergman's dream films. While each of the films provides a highly controlled and powerful experience, their relationship is uniquely fruitful; like the filmmaker himself, the canon moves inward toward greater realization by exploring and integrating the significant parts of a complex and fluid whole.

Footnotes to Chapter One

1. Ingmar Bergman, as quoted in "A Visit with Ingmar Bergman," by A. Alvarez, *New York Times Magazine* (Sunday, Dec. 8, 1975), 104.

2. Ingmar Bergman, as quoted in *Introduction to Ingmar Bergman*, produced for television by Lewis Freedman, 1967.

3. Ingmar Bergman, "Introduction," *Four Screenplays of Ingmar Bergman*, trans. Lars Malmstrom and David Kushner (New York: Simon and Shuster, 1960), p. xv.

4. Ingmar Bergman, "What is Film Making?" *Film Makers on Film Making*, ed. Harry M. Geduld (Bloomington: Indiana University Press, 1967), p. 184.

5. *Introduction to Ingmar Bergman.*

6. "What is Film Making?" p. 185.

7. "Introduction," p. xix-xx.

8. "Introduction," p. xiv.

9. "What is Film Making?" pp. 180-181.

10. Ingmar Bergman, "Cries and Whispers," trans. Alan Blair, *New Yorker* (Oct. 12, 1972), p. 46.

11. Ingmar Bergman, *Each Film Is My Last* (New York: Janus Films, a.d.), p. 4.

12. *Introduction to Ingmar Bergman.*

13. "What is Film Making?" pp. 187-188.

14. "Cries and Whispers," p. 55.

15. "What is Film Making?" pp. 178-179.

16. *Introduction to Ingmar Bergman.*

17. *Introduction to Ingmar Bergman.*

18. *Introduction to Ingmar Bergman.*

19. "Cries and Whispers," p. 38.

20. "Introduction," p. xxii.

21. "What is Film Making?" p. 182.

22. "What is Film Making?" pp. 180-181.

23. "Cries and Whispers," p. 66.

24. *Introduction to Ingmar Bergman.*

25. *Introduction to Ingmar Bergman.*

26. *Introduction to Ingmar Bergman.*

27. Sigmund Freud, "Creative Writers and Daydreaming," in *Critical Theory Since Plato*, ed. Hazard Adams (New York: Harcourt Brace Jovanovich, 1971), p. 752.

28. Ingmar Bergman, *Persona and Shame*, trans. Keith Bradfield (New York: Grossman Publishers, 1972), p. 74. All subsequent references to this screenplay will be included in the text. Since the screenplay is quite different from the film, we will quote dialogue only if it actually occurs in the film.

29. "Conversations with Bergman," in *Ingmar Bergman Directs*, John Simon (New York: Harcourt Brace Jovanovich, 1972), pp. 30-39.

30. Ingmar Bergman, "The Snakeskin," in *Persona and Shame*, p. 11.

31. *Each Film Is My Last*, p. 5.

32. In *The Interpretation of Dreams* (1900), Freud first proposed a two-part model of personality. Drawing its energies from the Id, the Ego was seen as part of that structure. Later in *The Ego and the Id* (1923), Freud began to give the Ego greater autonomy, suggesting that it has its own energy source.

33. Sigmund Freud, *The Problem of Anxiety*, trans. Henry Alden Bunker (New York: W. W. Norton & Co., 1936), p. 22.

34. Sigmund Freud, "The Anatomy of the Mental Personality," *New Introductory Lectures on Psycho-Analysis*, trans. W. J. H. Sprott (New York: W. W. Norton & Co., 1933), p. 107.

35. "The Anatomy of the Mental Personality," pp. 87-88.

36. *The Problem of Anxiety, p. 24.*

37. *The Problem of Anxiety, p. 18.*

38. *The Problem of Anxiety, p. 24.*

39. *The Problem of Anxiety, p. 24.*

40. *Introduction to Ingmar Bergman.*

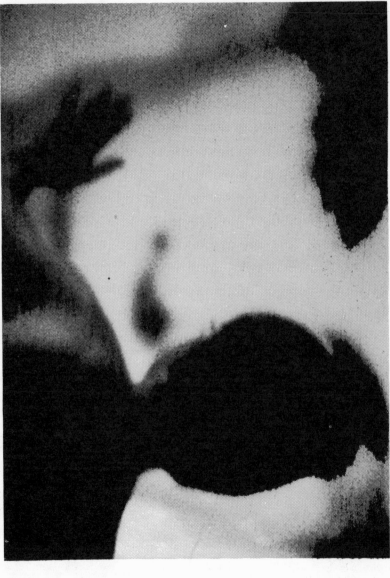

PERSONA. The germinal dream image in the opening montage is the small boy in shadow, reaching out his hand toward the illuminated screen on which gradually appears the blurred image of a woman's face, which represents for him mother, other, and plenitude.

Courtesy of United Artists Corporation.

PERSONA. The two women merge in a loving close-up where they occupy equal parts of the frame and where all black-white boundaries dissolve into muted grey tones.

PERSONA. Elisabeth cowers in the unreal half-light of the television.

PERSONA. Deep in the foreground, Elisabeth writes the letter that will separate their worlds while Alma is seen through glass, framed by the window in the separate space of the deep background.

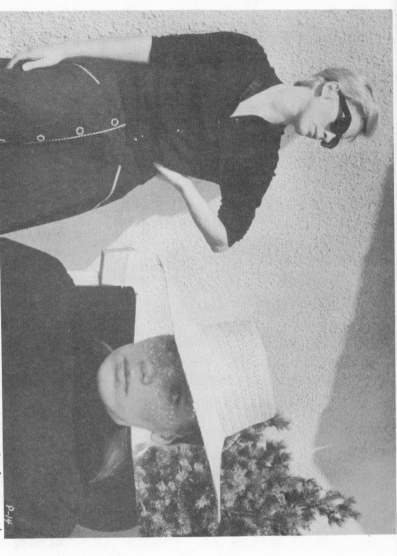

PERSONA. The two women gaze in opposite directions as posture, position in the frame, and high contrast of clothing and image suggest their volatile tension and the distance between them.

PERSONA. After one of the most ambiguous dream sequences, Elisabeth suddenly pops her head into the bottom of an exterior shot as if to take a picture of the audience and startle us with a form of direct address.

THE RITUAL. The formal portrait of the troupe of three players reveals them without their ominous masks, yet their faces wear expressions of contrived cheerfulness that disguise their true nature.

THE RITUAL. Thea and Sebastian stand behind a barred window, their faces revealing their first experience of entrapment and their desire to murder the judge. Sebastian's hidden eyes and Thea's elegant grooming ironically fail to mask the fear and anger revealed in their expressions. Courtesy of Janus Films Inc.

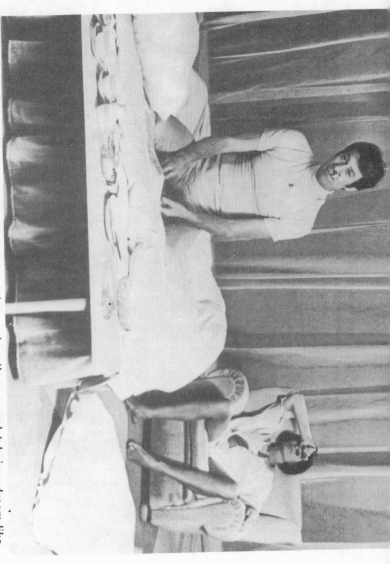

THE RITUAL. In the bedroom scene where curtains enclose them completely in a dream-like monochromatic world, Thea and Sebastian demonstrate a fluid power exchange between two childish equals who are playing dangerously with sexual fire. Courtesy of Janus Films Inc.

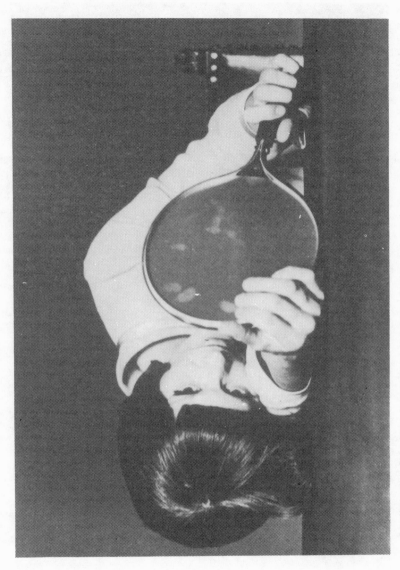

THE RITUAL. Thea narcissistically studies her own face as if fashioning new seductive strategies. Courtesy of Janus Films Inc.

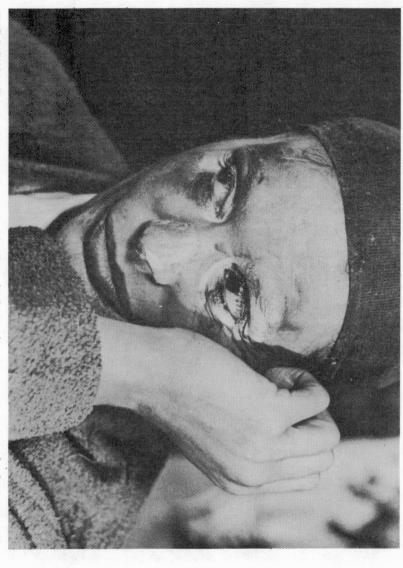

THE RITUAL. Thea's clown make-up ironically substitutes her true grotesquery for her outward beauty. Courtesy of Janus Films Inc.

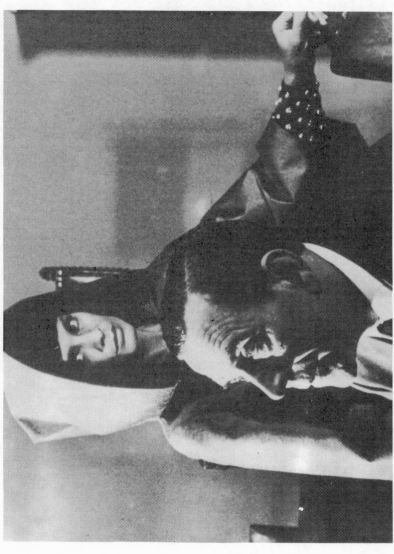

THE RITUAL. Reversing the power relationships in previous scenes, the hooded Thea now stands behind the frightened judge, extending her hand as if to take control. The expressions on their faces silently reveal the dynamics. Courtesy of Janus Films Inc.

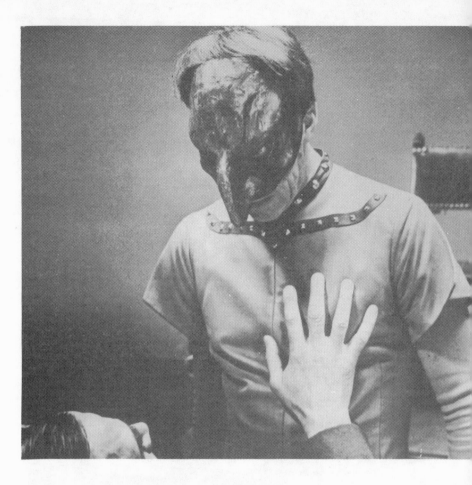

THE RITUAL. The judge pleads for mercy from the masked, dehumanized Sebastian. As in the opening montage of PERSONA, the gesture of the outreached hand suggests many meanings—a desperate plea for human contact, a desire to protect the self from the outside world, an attempt to define or dissolve the boundary between the self and the other. Courtesy of Janus Films Inc.

2

Sex and Politics in *Weekend* (1967), *Sweet Movie* (1974), and *Seven Beauties* (1975): The Way Out

It is not the consciousness of men that determines their being, but, on the contrary, their social being that determines their consciousness.

Karl Marx

Millions of women are completely invisible because their reality is eaten away by powerful men.

Dusan Makavejev

It therefore falls to ... criticism to continue to compare the inside and the outside, existence and history, to continue to pass judgment on the abstract quality of life in the present, and to keep alive the idea of a concrete future.

Fredric Jameson

Weekend, Sweet Movie, and *Seven Beauties* explicitly focus on sexual politics in exploring the corruption and decline of Western civilization, in which economics, government, class structure, sex roles and art are all implicated. In these three films, sex is co-opted by a repressive society, to be used in exchange for survival and power, yet

all three also raise the question whether the culture and its sexually
opportunistic protagonists deserve to survive. All three are satiric in
mode, drawing on the potentially liberating power of subversive
humor. They shock and outrage their audiences in an attempt to raise
our consciousness, engage us in self-criticism, and move us toward
progressive or radical action.

The three films come together with a Marxist/Feminist perspective
in that they acknowledge that art is part of the larger material context
of history, economics, and politics. All films are political in the sense
that they reflect the dominant ideology of the society in which they
are manufactured. Although Marxist/Feminist criticism can therefore be applied to any work of art, it is particularly effective in
illuminating the unique value of works that were created out of a
similar conceptual framework. Jean-Luc Godard, Dusan Makavejev,
and Lina Wertmuller, the directors of these three films, identify
themselves as Marxists supporting the Feminist cause; they see their
films, not merely as vehicles for personal expression, but as products
of a particular economic system at a particular moment of history,
distributed and consumed in the capitalist, sexist marketplace.
Inevitably, these products reflect the economic and sexual exploitation of the context in which they were manufactured; yet at the same
time, each filmmaker sees art as having the potential to alter these
conditions by providing new models of behavior, developed through
innovations in form and content.

In this chapter, we hope to integrate elements of Marxist and
Feminist criticism that will demystify these films and lead us to
aesthetic and materialist discriminations among them. We will draw
most heavily on those contemporary Marxist critics whose theories
take a dialectic approach to form as well as content. While all
Marxists assume the primacy of economics—that the mode of
production in any society forms the infrastructure on which the
superstructure (including the arts) is built—some Marxists grant a
more significant role to art and are more receptive to artistic
experimentation. Fredric Jameson's *Marxism and Form* provides an
excellent overview of Marxist criticism, distinguishing between two
schools: (1) the older Soviet tradition that dominated literary
criticism in the thirties and is illustrated in the works of Christopher
Caudwell and Ernst Fisher and in the *Aesthetik* of Georg Lukács, and
(2) the "postindustrial Marxism" that is compatible with phenomenology and that is exemplified in the works of T. M. Adorno, Walter
Benjamin, Herbert Marcuse, Ernst Bloch, Jean Paul Sartre, and

Jameson himself. He describes "the rhetoric of the older Marxist criticism as *genetic* in its emphasis on historical evolution and on the emergence of capitalist institutions."[1] This older school is often limited in the kinds of art it values, favoring social realism and rejecting works that are experimental in form. In contrast, the new Marxist criticism sees the revolutionary potential of innovative form and is thereby more compatible with feminism and transformalism.

> Marxism as such, . . . does not seem to exclude the adherence to some other kind of philosophy; that one can be both a Marxist and an existentialist, phenomenologist, Hegelian, realist, empiricist, or whatever.[2]

Being both diagnostic and descriptive, the new Marxist criticism develops Hegelian themes that are central to the theoretical frameworks that we apply in other chapters—"the relationship of part to whole, the opposition between concrete and abstract, the concept of totality, the dialectic of appearance and essence, the interaction between subject and object."[3]

Despite Althusser's efforts to reconcile Marxism with structuralism and his acknowledgment that art plays a crucial role in society, we have consciously avoided his position, which we find incompatible with transformalism for the following reasons. First, in attacking Marxist humanism, he denies all freedom and intentionality both for the artist and the audience and wants to invalidate the phenomenological nature of the artistic experience, which are precisely the values that Jameson successfully reconciles with Marxism. Secondly, Althusser rejects the Hegelian emphasis on self-criticism and thus fails to subject his own point of view to critical analysis, a process which Jameson places at the center of dialectical thinking. Finally, Althusser argues for the primacy of pure theory and de-emphasizes practice (as he has acknowledged in his late auto-critique), which upsets the dialectical balance that Jameson carefully maintains. For these reasons, we have chosen Jameson rather than Althusser as our primary model of new Marxist criticism.

In this chapter, we will also explore these films from a feminist perspective. Although some feminists reject the alliance with Marxism because they see it as patriarchal, we will combine them for a number of reasons. First, sex roles are clearly interwoven with social, political, economic, and philosophical issues. Moreover, the dominant tasks of feminist criticism—the historical and formal demystification of films produced in a male-dominated industry, the search for a female iconography, the encouragement of films made by women, and the exposure of the means by which women have been excluded from production—are structurally similar to those of Marxist criticism. The combination of these perspectives allows both of them to expand the critical enterprise rather than narrowing it into a competitive fragmentation.

A unique body of feminist film theory has been emerging over the last several years, often in the form of an open-ended discourse among a number of writers in Great Britain and the U. S.[4] Drawing largely on new French psychoanalytic, structuralist, and Marxist theory (at the moment, especially the work of Lacan and Althusser), this thought focuses on: 1) radical analysis of camerawork and editing in deconstructing the erotic "look" for which women are typically set up on screen; 2) radical analysis of narrative with special attention to innovations moving away from the single-climax structure; 3) exploration of the bases for roles of limited subject-hood that are typically created for women; 4) deconstruction of an entrenched "realism" that naturalizes these representations of women and props up the patriarchal illusion that what is shown in film is correct and inevitable in the world as it is and must be; 5) reassertion of the role of primary experience in encountering works of art, and analysis of the audience's participation in shaping their impact and meaning. The fluid exchange of these ideas means that we cannot work from a single author or text; instead, we will draw widely from our reading in these areas to inform our feminist perspective.

In addition, over the last twenty years feminist writing outside of film has had a pervasive influence in all areas of study. Simone de Beauvoir's *The Second Sex* and Shulamith Firestone's *The Dialectic of Sex* remain fundamental to evolving feminist thought. Both writers attempt an historical and theoretical union of Marxism and feminism. Firestone, more materialist in her basic approach, argues that the biological divisions between male and female preceded even the construction of the economic infrastructure.

She predicts that feminism will be the first revolutionary movement effectively to combine the political and the personal because it involves not only the reorganization of social institutions, but the reintroduction into public life and esteem of such "private" qualities as emotion, concrete everyday experience, and individual judgment. Arguing that power relations in the biological family are the model and "first cause" for economics, she presents a new version of Engels' analysis of history. In the following passage, Firestone's additions and comments appear in italics, embedded in Engels' words:

All past history (*note that we can now eliminate "with the exception of primitive stages"*) was the history of class struggle. Those warring classes of society are always the product of *the modes of organization of the biological family unit for reproduction of the species, as well as of the strictly* economic modes of production and exchange of goods and services. *The sexual-reproductive organization of society always furnishes* the real basis, starting from which we can alone work out the ultimate explanation of the whole superstructure of economic, juridical, and political institutions as well as of the religious, philosophical, and other ideas of a given historical period.[5]

She acknowledges that the power relations among men and women are rooted in nature, in the "inherently unequal power distribution" of the biological family in which the woman and child are dependent on the father for survival for long periods of time. Hence the family and motherhood are the prime objects of revolutionary change.

Firestone's vision of the revolutionary goal involves the reintegration of the technological (male) and aesthetic (female) modes of human experience into a pan-sexual cultural androgyny:

The separation of sex from emotion is at the very foundations of Western culture and civilization. If early repression is the basic mechanism by which character structures supporting political, ideological, and economic serfdom are produced, an end to the incest taboo, through abolition of the family, would have profound effects: sexuality would be released from its straitjacket to eroticize our whole culture, changing its very definition.[6]

We will also draw on the ideas of Wilhelm Reich and Herbert Marcuse, who have done pioneering work in integrating Freud and Marx into a theory of sexual politics. In the early thirties, Reich criticized psychoanalysis for supporting the bourgeois ruling class within a capitalist society and attacked Marxism for ignoring sexuality and the institution of the family. Although he wanted to claim psychoanalysis for Communism, he was simultaneously rejected by both camps. Yet, as Juliet Mitchell emphasizes in her highly perceptive study, *Psychoanalysis and Feminism: Freud, Reich, Laing and Women*, he is extremely important from a contemporary perspective.

Reich was a pioneer of sexual politics (the term is his). As such his thinking in this area is crucial for current libertarian socialist politics, for anarchism, for student cultural revolutionaries and for women's liberation.[7]

Firestone agrees with this judgment, concluding: "Wilhelm Reich's

The Sexual Revolution could have been written yesterday."[8] Focusing his attack on monogamy and the nuclear family, Reich argued that Freud's supposedly universal theory of sexuality was actually a brilliant analysis of what occurred under capitalism:

> The 'Oedipus complex,' which Freud discovered, is not so much a cause as it is a result of the sexual restrictions imposed upon the child by society. Yet, wholly unconscious of what they are doing, the parents carry out the intentions of authoritarian society.[9]

Moreover, Reich realized that this form of repression could be adopted as a conscious strategy by a fascist government:

> Fascism involves the supreme exploitation of all that patriarchal capitalism has brought into being. Patriarchy deprives women and children and adolescents of sexual freedom, makes sexuality into a commodity and subordinates sexual interests to economic ones. . . . And Fascism plays on this situation, encouraging its practice while proposing to emulate a Platonic homosexual state; women are needed for reproduction for the militaristic build-up, hence the concept of 'pure' motherhood and a further refusal of female sexual expression. Hitler offered men the full dependence of women; he returned the wife to the home.[10]

Reich violently objected to Freud's assumption that the redirection of sexual energy contributed to the advancement of culture. This opposition between sex and good works has been basic to Western civilization, particularly in the classical epic and the writings of the Judeo-Christian church, which would have us believe that getting bogged down in sex is distracting, degrading, and downright evil. Although such behavior involves both sexes, women receive most of the blame—the Helens, Circes, and Didos, the Liliths, Eves, and Delilahs. Reich not only denied that sexuality was destructive, he insisted it was the most powerful source of energy and creativity for advancement of the culture and the species. Moreover, he was willing to acknowledge and glorify women's full sexual strength. Insisting that passivity and masochism were imposed on women by a repressive society, he denied that these characteristics were part of their biological nature. Instead, he identified female sexuality with a positive receptivity, which could be an important resource for human advancement:

> For Reich vaginal receptivity came possibly to represent a meeting of the self and the world in universal love; he postulated that it was a new and higher stage on the evolutionary road from

beasthood to godhead. In women's sexuality perhaps mankind
would at last rejoin the natural universe.[11]

Unlike Reich and Firestone, Herbert Marcuse accepted the fundamental conflict between Eros and civilization, but criticized Freud for
failing to integrate a concrete view of history into his psychological
theory. Highly influential on political thought and action of the
sixties, his *Eros and Civilization* argued that historically, societies
have been organized according to irrational models of domination
and subjugation:

> Domination differs from rational exercise of authority. The
> latter, which is inherent in any societal division of labor, is . . .
> confined to the administration . . . necessary for the advancement
> of the whole. In contrast, domination is exercised by a particular
> group or individual in order to sustain and enhance itself in a
> privileged position.[12]

Domination leads not only to "surplus repression," but to the
"performance principle," the stratification of society and the judgment of individuals according to their competitive economic performance. Both of these aspects of the "reality principle" under capitalism
distort human sexuality, which for Marcuse is "polymorphously
perverse." Although Reich granted a more central role to sexuality
than Marcuse, he insisted that genitality was the only true form and
hence identified a great variety of sexual behavior (including
homosexuality) as negative perversions. But Marcuse argued that the
human being who insists on performing sexual acts that do not use
the genitals for procreation is denying those in power the full range
of their control:

> Against a society which employs sexuality as a means to a useful
> end, the perversions uphold sexuality as an end in itself; they
> thus place themselves outside the domination of the perform-
> ance principle and challenge its very foundation.[13]

Marcuse sees the aesthetic experience as basically sensual;

> The nature of sensuousness is 'receptivity,' cognition through
> being affected by given objects.[14]

In addition, his theories invite integration of the social and the sexual
in concrete action, and his concept of "polymorphous perversity"
provides a theoretical justification for a variety of newly emerging
forms of female sexuality.

Employing the dialectical process at the center of Marxism, which moves from the intrinsic material fact (the film itself) outward to the cultural superstructure, we will perform the following critical tasks in analyzing *Weekend, Sweet Movie,* and *Seven Beauties.*

1. The Film Artifact. Our strategy in developing a Marxist/ feminist perspective on the film artifact from the basic ideas described above involves two emphases: the first on the referential and culturally coded dimension of film, and the second on those material characteristics and codes unique to the film medium.

Work begins with the demystification of the material represented in the film image. All films involving human characters reflect and shape sex roles in society. These roles are so deeply imbedded in our consciousness that we frequently fail to see them even when they are blatant. In analyzing these three films, we will examine the connection between sex roles and the social-economic structure, paying particular attention to the effect of the patriarchal nuclear family on the sexual attitudes and behavior of male and female characters. Perception of this powerful connection has led some Marxists to make important contributions to feminist thought. For example, Engels argued:

> The first class antagonism which appears in history coincides with the development of the antagonism between man and woman in monogamous marriage, and the first class oppression with that of the female sex by the male. Monogamy was a great historical advance, but at the same time it inaugurated, along with slavery and private wealth, that epoch, lasting until today, in which every advance is likewise a relative regression, in which the well-being and development of one group are attained by the misery and repression of the other.[15]

In the words of the new Marxist critics of *Cahiers du Cinema,* the goal is to show what the films "are blind to; how they are totally determined, moulded, by the ideology of the culture that produced them."[16] Since all three filmmakers are themselves consciously demystifying the ideologies of the societies they portray, we will raise this process to the second power by evaluating the connections they make.

This analysis must extend to the form as well as the content in revealing adherence to and rejection of conventions of the dominant ideology. Marxist criticism redefines the relationship between form and content as a dynamic process where the two elements interact dialectically to shape the future of the medium and of the society. Chairman Mao Tse-Tung agreed:

> What we demand is the unity of politics and art, the unity of content and form, the unity of political content and the highest possible perfection of artistic form. Works of art which lack artistic quality have no force, however progressive they are politically. . . . On questions of literature and art we must carry on a struggle on two fronts.[17]

In Jameson's terms, "Change is essentially a function of content seeking its adequate expression in form."[18] This is illustrated historically in Eisenstein's development of a new form and theory—dialectical montage—to express adequately the concept of dialectical materialism that guided the revolution. Yet, unlike the *Cahiers* critics,[19] we would not wish to offer Eisenstein's theory (or any other) as a prescriptive formulation that would limit contemporary film-making; such a view contradicts its own goals by freezing the spontaneous process of dialectical creativity:

> For a genuinely dialectical criticism, indeed, there can be no preestablished categories of analysis; to the degree that each work is the end result of a kind of inner logic of development in its own content, it evolves its own categories and dictates the specific terms of its own interpretation. Thus dialectical criticism is at the other extreme from all single-shot or univalent aesthetic theories which seek the same structure in all works of art and prescribe for them a single mode of explanation.[20]

Thus as Transformalists applying a neo-Marxist and feminist perspective, we will analyze and evaluate these films both aesthetically culturally, but without reference to static external criteria.

The process of demystification of forms must include analysis of the individual film artifact in relation to the material nature of the medium—how fully it exploits the progressive potentialities or transcends the historical limitations of cinema. In the case of Eisenstein, for example, not only did he develop a dialectical montage that transcended Griffith's dualistic crosscutting, but he also offered theoretical speculation about the interphasing of sound and visuals that went far beyond his own practice.

One of the most advanced of the early film theoreticians was the Marxist critic Walter Benjamin, who recognized the mixed potential of the new medium. On the one hand, through its invisible technology, it offered a "spectacle" unimaginable in any other art form or previous historical period. With the close-up, it could transform space; with slow and accelerated motion, it could transform movement. Thus potentially, it could expand our knowledge and make inner experience more accessible to the world outside: "The camera introduces us to unconscious optics as does psychoanalysis to unconscious impulses."[21] Yet, on the other hand, the power of the spectacle threatened to reconcile us to our entrapment in a decaying culture: "In the midst of its far-flung ruins and debris, we calmly and adventurously go travelling."[22] The mechanical reproduction and the elusive nature of the film image, he argued, inevitably lead to the sacrifice of the "aura" with which unique, authentic objects (such as paintings and sculpture) are imbued. In order to compensate, the studios have historically fostered the "cult of the movie star," employing advertising techniques to imbue the film with the "phony spell of a commodity." The cult of personality also extends to auteur criticism, where the aura is manufactured around the director as star. In contrast, however, Benjamin observes that the medium also has the potential for breaking down the barriers between artist and audience, for it could feature ordinary people rather than stars, validating every human being's "legitimate claim to being re-produced," rather than increasing alienation.

A Marxist/feminist film criticism is necessarily concerned with the representation of ideas in concrete images. Marxists have argued that the film medium offers a unique means of objectifying subjective experience, which could form the basis of communal understanding. Bela Balazs, whose early theoretical writing on film developed a Marxist formalism, defined this uniqueness as the recovery of the language of gesture, particularly through the facial close-up. Bertolt Brecht argued that film inherently demands "external action and not introspective psychology."[23] Actually, Brecht, Benjamin, and Balazs all imply that cinema, like dreams, is a medium that forces the artist to express abstractions and feelings though concrete visual images, embodying a realm of subjective experience that might otherwise be inaccessible. But Brecht explicitly compares film to a non-Aristotelian, non-mimetic Epic theater, which relies on construction through montage. He traces his theater back to the Epic because, like Georg Lukacs, he sees in that form the perfect fusion of essence or meaning and the concrete details of everyday life. This is precisely what Marxist theoreticians, critics, and filmmakers frequently offer as a primary social value for the film medium, and helps to explain why *Weekend, Sweet Movie,* and *Seven Beauties* use the epic journey as an important element in their narrative structures.

Therefore, like the new Marxist/feminist criticism, Transfor-malism assumes that political ideas, including sexual attitudes, are expressed in stylistic choices. We will examine these films to determine what aspects of structure and surface reveal the ideologies of the filmmakers and of the societies portrayed in their products. We will consider the relationship between the sex of the central characters and the narrative structures through which they move. We do not assume a simple correlation between the biology of the filmmakers and the sexual attitudes expressed in the style, nor do we assume that receptivity or penetration in non-sexual behavior is limited to one sex. In fact, the promise of freedom seems to lie in an androgynous mixture of qualities, in which sex roles in no way restrict individual development. We do not know where biology ends and socialization begins in determining behavior and attitudes. But we agree with Reich and Firestone that biological differences have been distorted and coded by a male-dominated society into value-charged stereotypes that read like this: Women are screwed; therefore all qualities associated with women are fucked. In other words, positive value is assigned to aggressive penetration, and receptivity is redefined as passivity and masochism. Characteristics of camera-work, editing, and misé en scène may reveal non-discursively how the material means of image-making are also implicated in maintaining this ideology. As Northrop Frye points out, even in the supposedly advanced university context, important props and characteristics of style are sex-role coded; therefore certain ones bring scorn on men as well as women:

> The dismal sexist symbology surrounding the humanities . . . says that the sciences, especially the physical sciences, are rugged, aggressive, out in the world doing things, and so symbolically male, whereas the literatures are narcissistic, intuitive, fanciful, staying at home and making the home more beautiful but not doing anything really serious, and are therefore symbolically female.[24]

Historically, artists and critics have often been among those able to manifest androgyny. The structure of our own criticism is rational and logically ordered, yet it purposely emphasizes the values of subtlety, open-endedness, and maximum receptivity to the widest possible range of films. We believe it is possible to rescue for the culture qualities that have been disvalued because of their link with female biology, but which are potentially life enriching for both sexes.

2. **The Means of Production.** Being a materialist philosophy, Marxism deals not only with a work of art as a product, but also with the processes by which it was manufactured. Dramatic features are

made, not by individual artists, but by a collaborative crew within an industry. Our second task as critics is to consider: a) the working relations among those making the film; b) the financing and marketing of the film. One of the primary contributions of Marxist/ feminist criticism is to lift film out of its traditionally splendid isolation and explore it within the contexts listed above. As Jameson points out, Aristotelian aesthetics and its formalist heritage are based on a simpler economic system of individual craft where the work of art is a made object rather than a product. In evaluating the product, Marxist/feminist criticism examines, not only what the film has to say about the nature of society, but also what social processes and values are embodied in the way it was manufactured. A film cannot criticize society without raising the question: are the artists and the industry exempting themselves from the attack, or have they accepted the responsibility of self-criticism?

3. The Film Audience. The critic's work is not complete without considering the consumption of the product. Who is the audience for the film: the largest possible mass, or a smaller group who may be moved to progressive action? In fact, there may be a gap between the desired audience and the one actually reached by the film. Closely related is the question of what kind of effect the filmmakers seek from their audience: does the film appeal primarily to the emotions or the intellect; will it cause its audience to be entertained, escaping passively into the dazzling spectacle, or will it challenge, disturb, incite to action? What can be determined about the audience's experience of the work, and/or their reconstruction of its meaning? From a Marxist point of view, the goal is dialectical thinking, enabling the audience to shift perspective and gain a more objective view of themselves and their society. Jameson insists:

> Without this transformational moment, without this initial conscious transcendence of an older, more naive position, there can be no question of any genuinely dialectical coming to consciousness.[25]

Filmmakers must decide how much and what kind of manipulation to employ, whether to work toward ambiguity and subtlety or explicitness and clarity, the verisimilitude of depth focus and long takes, or the constructionist tactics of montage.

The new Marxist/feminist exploration of these questions re-integrates self and other by showing that the raising of personal consciousness and the transformation of social institutions are inextricably fused. In Jameson's terms, effective criticism:

cannot be an external but only an internal affair . . . it is part and parcel of an increasing self-consciousness . . . it involves a judgment on ourselves fully as much as a judgment on the works of art to which we react.[26]

Weekend (1967)

The Film Artifact

Weekend demystifies the ways in which a community of response is manufactured—in a particular image, a work of art, a medium, a society, and an historical period. The film anatomizes the various means by which the medium communicates meaning and manipulates our response. It dismantles the visual and auditory tracks, displaying their separate components and arranging them in dialectical opposition. Throughout the film we are constantly reminded that the sound track is comprised of music, dialogue, and noise, all of which evoke different kinds of responses and communicate different, sometimes contradictory, information. Despite our critical awareness of this process, these components still manage to control our reactions. The visual track is similarly anatomized into color, camera angle and movement, settings, costumes, and a taxonomy of subjects— people, animals, objects, words. These analytic techniques force us to consider the relationship between reality and images, or images of images. Through this analysis, we discover what it takes to horrify spectators or turn them on. What has greater impact—hearing a rape or murder or seeing it happen? What stage in the violence do you show for maximum impact? *Weekend* does not merely examine a product, object, or image, but insists on exploring the processes by which it is produced and consumed. Every sequence creates a specific context which defines the identity of its components and controls our interpretations of every sound and image and its relationship to the cosmos. This is precisely what happens in the larger context of society. Every culture constructs a contextual framework that limits and evaluates the perceptions, ideas, and emotions of any individual. Hence, *Weekend* demonstrates Marx's claim that "It is not the consciousness of men that determines their being, but on the contrary, their social being that determines their consciousness."

The film suggests that every event in the diegesis (and in the real world) must be understood and evaluated from the broadest possible perspective; the subject matter of *Weekend* is the history of cinema and the history of Western civilization. The film develops a dialectical relationship between diachronic and synchronic conceptions of human development through the narrative line, the camera movement, and the merging of past, present, and future in the final episode. There is a dual temporal movement—both forward and backward. In analyzing the history of Western civilization, it goes back to the Greeks and to the birth of Christ. Yet the narrative moves forward; the overall plot is set in the context of a weekend, with titles periodically informing us of the day of the week and even the time of day. In addition, a digital chronometer measures the film footage, for in cinema, time moves at twenty-four frames per second. The explicit fragmentation of diegetic and film time embodies what Marcuse calls the "temporal dismemberment" of experience, which prevails at a late stage of capitalism when people must be trained to perform work that is no longer necessary; time is running out for this culture in which time is money. In the context of certain sequences, synchronic circularity asserts unity and integration, but in the narrative structure as a whole, it denies the view of history as progress and suggests that Western civilization has gone down the wrong road to a dead end of disintegration and self destruction.

This thematic focus is made explicit in the dialogue as one of the characters reads Engels' analysis tracing the evolution of Western civilization from the Greeks to modern industrialized capitalism through stages of primitive tribal barbarism, the confederation of tribes, a military democracy, and finally the class society. Godard's film implies that the process is being reversed, that we have already returned to a military democracy and are well on our way back to barbarism and savagery. In a sense, the film predicts the Manson Family, the SLA, the People's Temple, and other guerrilla tribes who believe we must use horror to confront the discreet horror of the bourgeoisie. The stage of tribal confederacy, which Engels linked with the Iroquois, is first made concrete in the Indian costume of the child who participates in the traffic violence of the opening sequence; it is more fully developed in the breakdown of several nuclear families, and their replacement by the band of cannibalistic hippies, also in Indian costume, who capture the bourgeois couple at the end of their quest. The youth of those wearing the Indian gear underscores that tribalism is the wave of the future; it marks the end of private property, the nuclear family, and the class society.

The narrative events are organized into a mock-epic journey in which a bourgeois couple makes an odyssey or pilgrimage through a nightmare traffic jam and a modern scrap-heap landscape littered with wreckage and dead bodies. On the road, they meet a variety of bizarre characters who threaten their privileged position, until finally they are captured by the tribe. Though women are usually not permitted to go on odysseys, the "heroine" in this case is more flexible than the man, and it is she who survives; in fact, as the superior consumer, she eats him up at the end.

Throughout the film, the two dominant images of the consumer society are eating and driving, or less neutrally, cannibalism and traffic jams. Both "drives" are basic to our instinctual animal nature, yet they have undergone sophisticated elaboration within our society, which fools us into thinking that we have progressed in satisfying our primal needs. Automobiles give us the illusion that we control our own fate and direction, that we have power and freedom, and that we gain power from belonging to a technologically advanced society. Yet, they actually expose us to deadly crashes, long waits, poisonous air, built-in obsolescence, and exploitation by oil monopolies (such as Shell and Esso, which are explicitly mentioned). The traffic fatalities are not really "accidents," rather, they are either the inevitable outcome of a corrupt society or acts of sabotage by revolutionary forces. They implicate the entire society, even the filmmakers who use automobiles for their tracking shots.

The eating imagery extends the economic dimensions of consumption by linking it with sex and death, suggesting that both Eros and Thanatos have been co-opted by a repressive economic system. Sex partners are transformed into edible objects that are marinated and garnished with milk, eggs, or fish (fertility foods) before being devoured. The creative power of the film derives not from erotic energy, but from the intellectual articulation of ideas in concrete images; sexuality is never portrayed positively. Though this may reflect the corruption of sex that Godard has found in the society around him, his artistic choices frequently reinforce it. The same dynamic operates in his treatment of women's exploited condition; they are the only ones used as delectable sex objects to make the spectacle more appetizing. In implicating their own art, the filmmakers seem to be bringing us closer to the dead end. But from a positive perspective, Firestone suggests that after the Marxist/feminist liberation of the species, art as sublimation will no longer be necessary; full satisfaction in human experience triumphantly will signal the death of culture.

The full title of this film introduces the subject and form of demystification:

WEEKEND
A FILM
ADRIFT
IN THE COSMOS

In the opening scene we encounter a bourgeois triangle, in which all three characters—the husband Roland, the wife Corinne, and her nameless lover—are plotting various murders against the background noise of Parisian traffic. The titles resume:

A FILM FOUND
ON A SCRAP-HEAP

As the strategies of murder are elaborated, we also hear a radio giving statistical information about traffic deaths; the juxtaposition implies that so-called accidents may be used to disguise murder. The culture's refusal to accept responsibility for its acts and choices is also self-reflexively revealed in the ironic denial of artistic control over a film that is "found" rather than created and "adrift" rather than moving toward a specific end. These violent actions are nationalized in the third rendering of the title, graphically reiterated in the Franco-American patriotic colors of red, white and blue.

END WEEK END
WEEK END WEE
K END WEEK EN
D WEEK END WE
EK END WEEK E
ND WEEK END W
EEK END WEEK[27]

This opening immediately reveals that the subject of the film is the weak/end of a totally corrupt consumer society whose fragmentation will be developed through the dismantling of word and image.

The first accident we actually see involves a red Matra coupe that has collided with a white and blue Mini. We observe it from Corinne's point of view as she stands on a balcony watching the chaos below with amused detachment while warring families defend their private property. The overhead angle distances Corinne and the audience from the action, making it seem as absurd and farcical as a Keystone comedy. The tone shifts abruptly with the sudden intrusion of an ominous musical riff, which provides us with a triple warning:

attend to the music—it will manipulate your feelings; beware of farce—it masks destruction; watch out for the traffic—it's deadly.

Our role as voyeurs is intensified in the next scene where Corinne sits on a desk wearing only panties and bra, as she tells her Friend about an orgy she experienced with another married couple. Both the story that she narrates and the interaction with her listener demonstrate the flagging sexual energy of the decadent culture. The couple, who have been married only two months, are using her to titillate their sex life and need her to talk dirty in order to get off. Her verbal account affects her Friend in the same way; he asks, "Were you thinking of me," and exclaims, "I adore you Corinne. Come and excite me." Neither Corinne, nor her Friend, nor we in the audience are sure that the events described really took place, but it doesn't matter because, as in the description of the orgy in *Persona*, the primary function of the narration is not to reveal the truth, but to evoke an erotic response in her listeners. This sequence shows us the erotic power of words in a culture that is alienated from its senses.[28] Though we identify with her Friend as voyeur, we are unsure of his identity; his suit and tie and his note-taking suggest that he is her analyst, yet her scanty clothes and his erotic comments indicate that he is her lover. This confusion suggests a false dialectic in which both relationships are suspect. Our response, too, involves an uncertain synthesis; we respond to her erotically as we criticize her character.

Before we get too carried away by her description, however, we experience a series of interruptions. Periodically, romantic music wells up, drowning out her words and intensifying the turn-on. Yet apparently, Corinne herself does not share our immersion; in the middle of her discourse, she wants a cigarette, and not the brand offered by her Friend. She gets up and goes off-sreen to get one of her own, telling us both visually and verbally how distant she is from her own experience, and satirically undercutting the audience's experience of her as object of the erotic gaze, for which she had been set up in her little undergarments. In the next interruption, the following word appears on the screen:

ANAL
YSIS

The visual dismantling of the word renders it comical but in the context of Corinne's story, it links Logos (rational analysis) with Eros (anal intercourse) and with shit (the anal product). It also

displays Godard's dialectical attitude toward his own processes: all
this analysis is the central motive of his film; at the same time it's shit.
The sex acts described are full of comical puns and cannibalistic
implications. At the husband's direction, the wife dips her "pussy" in
a bowl of milk and Corinne breaks an egg with her buttocks as she has
an orgasm; thus the women become edible. This anticipates a later
sequence in which the sexual consumption is fatal; another young
woman is ritually prepared for slaughter by a woman-eating chef
who breaks an egg between her legs and stuffs a live fish up her
vagina before butchering her with his big knife. Both sequences
imply that men do not choose dehumanizing words and actions for
women merely because they unconsciously assume they are sex
objects; rather, they consciously make these choices because they
believe dehumanization and objectification will enhance their own
pleasure. As Jameson observes:

> Pleasure under capitalism is simply the sign of the consumption
> of an object. . . . We begin to glimpse what is the profound
> vocation of the work of art in a commodity society; *not* to be a
> commodity, *not* to be consumed, to be *unpleasurable* in the
> commodity sense.[29]

Weekend fulfills this vocation and implies that women should do the
same.

The odyssey is launched in the next sequence of the traffic jam.
The camera tracks endlessly along a line of waiting cars, following
the progress of the aggressive couple who dart into openings to
advance their position. The stylistic treatment of the sequence
emphasizes the diachronic movement through several time references
(11:00 a.m., 1:40 p.m., and 2:10 p.m.) and by the horizontal camera
movement in one amazingly long take; whenever we reach a break in
the procession of cars, the camera teases us into thinking that at last
we have found the cause of the traffic jam, but then speeds up to the
next car, as if mocking our notions of causality and our desire to
move on. Like the hateful couple, the camera and we in the audience
are implicated in the futility of trying to get ahead in the narrative.
While we are all waiting, the cars and their occupants provide a
procession of entertainments. The ball games, chess games, and
sail-trimming offer other outlets for the competitiveness of the
bourgeois players and in the roadside context become side-show
attractions of a post-industrial Vanity Fair. This programmed play
disguises the real nature of the human condition under capitalism,

which is revealed in the key images of the caged animals of a traveling menagerie and the harnessed horse, hoof deep in its own shit. The vulnerability of mortals and the danger of their situation within this society are confirmed by the final image in which we at last reach the cause of the traffic jam: a multiple crash with bloody corpses carelessly strewn about like the bodies of dogs or other small animals left to rot on the road. It's no accident that this common experience devalues human life and trains us to accept the hit and run. The sequence has moved from parodic comedy to grim irony, which is underscored by the recurrence of the ominous musical motif; this scrap heap is no joke.

In the next sequence, Godard further demystifies the traffic jam through a class analysis of one specific crash—between a working man's tractor and a young bourgeois couple in a red Triumph with a Chrysler engine. Amused by the spectacle and indifferent to the bloody death of the sports car's driver, Corinne and Roland fail to see how this event foreshadows their own fate; Godard sets them up as bourgeois spectators to the violence of the class struggle, perverted models for our own response. Printed messages underscore the point:

SS	/	SS	/	THE
		STRUGGLE		CLASS
				STRUGGLE

The titles fuse fascist terror with the class struggle in which the proletariat and the bourgeoisie are both tyrant and victim. Despite their fierce arguments, the farmer and the urban whore suddenly become allies against Roland and Corinne, who refuse to be witnesses to the accident. Posed in front of an Esso tiger billboard, they use Marx like an advertising slogan for their self interest, shouting, "Aren't we all brothers like Marx said? Bastards! Bastards! . . . Jews! Filthy, rotten, stinking Jews!" Esso and Marx, the "stinking Jew," bring us back to "SS" in a circle of complicity within capitalism. This sequence trains us how to read this text; every fragment, every verbal and visual image must be understood in terms of the particular context in which it appears within the film and the social-economic context of the society in which it was produced. In the midst of this sequence, the title

COUNTER
FEITO
GRAPHY

warns us that images can lie, not only in advertising and propaganda, but also in Godard's own demystification.

The transformation of the journey into a pilgrimage through history is explicitly signalled as Corinne asks Roland, "When did civilization begin. . . . Aren't we all brothers, iike Marx said?" As a Christian anti-Communist, Roland replies, "It wasn't Marx. It was Jesus." Disjointedly, she remarks, "We're not living in the Middle Ages. . . . What's the time?" The rest of the film answers these questions. Jameson explicates the goals of Godard's conscious historicism:

> The ideological effect of such an approach . . . is to reorder our perception of the historical present, to restructure our vision of modern society. . . . The notion of historical evolution is thus essentially a *form* or pretext for a new politization of our thinking, which gives us to understand what kinds of future social renewal and regeneration are available to us by allowing us a glimpse of the healthier, socially functional art of the past.[30]

Their next encounter with a pair of hitchhikers evokes the history of Christianity and cinema. They meet a Surrealist Mary Magdalene and her boyfriend, Joseph Balsamo, who identifies himself as the offspring of a homosexual encounter between God and Alexander Dumas (no more miraculous than the straight version). In the context of the sequence, Godard also links this Joseph/Christ with André Breton, whom he evokes in a story; with Buñuel's *Exterminating Angel*, which is named in the graphics; and with a flock of sheep into which the automobiles are transubstantiated. This gun-toting, car-thief savior turns out to be an anti-Christ and a "minister of the interior," preaching to the bourgeois couple: "You don't even know who you are. Christianity is the refusal to know oneself. It's the death of language." Yet, for the future of cinema, Joseph appears to be a reliable Chaplinesque prophet of the divine words of God-ard: "I am here to proclaim to these *MODERN TIMES* the end of the grammatical era and the beginning of an age of flamboyance in every field, especially that of cinema." Godard claims Surrealism as his cinematic roots (particularly in Breton and Buñuel) because, as both Benjamin and Jameson acknowledge, it offers an historical precedent for exposing and subverting the collusion between artistic conventions and cultural restrictions. Through its disruption and dismantling of rational structures, Surrealism liberates the irrational forces of anarchy.

The Surrealist image is thus a convulsive effort to split open the
commodity forms of the objective universe by striking them
against each other wth immense force. . . . It is their theory of
narration which perhaps most strikingly illustrates the way the
Surrealists propose to reawaken the deadened external world
around us. It is in appearance a refusal of narration altogether;
for Breton hates novels, and holds the obligatory description of
physical surroundings to be the basest kind of surrender to the
reality principle, since in it that purely perceptual level of things
to which our most superficial waking consciousness corresponds
is taken for Being itself.[31]

The next two encounters with Jean-Pierre Leaud move us forward
in our dual history to the French Revolution and the Hollywood
musical. As if left over from *La Chinoise,* Leaud first appears as an
actor in the role of Saint-Juste, prophesying that "freedom will kill
freedom." In fact, as a title informs us, the French Revolution has
ultimately declined into "Weekends with De Gaulle." Next, Leaud
appears in a telephone booth, dressed like Gene .Kelly, singing
musical comedy lyrics into the void while the bourgeois couple tries
to steal his car. This scene alludes to frivolous French imitations of
American musicals like Jacques Demy's *Umbrellas of Cherbourg*
and *Young Ladies of Rochefort* (which actually starred Gene Kelly).
Yet in Godard's parody, both Revolution *and* Romance end in
violence as the bourgeois couple tries to strangle Leaud with his
sweater. By having Leaud play two such dialectically opposed roles
in close juxtaposition, Godard follows a Brechtian principle of breaking
dramatic illusion.

Godard continues his exploration of romance, surrealism, and
violence in the encounter with the next couple, Tom Thumb and
Emily Bronte, whose romance, *Wuthering Heights,* has defined for
our culture the vision of wild nature's inexorable triumph over
civilization. Pursuing what they consider to be their realistic goals,
Roland and Corinne want to know the way to Oinville, but Emily
Bronte wants to make philosophical observations: "All fish, except
for sharks, are kind to children. . . . No corpulent fish can dance the
minuet." Sounding more like Alice in Wonderland

(**DU CÔTE
DE CHEZ
LEWIS
CARROLL,**

the titles tell us) than the historical Emily Bronte, she clarifies the distinctions between nature and art, instinct and convention, empirical fact and logic, reality and fiction. As she reveals the absurdity of conventions by applying them to animals, she implies their equal absurdity for human behavior. As we see a close-up of a pebble in Emily's hands, she claims that humans have had little effect on nature, which potentially can escape co-option or coding by language and system:

> Poor pebble. . . . It dates from before mankind, and then, when man came along, he did not incorporate it either into his art or his industry. He did not manufacture it, assigning to it a humble, luxurious or historical status. The pebble perpetuates nothing save its own memory.

But since this is not the information wanted by Roland and Corinne, they contradict her by transforming the pebble into a weapon as they fling it at Tom Thumb and set fire to Emily. Like all fascists, they are equally willing to burn a book or its author. This act fulfills the prophecy implicit in the titles that appeared a few moments earlier:

**THE FILM
DISTRIBUTORS
AGAINST POOR BB**

The reference to Brecht continues the dialectical pattern of double implications from the SS/CLASS STRUGGLE titles. BB is the linking term between the two forms of artistic alienation that dominate this particular sequence: the persecution and exile of a radical artist by a fascist society, and a purposeful theater of alienation that forces the audience to perceive intellectually the relationship between a work of artifice and the outside world it demystifies. Like Godard, Brecht wanted to alter the audience's habitual response by creating a new, radical realism:

> What is "natural" must have the force of what is startling. This is the only way to expose the laws of cause and effect. . . .
> The dramatic theater's spectator says: Yes, I have felt like that too—Just like me—It's only natural—It'll never change—The sufferings of this man appall me, because they are inescapable—That's great art; it all seems the most obvious thing in the world—I weep when they weep, I laugh when they laugh.
> The epic theater's spectator says: I'd never have thought it—

That's not the way—That's extraordinary, hardly believable—
It's got to stop—The sufferings of this man appall me, because
they are unnecessary—that's great art: nothing obvious in it—I
laugh when they weep, I weep when they laugh.[32]

The distinction between art and reality is made explicit as Roland
criticizes the film, perhaps articulating what some members of the
audience may feel: "This film's crap. We're always meeting nut-
cases." Corinne replies: "There's nothing to stop you from leaving,"
which, ironically, is true of the audience, but certainly not of Roland,
who is trapped in the narrative structure. Expressing the mass
audience's obsession with filmic realism, she claims: "This isn't a
novel. It's life. A film is life," and thus she can shed crocodile tears
over Emily Bronte's murder. More sophisticated in his response,
Roland realizes that Emily is only an imaginary character, yet he
doesn't see how this is true of himself as well. While Bronte is an
author posing as a fictional character, her companion Tom Thumb
is a fictional character posing as an author. He, too, has a long record
of obscuring the lines between reality and illusion, particularly in the
eighteenth-century mock heroic tragedy by Henry Fielding—*The
Tragedy of Tragedies*, or *The Life and Death of Tom Thumb the
Great*—which, like Brecht's *Threepenny Opera*, followed Gay's
Beggar's Opera in breaking dramatic illusion and fusing biting
political satire with dramatic parody. Like Roland, we in the
audience see only some of the connections and distinctions; we can
laugh at these characters, interpret them as satiric caricatures without
necessarily acknowledging that we share their corrupt values,
oppressive behavior, and desire for escape into fiction. As Corrine
and Roland go off to pursue their crusade, leaving Emily burning
like Joan of Arc in the background, we hear the voice of Tom Thumb
passing judgment on the exterminators and prophesying their doom:
"They don't want progress, they want to be first. They will submit to
anyone so long as he promises that they can make the laws." This
statement signals the end of the aggressive, linear movement along
the diachronic axis and initiates the defeat of the bourgeois couple by
a series of reversals.

Time moves backward as the titles set the date of the action with
pseudo-precision: *"One Tuesday in the 100 Years War."* As we see a
huge close-up of an earthworm from an overhead angle, we hear
Roland and Corinne humbly acknowledging their self ignorance.
Now they become the hitchhikers—passive passengers in a lorry that
carries them to new adventures starring some of the same "nut cases"

in new roles and seen from new perspectives. The driver takes them to a barnyard Mozart concert where he is pianist and lecturer. The sequence develops dialectical interplay between unity and fragmentation, harmony and disruption. As we hear Mozart's highly structured sonata, the camera makes two slow, 360° pans of the farmyard, integrating all of the visual elements—workers and bourgeoisie, men, women, and children, tractor, trailer, and piano—in a harmonious circle. Elements that have previously been held in tension are integrated in this scene: work and play, workers and high culture, historical past and present moment. For the first time the music emanates from the action; Emily Bronte is even resurrected in modern dress to turn the pages of the piano music. We may begin to suspect that fish can learn to minuet after all. Both times the pan stops when the camera reaches the piano; after circling the barnyard twice, it goes round once again in the opposite direction. This self-conscious movement not only is analogous with the three-part structure of the sonata, but also suggests the material nature of movies—film wound on two circular reels, which must be rewound for the new showing. In the broadest sense, it also suggests the film's view of the history of Western civilization as it moves forward in repetitive cycles, only to be rewound back to its primitive beginnings.

The harmony that dominates this sequence is interrupted by elements that are difficult to interpret and evaluate. Once again it is language that provides the greatest complexity and ambiguity. Distracted by economic factors, the aesthetic judgments of the piano player are muddled and contradictory. He explains that the Beatles and Stones represent continuity with Mozart's harmonies. Yet when he died, Mozart, who would get "vast royalties" today, was "tossed into a pauper's grave like a dog." On the other hand, "serious modern music," which is trying to find new musical principles, is "probably the biggest flop in the whole history of art." However, the sequence as a whole develops the Marxist view that history moves by a series of disruptions, implying that in its own time, Mozart's music was as radical as the new music of today, and, like Godard's own work, each frightens its audience, defeating their expectations by breaking out of formulae. Today's pop success imitates yesterday's aesthetic challenge, while the new challengers starve like Mozart. Any work that succeeds in its own time is suspect. Every work of art must be reinterpreted in its individual and historical context, as the interruptions and the harmony of this sequence must be reinterpreted in relation to each other. Together they deny the deceptive simplicity of linear self-satisfaction, and create a necessary larger, self-critical unity for the piano player, the filmmaker, and the audience.

The following sequence moves us and the couple "straight on" to the ironic, self-reflexive art of the twentieth century. Their encounter with a group of Italian actors left over from an "international co-production" is interrupted by titles, which grow in length and meaning:

ONE FRIDAY
FAR FROM

seems to locate the scene in time and place, and perhaps alludes to the earlier political co-production *Far from Viet Nam* (1967), in which Godard had just participated. But the addition of **ROBINSON** redefines Friday as the exploited slave in Defoe's classic myth of capitalist imperialism. And the further addition of

AND MANTES
LA JOLIE

puns on Balsamo's destination in the earlier sequence (Mont-Saint-Gely) where he hijacks the bourgeois couple's car and reverses their direction. After doing a piggy-back vaudeville routine worthy of Footit and Chocolate, Corinne and Roland sit by the road like the two tramps in *Waiting for Godot,* and are quizzed by passing motorists, who force them to give absurd answers to absurd questions: "Are you in a film or are you for real? Would you rather be fucked by Mao or Johnson? Who attacked first—Israel or Egypt?" Like being forced to choose between Tweedledum and Tweedledee, Democrats or Republicans, they are repeatedly trapped into giving a wrong answer. The dramatic action confronts the audience with the same questions. As the camera watches Roland sitting indifferently by the road, a passing tramp asks for a light. Roland refuses but is utterly indifferent as the tramp rapes Corinne in a ditch off-screen. We wonder, since we don't actually see it, whether the rape really happens; whether there is much difference between being fucked by a tramp or by a husband she hates; and whether the aggression in this film is initiated by Roland and Corinne, the Robinson Crusoes of this quest, or by the Fridays they encounter on the road.

The theme of imperialism is elaborated in the next sequence when Corinne and Roland are picked up by two more Fridays—two garbage collectors, an Arab and an African—and driven to a dump that looks like the setting for *Endgame*. As in the concert sequence, this episode presents important rhetoric that must be reinterpreted according to the visuals with which it is juxtaposed. Forcing the bourgeois couple to work while they munch their lunch, the workers use the eating metaphor to give a lesson in economics—they grant the hungry hitchhikers token bites of their sandwich that represent "the proportion of its overall budget which the U. S. gives to the Congo." The sequence thus develops a dialectic interplay between the concrete and the theoretical, between garbage and progressive rhetoric, all of which together form the substance of revolution. The disjunction between sound and image begins as we hear the black man delivering a speech on Africa while we watch the Arab eating and picking his teeth; later the process is reversed. The revolutionary rhetoric is reinterpreted as the disjuncture is intensified by the introduction of flashbacks. As the black man describes "breaking the back of Nazism . . . destroying the evil where it had first taken root," the film cuts to a flashback of the Christ figure Joseph Balsamo hijacking the car; the juxtaposition makes it ambiguous whether this visual image illustrates Fascism or the resistance to it, and thereby comments on the failure of Christianity to avoid the faults of the system it overthrew. A few moments later, as the black man talks optimistically about the African revolution and its successful conclusion, there is a second flashback to Leaud as Saint-Juste declaiming in the field, reminding us that like Christianity, the French Revolution also failed. As the Arab insists, "It is no accident that we are studying the guerrilla tactics practiced by the Viet Cong," a flashback to the accidents on the road makes us wonder whether we should reinterpret this violence as sabotage. When the Arab quotes Engels' description of the development of Western industrialized class society, Godard uses a series of flashbacks (an armed family defending their car, the burning cars of the traffic violence, the flock of sheep blocking the road, and Tom Thumb declaiming over the charred remains of Emily Bronte) to show the reversion to barbarism. When he quotes Engels' analysis of the Iroquois, whose pure form of tribal confederation makes them fundamental to an understanding of the early history of the West, Godard flashes forward to the band of hippies in Indian drag; this juxtaposition reveals not only the reasons for their particular choice of life-style, but also Godard's reason for concluding his film with these barbaric characters. The fact that this is the only sequence in the film that uses flashbacks and flashforwards may lead us to conclude that it is central in providing an historical overview for the narrative, which in fact it does through the quotation from Engels' analysis of Western civilization. On a more practical level, it may be an effective means of making a very talky sequence more visual. Yet, the opening sequence with the erotic narrative needed no such diversionary tactics. Godard knows his audience's taste, which he simultaneously exposes and satisfies; we are more likely to be turned on by sex than by political rhetoric.

In the next sequence, as Corinne and Roland reach their destination— Oinville, home of Corinne's rich mother—the title *Weekend* reappears, signalling the beginning of a new cycle and the intensification of the film's focus on perverted myth and ritual. Like Greek heroes readying themselves for the climactic event, they prepare for the matricide of their dreams. While Corinne purifies herself in a bath (not even exposing her breasts, which are supplied by a painting of a bare-breasted woman hanging above the tub), she plots her mother's murder. Meanwhile, Roland tells a fable of a monstrous hippopotamus who fast-talks God into letting him live in the water (where he can gobble up all the fish) by promising to spread out his shit to prove it has no fish bones. Denying his obvious identification with the hippopotamus, Roland scorns the ugly creature for "the servile way he accepts collective life." Roland and Corinne actively rebel against the collective unit of the family by killing her parents and competing for individual profit. This sequence demonstrates how enlightened self interest under capitalism actually destroys the nuclear family in which it is rooted.

The matricide in the following scene has important implications for both history and cinema. According to Engels, the destruction of the matriarchy was an essential step for the formation of class society. Only when patrilineal ownership of children was established, was there a parallel division of property and classes and an active competition among the fraternity of men. Therefore, the achievement of the Communist Utopia depends on the destruction of the patriarchy. In this scene, the choice of the mother as victim of a spectacular murder rather than the father (who has gradually been poisoned off-screen) implies that in this new stage of history we have really moved backward rather than forward. The sequence also forces us to consider the art of murder—how to do it (not by "the methods of Doctor Tar and Professor Feather," but by stabbing), how to get away with it (by stacking a VW and an airplane into a beautifully composed bonfire with momma in the hot seat), how to represent it on screen (with screams and rivers of watery blood washing over a skinned rabbit that is really dead), and how to get a dramatic response (with wolves howling in the background, the formerly estranged couple is inspired by the ritualistic murder to declare their mutual love).

This lesson in ritual violence is expanded in the final section of the film, in which the narrative is captured by the barbaric terrorists and devoted to horror. After Corinne and Roland crash a family picnic, greedily striving to gobble as much food as they can, the bourgeoisie (both hosts and guests) are ambushed by the hippie tribe who complete the destruction of the family. Sorting out their captives by sex, size, and age, for execution, consumption, or co-option, this group of revolutionaries become the ultimate Nazis, which they themselves acknowledge: "We can only overcome the horror of the bourgeoisie by even more horror." Certainly this tribe presents no positive alternative.

This section continues and expands the film's on-going self-reflexive criticism; it marks the dead end, not only of Western civilization, but also of cinema. Even more than in the barnyard concert, the music becomes dominant in the narrative and the visual development. As we watch the changing of the drummers, we realize that music has now explicitly become a warning system and a means of radical communication, as in African and Indian tribal societies. There is a parallel explicitness in the use of movie codes, signalling that the heroes and villains of these hippies have been defined by films made in the USSR and the USA ("*Battleship Potemkin* calling *The Searchers*"), and by hybrids of the Western and French New Wave ("*Arizona Jules*." Similar coded messages are drawn from literature and Godard's own biography. In one scene we see Anna Wiazemsky, Godard's wife, posing as Mademoiselle Gide, the relative of another highly self-reflexive artist preoccupied with literary counterfeitors rather than "counterfeitography." The Franco-American pun *Lumière in August* points to two forms of artistic ritual in two media: Faulkner's sacrificial ritual of the American South and Lumière's pioneering efforts to capture the reality of the moving ocean on film. As the tribe's butcher brandishes his knife and prepares a girl for slaughter, we see the words *Totem and Taboo*, naming a work by Freud that has helped to code sexual violence for Western culture. In *Totem and Taboo*, Freud tried to establish archetypal roots for the incestuous nuclear family to prove it was universal. As in the matricide, the film continues its dialectical exploration of image and reality in presenting sex and violence. This time we see not a painting of breasts, but a nude female body being used as both subject and object—the (replaceable) canvas on which a male is expressing himself. After Roland has been gutted, Corinne says, rather casually, that it's horrible, but we see only the top of his body; similarly, we do not actually see the fish enter the vagina of the girl who is being marinated. Shortly after this comment on the medium's typical unwillingness to reveal the horror it suggests, a pig and a goose are killed on screen; they twitch and bleed, continuing the film's radical extension of marketplace realism.

The full horror to which the film has been building is developed by deconstructing some of our most deeply held romantic ideas about "human nature." As a drummer solos at the edge of a pond, we hear a rhapsodic eulogy to the ocean. The sweeping, circular movement of the camera, the musical accompaniment, and the incongruity between the visual and verbal tracks (we see a stagnant pond while we are told of the vast ocean) all suggest a parallel with the barnyard concerto sequence. Here, too, the speech is highly ambiguous, and must be interpreted in terms of the full aesthetic and historical context. The Ancient Sea is identified with "man's rude beginnings when he first learned the pain which has never left him since." He shares this environment with the treacherous hippopotamus, who is equally monstrous.

> I suppose that man only believes in his own beauty out of vanity,
> but in fact suspects that he is not truly beautiful.

Man also shares the ocean with fish, a symbol of potential fertility, with whom he has been mockingly linked throughout the film: the corpulent fish who can't minuet, the poor victims gobbled up by the hippo, the live fish with which the girl is stuffed, and the shark who hates children and shudders after death as we supposedly shudder after orgasm in self-loathing. The ocean is denied as a symbol of the unconscious, and is linked instead with the human heart, which is as stagnant as the pond.

> Allow me to say that, in spite of the ocean's depth, the depth of
> the human heart is on another scale altogether. Psychology still
> has a long way to go.

This denial continues the motif of the attack on Freud and depth psychology, made explicit in the allusion to *Totem and Taboo*. The placement of this discussion of the "Ancient Sea" at the end of the film has a number of ironic functions. It suggests that in the film's backward movement through history, we have arrived at the first cause, the "source of life." But this archetype of human identity and harmony with nature is constantly undercut, suggesting that instead of valuing it romantically, we must view the ocean suspiciously, since all that has come out of it is cannibalism and endless horror. Like the sentimental swan song of the dying female hippie whom the speaker anticipates—"Avoid any comparison between me and the dying swan"—the final sequence parodies false romance, art, and archetypes of the "eternally human" and provides a swan song for the girl, the hippie group, the movies, Western civilization, and the human species. As a final image, it offers us Corinne, munching on a mixed grill. When she learns that it includes leftovers of her husband, this insatiable consumer announces: "When I've finished . . . I wouldn't mind a bit more." But the titles reassure us that this, indeed, and in words, is:

END OF STORY   /   END OF CINEMA

The Means of Production

Working Relations.   Godard's working relations must be divided into two periods: before and after the May '68 political uprising in Paris. During Godard's April '70 tour of the United States with his collaborator, Jean-Pierre Gorin, he denounced *Weekend:*

> GODARD: There is no such thing as classical cinema, there is only capitalist cinema and revolutionary cinema.
> INT.: What do you consider something like *Z?*
> GODARD: An objective ally of Hollywood.
> INT.: What do you consider *Weekend?*
> GODARD: The same. Maybe more fun, but the same.[33]

The primary reason for his rejection of *Weekend* is that the working relations were dominated by the cult of personality, focused on Godard as the darling auteur of the French New Wave. In his early period, he also used big name stars like Brigitte Bardot, and helped to create new ones like Jean-Paul Belmondo. After his political conversion, he renounced them and his own stardom; unfortunately, he also sacrificed Raoul Coutard, his cinematographer on the earlier films, because "He is a reactionary mind. . . . We have nothing to say to each other."[34] Godard wanted to purge himself of his bourgeois background and of his associations with cult and ritual.

> I was raised in a bourgeois family, and then I escaped. I went to the Sorbonne for one hour. . . . I still had to escape . . . so instead of going to LSD or marijuana I got into show business. Then I discovered—and it took me fifteen years—that show business was an even more bourgeois family than the one before. . . . Then, after fifteen years of being a bourgeois fighting *other* bourgeois, when the May-June events arrived, I was ripe to make a definite break with what I was.[35]

Weekend is the borderline film in its conscious concern with the cinema of spectacle, ritual, and stars.

According to Godard, the problem of being an "auteur" is that it isolates the director from his crew and his audience:

> On *Pravda* (1969) we were three people and I finished it alone. But even if I was alone, my loneliness was very different from the loneliness when I made *Weekend* or *Pierrot le Fou* or *Breathless*. Because I felt more related to political events and mass events and students' struggle, I was not really alone.[36]

Moreover, Godard claims (unconvincingly) that this isolation seriously undermines the value of his political analysis in *Weekend* because it is limited to the expression of one individual's vision or feelings:

> The filmmaker just put his own feelings on the screen. Just because he puts it in a different way than James Bond or something, he thinks it is *really* different—just like when I was doing *Pierrot le Fou* or *Weekend*. But if you analyze it, you see that there is nothing more than an individual's own feelings.[37]

Yet to contradict Godard (or to support him against his own self-criticism), it cannot be denied that even these early films rebel against the bourgeois industry in handling the script:

> Jean-Luc used to improvise the dialogue from pieces of paper in his pockets. . . . He usually had a script to submit to the backer, but he didn't care about it, because he wasn't going to follow the script.[38]

And in transformation of narrative conventions:

> One thing that can really be proved is that the development of
> movies and the invention of the camera did not mean progress,
> but only different kinds of tricks to convey the same stuff already
> in the novel. . . . Novelists became incapable of transforming
> progress into revolutionary movement because they never
> analyzed where the narrative line was coming from. By whom
> was it invented? For whom and against whom?[39]

Despite his own reservations, all of his early films, especially
Weekend, clearly demonstrate his own later dictum that radical
cinema must have a radical form.

After *Weekend*, Godard acted on his self-criticism by entering a
new stage of working relations, forming with Gorin the Dziga Vertov
Film Group, dedicated to the following principle:

> It is necessary to stop making movies on politics, to stop making
> political movies, and to begin making political movies
> *politically*. It means maybe taking a gun one day, then the next
> day going back to a pen or the camera.[40]

After making this claim, the Group still had contact with the
bourgeois industry, but now they set out consciously to exploit it:

> INT.: If you have your film processed by Technicolor, a
> capitalist firm, it's necessarily a bourgeois film, isn't it?
> GODARD: No, not at all. Because you can have a gun, an M-17,
> and you can shoot Nixon with it. And it will not be a bourgeois
> bullet any more.[41]

At the same time, they consciously demystified relations with other
workers on the film:

> The economic reality is the lab and the studio. . . . For example, if
> you do fast editing, you know, a lot of shots, you have to be aware
> of the negative editing girl who is working at the lab. The boss of
> the lab is trying to get her to edit as fast as if there were a few
> shots. You see? She's just a worker on an assembly line and this
> assembly line is just a movie, frame after frame.[42]

Although Godard and Gorin claim, "Our personal lives are of no
interest," they are also aware that their private behavior must not
contradict the radical principles of their films. This is particularly
relevant to the sexual issue:

> The basis for *Struggle in Italy* was our attempt to organize our
> personal lives with our wives. . . . So we deliberately chose a
> subject which was strongly related to our ideology, because even

> when you speak to a woman you are in love with, or the women
> speaks to you, this is ideology. . . . Trying to work with our wives
> on movies, when they are not especially interested in movies, was
> correct at that moment.[43]

As is clear from this statement, Gorin and Godard take a very
patronizing attitude toward women. Why should the women work
on movies if they are not interested in them? The same attitude
informs *Letter to Jane*, which attacked Jane Fonda's "misguided"
participation in the anti-war movement, suggesting that the American press had exploited this "naive" star's visit to Viet Nam. Though
he has some theoretical understanding of women's exploited situation, his films make no contribution to the representation of women
as realized subjects in the realm of independent action. Godard
himself realizes his failure to deal effectively with the women's issue
and his problems in communicating with us:

> With this women's liberation thing, we were interested in trying
> to speak to a woman who was the leader of the takeover of Grove
> Press, and she said, "Well, for the moment my relationship with
> men makes it impossible to talk with you." And she was right,
> because that was a concrete situation, and we had nothing
> concrete to discuss with her.[44]

These limitations imply that half the world's population will have
trouble taking part in Godard's vision of community.

There is some question whether the Dziga Vertov Film Group was
really a communal enterprise, or just a couple of buddies. They
wanted "not just to work together as fellows, but as a political
group."[45] But when asked in 1970 how many people were in the
group, Gorin replied:

> For the moment, two—but we are not even sure. There is a left
> wing and a right wing. Sometimes he is the left and I am the
> right, sometimes I am the left and he is the right. It's a question
> of practice.[46]

In speaking of his working relations in 1976, Godard admits:

> We are in no way a group. . . . I never worked really with a group.
> When I worked with Gorin, it was not a group.[47]

The process of self-criticism and renunciation of earlier stages
continues.

Financing and Marketing. Godard realizes that no matter how radical a film may be in its content, form, and working relations, it can still be co-opted by the ways in which it is financed and distributed. The knowledge that one has to deal with bourgeois business interests at both ends of the production process fosters self-censorship, preventing many projects from even being proposed:

> I think it's impossible to make a film out of the Chicago trial, to make it a concrete analysis of a very specific situation, and to have the picture distributed by Metro Goldwyn Mayer. If it's possible, and if you make the picture, you get a Metro Goldwyn militant picture. Which is *still* a Metro Goldwyn picture.[48]

Godard is most fond of using supposedly political films like Z to illustrate this point:

> The Greek government is paid by the CIA—it lives on CIA money. And Hollywood is the agent of the CIA in that particular area of ideology which is the movies. So what does it mean if you make a picture on Greece, and this picture receives an Oscar in Hollywood? These are the two parts of the contradiction.[49]

The problem for Godard and the Dziga Vertov Film Group was to come up with alternatives to this financial trap. For *Weekend,* the solution was multiple producers; the film came out as a Comacico/Copernic/Lira/Ascot/Cineraid Production. In addition, Godard apparently located some money realized from insurance policy returns. With this financial structure, progressive capitalists could reduce the price and spread the risks of financing a "radical" film. In 1970 another solution was to deal with the most flexible, humane, and progressive element of the bourgeois establishment—in this case, Grove Press.

> GORIN: The only people who offer us money are Grove press. They are closely linked with Hollywood, but we can use the money.
> GODARD: We are very glad to receive money from Grove, and if they are glad, for the moment it's OK.[50]

Grove distributed several Godard films (including *Weekend*) both in 16mm for the college market and in 35mm for theaters and also advanced money for films not yet begun, yet Godard still acknowledged that this association would influence the content.

> Grove Press has already bought two pictures in advance. What
> does it mean for us? It means we can control the picture except
> inside the States. It means, since it is more money than we have
> had in the last two years, that we have the capacity to think and
> work on the picture for six or seven months. It means we have no
> bread and butter problems for six months, and we have more
> creative possibilities. It means to pay people on the same basis
> that we are paid. But still we know what Grove Press is, more or
> less, and we know, more or less, what we are. So the first picture,
> *Vladimir and Rosa*, will deal with sexuality. We know Grove
> Press is interested in erotic things as well as politics and avant-
> garde art. And since Barney Rosset is interested in that, we have
> tried to work within that, and to deliver the best picture we can.[51]

Another solution was to make films with an extremely low budget.
Although Godard had always made inexpensive films, he was now
carrying it to new extremes where he would be willing to sacrifice
conventional theatrical distribution entirely.

> Grove Press, for example, has given us $6,000 for *Pravda*. This is
> the right price, because it's reasonable that in two or three years
> Grove Press will be able to get eight or nine thousand dollars.
> But not much more, I think. So we have to manage to make
> pictures for that price—which is right too. . . . We think that
> pictures are too rich—not only that they cost too much, but that
> they have too many images, too many sounds, and this doesn't
> cost more than a few thousand dollars.[52]

The logical extension of this position is the 8mm "home movie" or
video, both of which Godard has explored. As another means of
raising money, Godard and Gorin have toured the college circuit
with the films. Now that Godard and Gorin have split, Godard
continues this tactic alone. However, he realizes that these are all
short-range and imperfect solutions, and that he may run out of
creative alternatives:

> It might mean that we will be obliged to stop making movies for
> economic reasons or maybe from political decisions. At a certain
> historical point we will know if it's more important not to make
> a movie.[53]

Film Audience

In discussions of Godard's films and their audience, he is frequently
accused of an important contradiction: if his goal is political action,
why does he make films that are inaccessible to mass audiences? But

that is somewhat unfair to Godard, who has a different audience in mind. In fact, he has relinquished the wider appeal of his earlier works for his political goals.

> A film is no more than a leaflet, and a leaflet is just shown to the people it's addressed to.[54]

Rather than dazzling a mass audience with spectacle and deluding himself that he is changing their political vision, he chooses a concrete effect on a specific audience. In speaking of his Super 8 projects, he says:

> We think the best way of projecting it is to project it to a very small group, a family, things like that. This is a militant work because it deals with personal problems and the relationship of personal problems to political or general problems.[55]

Ideally, Godard believes that significant political action can result from showing the right film to the right audience at the right time. When an interviewer pointed out to Godard that the student take-over at Columbia occurred two days after *La Chinoise* opened in New York, Gorin remarked:

> Don't tell him that. He has been noting—putting in a notebook—every student insurrection just after a showing of *La Chinoise*, and coming to me and saying, "Look! You see, it works!"[56]

Under the right circumstances, the results can be even more immediate. For example, Godard claims:

> When the film *The Green Berets* was shown in Jordan, they destroyed the movie theater—the only place in the world where the population destroyed a movie theater![57]

Yet Godard's films are so demanding and difficult that their select militant audience must also be an intellectual elite. This was vividly demonstrated on the 1970 tour during the appearance of Godard and Gorin at the Berkeley Community Theater following the showing of *British Sounds:*

> When the film was over, Godard, Gorin and Luddy approached the stage for the question-and-answer period, only to be met with a barrage of tomatoes. . . . The questions . . . were no more intelligent than the tomatoes. Godard was attacked for being arrogant, for being a male chauvinist (despite the fact that his film included a long statement on the oppression of women), for

getting rich by ripping off the Movement—on and on and on. He tried to answer calmly, but nobody in the audience was really listening.

Someone asked him if there was a place in the Revolution for "smoking dope and dancing naked in the streets." Godard replied that while there might be a specific situation in which such action would be a correct tactic, he didn't advocate it as a general movement. He spoke repeatedly about acting from logical analysis rather than from emotional feelings, but this just got people more upset. One young woman began a long, whining statement in which she kept returning to her "feelings," and was just coming around for the third time to, "and I feel," when Godard yelled, "Fuck your feelings!"[58]

Whether or not Godard's films succeed in moving audiences to direct action—tearing down a movie theater, throwing tomatoes, or taking over a university—their primary effect is in expanding consciousness, moving audiences beyond their habits and expectations in the medium and in society, and forcing them to participate actively in decoding the images and the concepts they embody. The films demand full participation of intellectual faculties rather than emotional identification. For Godard's style, the possibilites are open-ended since, for him, filmmaking, like the revolution itself, will take infinitely unpredictable concrete forms.

> People think we are aiming at a model, and this model you can print and then sell as a revolutionary model. That is shit.[59]

Sweet Movie (1974)[60]

The Film Artifact

Sweet Movie demystifies the ways in which "chaotic natural beings" are controlled and destroyed by art and ideology in both Communist and capitalist societies. It retrains its audience in how to consume this dangerous product:

> *Sweet Movie* is like halva—it is so thick and sweet that people can only eat one or two bites.[61]

Instead of depending primarily upon analytic techniques like Godard, Makavejev uses a mixture of tones in a collage structure to create a form of subversive anarchy which forces his audience to find their limits through gut responses and joyfully affirms instinct over intellect. Like *Weekend*, *Sweet Movie* presents a dark vision of experience, yet it comically celebrates life and survival. The refrain of the theme song (written by Makavejev) asks the paradoxical question: "Is there life after birth?" Although the film answers affirmatively, as in his earlier works (especially *Love Affair: or the Case of the Missing Switchboard Operator*, 1968 and *WR: Mysteries of the Organism*, 1971), Makavejev bombards his audience with intensely disturbing images, mixing sweetness and terror, hilarity and the macabre, pure ideology and sickening violence. In the opening scene, a woman croons, "I see something black. Is it my beloved, or is it cowshit?" Confidently, we giggle at the incongruity. But later we get rather edgy when we see inmates of a radical therapy commune prancing around with their shit on a platter (this image was eliminated by the American distributors) while the silly, victimized heroine moons in a corner before writhing sensuously in a vat of chocolate. The values have been reversed; showing your shit seems preferable to being chocolate-coated. But we are still revolted by the shit and turned on by the sugar. We feel uneasy because we are not sure how we are supposed to respond—to anything. We cannot revert to neat formulae or political rhetoric because they, too, seem to be under attack. From an anarchistic perspective, any system is dangerous because it destroys the natural force of organic life.

Like Godard, Makavejev forces us to explore our own judgments through the images he presents; it's impossible to have a passive response. Thus, while watching their films, at moments we may feel stupid, ridiculous, perverted, or counter-revolutionary. Yet *Weekend* and *Sweet Movie* evoke different kinds of reactions. Godard's film is highly puzzling, demanding that the viewer figure out the intricate connections among various elements and the concepts that gave rise to them; not being engaged on the emotional level, many viewers simply are baffled and angrily give up. In contrast, every segment of *Sweet Movie* engages its audience emotionally—either delighting them through its comic exaggeration of the familiar or disgusting them through taboo-busting—even if the viewer doesn't understand what it means, or why it's there, or how it relates to anything else in the film. Thus, although *Sweet Movie* may be as outrageous and offensive as *Weekend*, it is more accessible at this primary level. Whereas we come away from *Weekend*'s ironic prophecy of doom with tremendous respect for Godard's brilliance and originality, but contempt for the rest of mankind, *Sweet Movie*'s comic unpredictability sends us out with a desire to love and rescue our fellow humans from institutions and dominance. In describing Rabelais' genius, Mikhail Bakhtin also defines the source of Makavejev's revolutionary power:

> Laughter liberates not only from external censorship but first of all from the great interior censor; it liberates from the fear that developed in man during thousands of years: fear of the sacred, of prohibitions, of the past, of power. It unveils the material bodily principle in its true meaning. Laughter opened men's eyes on that which is new, on the future.[62]

Adapting this Rabelaisian spirit to the cinematic medium, Makavejev draws heavily on Eisensteinian dialectical montage; yet his unique collage technique and his parodic tone result in a Dadaist aesthetic. His use of the medium fulfills Benjamin's prophetic insight:

> Dadaism attempted to create by pictorial—and literary—means the effects which the public today seeks in the film. . . . One requirement was foremost: to outrage the public. . . . It hit the spectator like a bullet, it happened to him, thus acquiring a tactile quality. . . . By means of its technical structure, the film has taken the physical shock effect out of the wrappers in which Dadaism had, as it were, kept it inside the moral shock effect.[63]

Like Godard, Makavejev's achievement is to retain the moral effect of Dada, realized through the technical potentialities of cinema.

Of the three films under discussion in this chapter, *Sweet Movie* is most explicitly focused on sexual politics. This results primarily from Makavejev's study of Wilhelm Reich (who was the subject of *WR: Mysteries of the Organism*). For Makavejev as for Reich, sexuality is the measure of freedom, and female receptivity is the potential by which human beings can transcend the technocratic male civilization as we have known it. Hence *Sweet Movie*, like all of his films, is centered on female figures who, though limited and sometimes victimized, are further along the evolutionary road than their male counterparts. As a Reichian, Makavejev works to combine the Marxist and Freudian visions of human causality, while criticizing each for its narrowness and distortion. His plots highlight the destructiveness of Freud's bourgeois obsesssion with the Oedipal syndrome (the mother-son relationship in *Sweet Movie*) and of the repression exercised by Stalinesque killers (the ice-skater and Stalin himself in *WR*; the sanitary engineer in *Love Affair*; Anna Planeta in

Sweet Movie); Reich saw Stalin as "modju," a modern-day devil. The Reichian influence informs, not only Makavejev's ideas, but also his anarchic tone and collage structure. Reich's primary scientific method, which he called "functional identity," was based on the dialectical principle of unity in diversity. For Reich, all opposites, all apparent contradictions, are actually expressions of the same base, diverse applications of the same source. For example, the vagina taking the penis is functionally identical to the baby sucking the nipple. In *Sweet Movie*, this identity is realized in the commune scene where the Western herione tenderly rubs a man's cock against her face to the same lullaby by which she sucked a black woman's nipple, suggesting that nursing shapes our sexual tastes.

The concept of functional identity is central to his collage technique, where images and juxtapositions are Dada-like in their outrageous effect. In *Sweet Movie*, one of the most comically startling images is of the Western heroine being carried about Paris in a suitcase that wiggles as she struggles to release first a finger and then her head, which sticks out of the red plastic, then looks in astonishment at the bustling city around her. In an interview, Makavejev identifies this image with Solzhenitsyn when he was thrown out of Russia:

> I empathized with Solzhenitsyn when he was forced out of his country. I imagined his surprise when, after being put on the plane, he found himself in Frankfurt! The suitcase scene was my discrete "homage" to him.[64]

At another more conventionally "serious" level, he also identifies this shot and that of the girl emerging from a swimming pool as images of birth. Makavejev explains that in the final shots of *WR*, he was creating just such an identification between himself, Reich, and the film's heroine. In his collage technique, which combines allusions, newsreel footage, fiction film, multiple plots, documentary, interviews, black and white and color, the unique aesthetic power results from juxtaposition rather than the innovativeness or visual brilliance of individual shots. In this way, the films force the audience to transcend habitual perceptions and move them toward a new consciousness:

> My feeling is that I use cliches as bricks, as blocks. They are mostly exposed to critical examination and doubts, so they reveal their real nature, especially if you watch them several

times. Then you discover that cliches are disappearing, and they
reveal their real soul.[65]

Sweet Movie, however, more than any of his earlier films, also
develops dazzling visual pleasure so that the film's surface expresses
its special theme—the dangerous sweetness of art.

The structure intercuts between two plots of eight sequences each,
which follow the episodic adventures of two contrasting women: the
antiseptically pure Miss Canada, who is really the prize loser; and the
vivacious Captain Anna Planeta, soulful veteran of the Spanish Civil
War, who turns out to be a killer.[66] Each story contains an insert of
black and white documentary footage collected from both camps—
the exhuming of corpses of Polish officers killed by the Soviets and a
film of gymnastics for babies being trained for the Third Reich.
These contrasting plots suggest the dialectical poles of world politics—
the competitive commercialism of the U. S. A. and the death-loving
political romanticism of the U.S.S.R.

In the first Western sequence, our bourgeois heroine (Carole
Laure) is displayed in pure white fur at the Miss World contest, where
seventy-seven virgins from all over the world are subjected to a pelvic
examination under spotlights, before a huge audience. The contest is
sponsored by the Chastity Belt Foundation, a firm dedicated to
destroying "chaotic natural beings," and managed by a carnivorous,
dessicated platinum blonde mother determined to buy her son (Mr.
Kapital, the richest bachelor in the world) the best wife on the market.
This Holy Mother is accompanied by bopping, finger-popping
priests on conga and guitar. The other competing virgins represent
racism, the Third World, and Makavejev's own homeland: Miss
Southern Rhodesia, a white giggler who coyly cooperates; Miss
Congo, a powerful black giantess with a bunch of bananas dangling
from her belt; and a hefty Miss Yugoslavia who, although she comes
across like a Polish joke, also suggests an active subject with plans of
her own as she sits on the wrong chair and slugs the doctor and the
announcer. When our heroine, Miss Canada, spreads her legs, the
doctor's face is beatified, as if a soft light were coming from her cunt.
The contest makes comically explicit the Western cinematic and
cultural practice of fixing women with a gaze that sees only their
erotic possibilities and evaluating them from this perspective only.
Then the film cuts abruptly to a spectacular shot of Niagara Falls.
This juxtaposition works like a commercial that functionally
identifies women with their sexual organs and trains us to desire

marriage. Shulamith Firestone calls this the "Privatization of Sex,"
the "confusion of one's identity with one's sexual identity":

> Because the distinguishing characteristic of women's exploita-
> tion as a class is sexual, a special means must be found to make
> them unaware that they are considered all alike sexually
> (cunts).[67]

In the second sequence, as the camera dwells on impressive shots of
the Falls, a helicopter enters the frame, trailing a banner that reads:
"Happiness Forever." Makavejev forces us to reconfront the way in
which the power and beauty of the waterfall have been com-
mercialized into a honeymoon cliché. As in *Love Affair*, where the
male killer is a sanitation engineer, Makavejev uses this metaphor as
Mr. Kapital defines marriage: "A purified sanitation system for
unchecked waste." As the Western hero, the groom wears cowboy
gear and gives his bride a diamond crown from his mines in South
Africa. Although the bride had been judged the world's purest and
most beautiful vessel-virgin, on their wedding night (the third
sequence), she holds a bouquet of red lights in front of her crotch,
implying that even she is a whore. Thus the husband can still
consider her dirty; he rubs her down with alcohol, determined to kill
all germs and desire before he pisses on her with his golden cock. The
fast cut to Niagara Falls that follows confirms that in conventional
Western marriage, even the white man's sewage is monumentally
powerful.

Though she is still technically a virgin, this is only the first of a
series of violations. In the fourth sequence, Miss World is seen at her
husband's swimming pool stroking his toy lion, perhaps identifying
with this stuffed pussy. After being nearly drowned by her mother-in-
law and the family lawyer, she is then turned over to Jeremiah
Muscle, a black body builder, who stashes her in a giant white milk
bottle. Now the female victim is pitted against the black victim, who
has also been trained to see himself only as a body and a sexual
performer. Instead of realizing that Mr. Kapital is their common
oppressor, they call each other names—"Hitler! Filthy Jew!"—and
attack each other. Trying to get at her still unconsumed cherry, Mr.
Muscle offers himself as another delectable: "Try me. I'm delicious.
See this chocolate complexion?" Beginning to develop her taste for
chocolate, she licks his face and smiles, "It's sweet." "Finger-lickin'
good," brags Mr. Muscle. To preserve her virginity ("My only
property . . . my diamond") she slyly offers him a diversion: "I'll do

something to you my father taught me." She jerks him off; but instead of thanking her, he knocks her out. To get rid of the body, Jeremiah stuffs her into a red plastic suitcase. As it bumps its way along the conveyor system, the film forces us to re-examine a familiar perception. Now that a person is involved, the whole process is humanized and we watch with careful attention. When the airline clerk asks him why his bag is so heavy, Mr. Muscle claims it is full of Marcuse, Vranicki, Supek, and Sartre, using lofty ideas to disguise an act of violence, a popular strategy in the West.

In the fifth sequence, our heroine is reborn. As we hear the theme song, "Is there life after birth?" we watch the car carrying the red suitcase drive through a long tunnel and then emerge near the Arch of Triumph. Miss 1984 begins to crack the zipper of the suitcase like an embryo breaking out of its egg. Once out of the shell, the hatching chick establishes herself as a new female subject through her "look" directly at the audience, but then she is imprinted by the first man she sees, who happens to be El Macho, a narcissistic brown glitter star shooting a film on the Eiffel Tower. An effeminate British director coaches the star: "Look terribly Mexican!" As an androgynous fake radical (perhaps evoking Mick Jagger), the singer moans his masochistic manifesto: "To see this world full of so much suffering turns me on . . . like the motor of history . . . I'm a wild stallion, hooves of gold, flying mane . . .with thrusting sword . . . revolt here, revolt there . . . so wild and not afraid." Makavejev uses this pop Zapata to illuminate the connection between sadomasochistic chic and worldwide oppression. El Macho enfolds Miss World in his swirling black cape, trimmed with multi-colored hands reaching up at the star from the hem. He fucks her on the tower as a gaggle of groupie nuns watches adoringly. Unfortunately, Macho and World get stuck together like dogs with "lover's cramp," and have to be carried to a restaurant kitchen and laid on a table with other hunks of meat to be separated. This indignity is one too many for Miss World. After they are separated, she breaks eggs over her head and smears them on her face while El Macho weeps sentimentally. As in *WR* and *Love Affair*, the egg is a key image as the perfect food and symbol of life; here, it is wasted.

The sixth sequence begins as Miss World is dumped out with the rest of the garbage into Otto Muehl's radical therapy commune (called "La Voie Lactee," or The Milky Way), which outrages everyone in the audience, but which Makavejev describes as,

Very nice people. It is the only alternative community that I have

met that is not heavily into drugs. . . . Very normal, and highly
educated people. In the commune they became warm and happy
and rid of all their social rigidities.[68]

Here Miss World is restored by a loving black Momma Communa
who suckles her, and by the whole group who use food to integrate
her into their community. Yet their eating habits violate every
manner known to civilized man: they throw food, spit, and vomit on
the table.

> We are not conscious of how we are affected by millions of
> taboos, not only about sex and death, but even about the edges of
> plates. If you spill food on the table, you are not supposed to eat
> it. If something falls into a glass of water, you are not supposed
> to drink it. There is incredible embarrassment when food is spilt.
> But you can just look around and see how parents are eating
> their children, and how people are eating each other emotionally.
> Really in our society I think people are scared and this reminds
> them of what happens in families.[69]

In this commune every member regresses to infancy. We watch one
grown man lie on his back, kicking his legs in the air, cooing and
pissing while his helpmates caress him and sprinkle his body with
baby powder; then others shit on stage to enthusiastic applause and
joyfully waltz with shaved heads in the nude as Miss World sulks in a
corner. Between the two ends of the biological process Makavajev
inserts the documentary footage of the baby gymnastics, where a
healthy blond baby looks astonished as it balances on the hand of a
training doctor with the strains of *Eroica* playing in the background.
This juxtaposition underlines the revolutionary nature of the
commune's attitude toward infantile regression. As a Reichian,
Makavejev insists that the sphincter is a political muscle; once it is
controlled, the whole organism is prepared for Fascist domination.
We learn discipline one muscle at a time, starting in infancy with
toilet training but then moving on to calisthenics or the goose step, as
the newsreel clearly demonstrates. Makavejev sees children as the
victims of society and the potential agents of revolution. Hence, the
regression to infancy can be an act of political liberation whereby one
discards all cultural imprinting and once again becomes a chaotic
natural being with unlimited potential. Although Makavejev intended Miss World to achieve this transformation, the actress Carole
Laure was too frightened by the "crazies" and thus chose to remain
the masochistic victim to the end.

The brief seventh sequence (which has been cut out of some prints) shows the commune singing around an organ, where props like breath spray and a boot perhaps parody the values rejected by this radical community. However, the capitalist conclusion that follows in sequence eight shows the commercial forces triumphant. The commune now becomes the setting for a TV commercial selling chocolate, with Miss World starring as an erotic Bon Bon.

> People are very corrupt and as soon as they feel that people are sexually free, they run to them just to profit from sexual freedom, just to steal some sex.[70]

The liberating use of food in the commune is now co-opted into the cannibalistic metaphor of female exploitation as the director tells Miss World: "I want them to feel they're eating you." As Makavejev says:

> Millions of women are completely invisible because their reality is eaten away by powerful men.[71]

This scene brings together elements from Miss World's earlier violations: she, rather than El Macho, is now the media star; she performs before a prop that helps to turn her on—a statue of a black man in boxer shorts with burning red-light eyes that evokes her wedding night and Jeremiah Muscle, who first taught her to lick chocolate; finally, she is drowned again, this time successfully, in chocolate, as the director says: "Beautiful." As her mother-in-law's voice-over tells us: "Let everything be known. Let everything be clean," we see that Miss World is no longer white and pure, but she is still the sweet victim.

The plot reveals that Western ideology trains women to be delicious masochists and men to be egomaniacal power lovers. As Reich affirmed:

> Masochism flourishes like a weed in the form of the diverse patriarchal religions, as ideology and practice, smothering every natural claim of life.[72]

As a materialist, Makavejev prefers an eating metaphor:

> The whole family represents emotional food for the father. They are sacrificing some emotions and the father is like a monster eating them, kind of making them smaller.[73]

The western world is dominated by phallic power: Mr. Kapital's golden cock, Mr. Muscle's giant white milk bottle, and El Macho's Eiffel Tower. But throughout Makavejev's films, the power of these phalluses is undermined by castration imagery: the plaster casting and sex-change operation in *WR*; the pulling down of spires and the downfall of the tower-dwelling hero in *Love Affair;* and most powerfully, the slicing of the pseudo penis in the commune scene of *Sweet Movie*. One of the men puts a beef tongue in his fly and slaps it on the table and begins to cut it. The reason this action is so shocking to the audience is that western civilization cooperates to shield men from castration anxiety, which they have because, in fact, their genitals are so vulnerable, and because, in patriarchy, the penis is their sign of exclusive ownership of all the cultural apparatus. This is visually confirmed a few moments later as Miss World rejects the big piece of meat and takes out the actor's real penis and rubs it gently against her cheek:

> MK.: This was not done by the group, but by an Argentinian actor I brought into it. So he's part of, let's say, my play. I liked it because it is a kind of self-castration, a self-criticism play. There is also the idea that we have enormous cocks. I like this setting because not only am I confronting us with castration fears, but because a second later when we see the real thing it is so vulnerable.
> Int.: And small. . . .
> M.: But still big enough for her. It is a pity we are not able to go further.[74]

As a Reichian, Makavejev would undoubtedly argue that castration fear is fostered by the western economic structure:

> The fear of castration, which Freud discovered in bourgeois men, is historically rooted in the economic interest of the budding patriarchate. And the same motives which originally created the basis for the castration complex maintain this complex in capitalism today; the patriarchal private enterprise system's interest in monogamous permanent marriage—an interest in which parents, totally on an unconscious level, function as the executive organs.[75]

The commune returns us to Engels' and Reich's vision of a matriarchy where children no longer belong to a single father (Makavejev tells us that "each baby has twenty-five fathers") and where the leader is the film's most positive figure, the good mother, Momma Communa, who guides the others along the Milky Way. In Marcuse's terms, the commune is revolutionary at the primordial level, rejecting the father-dominated reality principle and regressing to a pregenital "superid":

> The psychical phenomenon which, in the individual, suggests such a pregenital morality is an identification with the mother, expressing itself in a castration-wish rather than castration-threat. It might be the survival of a regressive tendency: remembrance of the primal Mother-Right. . . .[76]

Meanwhile, the revolutionary counterculture plot seems to establish a black and white contrast with the West, with the Revolutionaries as the good guys and the Capitalists as the villains. A number of oppositions emerge:

Revolutionaries	vs.	*Capitalists*
Sugar		Chocolate
Old World/Experience		New World/Innocence
Earthiness		Cleanliness
Blood		Gold
Death		Birth

Moreover, the sexual politics seems to be reversed. Though a woman is again the central figure, she is the killer and men are her victims. Yet on closer examination, we see that Makavejev has carefully linked the two plots with a series of common terms. There is a growing integration until they are finally synthesized into a functional identity.

In the first revolutionary sequence, our heroic Comrade Anna Planeta (Anna Prucnal) is a proletarian Cleopatra, riding on a barge called "Survival." The head of Karl Marx, her own Mr. Kapital, dominates the prow. In the Western sequence that follows, Mr. Kapital smokes a Lenin pipe and quips: "He's the guy who shot the Tsar and started World War I," conveniently leaving out the Revolution in his garbled history. On the sound track, old Italian anarchist songs introduce the theme of revolutionary romanticism, singing: "For an idea we leave our beloved. . . . Our country is the whole world. . . . Our law is liberty. . . . Rebellion beats in our hearts." While at this point we may take these lyrics straight, they are later undercut by El Macho's parody. In this version of boy-meets-girl, Anna is pursued by a sailor (Pierre Clementi) who bicycles along the shore; his shaved head links him with the inmates of the therapy commune. In the second sequence, in contrast to Mr. Kapital's taking his bride for a ride in his private helicopter, the sailor hitches a ride on Anna's revolutionary barge.

In contrast to the antiseptic wedding night of the Western plot, this coupling (in the third sequence) is frantic and comically lustful. As the sailor relieves himself on the shore, he, too, tosses a little piss her way, but in this case it's only foreplay, and causes Anna to wave him on board. This pair also has an audience along the river bank who shout encouragement: "Stick your sword in to the hilt! It won't hurt her!" Her own comment: "Man! How proud that sound!" continues the theme of phallic glorification, showing that macho is not restricted to the West. In the background, the chorus sings the familiar "Life after birth" theme, including the lines: "It's sweet to be hungry. It's finger-lickin' good," anticipating Mr. Muscle's self-advertisement. Anna welcomes the sailor as an "authentic sexual proletarian": "Hey, Potemkin. Aren't you from the Revolution that failed? I mean the one in 1905?" As he fucks her on the stairs, she shouts, "Fascination! Forward! Optimistic Tragedy!" Despite the comic glee, however, the dialogue is full of turgid romantic illusion and hints of the male masochism to come:

> SAILOR: I'm your new lover. I'm starving for love.
> ANNA: People who starve know how to make love.
> SAILOR: Where does the boat go?
> ANNA: To the end. The bottom.

But despite these clues, we still like the earthy, independent Captain Planeta and her eager lover far better than the perverted Kapital and his tortured bride.

The turning point comes in sequence four. The Revolution's susceptibility to commercial co-option is displayed as the lover presents Anna with gifts from "romantic foreign ports": an Arabian carpet made in China, vodka from Berkeley, and a white mouse named Leonid. The sailor reveals his name is Bakunin. While Anna and a friend playfully bathe the sailor, she warns him explicitly: "Do not trust your fate to anyone. . . . This boat is full of corpses." He replies: "The whole world is full of corpses," and sinks back into the tub as if he were dying, evoking the near-drowning of Miss World in the previous sequence and foreshadowing his own murder. Makavejev cuts abruptly to documentary footage of the corpses of ten thousand Polish officers allegedly murdered by the Soviets during World War II.

My feeling is that the main reaction to this kind of necrophiliac

> exposure of death is shock. The material is showing that death is
> something to be displayed.[77]

Although Makavejev believes that "the revolution is always alive,"
he still attacks its murderous deeds—particularly under Stalin—that
betray the spirit of Bakunin:

> Trotsky was just one of the tens of thousands of good people who
> were carefully picked out and killed by the movement. Obviously
> something monstrous had happened in the movement. The
> movement shaped itself in such a way that whoever was creating
> had to be killed. It's quite terrifying, and I think that this terror is
> still not expressed.[78]

This newsreel insert is the first clear signal that our early admiration
for the revolutionary heroine was naive and that she is just as
dangerous as Mr. Kapital.

> This is the point when my fiction story becomes documentary.
> All this black and white footage then changes back into color to
> show that there is some kind of process of transformation; a
> transformation of Anna from a love-bringing woman to a fear-
> bringing one.[79]

To underscore this transformation, Makavejev cuts to a close-up of
thick red liquid that foreshadows the pool of blood in the sugar bed;
Anna forms this red sugar into a rose, sealing the two plots together
by evoking Mr. Kapital's Rosebud insignia. Above the blood appears
a printed message to Anthony Eden from the British ambassador to
Poland: "Let us think of these things always and speak of them
never," almost the dialectical opposite of Makavejev's prescription.
But the visuals follow the advice to Eden as we cut back to the sailor
laughing and singing as if he's been reborn in the water. He runs into
an inviting bed of sugar, with bright lollipops dangling overhead.

In sequence five, we see two sides of Anna as the embodiment of the
Revolution—heroic underdog and dangerous aggressor. Following
the breaking and wasting of the eggs in the previous capitalist
sequence, the fragility of life and ideals is now demonstrated. With
tearful self-pity, she tells the sailor how she tried to keep her
Communism pure, but "All have deserted me . . . only a few old
soldiers come to visit me." Although she claims that liberty,
Communism, and love start today, she has become a callous survivor:
"The one who falls and dies is a schmuck, an idiot." Again she warns
the sailor not to stay with her, and this is good advice.

The next scene reveals her, not as a victim, but as a predator. Dressed in a virginal white bridal dress (with suspenders over her breasts and a blue bow tucked into her pubic hair), Anna entices four little boys with her colorful lollipops and bins of bright jellybeans displayed around her sugarbed. As she performs a seductive strip-tease, one boy caresses her pink platform shoe and she loops her stocking around his neck, anticipating the fetishism in the long takes of the boot on the organ in the commune scene and of Miss World's feet as she undresses for her chocolate bath. Some of the props seem strangely familiar: the stuffed tiger and the black death's head with sugar eyes evoke the statue of Mr. Muscle and the stuffed cat in the poolside scene. Her walls are covered with a photomural combining blow-ups of Revolutionary heroes with Western stars—a nude poster of the Mommas and Poppas (a slick version of the commune) and Marlon Brando as the Wild One. This glamorous overlay on Lenin and Trotsky transforms them into decoys for dangerous seduction, like the lollipops and bon bons:

> Lenin was very passionate, very alive, so can you do anything worse to him than to turn him into a beautiful corpse, like a piece of pink pastry?[80]

The same treatment is given to Jesus, who also hangs on the wall; his star power is augmented by the religious ceremony that dominates the sound track, sanctifying the seduction. Religion seems to be exploited for the same ends in both worlds.

Although we do not actually see the boys being harmed in this scene, we feel vaguely uneasy and suspect they may be in danger (as in the documentary footage of the baby gymnastics that immediately follows). Under Makavejev's direction, however, the scene is a turn-on and the little boys seem to be enjoying themselves. The "Survival" barge may turn out to be the "Good Ship Lollipop," yet we have all been taught that children should not take candy from strangers. We are unsure how to react. We don't want to be prudish, yet if the sexes were reversed (if the adult seducer were male and the children female) we would probably condemn it as child-molesting and might even object to child actors being exposed to such eroticism. In fact, many of the images do suggest child pornography. Anna opens one boy's fly; she straddles the head of another as he looks up at her, and finally climbs onto a bunk bed with a third, telling him he can fuck her. He pulls the curtain to hide from the audience the actual deed. This scene is the peak of "outrage" in the counterculture plot as the

infantile behavior of the commune scene was in the other; both
challenge some of the audience's most deeply held taboos, and Anna
demonstrates that mother/son incest is not limited to the West. But
this treatment of child sexuality is to be sharply distinguished from
exploitive pornography, especially when viewed in the context of
sexual politics as defined by Reich and Firestone. Reich advocated
liberation from patriarchal dominance for children as well as for
women, arguing that the sexual impulses of children should be
fostered and satisfied rather than discouraged. He insisted that

> The "Oedipus complex," which Freud discovered, is not so
> much a cause as it is a result of the sexual restrictions imposed
> upon the child by society. Yet, wholly unconscious of what they
> are doing, the parents carry out the intentions of authoritarian
> society.[81]

As Firestone points out, this is part of our power psychology by
which we alienate and repress children so as to control them into
inheriting the father's name and perpetuating the nuclear family.
Since both children and their mothers are subjugated, mother/son
incest is a way of rebelling against the father. Repressed parents
compensate for their own lack of sexuality by inducing it in their
children. Especially frustrated by her total impotence, the mother
alternately caresses and disciplines the child, trying to re-create the
relationship she hoped for with her husband, but in fact, arousing a
perverted mother-fixation. Because the father so jealously guards his
power, the male child's desire leads to a strong fear of castration,
trapping him in a frightening double bind. It is part of Makavejev's
explicit attack on the failure of the Revolution that it never created
the slightest deviation from the Russians' puritanical, Czarist
orthodoxy in which child sexuality indicated moral breakdown
rather than movement toward a freer human condition. The ambiguity is essential: while Makavejev displays the potentially positive
value of child sexuality, he nevertheless exposes Anna as one who
exploits it because she, herself, is the victim of a perverted revolution.

Our worst fears about Anna are confirmed in the next sequence.
After looking at her pop heroes, she complains: "All the ones I loved
have died." Like the proverbial killer who murders his parents and
then pleads for mercy because he is an orphan, Anna is soon revealed
to be guilty of killing those she loves. The sailor rises out of her bed of
sugar, exclaiming, "I feel good." She remarks, "It always starts that
way," confirming that these ritualistic killings are a habit. They
make love in the sugar, lick the sweetness from each other's bodies

and scoop up spoonfuls to sweeten their coffee; nevertheless, she warns: "Sugar is dangerous." Throughout the film, Makavejev has been showing us how our culture gets us hooked on sugar in order to make us more susceptible to political and commercial manipulation. Sugar is biologically related to both energy and anxiety. Its whiteness misleads us into assuming it is symbolic of goodness, but *Moby Dick* presents a strong counter example. Like Melville, Makavejev insists on the ambiguities. After confessing that sugar doesn't take away the bitter taste, Anna bites her lover near the neck and draws dark blood, which drips from her mouth. Seeking no explanation from this sexual vampire, the masochistic sailor who loves "to live dangerously" ecstatically moans: "I felt so jealous when Vakulinchuk died." Film buffs will recall that Vakulinchuk was the martyred sailor in Eisenstein's *Potemkin*. She obliges his romantic desire for death by plunging a dagger into his gut. As the camera lovingly dwells on the sensuous pool of thick red blood bubbling up through the sugar, she twists the knife and stirs the red and white substances as if making a delicious "pink pastry." He dies laughing and she sugarcoats his corpse. This sensuous murder evokes the erotic secret-room romanticism so popular in Capitalist countries where the woman slays her lover either to escape (as in *Last Tango in Paris*) or to attain total possession (as in *In The Realm of the Senses*). Makavejev claims that the actor Pierre Clementi took the masochism much further than was originally intended. Having just been released from prison after a dope bust in Italy, Clementi brought to the film the aura of the victim. Yet the final line that Makavejev gives him concerning Vakulinchuk, which is repeated in a voice-over as he dies, puts the erotic masochism in the context of political idealism, functionally identifying them in a Reichian spirit.

> The striving for non-existence, for the Nirvana, for death, then, is identical with the striving for orgastic release, that is, the most important manifestation of life. There can be no idea of death which derives from the actual dying of the organism, for an idea can only render what has already been experienced, and nobody has experienced his own death.[82]

Sequence seven presents various kinds of sentimental hypocrisy. Anna hangs a plastic bag full of water as a tear on the Marx figurehead of her ship, showing how the Revolution publicly mourns those it has murdered. To the accompaniment of sirens and sad music, the police arrive and remove the four boys, whom Anna has also killed. The local citizens are outraged and throw stones through the windows of the boat as the boys' bodies, wrapped in plastic, are lined up neatly on the riverbank. But the presence of newsmen and photographers shows that such "tragedies" immediately become ghoulishly popular media carnivals, strengthening the connection with the Capitalist world of deadly media coverage and slick packaging. In the final shot of the sequence, the four boys watch their own dead bodies being taken away, foreshadowing their later rebirth out of the plastic cocoons and implying that the Revolution still has potential for life.

The two plots are fully integrated in the last two sequences. While Miss World is drowning in chocolate, the resurrected sailor voyeuristically peers through a window as Russian music dominates the sound track. The off-screen voice of Kapital's mother ("Our boys did quite a job!") bridges the two sequences and comments not only on those who have exploited the pathetic heroine of the West, but also on the victims of the post-revolutionary corrupted mentality; Makavejev cuts back to the newsreel footage showing the corpses of the Polish officer[83] and then to black and white footage of Anna's victims lined up on the shore. In order to assure us that there is still some hope for the Revolution, he uses a number of codes to accentuate the rebirth of the young boys. As they revive, color gradually seeps into the black and white image, as if helping in the regeneration. The piercing whistle of a train passing over a bridge announces the miracle. The shot of the boys freezes and as the visual image returns to full color, a children's chorus sings the theme song, reaffirming that there is, indeed, life after birth.

Makavejev also develops the dialectic on a self-reflexive level by contrasting two cinematic styles. The Western plot is sprinkled with a number of film allusions (perhaps both mocking and affirming the West's contribution to the world's store of images). At the Miss World contest, the mother explains how clean capitalists can kill the beast within them by a simple "Triumph of the Will," evoking another documentary of Fascist gymnastics like the baby calisthenics of the insert. The entrance to the contest stage is shaped like an enormous vaginal "Rosebud," an image we see again on the helicopter. In case we don't recognize this allusion to *Citizen Kane*, Kapital's huge mansion clearly evokes San Simeon or Xanadu. Since Makavejev makes his millionaire into a caricatured villain, one suspects he is parodying Welles, who cultivated an ambiguity that allowed him to criticize Hearst while simultaneously glorifying him, an ambivalence typical of a Yankee romanticism still hooked on the American dream. As Mr. Muscle carries Miss World to the top of *his* tower, the *King Kong* allusion hints at the ape image hidden in the heart of American racism. The verbal evocation of Buñuel's *The Milky Way* in the title of the commune calls attention to shared qualities and values like the absurdist tone and the anarchistic mockery of the Church and cultural taboos. The chocolate commercial scene, where the cinematographer smiles obscenely, obviously turned on by his drowning model, extends the situation from *Blow-Up* where the photographer straddles Varushka in a surrogate sex act and is merely indifferent to, not actively excited by, the death that may have taken place in front of his camera.

The film also parodies a number of techniques typical of Western cinema, exploring some of the values implicated in these formulae. The slow-motion treatment of Miss World's near-drowning in Kapital's pool evokes the beautiful handling of subject matter that is inherently ugly (like Peckinpah's choreographed violence with blossoming blood and gracefully falling bodies), only here the object of the long look is our favorite sufferer—the female. On the Kapitals' wedding night, the film cross-cuts between husband cleaning his ass and wife waiting expectantly, parodying Griffith's intense crossing-cutting (with its false implication of unity and omniscience) by the absurdity of the images and the anti-climax of urination instead of penetration. The sequence reminds us comically how our viewing experience can be manipulated, expecially though techniques of simple bi-polarity (as is parodied in the film's structure). Makavejev randomly chooses a movement of the wife to repeat through looping, parodying the inflation of trivia through sophisticated technique used for its own sake. He suggests the burned-out search for the realistic thrills of "cinema vérité" when the silly director on the Eiffel Tower squeals: "At last! Instant cinema!" as he spots the couple fucking. The overall pattern of filmic references suggest that western cinema has declined from innovative classics like *Citizen Kane* to exploitive "snuff films" like the chocolate commercial.

On the revolutionary side, the parody focuses on Eisenstein, particularly his silent classic on the abortive 1905 revolution— *Battleship Potemkin*. Not only does it provide the source for the hero, who is called Potemkin and who worships Eisenstein's martyr Vakulinchuk, but Makavejev also emulates its style, especially in the encounter between Anna and the sailor. While she floats down the river, on shore he performs exaggerated gestures characteristic of silent films. The film then intercuts between the barge and the sailor on his bicycle moving in opposite directions, accentuating the dialectic of the montage. The synthesis builds on images of spectators—common people rather than actors—amassing on the shore to witness the heroic coupling and evoking the scene in *Potemkin* where the crowds stream forth to honor the martyred Vakulinchuk. All this manipulative power is further parodied as it serves, not an event of historical significance, but a romantically elevated fuck. The film also draws on the heroic socialist realist films of the forties. For example, as Makavejev says, "When the woman shakes hands with the children, this is the typical gesture language of 'revolutionary' bureaucrats."[84] Parody of both Russian and Western styles is dropped in the commune scene where the film successfully interweaves color documentary footage into the fiction to record authentic people living out the Reichian revolution.

The Means of Production
   Working Relations. Although Makavejev is definitely an auteur with a small, joyful following, he mocks the cult of heroism and stardom in both his films and his filmmaking process. Though he apparently had the opportunity to use stars in *Sweet Movie* (according to the *Hollywood Reporter* and *Variety*, Jean Seberg and Dominique Sanda both signed at various stages), he wound up using the relatively unknown Carole Laure, who later sued him and his main producer for personal damages inflicted on her during the shoot. According to Makavejev, she was just trying to capitalize on publicity to build her star aura, as Sami Frey does as El Macho within the film. However, his best working involvement lay with the non-professional members of Otto Muehl's real-life commune:

> Part of the script included a kind of anti-psychiatry mental hospital. When I met them, I wanted to do part of the film in Vienna, but we brought them to Paris instead.[85]

He substantially altered the script to include their greater participation because their involvement with each other represented the antisocial communal spirit at the heart of the film:

> Individually they have no money, they share everything . . . They get into real regression, but with real mutual support. They are very conscious of what they are going through, and are very often discovering things from their childhood . . . They also do it publicly because they know it turns others off, and that's a way

for them to defend themselves, because whenever they are nice,
people come in flocks.[86]

Makavejev's receptivity to the spontaneous is one of the greatest
strengths of his filmmaking process.

> I had wanted to make it much more positive. It was planned as a
> hilarious comedy, and I believe it would not have been so strong
> and heavy. When making films I always follow what happens
> around me, and in this case some doubts kind of crept in and they
> became heavier and heavier.[87]

This helps to explain why the commune was such a valuable resource
for him.

> Once by accident we ran the screams of this man in therapy and
> we got a baby's cry. Incredible! A baby's cry, but because he's an
> adult we don't recognize it. It is the basic way of breathing under
> a stress situation. They do this kind of thing as part of their
> regular therapy.[88]

We can infer from the lawsuit that Carole Laure was very threatened
by the commune; her reaction caused Makavejev to omit her
regeneration scene and create new alternatives.

> Carole was not able to follow through . . . because she started
> having problems with nudity. She was able to be naked in a
> number of scenes, but mostly when she was alone. She believed
> that she was going to be fucked by all of them in front of the
> camera. The idea was that they were going to undress and bathe
> her, and treat her in a very sensual and gentle way. Then one tear
> was going to appear in the corner of her eye. The next step was
> the awakening of the mouth, then a food orgy that persuaded her
> to be gentle with sex. So a whole series of events were very
> carefully planned to bring her back to life in a number of very
> small steps.[89]

Just as he was able to draw on Pierre Clementi's masochism in the
murder scene, Makavejev was also able to use Anna Prucnal's
strengths creatively:

> Anna came out from the kitchen carrying this salad and they
> started throwing it around. It was very nice because suddenly the
> connection between the food and the girl appeared completely
> improvised and unplanned.[90]

Makavejev does work with a script, but his kind of daily planning is
consistent with his use of improvisation because it is focused on
immediate sensory experience.

> I planned a program with a day of eye contact, a day of food , a
> day of piss, a day of shit, a day of sex, and a day of death.[91]

Like the films, his working relations are clearly informed by the
spirit of Dada and anarchy.

Financing and Marketing. Like *Weekend, Sweet Movie* was made
possible by a group of producers who are self-conscious about
finding alternatives to the monolithic industry. It came out as a
VM/Mojack/Maran Films production, involving cooperation between French and Canadian financing. In 1973-74, Vincent Malle's
French company co-produced thirteen films at an average budget of
$250,000 each, with government seed money for seven of them.
Though this is a highly risky situation, Malle feels strongly that the
aesthetic and social possibilities are worth the risk. The Canadian
Film Development Corporation also receives sizable government
grants for its operation, and then feeds the profits back into the
corporation. Though insisting that government support is necessary
to get good films from the industry, CFDC does not choose projects
that will suit the government. In fact, its executive director says of
their selection process:

> We try to keep everyone reasonably discontent.[92]

Makavejev has had considerable trouble getting distribution. His
censorship problems began with *Love Affair*, but fully blossomed
with *WR: The Mysteries of the Organism*. Not only was he forced to
change the last word in the title from *Orgasm* to *Organism*, but the
film was totally suppressed in Yugoslavia:

> I think it was clearly understood as being anti-Stalinist. Basically
> I think that people thought my questioning of everything was
> unacceptable. It was not even specifically political or sexual.
> There is a sentence in Marx where he says that it's very important
> to practice ruthless criticism on everything that exists. Now this
> type of thinking was considered by some politicians as not only
> relativistic but kind of undermining. That's not true, because
> whatever is going to endure does so in spite of being questioned.[93]

Forced to leave his homeland, he made his next work *Sweet Movie* in
Canada and Europe,[94] where he encountered new distribution
problems. After its premiere showing at Cannes in 1974, the mass
defecation scenes were cut from the commune sequence, and never
appeared again in theatrical exhibition. The Italian producers, who
distributed the film in Italy, made further changes and released the
film:

> As adapted for the Italian mentality (and censors) by Pier Paolo
> Pasolini and Dacia Maraini. Censors intervened just enough to
> help box office considerably.[95]

Makavejev responded to these cuts with remarkable (and somewhat
Dadaist) flexibility:

> I also think that with clever distribution I could make different
> versions for different countries. . . . I discovered that the French
> are most concerned with food, the Scandinavians with violence.
> The Italians are more political so in Italy it was shown with five
> titles, Pasolini did one with my approval. It was *Infantile
> Malady of Left Communism.*[96]

Like his use of spontaneous reality in making his films, his
acceptance of these cuts seemed to pay off:

> My great success in Italy was very useful, and *Sweet Movie* was
> about sixty per cent more successful in France than *WR*. Still,
> *WR* brought me a much better reputation in France than *Sweet
> Movie*, which turned some people off.[97]

In the U. S. A., a censored version of the film eventually received
limited distribution, mainly in art houses, by Biograph Films, a local
operation based in Berkeley. The American mainstream, however,
failed to distinguish *Sweet Movie* from the sleaziest, hard-core
pornies. In a muck-raking cover story titled "The Porn Plague,"
Time Magazine lumped the film with *Deep Throat* and *Behind the
Green Door*, using its most superior, arch tone to express its moral
outrage:

> One current porn film, *Sweet Movie*, features a striptease for
> children, intercourse plus murder on a bed of sugar, grisly
> exhumations, and a band of rollicking adults who vomit,
> defecate and urinate on one another to the strains of Beethoven's
> *Ninth Symphony*. The director, Dusan Makavejev, professes to
> see the film as socially beneficial. Says he: "It is meant to have a
> lasting aphrodisiac effect and generally tone up the orgasm.[98]

Since *Sweet Movie* has such limited distribution in the U. S. A., we
realize that our lengthy discussion of it may be of limited interest to
many of our readers; but we believe it is part of the critical task to help
outstanding progressive films reach a wider audience.

The Film Audience

Makavejev realizes his films will not be widely seen. But unlike

Godard, who wants to reach a group that is ideologically and historically correct for the material, Makavejev assumes that the size of the audience is directly linked with the intrinsic aesthetic qualities of his works, particularly their density. In order to make them more accessible, he would have to thin out the material:

> I think that if I want to reach large audiences, I have to produce three films a year instead of one *Sweet Movie*, but with the same actors and the same story.[99]

His films must be seen many times if the full richness is to be savored and the nutritional values digested.

> My films are not for just one viewing. They change the more they are seen.[100]

Yet he does not really demand from his audience that they adopt his point of view, transform their own ideology, or storm the Pentagon. What he expects is an openness (Reich's female receptivity), which would necessarily enrich one's experience and enlarge one's perspective.

> I think it's important not to be apparently political, because if you believe in film as a kind of action-created structure, then it has to be as neutral as possible so that people can be free to accept or refuse ideas. As soon as you start promoting ideas, then you are trying to seduce people to your point of view. If I'm going to seduce people, I want to seduce them for themselves—to do something for them.[101]

Although he hopes that his films will "influence social situations," he is not disturbed when some viewers accuse him of being "counter revolutionary."

> That I am not offended by this kind of labelling tells me I know what I'm doing.[102]

When Makavejev brought his film to the U. S. A. to seek distribution, he premiered it at Berkeley's Wheeler Auditorium, probably assuming that here he would find his most sympathetic radical audience. But he fared no better than Godard. Though the response was varied, it was uniformly passionate: *Sweet Movie* was attacked as an homage to Hitler, ridiculed as a forty year old's wet dream, and celebrated as a brilliant work of revolutionary anarchy. Yet he did not get angry like Godard. As if energized by their attack, Makavejev met the hostile remarks with comic resilience—smiling,

shrugging, joking, trying to implicate even the shrillest objectors
into his human predicament. Apparently audiences need such films,
because many are unable to grant him the freedom that is offered
them and that he and his co-workers courageously expand by making
such dangerous movies.

Seven Beauties (1975)

The Film Artifact

The prologue to Seven Beauties suggests that the film will demystify
the Fascist idealism and patriarchal authoritarianism that lead to
world wars and the cowardice and stupidity of the silent majority
who support this corrupt power structure in exchange for personal
survival. Over the titles, we see a montage of brown-tinted WWII
newsreels of exploding bombs, Hitler and Mussolini shaking hands
on the German-Italian alliance, Nazi guns and flags, crashing planes
and amassing crowds as we hear an upbeat rock 'n' roll parody with a
series of "oh yeah's," and a male voice cataloging those to whom the
film is satirically dedicated: "the ones who support the corporate
image without knowing it, the ones who would have been better off if
they had been shot in the cradle, the ones who say we Italians are the
greatest heroes in the world, the ones who vote to get rid of strikes, the
ones who still support the king, the ones who believe Jesus is Santa
Claus as a young man, the ones who keep going just to see how it will
end, the ones who are afraid of flying, the ones who are in garbage up
to here, the ones who lose by the skin of their teeth." Yet, it is highly
questionable whether the film fulfills the iconoclastic expectations
raised by the prologue, or actually winds up affirming survival at any
cost. Whereas Godard and Makavejev control their subtext so that it
expresses their subversive ideology, the subtext in Seven Beauties at
times contradicts its announced political goals. Despite this
ambiguity, the self-righteous tone of Wertmuller's singing spokesman implies that it's easy to separate one's self from the list of those
who should be scorned and that the makers of this film clearly are not
implicated. In her confident detachment, she lacks the self-criticism
of Godard and Makavejev and thus fails to raise the consciousness of
her audience to the second power. Both Weekend and Sweet Movie

explore the difficulty of making moral distinctions and judgments but affirm the necessity of doing so. Their strategy prevents the viewer from facilely condemning others or naturalizing one's own corruption, which is apparently what *Seven Beauties* encourages its audience to do.

The film follows the picaresque adventures of its antihero Pasqualino, nicknamed "Seven Beauties," who is introduced in the prologue as he escapes from a Nazi transport and bumps his head on a tree, establishing him as the engaging bumpkin whose fate is inevitably out of his own control. The narrative intercuts between two kinds of Fascist terror which threaten him in the past and present. In Italy where the Mafia controls "peaceful" domestic crime, Pasqualino kills his sister's pimp to save the family honor, pleads insanity to save his neck, and enlists in the army to escape his imprisonment in an asylum. In Germany, whose wartime "order" is directed by the Third Reich, he is imprisoned in a concentration camp and earns his survival by fucking a female commandant (Shirley Stoler) and shooting a number of fellow prisoners, including his best friend. In an epilogue, he returns home to find that his mother, sisters, and fiancée have all become whores, and decides to marry his tainted bride and start having as many kids as possible to create his own private army. Wertmuller skillfully cuts from one plot to the other whenever Pasqualino's predicament gets most desperate, as if offering him and the audience escape through imaginative diversion. Wertmuller's most passionate supporter, John Simon, argues that this crosscutting achieves not only suspense and dramatic exposition, but

> Rather it is to show that the life of the preening little Mafioso was just as preposterous, in its own way, as that of the escaping survival artist, except that the weird things are now being done in the name of staying alive and not in that of *onore* and *dignità*—and survival is probably a worthier cause.[103]

Bruno Bettelheim, on the other hand, believes that the intercutting falsely implies that life in the camp and in the town are functionally identical in their corruption and violence and further distorts the moral vision by making the horror serve the comedy:

> We experience horror, then something grotesquely comic or funny.... the horror becomes background for the comic scene, and the comic scene wipes out not the fact of the horror, but its

emotional impact. . . . The film induces us to commit ourselves
to not taking any event or situation seriously—not even one that
would ordinarily upset us greatly or move us deeply.[104]

While Godard and Makavejev also juxtapose horror and comedy, the
effect that they achieve is not to weaken the impact of the horror, but
rather to use it in exposing the terrible consequences of what we have
been trained to accept and desire. We are not denying that there is a
valid connection between the Fascism in the camp and that in the
Mafia, which Wertmuller reinforces by a number of self-reflexive
allusions. Pasqualino and the pimp call each other "pig" and
"worm," foreshadowing the exchanges with the commandant. When
Pasqualino meets with the Mafia boss, their male posturing and
pompous talk of respect reminds us of the opening footage of
Mussolini and Hitler. The meeting takes place in a huge, station-like
building that has its parallel in the enormous terminal space of the
camp's interior. However, we agree with Bettelheim that the simplistic intercutting glosses over all distinctions. (If we had to choose
between life in the camp and in the town, the decision would be easy.)
Wertmuller's editing resembles Griffith's crosscutting more than
Eisenstein's dialectical montage used by Godard and Makavejev,
which perhaps partly explains why her films are so much more
accessible and popular in the U. S. A.

   In both Fascist contexts, Pasqualino is corrupted and despicable,
but he survives. Thus in its ironic detachment, the film presents us
with nothing more than a despicable survivor. One way that
Wertmuller increases the distance between audience and characters is
through a series of role reversals. Pasqualino fluidly alternates
between killer and victim, aggressor and worm. While most war films
train us to expect men to function as heroic idealists with women as
the practical survivors, Wertmuller performs a sexual reversal in
which the female commandant is the ironic spokesman for German
romanticism while Pasqualino crawls home sullied but intact. None
of the characters is really a fully developed human being; as they
switch personae, we see no humanity beneath the posturing. Even in
the death camp, the victims are more like animated cartoon figures
whose misery is never convincing. Pasqualino emerges from this
nightmare like the little mouse in *Tom and Jerry*, who always
bounces back. Kosinski sees the entire film as "a cartoon trying to be a
tragedy," making contradictory emotional demands.

   By making him bigger than life in the comic strip sense, the film

> denies him any larger human dimension. . . . Wertmuller's error
> is not only in trying to pass off a shell as a viable tragic character,
> but in manipulating us into expending emotion on a vacuum.[105]

Despite her detached handling of the other characters, Wertmuller's
aesthetic choices also set us up to be charmed and seduced by
Pasqualino. His position as starring protagonist, the camera's loving
attention to his poignant expressions and clowning gestures, and his
indomitable resilience make us root for him to the very end.
Wertmuller seems to be so engaged with Giannini's Chaplinesque
talents that the film actually affirms a character whose behavior
invites condemnation; in this contradiction lies the film's central
failure of irony. Kosinski correctly perceives the ways in which
Giannini's aura confuses the film's moral vision:

> It is too easy to be inveigled by Giannini's presence into
> dismissing Pasqualino's morality. In fact, the character's per-
> sonality seems almost to have been shaped to conform to
> Giannini's extremely marketable persona.[106]

Wertmuller defends her decision to save her corrupt hero on moral
grounds:

> It is very dangerous in a movie when the bad guy dies, if the bad
> guy is a Hitler or a Mussolini, because the viewer can feel that he
> has actually killed him, that now he is free. . . . We must
> remember that even in real life, although the Hitlers and the
> Mussolinis may be dead, their legacy is still inside all of us.[107]

Although she convinces us that this legacy lives on in Pasqualino,
who actually impersonates Mussolini and is visually compared with
Hitler, her treatment of him and the other characters merely
reinforces our cynicism.

To demonstrate that this is not an inevitable consequence of the
material, one need only compare *Seven Beauties* to Ingmar Bergman's
Shame, which deals with similar issues and also ends with the
survival of its murderous, cowardly protagonist.

> *Shame* originates in a panicky question: How would I have
> behaved during the Nazi period if Sweden had been occupied
> and if I'd held a position of responsibility or been connected
> with some institution? Or had even found myself threatened as a
> private person? . . . Every time I've thought about such matters,
> I've always come to the same conclusion: physically and
> psychically I'm a coward—except when I get angry. . . . But I'm
> always a coward. I've a strong instinct for self preservation.[108]

We are moved by *Shame* because Bergman forces us to acknowledge these despicable traits within ourselves and yet condemn them; Wertmuller, on the other hand, mocks her characters from a superior vantage point for the same qualities, yet she presents them as "human" and inevitable. One is more likely to associate her with the Nazi commandant who toys with the "macaroni" and exposes his selfish cowardice, rather than with the heroic socialist or anarchist who are both defeated. Wertmuller, like the commandant, understands the appeal of Pasqualino's pathetic yet deadly powers of survival.

Perhaps it is unfair to compare Wertmuller with Bergman or to accuse her of failing at tragedy, for she has obviously chosen her satirical tone quite carefully. She develops a distinctive mixed form that both draws on and parodies the conventions of tragedy, comedy, and farce. In both plots she selects material with tragic potential: Pasqualino's murder of his sister's seducer to defend family honor is a traditional theme of domestic tragedy; the extermination of the Jews is undoubtedly one of the most tragic events in modern history. Yet she mocks those who are committed to tragic idealism because it leads to actions that are either absurd (Pasqualino butchers the pimp, whom his 37-year-old sister dearly loves) or horrendous (the commandant uses the Nazi dreams for a master race to justify the extermination of "worms" who "have no ideas or ideals").

From archetypal comedy, Wertmuller draws the conventions of the low-class picaro who gets by on his wits, and who demonstrates his resourcefulness through his comic adaptability. In the traditional manner, she ends with Pasqualino's marriage and his announced intention to build a new society. However, she parodies these comic conventions by showing the grim price of survival In the final sequence, his mother comforts him: "You're beautiful, Pasqualino. You're alive." Looking in the mirror with his face partially obscured, he replies glumly: "Yes, I'm alive," as if questioning whether it's worth it anyway. The new society he plans to build with his virgin/whore wife holds little more promise; he presents it as an island of armed safety, a perverted Eden, in a society that will decay further: "I want kids, 25 or 30. We've got to defend ourselves. See all these people. Soon we'll be killing each other for an apple."

Farce is conventionally a form of slapstick comedy in which resilient creatures survive one disaster after another. It is basically comic because it shows life triumphing over death as in the case of the farcical Pasqualino. Yet the consequences for many of the other characters in *Seven Beauties* are deadly, especially for the pimp, who is murdered, and the Anarchist, who drowns in a vat of shit, inevitably reminding us of the death of the Western heroine in *Sweet Movie*. But whereas her drowning makes a satirical point about media exploitation and evokes the central bi-polarity between shit and sugar, the choice of this particular form of death in *Seven Beauties* merely enhances the spectacle. Throughout *Sweet Movie*, the comic exaggeration of physical imagery is used to show both the distortion of bodily life under economic and political exploitation and its possibilities in a state of freedom. *Weekend*, too, draws heavily on body imagery but its uses are more closely linked to the analytic perspective of traditional satire: the burning, cannibalism, and blood function metaphorically to predict the most horrible possibilities of human life as the society disintegrates. *Seven Beauties* relies equally heavily on such images—e. g., the fatness and moles of the ugly women, the shit, the dismemberment of the pimp, the greenish corpses, and the emaciated living dead—but they do not work in a unified way to enrich the film's resonance. Instead, they merely titillate us visually and expose grotesque weaknesses, which suggest that we can expect little from these characters. We regard them with a mixture of indulgence and contempt, a form of sentimentality common in farce, which prevents us from taking them seriously or evaluating their behavior.

This blending of various forms of parody works particularly well in the sequence where Pasqualino murders the pimp. As we hear loud snoring, we see Pasqualino with gun in hand sneaking into his enemy's room in the dead of night. He snaps on the light and wakes up the pimp, who blurts out: "Don't shoot, pig." This insult, his snoring, and the seediness of his room comically identify this ugly little man with an animal and make his seductive power (which got him in trouble in the first place) seem totally absurd. Thus far the tone of the encounter is pure farce. As the nervous Pasqualino postures as an aristocrat pursuing honor, he nobly tells his enemy to get his gun as if challenging him to a duel, and then shoots him by accident, confirming that he's just a bumpkin after all. When he sees the blood and realizes that he has actually committed a murder, he panics and gets sick. The gap between the surface melodrama and the underlying physical reality is the source of both the comedy and the grimness of the scene. The real horror is that one can commit such a brutal act through absurd role playing, as we realize that on a larger scale the heroic posturing of Hitler and Mussolini that we laughed at in the prologue led to deadly consequences for millions in World War II. Thus this scene skillfully exposes the limits of all three modes—farce, which denies the consequences of sex and death; comedy, which refuses to acknowledge the full price paid for survival; and tragedy, which inflates questionable values like family honor and patriotism.

The successful control of tone is unfortunately not sustained in the dismemberment sequence where the slapstick farce is allowed to take over, possibly because of its popular appeal, even though it undermines the moral vision. The sequence opens with a cut to a close-up of a tool kit. Then the camera pulls back to reveal Pasqualino dressed as a butcher, nipping from a bottle of vodka to bolster his courage as he tries to cut up the body of his victim. He struggles with the corpse, which keeps falling on top of him, and bumps his head on the table as he takes up the hatchet, evoking the pantomime of both Chaplin and Keaton, which Wertmuller earlier used in the notorious sex scene in *The Seduction of Mimi*. In both cases, she pits little Giannini as a pathetic Chaplinesque bungler against monstrous opponents whose physical grotesquery (she has an enormous ass and the corpse keeps farting) prevents us from feeling any sympathy for them despite the fact that they are really his victims. Thus we are encouraged to laugh at deformities and carnage without compunction. In his one line of dialogue, Pasqualino clearly articulates the contemptuous attitude that rationalized both his and Wertmuller's treatment of these bodies as dehumanized objects: "O God what un ugly slob!"

Wertmuller develops parody most fully by making *Seven Beauties* an anarchistic mock epic. As an extended narrative, the traditional epic defines what it means to be civilized within the boundaries of a particular culture by following the exploits of a culture hero whose deeds are essential to the survival of his people. It includes combat with an uncivilized monster (like the Cyclops or Grendel or Satan), an outsider who embodies the forces of anarchy. His destruction justifies the temporary suspension of civilized behavior (murder, treachery, whatever it takes) on the part of the culture hero in order to preserve the social and moral status quo. The epic requires a highly elaborate, formalized style in order to give the civilized codes an aesthetic appeal, but the rules must come to feel like human nature rather than contrived conventions. Hence, on all levels, it's an establishment genre, opposing the disruptive, radical forces of irrationality and chaos. Epics are male-dominated forms where women are deceptive (Helen, Circe, Penelope), distracting (Calypso,

Dido), dumb (Eve), or destructive (Scylla and Charybdis). At best, they sit home demurely and wait like Penelope, futilely weaving and unweaving their tapestries, dreams, and tales. Only divine females like Athena share any of the action and even *she* has to travel in drag. Women are seen as dangerous because they drag men down to the physical level of animals and tempt them to violate their own idealistic culture codes, which the epic defines as the basis of humanity. Thus, the women are symbolically associated with counter-culture monsters (Grendel is supported by his mother, Satan corrupts Eve, Circe turns men into swine, and even Penelope encourages the riotous guests).

Seven Beauties turns these values upside down by supporting the forces of anarchy and reversing many of the important roles and values. The mock epic begins with the traditional invocation, not to the muses who inspired the film, but rather to those it attacks; the visuals of the prologue state the military theme central to all epics and demonstrate that civilized order is maintained by brute force and propaganda. The narrative begins *in medias res* and uses the flashback structure of *The Odyssey*. Like Odysseus, this culture anti-hero relies on his shrewd wit and is never at a loss; he is the only one of his companions to get home alive. The Nazi monster he combats does not represent anarchy, but a maniacally rigid order that poses as a superior civilization. *Seven Beauties* affirms a neo-primitivism where the anti-hero fights back with his subhuman "thirst for life." Not only has "human nature" decayed to the point where rules and values have no meaning, but, unlike the tribalism in *Weekend*, this new "truth" remains unanalyzed, and therefore is given the force of the "natural" or "inevitable." Like all epic heroes, his journey takes him to the underworld—here it is the deathcamp where he receives a prophecy, not from a blind Tiresias, but from an impotent anarchist who predicts overpopulation and proclaims "Man in disorder!" as the only hope for the future. The deathcamp is introduced by the demonic strains of Wagner's *Ride of the Valkyries* and by a montage of images in muted monochromatic tones, which, like the brown-tinted newsreels of the prologue and the misty gray landscapes of the forest, impose a dreary uniformity that opposes the vital spirit of anarchy. Extending the sexual reversals to the underworld, in this mock epic all of the lost souls are male and the reigning power is female. In this clearly intentional deviation from historical reality, perhaps Wertmuller hoped to benefit at the box office from the stereotype allegedly held by Italian men that mature female power is devouring and murderous; perhaps she herself is the victim of this ideology.

Though he is not as handsome as Odysseus, Pasqualino is mysteriously attractive to women, who also have considerable benign power in controlling his fate. He is aided by a series of older women who function like perverse Athenas: in the asylum, although he rapes a helpless madwoman, an elderly female doctor arranges for his release; while starving in the forest, he steals food from a mysterious aging beauty and her silent maid; in the death camp, he remembers his mother's teaching that "all women are women" and can be reached through love; he relies on visions of women he has known to generate an erection so that he can carry out his bold scheme of seducing the monstrous commandant. Although the commandant is a powerful witch like Circe, who captures men and turns them into animals or worms (he explicitly asks her if she is a "witch" or "enchantress"), the sex roles are reversed since he is the one who tries to drag her down to the physical level away from her lofty idealism. Although they call each other "pig," he tries to court her as Odysseus was wooed by Circe and Calypso. The sound track links her with the sirenous, satin-clad woman in the forest, who uses the commandant's voice to sing Wagner's *Traume (Dreams)*, which recurs in the deathcamp seduction. Simon says:

> Lina could have dubbed in someone authentically German, but ... what she wanted to convey was a certain pro-Germanism, the mystical identity of those two voices.[109]

Pasqualino's odyssey through Germany is framed by his encounters with this Scylla and Charybdis, who are dangerous but certainly not very seductive. As in the *Odyssey*, the journey ends with the hero returning home to his women and family. Though it is not one Penelope and a houseful of suitors, but rather one slightly tarnished fiancée, a houseful of sluttish sisters, and a town overrun by rutting Yankees, practically all of the women follow their conventional epic role of sitting and waiting. The entertaining of their suitors has been more profitable, however; the house is full of American souvenirs and Pasqualino's fiancée can now afford to support him.

Ironically, upon returning to Naples, the hero acts exactly against the anarchist's prophecy of overpopulation as he prepares for the future by spawning as many children as possible for his self-interest.

His acceptance of his whorish fiancée suggests that he has relinquished all hope of preserving codes in the decadent culture:

> According to whether man feels himself overwhelmed by the
> encircling forces or proudly believes himself capable of taking
> control of them, he declines or demands to have his wife
> delivered to him a virgin.[110]

His mother also gives him advice: "Don't think of the past. What's
done is done," which evokes Marx's famous warning that those who
fail to remember history are doomed to repeat it. As Marcuse suggests,
her advice is well designed to serve expediency:

> This ability to forget—itself the result of a long and terrible
> education by experience—is an indispensible requirement of
> mental and physical hygiene . . . but it is also the mental faculty
> which sustains submissiveness and renunciation. To forget is
> also to forgive. . . . Such forgiveness reproduces the conditions
> which reproduce injustice and enslavement.[111]

This mock epic defines how one insures his own survival within a
totally corrupt civilization that has destroyed all communal values.

One way in which *Seven Beauties* tries to preserve some traditional
values while at the same time appraising their moral worth is in the
exploration of art. Since the network of filmic allusions in *Seven
Beauties* has received much critical praise and certainly helps to
enrich its surface, it is important to examine how they are used. One
group of clearly intentional references to familiar film heroes is
highly significant in the comic development of Pasqualino's character. When he enters the theater where his sister is singing, he is lit in
red like a cabaret star and wears the slick light suit, hat, and cigarette
holder that evoke both George Raft and Marcello Mastroianni in
Divorce Italian Style (where Mastroianni's appearance is already a
parody of Sicilian gangsterhood). His sneering face-off with the
pimp in his sister's brothel is like a *mano a mano*, the confrontation
between two tough guys without which no Western is complete.
Pasqualino's escape from the mattress factory after killing the pimp
draws on the swashbuckler, as he swings on sheets from building to
building and makes a glorious speech from one of the windows. On
the one hand, all these heroics mock Pasqualino's deadly efforts to
protect the social code of family honor. Yet at the same time, the
enjoyable familiarity of the allusions increases our indulgence
toward him: how can he help it, poor thing? We have all been

similarly imprinted. But at the end, his choice of individual preservation promises no better than these communal models of behavior. Thus the goal in using these borrowings is not clear; while the film suggests they must be abandoned because of their danger, it simultaneously exploits their popular appeal and fails to offer any real alternatives. The casting of Fernando Rey as the anarchist is similarly linked to a confusion that is central to the film. The reference to Buñuel is clear, since Rey has played leading roles in a number of his works. But in *Seven Beauties*, his ideas are so undeveloped that we have little interest in them or him as a moral alternative, and his grotesque death hardly affects us. So despite the verbal support of anarchy, we cannot tell whether the film is affirming Buñuel's vision, or suggesting that his work has been as futile as the anarchist's.

Finally, another important group of allusions draws on the conventions of silent comedy with considerable originality. In the scene where he steals food, Pasqualino rushes out and the camera holds on the doorway as he dashes back and forth, trying to figure out what to do next. Like Keaton or Chaplin in the familiar "wrong way" scenes, the hero conveys a silent, underdog ineptitude together with wild energy, but Wertmuller adds Pasqualino's verbal resource-fulness (he talked steadily and cleverly to distract the woman as he stole the food). This combination now seems appealing to us; he has hurt no one and is trying to help his friend. In the courtroom scene, silent conventions are used with greatest dexterity and resonance. Conveying information and emotions entirely through visual means—the sisters' clothes tell us they have all become whores; Pasqualino and the young girl decide their future with an exchange of looks; the lawyer carries messages back and forth between the judge and the Mafia Don, showing us how local justice really works—the action is orchestrated to the strains of utterly Italian mandolin music. Through the rhythmic movements of this successful silent treatment, the sequence comically suggests that Italian justice has become a ritual performance whose verbal forms are empty, absurd, and completely unnecessary. It also boldly emphasizes that images are the real source of the medium's power and this film's greatest strength, providing a reservoir of common experiences.

Another way in which art is explored in *Seven Beauties* is by repeatedly evaluating the characters' performance as if they were creative artists. In the opening sequence, when Pasqualino is escaping from the Germans and deserting the Italian cause, his friend praises him for the authenticity of his fake wound as if it were a work of art. Pasqualino confesses that he stole the bandages off a dead soldier: "I feel bad about it, but I had to do it." Later when they see helpless Jewish families being gunned down by Germans, he uses the same kind of argument ("It would have been suicide") to rationalize his own detachment; his friend contradicts him with his words rather than with his behavior, introducing the theme of resistance: "You've got to say NO." This incident helps to illuminate Wertmuller's own moral stance as an artist. While she verbally professes to be innovative and radical, her behavior is often more like Pasqualino's: she uses expediency to survive within the competitive marketplace of the film industry and extensively borrows from other filmmakers, both living and dead.

Later, Paqualino is cast in the role of critic as he evaluates the singing of three would-be sirens. Despite her patriotic lyrics and costume (a garter of red, white, and green), the fat legs and clumsy dancing of Pasqualino's chubby sister bring no glory to the family or the fatherland. Wertmuller gets us to support the condemnation of her performance on aesthetic grounds, although her brother's moral reasons are preposterous, thereby confusing the two perspectives. We are led to agree with the preening Pasqualino that only an elite of the young and beautiful deserve to seek love. This judgment is reaffirmed in the second encounter, where he tells a lovely young girl, who is crying because everyone laughs at her terrible singing: "If anyone bothers you, say you're my fiancée." Thus he becomes the Fascist critic who protects his protégé with brute force—a position analogous to that of the pimp who has offered Pasqualino's sister the same encouragement. The morality and the quality of the singing are the same; only physical appearances differ. In the third encounter the political implications of aesthetic judgments are developed even further as Pasqualino's role shifts from powerful backer to poor hungry spectator. While starving in the woods, he chances upon an idyllic scene that at first looks like a fantasy; in an elegant country mansion a lovely, amply fleshed lady sits at a piano in a backless white satin gown singing a Wagnerian aria. Only the quality of her singing seriously deviates from perfection. Like his sister and fiancée, this singer is undoubtedly the protégé of another authoritarian critic—her aristocratic husband away at the war or perhaps even the Fuhrer himself—for she performs according to what Susan Sontag defines as the Fascist aesthetic.

Fascist art displays a Utopian aesthetics—that of physical

perfection. Painters and sculptors under the Nazis often depicted
the nude, but they were forbidden to show any bodily imper-
fections. Their nudes . . . are both sanctimoniously asexual and
(in a technical sense) pornographic, for they have the perfection
of a fantasy. . . . Nazi art is both prurient and idealizing. . . . The
fascist ideal is to transform sexual energy into a "spiritual" force
for the benefit of the community. The erotic is always present as
a temptation, with the most admirable response being a heroic
repression of the sexual impulse.[112]

Apparently Pasqualino manages to resist the sexual temptation and
pursue his duty of gathering supplies for himself and his friend, but
certainly without any heroic motives. He rejects the siren's charms,
not because her song is too Germanic or her figure too voluptuous, or
because his morality or his ear is too delicate, but rather because his
proletarian taste buds are more aroused by the sumptuous game
hanging on the walls and by the smell of onions that lures him to the
kitchen.

The theme of Fascist art is elaborated in the scene where Pasqualino seeks an audience with Don Raffaele, the local Mafia
bigshot, to tell him that he has murdered the pimp. The opening shot
reveals a huge Roman statue of Hercules, which expresses the brute
strength of an imperialist culture and provides a classical source for
the heroic posturing of Mussolini and Hitler. Later in the courtroom
scene, we see similar oversized statues, implying that this form of
posturing again dominates the Italian system of justice. But in this
scene, as Pasqualino and Don Raffaele strut beneath the giant models
within the cavernous room, the dehumanized scale dwarfs the two
little men who are lesser versions of even their human heroes. Don
Raffaele advises Pasqualino on how to get rid of the body, making it
both an artistic and sexual challenge:

A real man knows how . . . you need imagination. The man who
wants to be more has to do more . . . what normal people can't
even imagine. . . . This is your chance to be a real man. Naples is
a land of imagination.

Just as Pasqualino was led into committing the murder by following
movie heroes like George Raft, now he must turn back to the same
movies to learn how to dispose of the body. The Don offers him a
short course on methodology, which is illustrated by a montage of
imaginative techniques familiar to most gangster buffs: iron shoes in
the river, popular in the U. S. A.; stuffing oversized coffins, an
international method; and sneaking new bones into the old bone

house, an Italian specialty. The art of murder depends on progressive technology like all other art forms in the West. Despite these private lessons, Pasqualino proves he is an amateur who has not yet mastered the disappearing act: he breaks the unities in his murder drama by dividing the corpse into three acts, each of which is sent to a different destination, tripling his chances of getting caught. But he doesn't give up, not even in prison, where in order to plead insanity, he imaginatively imitates Mussolini, proclaiming: "a breed of artists and warriors that challenges the world." Though he draws catcalls from his fellow inmates, they also recognize his impersonation, chanting, "Duce, Duce, Duce" as they encircle him like an audience. Though his performance succeeds, he is merely transferred to another prison—an asylum, where he is presented with war as another means of escape. Yet the doctor warns him, "This war may be worse than you imagine." It is precisely because Hitler is abnormal that he became the most imaginative war artist the world has ever known, inventing the most extravagant forms of torture and misery that could be performed on the inferior masses. Yet, we don't praise him for these talents because, unlike the Fascists, we are able to distinguish between aesthetic and moral criteria. Art stripped of all morality is bound to be corrupt. As Walter Benjamin argues:

> The logical result of Fascism is the introduction of aesthetics into political life. . . . All efforts to render politics aesthetic culminate in one thing: war. . . . Marinetti says in his manifesto on the Ethiopian colonial war: "War is beautiful because it combines the gunfire, the cannonades, the cease-fire, the scents, and the stench of putrefaction into a symphony. War is beautiful because it creates new architecture, like that of the big tanks, the geometrical formation flights, the smoke spirals from burning villages. . . . Poets and artists of Futurism! . . . remember these principles of an aesthetics of war so that your struggle for a new literature and a new graphic art . . . may be illuminated by them!" . . . Mankind, which in Homer's time was an object of contemplation for the Olympian gods, now is one for itself. Its self-alienation has reached such a degree that it can experience its own destruction on an aesthetic pleasure of the first order. This is the situation of politics which Fascism is rendering aesthetic. Communism responds by politicizing art.[113]

Wertmuller seems to waver between these two poles, occasionally beautifying her politics and sometimes politicizing her art, depending on which has greater popular appeal, but without really committing herself to either position.

Since Pasqualino is a worm rather than "a real man," he lacks
Hitler's genius for war, which demands a perverted tragic idealism.
Instead, Pasqualino is like a low comic parody who would traditionally be confined to a subplot, but Wertmuller puffs him up to be
the star. As the inflated braggadocio, his greatest exploit is the
outrageous scheme of seducing the commandant and trying to
convince this cold, pig-eyed Nazi that she has inspired a burning
passion in his heart. With staggering macho arrogance, he gambles
his life on his powers as a sexual performer. The worm has guts!

Bringing together the main domestic and historical themes, the sex
scene between the hero and the monster in the death camp is perhaps
the most successful in the film. Though it continues to exploit female
physical grotesquery (as in *Seduction of Mimi*), this is mitigated by
its development of complex issues and techniques that have been
important throughout the film. The breakdown of traditional sex
roles is basic to the fluid exchange of roles that characterizes the entire
sequence. Pasqualino is planning to "seduce" her, but she holds all
the power to evaluate whether he suits her or not. At one point she
even warns him, "You'll never complete this performance." In the
preliminary courtship, his practical goal of survival demands that he
use the language of romantic idealism: "Who are you really? Maybe
you're just a victim of your own sense of duty . . . like us . . . Your rosy,
delicate flesh . . . is meant to be caressed." Though she has just put on
a romantic song by Hitler's favorite singer ("Only do not weep for
love . . . "), she now becomes the earthy, practical one, telling him:
"Eat, Naples." She orders him to strip and walks around his naked
body, coolly appraising his sexual possibilities. Like the scene where
Pasqualino murders the pimp, this sequence also powerfully combines a variety of tones and generic characteristics. Pasqualino is
farcical in his arrogant assumption that all women want to be fucked
by him, even in his present condition (like the Lilliputian queen who
fantasizes about scandal with the giant Gulliver). At the same time,
Wertmuller evokes pathos and fear through the Swiftian size
relationship. After the commandant strips down to her thermal
underwear and boxer shorts and whips Pasqualino in time to the
music, he frantically kisses his way up her arm and collapses on her
bosom; he's like an exhausted little puppy that gets lost in her ample
flesh. But the grunts and flailings of his comical struggle to perform
contrast sharply with her ominous impassivity as, a moment later,
she warns him coldly that if he fails at fucking, he will die. Susan

Sontag might be describing both the serious and parodic dynamics of this scene in her explanation of Fascist aesthetics:

> They also flow from (and justify) a preoccupation with situations of control, submissive behavior, and extravagant effort; they exalt two seemingly opposite states, egomania and servitude. . . . The fascist dramaturgy centers on the orgiastic transaction between mighty forces and their puppets. Its choreography alternates between ceaseless motion and a congealed, static, virile posing. Fascist art glorifies surrender, it exalts mindlessness: it glamorizes death.[114]

In contrast to the rape of the asylum inmate, Wertmuller now shows that the degradation of the act itself has only been a warm-up. As the commandant tosses him off her after his "success," she tells him he must choose six fellow prisoners to kill or she will shoot them all: "Understand? It's up to you. . . . It's your turn to play butcher." She forces Pasqualino and the audience to confront a savage role reversal, revealing the tragic price of the survivor's adaptability.

The richness of visual style and allusion successfully conveys much of the scene's impact and significance. Pasqualino watches, groaning, as the commandant sits in a chair, grotesquely parodying Marlene Dietrich's seductive pose in *Blue Angel*. Bronzini's "Cupid and Venus" couple incestuously on the wall, reinforcing the horrible danger and taboo of making it with the "terrible mother." Sharing wall-space is another perverter of mythology, the Fuhrer himself, a "little worm" whose grand performance provides inspiration for the commandant as she gazes at him, and reminds us that Hitler has been linked with our pathetic hero throughout the film. A number of elements in this sequence strongly evoke Visconti's treatment of similar themes in *The Damned*. Recall that in the music hall sequence with his sister, Pasqualino was introduced in red; the commandant is now lit in the green that has signalled oppression and death throughout the film. In *The Damned*, the Nazi mother and son were also introduced in red and green theatrical lighting, but with the colors reversed, perhaps suggesting here a reversal of power. Helmut Berger, in drag, also does a Marlene Dietrich imitation. But even more powerful emotional links with the earlier film lie in the physical grotesquery, the perverse hero worship, and the suggestion of incest that pervades this scene. It is very difficult to watch this obscene encounter, which is somehow even more taboo than incest. A number of elements contribute to this effect: the concentration camp setting intimately linking sex and death; the cold sadism of the mother figure; her smooth, freckled fatness; the degradation of the sex performance under pressure; the total reliance on fantasy as a source of arousal; and the sexual power reversal—but perhaps most difficult and ominous is the terrible inequality of power, which generates the archetypal sado-masochistic situation with its repertoire of torture and humiliation.

Though this is undeniably Wertmuller's most impressive film, its moral ambiguities prevent it from being a reliable catalyst for dialectical self-criticism or a progressive source for radical sexual and political alternatives.

The Means of Production

Working Relations. Wertmuller is certainly a star; in fact, she is practically a constellation, surrounded as she is by other glittering luminaries. Since she made stars of Giancarlo Giannini and Mariangelo Melato, she has taken them and a number of good second leads with her from film to film. Her latest film, *Night Full of Rain*, again stars Giannini, this time with Candace Bergen. She also claims the personal aesthetic integrity that is traditionally assigned to the auteur:

> I do everything myself. I write, direct, and cut. Furthermore, I'm the most political author of the Italian cinema and never compromise with myself.[115]

Yet in the next breath, she describes the ease with which she relinquishes her unique vision:

> I also do secret things to earn extra money like Westerns and commercials—naturally signed with another name, generally something like Hank Walker or Jimmy Steel because Italians believe an English name makes the product better.[116]

Unlike Godard, she is grateful to be a powerful member of the bourgeois show business family. In her relations with crew and actors, her goals include neither Godard's pained search for community nor Makavejev's openness to the creativity of others. Her role is the traditional one of charismatic genius manipulating and driving people to fulfill her vision:

> Before, she was screaming, working in a fury. Now we're doing the intimate scenes, she looks stricken, almost quiet. . . . A gentle

voice. "Now Candina." I am a fly in Wertmuller's web, and my
own. I never used to be neurotic, now I'm neurotic and see she's
controlling it. I don't think I'm totally insane, but I've never
experienced anything like this.[117]

Even her most ardent fan, John Simon, feels it necessary to defend her
against the frequent charge of temperamental tyranny:

Not so, she says. It's just that she operates on a tight schedule,
and some (usually less experienced) actors have to be aroused to a
certain emotional pitch, so she yells, and cries, and has fits. "The
performer's reaction isn't always what the script specifies, but
for all practical purposes it looks just like it. (Lina laughs.) I will
use all available means, even violent ones."[118]

It is more difficult to sympathize with her scheduling problems,
however, after one learns that she shot *Seven Beauties* at a ratio of
about 50 to 1. (Years ago, Godard once remarked that when his ratio
went up slightly after *La Chinoise*—which he shot at about 3 to
1—he felt that he was getting old.) Maureen Orth, her production
assistant on *Seven Beauties*, however, describes certain well-known
exceptions to Wertmuller's usual handling of personnel:

With Enrico [her husband] . . . Lina was almost childlike in her
adoration. She also adores Giancarlo Giannini, the only other
person to whom she never raised her voice.[119]

While Giannini was getting star treatment, the real Pasqualino—
"an Italian-Jewish survivor of a concentration camp who had
murdered his sister's pimp, . . . was cast as a prisoner. . . . While
everyone else was straining to recreate his life, the real Pasqualino sat
around every day virtually unnoticed—a gnarled, hook-nosed
extra."[120] Some of the women on the set also complained about
Wertmuller's casting.

When Luch [her other assistant, a "young radical from California"] resisted being cast as a topless Nubian slave in a
whorehouse scene, Lina scoffed: "Cinema is all tricks and
fantasy. If you don't want to participate in the fantasy, go back to
the university."[121]

Wertmuller also cast Orth and her mother in the brothel scene.

Though she will, of course, change a script when the unpredictable occurs during shooting, she makes far more extravagant
claims for her anarchistic flexibility:

> In my films I show my fear of all fixed structures, whereas all
> structures should be mobile. I believe in democracy with all its
> risks.[124]

However, Candace Bergen's is only one of many statements about her
working methods that bear little resemblance to her self-portrait:

> This way of working, where everything is calculated, it's like
> working in an iron lung.[123]

Financing and Distribution. Wertmuller is probably the only
female director in the world who has no trouble getting backing for
high budget feature films. When asked how she accomplished this
miracle, she responds in the language of sexual attack:

> It took a lot of effort. . . . Do you want to know the method? The
> first rule of all, break balls a lot. The second rule—break their
> balls again. The third rule—again.[124]

But she denies Feminist issues with astonishing naivete—as if all
sexes and classes had equal access to the goodies:

> If a woman can make you $20 million, there are no longer
> problems of uterus or testicles.[125]

The sexual and economic patriarchies that she "attacks" in the films
have long since realized that in her work they have nothing to fear.
On the contrary. Helped by the huge advertising budgets and critical
raves typical of star products, Seven Beauties is the only film under
discussion in this chapter to make Variety's of million-dollar
grossers, and that, of course, was only the beginning. Courted by
Universal, Columbia, and United Artists, she finally signed a four-
picture deal with Warner Brothers, with Giannini as an important
part of the stellar package, which may be somewhat undermined by
the box office failure of Night Full of Rain. Actually, her rise to
power within the industry would be worthy of little comment (except
for her sex) if she had not been blown up there partly by her own cries
of radical commitment, and by the underdog glamour exploited in
her films. Thus it seems appropriate to point out that every aspect of
her career works to maintain the existing sexual and economic power
structure.

The Film Audience

Unlike Godard and Makavejev, Wertmuller insists that her primary goal is to reach a mass audience of proletarians and that she is willing Western film desire shape the aesthetic qualities of her films.

> My real audience [is] not the critics or the intellectuals or the bourgeoisie. . . . My greatest desire is to make popular cinema. I continue to do all that I can to avoid addressing an elite, intellectual or otherwise. . . . I have succeeded in many parts of the world. . . . I hope I can do the same in America without resorting to sharks or flaming skyscrapers—but if it proves necessary, I'll do this too.[126]

These statements are consistent with her actual behavior. Although her first film *Lizards* was a critical success, winning fourteen international awards, it did not do well at the box office; hence, she immediately changed her style.

> It followed the conventional road of the cinema today; it was for the intellectuals. Considering the problem, I changed my politics; I changed my approach, searching for a popular cinema while trying not to reject anything which might enable me to communicate with people.[127]

In her subsequent films, she has tried to adapt these same political issues to more popular genres, while apparently indifferent to the resulting changes in content.

> What's important is to agitate the big problems in the kind of film that the masses will run to see just as they will run to see a Western or a dirty movie.[128]

Hence, she has chosen a comic tone and claims it is compatible with her progressive political goals.

> The serious approach may make its point less effectively than the comic. In fact, in Italy, the severe, macabre approach to politics drives people away . . . making them feel politics is only for the experts. . . . Every familiar experience partakes of all of life—which is tragic and horrendous, yes, but also wonderful. Why should we choose only to look at the tragic and heavy face of politics? I always fear the representation of power in a totally serious light because power itself requires this seriousness to be terrifying.[129]

While Godard and Makavejev also combine humor and politics, Wertmuller can give the pairing an exploitive twist, using it condescendingly to bring her ideas down to the mass audience level, a strategy that reinforces rather than destroys class stereotypes.

Cheerful vulgarity is the wit of the poor, their last and extreme defense.[130]

The density that she sacrifices in her films is precisely what distinguishes *Seven Beauties* from *Weekend* and *Sweet Movie* and prevents it from achieving dialectical thinking, creating an authentic transformation of the audience, and leading them to a higher level of consciousness. As Jameson points out, a dialectical mode of thought results in a challenging complex style.

> Density is itself a conduct of intransigence: the bristling mass of abstractions and cross-references is precisely intended to be read in situation, against the cheap facility of what surrounds it, as a warning to the reader of the price he has to pay for genuine thinking.[131]

Yet Wertmuller undeniably succeeds in pleasing a mass audience and in convincing a number of bourgeois critics that her films are expressing "deep" or "profound" political analyses. *Seven Beauties* was a smash box office hit, particularly in the U. S. A., and drew extravagent praise from the very publications that regularly pan or ignore Godard and Makavejev: *Time* and *Newsweek*, *Variety* and *The Hollywood Reporter*, *Cosmopolitan* and *Playboy*. The film drew the most enthusiastic reviews from reactionary critics, who usually pride themselves on squelching self-indulgence: John Simon of *New York Magazine* dubbed Wertmuller "the most important film director since Bergman" and ranked her with Goya, Delacroix, Debussy, Stendahl, Proust, and Rodin as one of those rare geniuses who combine taste and innovation; Judith Crist myopically saw *Seven Beauties* as "an Italian *Sorrow and the Pity*" (an association that undoubtedly made Marcel Ophuls despair); and Rex Reed and William Wolf gushed and raved in *Vogue* and on *Cue* respectively.

Yet the praise was not universal. *Seven Beauties* was attacked on the right by reactionary publications that accused it of having "too many ideas" (L. A. *Herald Examiner*), being "too confusing" (*Wall Street Journal*), and becoming "doctrinaire rather than stirring" (*L. A. Times*). On the left, her critics included distinguished liberals who usually do not bother to write film reviews—Jerzy Kosinski, the Polish novelist, who accused her of "an elitist disdain" in representing the lower classes by a dehumanized comic strip dummy, whom she exploits for easy laughs; and Bruno Bettelheim, the noted sociologist and deathcamp survivor, who attacked Wertmuller for exploiting the concentration camp tragedy as spectacle and falsely suggesting that only the odious survived. New York film critics Molly Haskell and Pauline Kael deflated Simon's puffery for similar reasons (the latter wickedly titled her review, "Seven Fatties").

Feminists have been especially outraged by Wertmuller, particularly because she claims to be one of them.

> I have genuine feminist sentiments. I love women—and men, also. I think the feminist critics have misunderstood my intent and it's a pity because I'm very disposed to working for women— but within my own framework.[132]

The attack has focused on her exploitation of the female body as an object of laughter, particularly when swollen to gargantuan grotesquery (as in the mountainous Nazi commandant, Pasqualino's family of fatties, and the big-assed adulteress in *The Seduction of Mimi*), and by her focus on female masochism, which either encourages the tendency through a perhaps unintentional glamorization (especially in *Swept Away*) or coldly displays it as a contemptible object of ridicule without any compassion for the victim. The sex act in Wertmuller's films often involves sympathy for the macho obligation to perform despite the hapless male's "natural" fear of his sexual object (though Wertmuller herself believes the roles of performer and judge are reversed in *Swept Away*). With no material perspective on this performance ethic, *Seven Beauties* reinforces the link between female sexuality and the overwhelming or destruction of the male. Makavejev, though male, tries to redefine the unique values of being female and to show without condescension how they can transform and enrich the entire culture. Though Wertmuller has had the opportunity to demonstrate those values, instead she proves that she can cheerfully perform exactly like a socially approved male within the system:

> I want women to know that I was able to make these films not because I'm some sort of witch with supernatural powers, but rather because I have analyzed and come to understand the true law which governs our society. This is not the immutable law of the all-powerful patriarchal god of the Old Testament, but a law which is purely economical. . . . it's the same law for everyone, men and women.[133]

Like her predecessor Leni Riefenstahl, she is proud that no one can call her a "women's director," for her brand of androgyny leads her to outdo her male counterparts in mysogyny. Hence, she may succeed in proving that she is an exceptionally shrewd and talented individual,

but she in no way helps the plight of women or helps to alter the
sexist, racist society.

> I haven't had an easy career. But I maintain that when you really
> get down to work the sex thing is overcome. Look, I also think
> there's a slightly racist mentality in women themselves, in
> feminism. We are the first ones who should make no sexual
> distinctions for the jobs. I find it racist when there are things just
> for women. We're the first ones to feel blacker than the blacks.[134]

Even a moderate like Pauline Kael is angered by Wertmuller:

> For all the political babbling of her characters, the meaning of
> Seven Beauties is deeply reactionary and misogynous. It gets an
> audience response by confirming what people, in their most
> superstitious recesses, already believe: that "human nature"
> stinks and nothing can be done about it.[135]

Marxist critics have thus far provided the broadest context in
which to evaluate Wertmuller's politics, particularly since she
advertises herself as a leftist. The Marxist journal Cineaste accused
Wertmuller of reinforcing racism against Neopolitans at home (a
serious problem in Italy) and dressing up conservative ideas in slick
packaging for American consumption.

> "I dedicate my film to the masses," has become almost
> emblematic of Wertmuller's work in the U. S., reported in nearly
> every interview. In Italy, however, that notion has often been
> challenged. . . . Such criticism—in contrast to the overwhelming
> enthusiasm of America's response—must be seen within an
> overall political context. Almost by definition, artists and
> intellectuals in Italy are "on the Left. . . . " In the U.S., however,
> where the act of coming out publicly as a radical, a Communist,
> or a Socialist still has the power to terrorize large segments of the
> population, being "on the Left" also carries a certain mystique.
> Wertmuller's work may appear politically outrageous, ultra-
> committed or exceptionally sincere in America where political
> themes are rarely directly confronted on film; seen in her native
> context, she's just one among many talking, writing and filming
> about "the exploited masses." Actually, in the extraordinary
> realm of Italian politics, her official stance is not very far to the
> left of center. . . . Giacomo Mancini, leader of the conservative
> faction of a by no means revolutionary Socialist Party, is Lina's
> political idol.[136]

Wertmuller's commercial success in America would, of course,
make her work highly questionable to most leftwing critics. While

Jameson deviates from earlier Marxists to defend avant garde forms of modernism for advancing the culture's consciousness, even he is suspicious of works that flourish within the capitalist marketplace.

> That older modernism was in its essence profoundly antisocial, and reckoned with the instinctive hostility of the middle-class public of which it stood as a negation and arefusla. What characterizes the new modernism is however precisely that it is *popular*: maybe not in small mid-Western towns, but in the dominant world of fashion and the mass media. That can only mean, to my mind, that there has come to be something socially useful about such art from the point of view of the existing socio-economic structure; or something deeply suspect about it, if your point of view is a revolutionary one.[137]

Although he included the early Godard in his list of new modernists, *Weekend* and *Sweet Movie* both seem to fit Jameson's description of the older antisocial modernism while the more accommodating new modernist label perfectly suits *Seven Beauties*. Marcuse would probably see this film as dangerous because it co-opts radical ideas and transforms them into harmless, fashionable entertainment. The adorable rapist and murderer outlives the Socialist, who rots in jail, and the anarchist, who dies in the lumpy chocolate. The masses can sneer at her characters, enjoy the spectacle, and think that we have encountered a profound statement about the inevitability of corruption. But, in Benjamin's terms, the spectacle actually reconciles us to the "far-flung ruins and debris" in which we are trapped instead of helping us to find a new way out.

Footnotes to Chapter 2

1. Frederic Jameson, *Marxism and Form: Twentieth Century Dialectical Theories of Literature* (Princeton: Princeton Univ. Press, 1971), p. xvi.
2. Jameson, p. 207.
3. Jameson, p. xix.
4. Some of the journals carrying these exchanges are *Women and Film* (now defunct), *Jump Cut*, and *Camera Obscura* in the United States and *Screen* and *Screen Education* in Great Britain. Some of the major theorists and critics now writing are Julia Lesage, Clare Johnston, Pam Cook, Laura Mulvey, and Christine Gledhill. For an overview and valuable references to this material, see Christine Gledhill, "Recent Developments in Feminist Film Criticism," *Quarterly Review of Film Studies*, Vol. 3, no. 4 (Fall 1978).

5. Shulamith Firestone, *The Dialectic of Sex* (New York: Bantam, 1971), p. 13.

6. Firestone, p. 60.

7. (New York: Random House, 1974), p. 197.

8. Firestone, p. 70.

9. Wilhelm Reich, *The Mass Psychology of Fascism*, trans. Vincent R. Carfagno (New York: Farrar, Straus and Giroux, 1970), p. 56

10. Mitchell, pp. 211-212.

11. Mitchell, p. 201.

12. (New York: Vintage Books, 1962), pp. 33-34.

13. Marcuse, pp. 45-46.

14. Marcuse, p. 161.

15. Friedrich Engels, *The Origin of the Family, Private Property and the State* (1884), "Preface" to the Fourth German edition, in *Selected Works*, Vol. III, p. 240.

16. Jean-Luc Comolli and Jean Narboni, "Cinema/Ideology/Criticism," editorial originally printed in *Cahiers du Cinema*, no. 216 (October 1969), trans. Susan Bennett, in *Movies and Methods*, ed. Bill Nichols (Berkeley: Univ. of Calif. Press, 1976), p. 28.

17. "Talks at the Yenan Forum on Literature and Art" (May 1942), *Quotations from Chairman Mao Tse-Tung* (Peking: Foreign Language Press, 1966), p. 302.

18. Jameson, p. 328.

19. "To us, the only possible line of advance seems to be to use the theoretical writing of the Russian film-makers of the twenties (Eisenstein above all) to elaborate and apply a critical theory of the cinema, a specific method of apprehending rigorously defined objects, in direct reference to the method of dialectical materialism." Comolli and Narboni, p. 29.

20. Jameson, p. 333.

21. Walter Benjamin, "The Work of Art in the Age of Mechanical Reproduction," in *Illuminations* (New York: Harcourt Brace Jovanovich, 1968), p. 239.

22. Benjamin, p. 238.

23. Bertolt Brecht, *Brecht on Theater*, ed. and trans. John Willett (New York, 1964), p. 50.

24. Northrop Frye, "Expanding Eyes," *Critical Inquiry*, II, no. 2 (Winter 1975), pp. 201-202.

25. Jameson, p. 307.

26. Jameson, p. 414.

27. Jean Luc Godard, *Weekend/Wind from the East* (New York: Simon and Schuster, 1969), p. 17. All future citations of dialogue will come from this text.

28. For an illuminating discussion of *Weekend* from a Marxist perspective, which includes a perceptive analysis of Godard's erotic use of words, see James Roy MacBean, *Film and Revolution* (Bloomington, Ind. and London: Indiana Univ. Press, 1975), Part One.

29. Jameson, p. 395.

30. Jameson, p. xvi.

31. Jameson, pp. 96-97.

32. Brecht, p. 71.

33. Michael Goodwin, Tom Luddy, and Naomi Wise, "The Dziga Vertov Film Group in America—An Interview with Jean Luc Godard and Jean Pierre Gorin," *Take One*, II, no. 10 (March-April 1970), p. 16.

34. *Take One*, p. 16.

35. *Take One*, p. 22.

36. *Take One*, p. 12.

37. *Take One*, p. 19.

38. Barbet Schroeder and Suzanne Schiffman, quoted in "The Urgent Whisper," by Penelope Gilliatt, *New Yorker* (Oct. 25, 1978), p. 56.

39. Kent E. Carroll, "Film and Revolution: Interview with the Dziga-Vertov Group," in *Focus on Godard*, ed. Royal S. Brown (New York: Prentice Hall, 1972), p. 58.

40. *Take One*, p. 23.

41. *Take One*, p. 22.

42. Carroll interview, pp. 55-56.

43. *Take One*, p. 10.

44. *Take One*, p. 26.

45. Carroll interview, p. 50.

46. *Take One*, p. 10.

47. "The Urgent Whisper," p. 56.

48. *Take One*,, p. 17.

49. *Take One*, p. 24.

50. *Take One*, p. 24.

51. Carroll interview, pp. 59-60.

52. *Take One*, p. 12.

53. Carroll interview, p. 56.

54. *Take One*, p. 17.

55. *Take One*, p. 15.

56. *Take One*, p. 12.

57. *Take One*, p. 17.

58. *Take One*, p. 24.

59. Carroll interview, p. 54.

60. This discussion draws heavily from "Life and Death in the Cinema of Outrage: or, the Bouffe and the Barf," by Marsha Kinder, *Film Quarterly* (Winter 1974-75), pp. 4-11.

61. John O'Hara, "Dusan Makavejev: Interview," *Cinema Papers* (Nov.-Dec. 1975), p. 237.

62. *Rabelais and His World*, trans. Helene Iswalsky (Cambridge, Mass. and London, 1968), p. 94.

63. Benjamin, pp. 239-240.

64. O'Hara interview, p. 237.

65. O'Hara interview, p. 240.

66. Makavejev says: "You never see her kill. You see, when the corpses are dug out from the sugar and laid on the riverbank, our four kids are *watching* from the nearby bridge. In my mind she was just riding a boat full of corpses. Her part in the crime was left unclear intentionally. . . . In the play, "The Wardrobe of Historic Importance," my friend Rasa Popov turns the story

around the locked wardrobe in the family living room. When the son discovers that the wardrobe is full of corpses, the father argues that yes, they are there, but they are *not* in the room, because the wardrobe is locked and should stay closed forever. When critical, analytical minds criticize and dissect movies (or dream images or symbols), raised awareness of hidden meanings must be accompanied by raised awareness of disguising techniques— the artist is the author of both the concrete image *and* of *whatever is left out*. The poet speaks with words *and* empty space, *and* the *length of the pauses*." (Letter).

67. Firestone, p. 148.
68. O'Hara interview, pp. 238-239.
69. O'Hara interview, pp. 238-239.
70. O'Hara interview, p. 238.
71. O'Hara interview, p. 240.
72. Wilhelm Reich, "The Breakthrough into the Vegetative Realm," *Selected Writings* (New York: Noonday Press, 1961), p. 111.
73. O'Hara interview, pp. 239-240.
74. O'Hara interview, p. 238. Interview corrected from Makavejev's letter, where he adds: "American interviewers so often do not feel obliged to check their written interview with the interviewee. I find this arrogant and, if you wish, 'culturally imperialistic' when done to people who do not speak English as a mother tongue. Spoken language has a melody of expression and *can be clumsy*. They take your words literally and crucify you on the printed page. You are simply not allowed to make mistakes or they publicly punish you for not knowing *their* language well! (And they do not speak *your* language.)"
75. Wilhelm Reich, *The Imposition of Sexual Morality* (New York: Farrar, Straus and Giroux, 1971), p. 170.
76. Marcuse, p. 209.
77. O'Hara interview, p. 240.
78. O'Hara interview, p. 235. Makavejev adds: "The words 'good' and 'carefully' bother me, but I don't know how to cope with it. When I write myself, I am careful not to be judgmental, or at least not in an apodictic fashion. Trotsky, embracing the concept of revolutionary violence, engineered his own destruction two decades later, but this does not change the fact that he was killed by criminals. If, instead of 'good people,' you place 'revolutionaries,' it would be a little more precise." (Letter).
79. O'Hara interview, p. 240.
80. O'Hara interview, p. 237.
81. *The Mass Psychology of Fascism*, p. 56.
82. Wilhelm Reich, *Character Analysis*, trans. Theodore P. Wolfe, 3rd ed. (New York: Orgone Institute Press, 1949), p. 340.
83. Makavejev says: "The Polish officers were not caught fighting anyone. They ran away from the Germans. They were killed because they were not needed, and maybe they were reactionaries politically, but they were foreign subjects who looked for protection. This case was a blatant and arrogant massacre motivated nationalistically and bureaucratically, but there was no revolutionary violence involved. These foreign officers were not shooting at the Russians; they ran to them as to brothers." (Letter).

84. Letter.
85. O'Hara interview, p. 237.
86. O'Hara interview, p. 238.
87. O'Hara interview, p. 238.
88. O'Hara interview, p. 238.
89. O'Hara interview, p. 240.
90. O'Hara interview, p. 240.
91. O'Hara interview, p. 240.
92. Michael Spencer, *Los Angeles Times*, May 24, 1974.
93. O'Hara interview, p. 237.
94. Since then, Makavejev spent a year teaching at Harvard, returned to Yugoslavia, and is now living in Paris.
95. O'Hara interview, p. 240.
96. O'Hara interview, p. 240.
97. O'Hara interview, p. 240.
98. *Time* (April 5, 1976), p. 61.
99. O'Hara interview, p. 240.
100. O'Hara interview, p. 240.
101. O'Hara interview, p. 237.
102. O'Hara interview, p. 237.
103. John Simon, "Wertmuller's *Seven Beauties*—Call It a Masterpiece," *New York* (February 2, 1976), p. 26.
104. Bruno Bettelheim, "Surviving," *New Yorker* (August 2, 1976), p. 48.
105. Jerzy Kosinski, *"Seven Beauties*—A Cartoon Trying to Be a Tragedy," *New York Times* (March 7, 1976).
106. Kosinski, ibid.
107. Gina Blumenfeld, "The (Next to) Last Word on Lina Wertmuller," *Cineaste*, Vol. VII, No. 2, p. 9.
108. Ingmar Bergman, *Bergman on Bergman* (New York: Simon and Schuster, 1972), p. 228.
109. Simon, p. 30.
110. Simone de Beauvoir, *The Second Sex* (New York: Bantam, 1961), p. 141.
111. Marcuse, p. 212.
1·12. Susan Sontag, "Fascinating Fascism," *Movies and Methods*, ed. Bill Nicholas (Berkeley: Univ. of Calif. Press, 1976), pp. 40-41.
113. Benjamin, pp. 243-44.
114. Sontag, p. 40.
115. Peter Dragadze, "Movies Italian Style," *New Times* (October 1976), p. 122.
116. Dragadze, p. 122.
117. Candace Bergen, quoted in Mary Blume, "Wertmuller: 'I Love Chaos,' " *International Herald Tribune* (Feb. 19-20, 1977).
118. Simon, p. 30.
119. "Look This Way. Breathe. Brava," *Newsweek* (Jan. 26, 1976), p. 79.
120. Orth, p. 79.
121. Orth, p. 79.
122. Dragadze, p. 122.
123. Bergen, *Herald Tribune*.
124. William Wolf, *Cue* (Jan. 17, 1976), p. 30.

125. Simon, p. 29.

126. Blumenfeld interview, p. 7.

127. Blumenfeld interview, p. 7.

128. E. Servi Burgess, "Towards a Popular Feminist Cinema: An Interview with Lina Wertmuller," *Women and Film*, Vol. I, nos. 5 and 6, p. 7.

129. Blumenfeld interview, p. 7.

130. Burgess interview, p. 6.

131. Jameson, p. xiii.

132. Blumenfeld interview, p. 8.

133. Blumenfeld interview, p. 8.

134. Burgess interview, p. 8.

135. Pauline Kael, "Seven Fatties," *New Yorker* (February 16, 1976), p. 105.

136. Lucy Quacinella, "How Left Is Lina?" *Cineaste*, VII, No. 3 (Fall 1976), pp. 16-17.

137. Jameson, pp. 413-414.

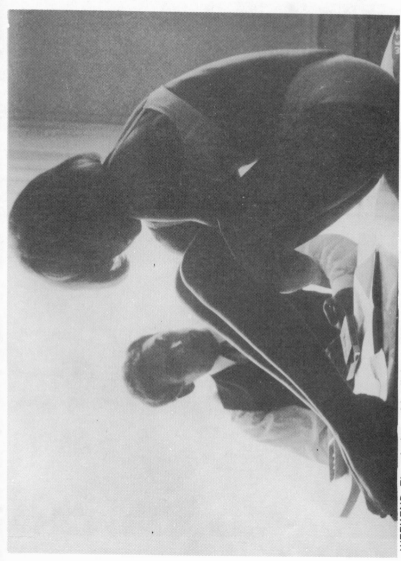

WEEKEND. The glaring white light and Corinne's self-protective posture obscure detail and ironically force us to gaze even more intently as audience and Analyst/Friend become voyeurs while Corinne tells about an orgy. Courtesy of Grove Press.

WEEKEND. The bourgeois couple takes a nightmarish odyssey through a weekend traffic jam where corpses and burning autos are surrealistically strewn along the highway. Although they are the only living humans in sight, husband and wife remain distant from each other as they relentlessly pursue their own selfish ends. Courtesy of Grove Press.

WEEKEND. Unable to bear the sudden appearance of another fictional reality within the local woods, the bourgeois husband accosts "Emily Bronte" and "Tom Thumb." Courtesy of Grove Press.

WEEKEND. The bourgeois couple tries to strangle Jean-Pierre Leaud with his sweater.

Courtesy of Grove Press.

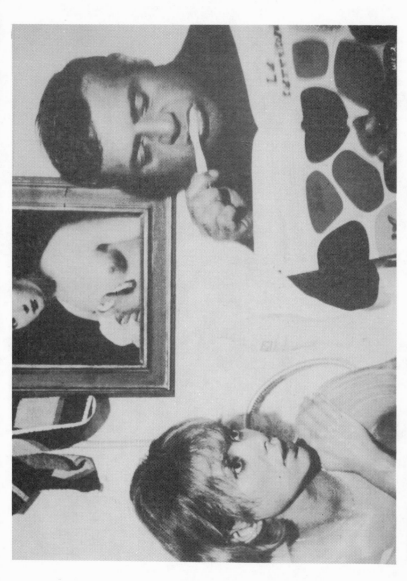

WEEKEND. While the image of the bathing Corinne is decorously cut off just above the breasts, the painting behind her supplies the missing part. Courtesy of Grove Press.

WEEKEND. The murderers dispose of their mother's corpse on the technological trash heap, which is incongruously stacked in the natural setting: Courtesy of Grove Press.

WEEKEND. Corinne is captured by the cannibalistic band whose pseudo-tribalism makes the woods as dangerous as city and highway. Courtesy of Grove Press.

SWEET MOVIE. Captain Anna Planeta defies the world with the rousing music and bold Karl Marx figurehead of her Survival barge, hiding the dangerous corruption at the heart of the ship. Courtesy of Biograph Films.

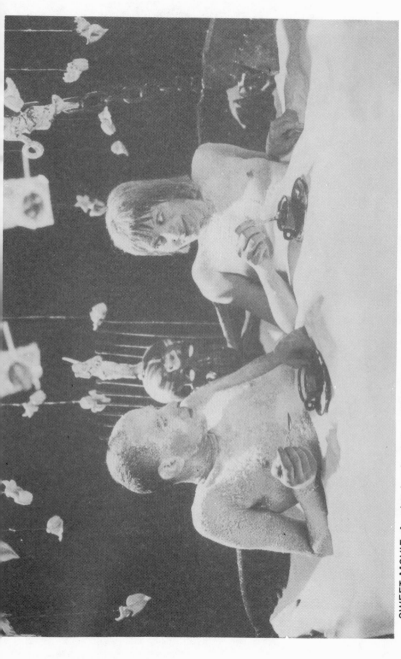

SWEET MOVIE. Awakening in their bed of sugar, Anna and her sailor scoop up spoonfuls to sweeten their coffee. Yet she tells him that "sugar is dangerous," a warning that is confirmed by the skull that stands between them. Courtesy of Biograph Films.

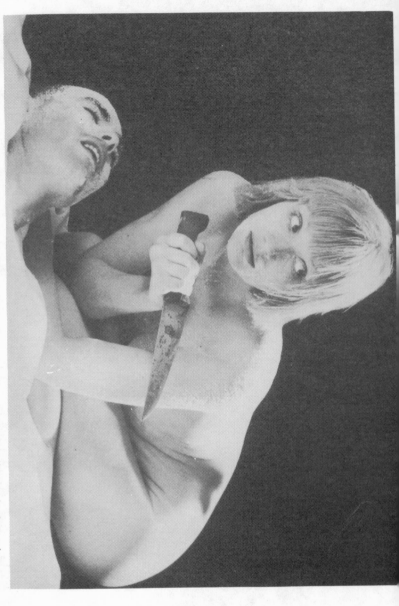

SWEET MOVIE. Anna Planeta's knife and her wicked expression contrast with the lush, grainy whiteness of sugar and skin. The masochistic love/death ecstasy of Luv Bakunin's expression mirrors the double reality of the sugar bed. Courtesy of Biograph Films.

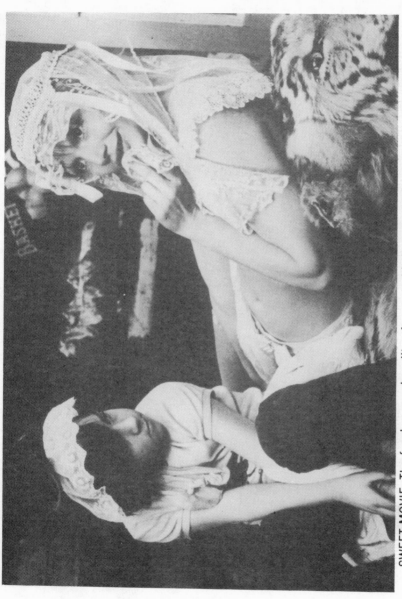

SWEET MOVIE. The fur, lace, and nudity of a masochistic seduction now serve the incest fantasies of a mad "bride" and her entranced child-partner—both sexual products of a failed revolution. Courtesy of Biograph Films.

SWEET MOVIE. After her ecstatic coupling with El Macho, Miss World cracks an egg on her head. This union with a pop star brings no baby, but it does bring rebirth for Miss World who is delivered at the Milky Way Commune. Courtesy of Biograph Pictures Corp.

SWEET MOVIE. Miss World is transformed into an erotic chocolate Bon Bon to be consumed by the TV masses. Courtesy of Biograph Pictures Corp.

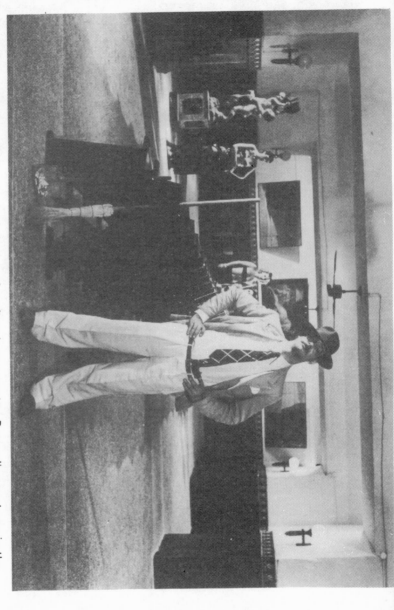

SEVEN BEAUTIES. Doing a poor imitation of an American gangster, Pasqualino postures in the sterile, impersonal space of the brothel, at once expansive and entrapping. Courtesy of Cinema 5.

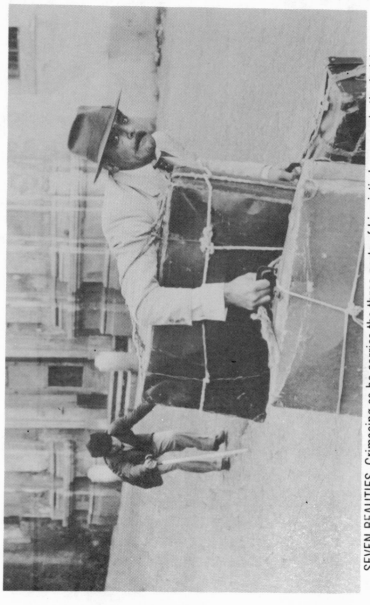

SEVEN BEAUTIES. Grimacing as he carries the three parts of his victim's corpse in the bulging suitcases, Pasqualino tries to sneak away inconspicuously but is pursued by an angry blind man who calls his bluff. Courtesy of Cinema 5.

SEVEN BEAUTIES. In undershirt and boxer shorts, the Commandant grotesquely evokes Marlene Dietrich's pose in BLUE ANGEL as she sits in front of the baroque eroticism of Bronzini's "Cupid and Venus." Both allusions evoke and contrast ironically with the "terrible mother" coupling about to take place. Courtesy of Cinema 5.

3

Experience and Behavior in *Red Desert* and *Une Femme Douce:* A View from Inside Out

If you prick me,'you don't suffer.

Giuliana in Red Desert

I cannot experience your experience. You cannot experience my experience. We are both invisible. . . . Only experience is evident. . . . Psychology is the logos of experience.

R. D. Laing, The Politics of Experience

It is fairly certain that every bird is predisposed to sing like its species.

The wife in Une Femme Douce

A person is a member of a species shaped by evolutionary contingencies of survival, displaying behavioral processes which bring him under the control of the environment in which he lives . . . which he and millions of others like him have constructed and maintained during the evolution of a culture . . . a person does not act upon the world, the world acts upon him.

B. F. Skinner, Beyond Freedom and Dignity

The films and the approach in this chapter come together in their focus on the gap between experience and behavior. Michelangelo Antonioni's *Red Desert* and Robert Bresson's *Une Femme Douce* both present an alienated woman whose experience is not perceptible to those around her. Through experimentation with subjective point of view, both filmmakers force the audience to experience this alienation from the *inside*, so that the viewing process is extremely painful. Yet, film is a medium that has the power to document visible behavior with great accuracy, and both works employ a visual style that accentuates the *external* surface of the world.

The intensity of alienation, the lack of real contact with others, and the striving for inner peace that lie at the center of these films are familiar to people everywhere. We know something is wrong. The question is, what do we fix—the self or the social structures? Disillusioned with corrupt institutions, impotent political action, failed communities, and disintegrating relationships, thousands have turned to "self-realization"—transcendental meditation, radical therapies, scientology, est, and scores of other inner-directed isms and ologies. On the other side are those who deplore this obsession with the self and urge us to change the outside—to organize, to control our environment, to put our energies into political action and social reform.

Within academic psychology, this dichotomy has reached an acute state of polarization—behavior modification and humanistic psychology. B. F. Skinner and R. D. Laing, whose ideas have become as widely popularized as the movements alluded to above, represent the most extreme forms of these positions, especially in *Beyond Freedom and Dignity* and *The Politics of Experience.*

Skinner the behaviorist and Laing the existentialist psychotherapist both believe that civilization and the human species are threatened with extermination from overpopulation, pollution, and nuclear war, and must make radical changes in order to survive. For Skinner, the solution moves from the outside in—scientifically designing a rational social framework to control the behavior of individuals. For Laing, this is anathema. Change must come from inside out:

> Everyone will be carrying out orders. Where do they come from? Always from elsewhere.[1]

He believes that social progress can come only from individual change, from greater access to inner experience. Laing bases his hopes for regeneration on the "autonomous inner man;" Skinner totally denies the value of this element of individual personality, and wants to destroy it.

> A small part of the universe is enclosed within a human skin. It
> would be foolish to deny the existence of that private world, but
> it is also foolish to assert that because it is private it is of a
> different nature from the world outside. . . . The picture which
> emerges from a scientific analysis is not of a body with a person
> inside, but of a body which *is* a person in the sense that it displays
> a complex repertoire of behavior. . . . It is the autonomous inner
> man who is abolished, and that is a step forward.[2]

According to Laing, the destruction or undermining of the inner
person leads to ontological insecurity, which he diagnoses as a global
epidemic.

> As a whole, we are a generation of men so estranged from the
> inner world that many are arguing that it does not exist; and that
> even if it does exist, it does not matter . . . without the inner the
> outer loses its meaning, and without the outer, the inner loses its
> substance.[3]

Both psychologists are highly concerned with art: Laing because
he sees it as one of the most powerful ways of gaining access to
someone else's experience, and Skinner because he sees it as a means
of diagnosing and shaping society. In fact, both have tried to render
their theories in artistic form (Skinner in *Walden Two;* Laing in the
last chapter of *The Politics of Experience,* and in *Knots*). In Skinner's
hierarchy of personal and social values, neither art nor the artist is
especially important, for neither is essential to survival. He envisions
the creation of art as a kind of leisure therapy for the future in which
all can engage equally because he denies the existence of unique
talent. Social change would invalidate much of present art, especially
the "literature of freedom and dignity," which would undoubtedly
include *Red Desert* and *Une Femme Douce.*

> We shall not only have no reason to admire people who endure
> suffering, face danger, or struggle to be good, it is possible that
> we shall have little interest in pictures or books about them. The
> art and literature of a new culture will be about other things.[4]

He explicitly expels from his utopia artists who celebrate uniqueness
and extreme states of being. These are precisely the artists whom
Laing most values for their ability to risk the dangers of the journey
into the self; he sees the madness that may result as a potential source
of insight.

Small wonder that the list of artists, in say the last 150 years, who

have become shipwrecked on these reefs is so long—Holderlin,
John Clare, Rimbaud, Van Gogh, Nietszche, Antonin Artaud.
Those who survived have had exceptional qualities—a capacity
for secrecy, slyness, cunning—a thoroughly realistic appraisal of
the risks they run, not only from the spiritual realms they
frequent, but from the hatred of their fellows for anyone engaged
in this pursuit.[5]

In their different views of art, the central issue is freedom, which
Laing celebrates as the *sine qua non,* and Skinner condemns as a
neurotic symptom. For both of them, Dostoevsky (who wrote the
story on which *Une Femme Douce* is based) is an important symbolic
figure. For Laing, he is one of the great visionaries of existential
freedom; for Skinner, like the other artists Laing mentions, he is a
dangerous enemy.

> Even if it could be proved that human behavior is fully
> determined, said Dostoevsky, a man "would still do something
> out of sheer perversity—he would create destruction and chaos—
> just to gain his point. . . . And if all this could in turn be analyzed
> and prevented by predicting that it would occur, then man
> would deliberately go mad to prove his point." The implication
> is that he would then be out of control, as if madness were a
> special kind of freedom or as if the behavior of a psychotic could
> not be predicted or controlled. There is a sense in which
> Dostoevsky may be right. A literature of freedom may inspire a
> sufficiently fanatical opposition to controlling practices to
> generate a neurotic if not psychotic response. There are signs of
> emotional instability in those who have been deeply affected by
> the literature.[6]

Although they are diametrically opposed, Laing's and Skinner's
views of art can both be traced back to Plato, who apparently
struggled with the same dichotomy. In his utopian *Republic,* he
argued for censoring poets and dramatists lest they violate his chosen
social and religious rules; created as an imitation of an imitation, art
excites and strengthens the emotions to the possible detriment of
reason. Like Skinner, Plato made poetry's admission to his utopia
contingent on its social usefulness. Yet in the *Ion* he argued that the
poet is in special touch with the gods and creates not by craft but
because he is inspired and possessed, emphasizing the unique quality
of creative genius and its association with madness. Magnetized by
this divine contact, the poet transmits the force to his rhapsody, who
then transmits his ecstatic experience to the audience in a chain
reaction of responsiveness. In this way, the poet teaches the audience,
not through rational instruction, but through experiential posses-

sion. The possessed poet of Laing and Plato may gain his insight through the terror of gazing into the abyss; but the danger is that he may never return to the commonplace world. This paradoxical risk lies at the center of tragedy, but in the optimistic world of Skinner's utopia, there are no abysses and no paradoxes. All problems are soluble; risk is unnecessary; all human suffering can be eliminated. The new society is formed around the comic values of adaptation and survival.

Red Desert and Une Femme Douce are clearly works of "freedom and dignity." Their creators, Antonioni and Bresson, are explicitly concerned with the relationship between experience and behavior, and with problems of freedom and survival in a contemporary context. We wish to explore these films in their own thematic and formal treatments of these issues, and also through the polar perspectives of behaviorist and humanist psychology provided by Skinner and Laing.

Red Desert

Michelangelo Antonioni is an impersonal director whose films are highly controlled and analytical, not autobiographical; at the same time they have an extraordinary ability to convey the emotional intensity of subjective experience. Like Deserto Roso (1964), the earlier films—Il Grido (1957), L'Avventura (1959), La Notte (1960), and L'Eclisse (1962)—all deal with the basic problem of self-realization. The focus is on the struggle for sanity and the personal center necessary for survival in a modern universe. In all of the films, Antonioni is concerned with the emergence of a new kind of industrial society dominated by business and technology, in which the old kind of emotional relationships can no longer function. The new world has many important values—the power, efficiency, and mobility needed to master the environment, and an abstract beauty in the new structures. Yet these structures dwarf us, making us feel that the world is no longer geared to our needs. Further, certain traditional values—long term personal relationships, the uniqueness of the individual—are actually disfunctional.

In Il Grido, the world of the central character Aldo (Steve Cochran) collapses when his mistress abandons him, and he realizes that he has no center, that his identity and survival have depended entirely upon another person. This ontological void makes it impossible for him to understand the experience of his daughter or other individuals he encounters; nor can he participate in the efforts of his community to reshape itself for survival with the new technology, and he finally commits suicide.

L'Avventura also emphasizes the sense of loss, which begins with the mysterious disappearance of Anna (Lea Massari), who is never found. In the process of searching for her, Claudia (her best friend) and Sandro (Anna's fiancé) begin an affair. Although they go through the motions of looking for her, they actually fear that she will be found. Claudia (Monica Vitti), who began with naive belief in the old humane values, comes to realize that her affair with Sandro (Gabriele Ferzetti) implies that people are interchangeable. An architect who has sold out to business, Sandro (like Aldo in *Il Grido*) tries to fill his own emptiness by making love to the nearest woman. When Claudia finds him with a prostitute, she realizes that she, too, is replaceable. Trying to maintain as much human contact as possible, she settles for a limited relationship with Sandro. Ironically, in the process of searching for Anna, Claudia has discovered herself and gained new awareness of her needs.

La Notte is a darker film without even the glimmer of hope at the end of *L'Avventura*. It focuses on the end of a loveless marriage between Lidia (Jeanne Moreau) and Giovanni (Marcello Mastroianni), which began with more hope than existed between Sandro and Claudia. Like Sandro, Giovanni is an artist (this time a writer) who has lost his creative power and who is about to sell out to business, linking his artistic failure with the emotional failure of his marriage. In this film the second woman in the relationship is Valentina (again Monica Vitti). She possesses both Claudia's vitality and Anna's awareness of the limitations of love. Unwilling to accept limited contact, she remains emotionally detached; her knowledge does not prevent her from longing for the impossible, yet it preserves her from disillusionment.

In *L'Eclisse*, Vittoria (Monica Vitti), like Valentina, knows about the limitations, but, like Claudia, is willing to accept them. Although this combination makes her the most stable and realistic of all the central characters, Vittoria does not have a capacity for feeling that is superior to her lover's as Claudia's was superior to Sandro's—a trade-off of values necessary for the survival of the modern heroine. The film opens with Vittoria ending an affair with one lover, and then moving on to another. We don't have to see how the first one begins or the last one ends, because in this film human relationships are like an eclipse—a temporary conjunction of two bodies moving in different orbits. Vittoria, a translator, moves at a slow pace within the world of the old humanistic values. Piero (Alain Delon), her new lover, belongs to the world of the stock market, which is concerned with present and future and races at a frantic pace. The film ends with a long montage of objects and settings no longer inhabited by the lovers. This implies not only that their affair is over, but that people and objects are interchangeable. Finally, only the objects remain.

In these early films, Antonioni seems to accept the new world as inevitable although it means a sacrifice of important values from the past. The only hope is understanding and sympathetic acceptance of whatever human contact is possible. Understanding alone won't suffice, as Anna and Valentina demonstrate. Nor will an unthinking acceptance, as in the case of Sandro, Giovanni, and Piero. The most positive characters must achieve both, as Claudia and Valentina ultimately do.

In the three films after *Red Desert—Blow-Up* (1967), *Zabriskie Point* (1970), and *The Passenger* (1975)—Antonioni concentrates on the problems of alienation and limited human contact in the new world. He sacrifices inner exploration of character and focuses, instead, on new modes of visual perception developed through experimental use of color, editing, and camera movement. All three films focus on male protagonists who want to shed old identities and relationships and perform significant actions in the new world. All three desire personal power, but they seem totally indifferent to the moral, social, and philosophical implications of their actions. They are more successful at destruction or escape, as presented through the airplane imagery to be found in all three films. In *Blow-Up*, Thomas (David Hemmings) is a photographer who wants to document poverty, but is more attracted to the surrogate sexuality of the fashion world. When he accidentally photographs a murder, he's less interested in discovering the killer than in the aesthetics of his soft-focus product. In *Zabriskie Point*, Mark (Mark Frechette) longs to take radical political action, but he is isolated, even within the movement. From the very beginning, he claims he wants to die alone, and ultimately takes flight to Death Valley to fulfill his desire. In *The Passenger*, David (Jack Nicholson) is a disillusioned documentary filmmaker who takes over the identity of a gun runner, hoping to gain his power, but without knowing anything of the political issues involved. In all three films, human relationships are even more tenuous than they were in the earlier works. Each man encounters a mysterious woman whose feelings and motives are never clarified.

Ambiguity prevails at the end of all three films. Though relationships dissolve and attempts at action fail, one value remains: the ability to see. Perception is expanded both for the protagonists and the audience. This is developed particularly through the idea of the desert. While in *Red Desert* and the Los Angeles sequences of *Zabriskie Point*, the desert is identified as the urban wasteland, in the Death Valley scenes and the Sahara sequences of *The Passenger*, the muted, subtle qualities and horizontal openness of the true desert evoke a free and heightened response; they invite perception rather than projection.

The concern with diminished human contact is developed with greatest subjectivity in *Red Desert*, which focuses on a woman's alienation from the world around her. The central figure, Giuliana (Monica Vitti) is struggling to maintain her sanity after a suicide attempt. At the beginning of the film she is unsure of her own center and out of touch with the communal actions that surround her. Wife of a successful industrial executive and mother to a child whose mechanical toys are preparing him for the new world, Giuliana is frightened and baffled by the disparity between her own experience and the demands of external reality. In the first scene outside the factory, she is completely out of control. Leaving her son Valerio and darting across the road, she buys a half-eaten sandwich from one of the strikers and retreats to some bushes where she snatches bites, while peering about her like an animal in danger. In an attempt to find satisfaction in some activity, she prepares to open a shop but can't decide what to sell; her vague needs and feelings do not allow her to find significance in anything. She is constantly distracted from her tasks, which fragments her experience and makes it impossible to complete any action. Repeatedly she expresses her desperate fear of sinking, of the floor becoming quicksand with no one there to help. When she seeks comfort from her lover Corrado (Richard Harris), she is fully in touch with her terror: "Help me please, I'm afraid I won't make it." When he asks her, "What are you afraid of?" she says: "Of streets . . . factories . . . of the colors . . . of everything." Much of her behavior expresses this overwhelming fear—her constant writhing, her unsure footing, her habit of standing with her back to a wall or corner as if to gain additional support, her constant gestures of touching herself to reaffirm her existence. Her fear is partly justified by the actual dangers in external reality. As they stand in her shop in the glare of a naked light bulb, she tells Corrado: "I can't take it anymore, I've done everything to adjust to reality. . . . I even managed to be an unfaithful wife. There's something terrible about reality. . . . I don't know what. Nobody tells me."

Giuliana is unable to separate the elements of her experience; she has two conflicting desires. The story she tells of a young girl alone on an island reveals her fantasy of complete emotional independence (reminding us of Anna, the girl in *L'Avventura* who disappears on the island); but she also desires to be surrounded by the comforting presence of others. She tells Corrado, "If I were to leave, I'd take everything—all I see and touch." And later, "I'd like all the people who ever loved me here around me like a wall." This conflict is also expressed in *L'Eclisse* when Vittoria tells Piero, "I wish I didn't love you . . . or that I loved you more."

Giuliana tries to follow the advice of her doctor who told her, "You must learn to love *something*—your husband, your son . . . even a dog . . . not husbandsondog," but her relationships with others reveal that she is isolated in her chaos. Her feelings for her son Valerio seem clearest and help anchor her to reality (she describes the center of her madness with a story about "another girl" who didn't even have a son). Yet the child's alienation from her is developed in several ways; accepting the world of his father, he is fascinated by mechanical robots, gyroscopes and his chemistry set, which he uses to trick her into seeing that "one and one is one." She interprets his feigned paralysis as his willingness to bring her fear and pain, showing that he does not need her love, while she desperately needs his.

Her husband Ugo is a good man who provides very well for her, yet he is utterly unaware of her actual experience, responding only to the signals of her external behavior. He does not return from his trip to see her after her accident because he has been told it is "not serious." One night as she sits in the hallway, writhing in terror after a nightmare in which the bed was "quicksand and sinking down," he comes out, clinical and crisp in his white pajamas, and begins to comfort her. However, the contact turns him on and he begins to make love. Confused and full of need, Giuliana is susceptible to this potential contact and, her body tensing with conflict, she allows herself to go along with his sexual interpretation of her need. Later at a party when she actually does want to make love, he is embarrassed by the social difficulties of leaving and responds, "How can we?" In this brilliant sequence, she comes closest to her fantasy of being surrounded by everyone who loves her as she and all her friends crowd into the tiny, enclosed bedroom. But the physical fact of their closeness is ironically misleading; later, when they rush outside after she is frightened by a smallpox quarantine, they stand far apart in white mist, arranged in isolation from each other like figures in a Giocometti group. The arrangement shows their actual relationships. Giuliana stands in the foreground facing the others with Corrado, who seems more in touch with her at this moment. The camera cuts to a close-up of each face as if Giuliana is searching for some sympathetic signal. When the camera pulls back to reveal the entire group, the fog envelops them, rendering her isolation literal. Finding no help in the people who surround her, she desperately reverts to "independence" and rushes to escape in her car. When she almost drives off the end of the pier, the others go to her and she begins apologizing; it was the fog that isolated her and made her desperate. She fears that Ugo, who cannot understand her experience, will condemn her behavior as another insane attempt at suicide.

Giuliana's relationship with Corrado is extremely complex and developed with extraordinary subtlety. When they first meet in the factory, he is immediately drawn to her. In the shack sequence, the intensity of his desire is appealing, especially in contrast to Ugo's coldness. When Giuliana spontaneously leans against Corrado, his whole body tenses with sensual awareness; after she moves back to Ugo's side, he quickly changes position, kicking his foot through the wall in frustration. In the scene on the ship, she says to him: "Had Ugo looked at me the way you do, he would have found out a lot." Corrado realizes that the girl in the hospital was Giuliana and his apparent understanding of her accident leads him to question Ugo sharply, as if angered by his insensitivity. Antonioni carefully makes it appear that Corrado can offer her the understanding and sympathy that she so desperately needs, yet in reality he uses this knowledge to exploit her, which ultimately leads her to cry out, "You haven't helped me." This combination of sensitivity and selfishness makes him a dangerous predator. The first time they are alone, their conversation reveals that he is consciously on the make:

    CORRADO: I don't want to start with a lie.
    GIULIANA: Start what?
    CORRADO: Nothing . . . to talk. (He lies after all.)

In the guise of empathizing with her feelings, he actually denies her uniqueness and invalidates her experience. At the party in the shack when she momentarily stands at the window, pleading for recognition of her personal confusion, he remarks: "You wonder what to look at, I wonder how to live—the same thing." Later in the bedroom sequence he repeats this kind of response and we realize its undermining quality. When she moans, "I'm not well, I'll never get well," he is matter of fact about her illness, observing, "We all suffer from it . . . more or less," thus denying her very state of being. This brilliant sequence, extremely painful to watch, reveals with subtle richness Giuliana's conflict and the destructive limitations of Corrado's response. The humanity of his feeling for her is tested as she comes to him in extreme panic, after learning of her son's deception. Her behavior is dominated by her constant writhing, fragmented gestures, and sudden shifts of attention: she stares at the map, darts to the window and later, when they are already making love, suddenly jumps up to close the closet door. But even in her anxiety, she reveals her desire: she takes off her sweater; she lies down on the bed; and in a mixture of fear and seductiveness covers herself with the sheet. Yet between these acts of invitation, she curves her body into the foetal position, tries almost symbolically to hold him away with her outstretched arms, and twists her limbs around each other as if her body were intolerable to her because "Everything hurts . . . even my hair." Ironically, Corrado reacts much as Ugo did after her nightmare, with a soothing that becomes seduction. He caresses her hair as if to comfort her and winds up removing her blouse. He ignores all visual, tactile, and verbal signals of her panic, responding only to the ambivalent sexuality of her behavior. He may be more sensitive than Ugo, but acts only on what he chooses to see. This gap between his awareness and behavior is particularly ironic in light of one of his many inflated speeches. Acknowledging that life involves "big questions" and that "the answers aren't easy," he professes to believe in humanity, in justice a little less, and in progress a little more. But the most important thing to Corrado is that your behavior support your beliefs, that you act in a way that is right for the self and others; on these points, he feels his "conscience is at peace." Although Giuliana is playfully accepting, her response reveals the truth about Corrado: "That's a nice group of words."

Giuliana's encounter with the Turkish sailor aboard the quarantined ship can be seen either as a fantasy of escape or an attempt to make contact with others. Visually this scene is very abstract, almost surrealistic; it is difficult to identify objects or spaces. She has come to ask whether the ship takes passengers; like David in *The Passenger*, she wants to escape into a new identity. She carries on a conversation although the sailor cannot understand a word she says. Aware of this language barrier, he tries the one English phrase he knows, the conventional response to the prostitute, "I love ya." Despite all these signs of unreality, Giuliana is able to gain a new understanding of her emotional situation and move toward an acceptance of her life:

> I'm not a woman alone, but at times I feel separate—not from my
> husband—no—the bodies are separated. If you prick me, you
> don't suffer. I have been sick but I must not think of it . . . that is, I
> must think that all that happens to me is my life. That's it.

Although she has not been understood by the sailor, she has expressed herself and thereby gains greater access to her own experience. The final sequence parallels the opening: Giuliana and Valerio are walking outside the factory, but instead of being out of control she is motherly and reassuring. Valerio asks why the smoke is yellow; she replies, "Because it's poisonous," acknowledging that reality can be dangerous. Valerio asks, "Then if a little bird flies through there, will it die?" and Giuliana answers: "By now, the birds know. They don't fly through the smoke any more." These two final sequences demonstrate that she has begun moving toward understanding and acceptance, the combination that was the basis for hope in *L'Avventura* and *L'Eclisse*. Although little change has taken place in observable reality, within Giuliana the balance has shifted slightly toward survival.

To give us access to Giuliana's experience, the film offers much more than merely what she says and does. The point of view is highly subjective, enabling us to share Giuliana's experience through Antonioni's handling of sound, focus, color, imagery, editing, and camera work.

The opening sounds of the film are shocking and difficult for many in the audience to endure. With the factory complex out of focus in the visuals, we hear what sounds like a piercing female voice singing a weird melody, without vibrato or depth of sound; behind this loud wailing, we hear the other-worldly strains of electronic music, providing a perfect parallel for the visual and existential situation in which Giuliana, taut with anxiety, stands alienated from the world behind her. Later in the shack, behind the melange of chattering voices, radio music, and shrieks of horn and whistle from the ship outside, Giuliana hears the sound of a scream so faint that we in the audience are tested by it too. Giuliana's tension actually makes her highly sensitive to the human voice, but her extreme states of anxiety are usually signalled by the inhuman electronic music as in Corrado's hotel room and her encounter with the Turkish sailor. In the hallway sequence she is awakened from her nightmare by unidentifiable clicking and banging sounds: we discover that the mechanical robot with electric eyes is rolling back and forth in Valerio's bedroom. After she stops the sound, she moves up and down the stairs in a state of confusion and the electronic music begins. As her tension increases, the sounds throb and grow louder: the moment Ugo appears on camera, they suddenly stop. As she tells him about the quicksand nightmare and he begins to embrace her, the music begins again. The sounds of her anxiety (which may be auditory hallucinations) are not human expressions but mechanical, like the industrial noises which overwhelm her in the early sequences in the factory. Antonioni contrasts her reaction (which is to give up attempts at conversation and run away) with those of the men. Although the noise is deafening, they continue talking: in fact, one of the foremen carries on a telephone conversation, emphasizing the immunity which they have apparently developed. In the final scene, after Giuliana answers Valerio's questions, the factory goes out of focus, they walk out of the frame, and the electronic music begins: this time there is no lone soprano voice and the electronic music now suggests an accepted reality rather than signalling Giuliana's terror.

Like sound, focus is used subjectively, revealing Giuliana's feelings, especially her anxiety. When she is in a state of fear or tension, we frequently see the back of her head in clear focus against a blurred background as in the scenes in the hallway, in the shack, and in Corrado's hotel room. Sometimes the image slips out of focus, actually showing us the intensification of her anxiety, as when she admits to Corrado that she was the girl who attempted suicide in her hospital story, and when she discovers Valerio's deception. Other times it indicates a momentary change in her state of being, as the street vendor slips in and out of focus when she and Corrado come out of her shop, and the face of the hotel clerk blurs as she is unable to remember Corrado's name. During the long and complicated encounter in the hotel room, various shifts in color and focus indicate changes in her condition. Like the mist and fog, soft focus obscures objects, rendering them abstract even when they are not negative or threatening, like the pink flowers in the foreground when Giuliana and Corrado arrive, happy and playful, in Ferrara. Late in the party at the shack as everyone lies on the bed, the blurred focus blends their quiet bodies. Suddenly Giuliana sits up in sharp focus and looks around; as Corrado looks at her, he comes into focus too, and they are united as the rest of the scene provides a background for their relationship. Like the sound, focus plays an important part in contrasting the opening and closing images. The film opens with an extremely blurred image of the factory. As Giuliana and Valerio walk offscreen at the end, the image goes out of focus. Then we see with extraordinary clarity not the factory, but a carefuly composed shot of a storage yard, triangular in shape with orderly rows of barrels and, in deep focus, the smokestack from the opening sequence, emitting bursts of yellow flame. The clarity of this image underscores Giuliana's recognition of reality, and the need to cope with its dangers.

In his first use of color, Antonioni is master of its expressive possibilities, making it almost impossible to describe in language the subtlety with which he paints his images. Like many other things, colors frighten Giuliana; but Antonioni uses them to convey her emotions. The pale neutral walls of Giuliana's shop are striped with patches of cool greens and blues. More concerned with the shade of her environment than the objects for sale, she says: "I'd better use blue, that shouldn't disturb." Her desire to paint the world in pale and undisturbing colors is exaggerated in her subjective vision of the street where everything—buildings, cobblestones, a vendor and his wares—is a lifeless greenish gray. When she goes to Ferrara with Corrado and begins to experience spontaneous pleasure and hope in her new companion, the colors become more vivid—bright green grass, chartreuse walls, pink flowers, flaming red apron, bright floral couch, orange background, green house plants. Whereas in the colorful apartment, her beige sweater is pale in contrast, in the earlier street scene even the muted greens and browns of her clothing stood out from the monochromatic background. The shack sequence is introduced by a burst of glowing red. As a stockinged foot moves into the frame, we recognize the burning coals inside a stove. The small bedroom encloses the many bodies in bright red walls. Throughout the film, red is identified with passion or intensity. It is one of those colors that disturb; we find it in the apron of the Ferrara housewife who "nearly went mad with fear" when her husband once went away, and in the ship where Giuliana talks at the Turkish sailor. We also find it in the film's title where it designates the contrast between the turbulence of inner life and the bleakness of the modern wasteland. Even the medium blue exterior of the shack contrasts with the saturated red of the interior. Milli, the "lone woman" in the party, and Corrado are linked by the contrast between their inner and outer colors. Unlike the others who are dressed predominantly in black and white, these pale-skinned strawberry blonds are both wearing green. But inside they are both sexually frustrated predators who participate most vigorously in breaking off the red boards to feed the fire. In the hotel sequence color is used with a great variety of effects. Giuliana moves along the sterile white neon-lighted hall. Corrado, a small dark figure, waits at the end of the hospital-like corridor. When they enter the room, they are surrounded by the deceptive warmth of rich brown walls. As the background slips in and out of focus, Giuliana sees blurred pastel shades which have no counterpart when the image is clearly in focus. When she awakens after the lovemaking, the room is washed in pale pink. Giuliana "sees" monochromatically, reducing her anxiety by denying the conflict among colors, as she did by "seeing" the grey green street outside her shop. Yet, perspective is distorted, as it was in the hotel corridor, suggesting the deceptive quality of this tranquil moment. We see her anxiety return as she runs outside on the street and stands momentarily against the bright red of a store window.

Besides expressing Giuliana's subjective vision, color is also used to help define the nature of external reality. The factory and ships use vibrant primary colors, as if draining natural color from the landscape, leaving only sickly greys and browns. The bright yellows in the factory are associated with the poisonous smoke and the quarantine flag. When the red and blue piping reappears in Giuliana's home and Corrado's bedroom, these environments are linked to industry rather than individual life. In both the opening and closing sequences, Giuliana in green and Valerio in brown introduce color into the drab greyness of the environment, stressing the importance of their humanity.

Recurring imagery of railings, windows, and ships also helps to define the relationship between individuals and their environment. The industrial world they inhabit is full of bars and railings that create orderly boundaries but also entrap people. These lines dominate individuals in several ways. In an overhead shot in the factory, we see Ugo and Corrado through an iron grating, which seems to imprison them. Frequently these lines are in sharp focus, emphasizing their definite reality in contrast to the blurred individual they enclose. At the radar towers Giuliana's blurred face is seen through the sharply defined red grillwork. While she and Corrado make love, her anxiety makes the room go out of focus, but the red railing behind her head remains clearly defined. At times these abstract lines seem to compete successfully with the individuals for the attention of the camera. On the ship the camera slowly pans along piping, which it examines in close detail before finally turning to Corrado. In the bottle factory as Corrado answers questions about the South American project, the camera slowly pans the men's faces, focusing on one at random, and moving along the wall to follow a mysterious blue stripe, as if to suggest how easily Corrado is distracted from human concerns.

   In the world of *Red Desert*, windows seem particularly important in shaping and expressing the characters' vision. In a chaotic universe, windows define what shall be looked at; they frame people or objects as if fragmenting elements of reality and contributing to the feeling of alienation. Early in the film, we look out a factory window at a landscape that has been transformed with industrial structures (composed of artful geometric shapes) and then softened with rows of neatly planted trees. When Corrado first seeks out Giuliana, he peers through the clouded, barred window of her shop and then begins to walk away. The window does not reveal her presence within and helps to accentuate the tentativeness of his approach. In Ferrara, as Giuliana gathers her courage to tell Corrado of her terror, she is framed by a glass door, intensifying our awareness of her pain, and emphasizing her fragility. At other moments of crisis, too, Giuliana gazes out the window. When she enters the lobby of Corrado's hotel in a state of panic, we see the image of a car in the window. The confusion of this sudden visual shift is intensified by our inability to tell whether we are looking at the car through the window, or at its reflection in the glass. Inside his room, Giuliana darts to the window as if blindly seeking escape; outside, she sees a lone old man whose isolation reflects her own. In the sequence of heightened anxiety during Valerio's feigned illness, there are three important window shots. The situation opens with a cut to a narrow, horizontal window through which Giuliana sees a ship which she uses to try to interest Valerio and coax him out of bed; in the doctor's office, an out of focus hand passes in front of a window framing the grey muck of a slag heap; when Giuliana discovers Valerio's trickery, she weeps and looks through a window where the exterior is out of focus. In the shack sequence, several window shots emphasize the separation between inner and outer experience. Though we have seen boats in the harbor as the worker and his girlfriend leave the shack, we are still astonished at the first window shot, where a huge ship appears, gliding by so close to the shack that our perception is disoriented. All eyes are focused on this amazing sight, which evokes characteristic responses: Max thinks of sex—"Those men on board haven't seen a woman in six months"; Corrado thinks of how he can use this cheaper loading dock; Giuliana responds with instinctive fear. After a while, she returns to the window and the camera looks at her from outside, through the doorway and window, emphasizing her isolation in the crowded shack. Gazing out the window at the sea, she says tearfully: "It's never still—never, never. I can't look at the sea for long without losing interest in what's happening on land. . . . My eyes are wet . . . what should I use my eyes for? To look at what?" Ironically the window, which seems to select and frame objects for attention, only moves her further into confusion. Later, as everyone gazes out the window watching the arrival of the doctors and the raising of the quarantine flag, the others acknowledge the validity of her instinctive fear.

The mysteriousness of the ships that reappear throughout the film links them with the possibilities of the unknown and with fantasy, particularly Giuliana's desire for escape and fascination with the sea. The greatest mystery surrounds the first ship, which glides silently through the trees shrouded in mist. Its vastness is enhanced by comparison with a truck moving in the opposite direction along a road that parallels the canal. Standing by the stagnant water, Giuliana is the only one who sees the ghostly ship. This sense of mystery is maintained in the window shots. Ships also involve human contact, which can be dangerous, as the quarantine proves. But they also provide the setting for important moments when Giuliana succeeds in making contact. On the ship, she expresses her feelings for Corrado: "If I were to leave, I'd take you too because you're part of me." The qualities of mystery, fantasy, and meaningful contact are all present in the scene where she asks the Turkish sailor, "Does this ship take passengers?" Like the airplanes in the later films, ships seem to free Giuliana's imagination, enabling her to see beyond the limits of her present life.

Editing and camera work are very important means of developing Giuliana's subjective experience. Not as immediately accessible to our understanding as the blurred focus, use of color, or recurring imagery, they force us into kinesthetic awareness of Giuliana's panic and disorientation. The film moves from sequence to sequence through flat cuts, offering no visual or temporal transitions. The jarring cut from the great cloud of steam at the factory to Giuliana's terrified awakening prepares us for the disorientation that follows. Camera position is the source of discontinuity in the scene where Giuliana begins to pack for Ugo's business trip. As Ugo sits on the bed, the camera, behind him, watches her walk toward the cabinet. As the camera moves forward, eliminating Ugo from the frame, he suddenly appears through a doorway on Giuliana's right without benefit of cutting. In the two most powerful sequences, editing and camera work express Giuliana's confusion; she cannot integrate her fragmented experience. In the tiny bedroom at the shack, as she takes

a bite of the quail egg, the camera makes a series of quick cuts:
Corrado watching her; a close-up of Max's hand on Milli's leg,
sliding under her skirt; Linda half-watching; Giuliana leaning on
Corrado. Later, a great variety of actions are presented through a
series of rapid cuts. We see fragments (arms, legs, backs; discontinuous
movements and gestures; parts of walls, tables, chairs, and stove) shot
at various distances and from radically different angles, making it
impossible to perceive the situation as a whole. The effect is most
kinesthetic in the part of the hotel room sequence where Giuliana is
lying on the bed. The camera follows her eyes, looking upward at the
ceiling to avoid seeing Corrado. As she turns her head frantically
from side to side, the camera rolls with her, tilting the room and
communicating her vertigo; as the focus blurs, new colors appear,
and only the red railing can be identified.

The story that Giuliana tells Valerio is another means of conveying
her subjective vision and her conflicting desires for emotional
independence and human contact. In this sequence, sound, focus,
color, imagery, editing, and camera work are used in ways that
contrast with the rest of the film, suggesting another dimension of
Giuliana's inner reality. At first, the story seems to be purely an
escape fantasy. A young girl "who is bored with grownups" spends
her days alone (except for a rabbit scurrying across the surf) in an
idyllic lagoon. The opening image is of a blurred landscape, but then
everything is clearly in focus throughout the rest of the sequence. The
camerawork is very smooth; there is constant panning and a steady
flow of images instead of fragmented cutting. The bright, clear colors
contrast sharply with the muted tones and patches of primary colors
that characterize the rest of the film. The girl's bronze body
harmonizes with the natural landscape. The pinkish white sand and
the flesh colored rocks remind us of the moment of peace experienced
by Giuliana in the hotel room. But the predominant colors are the
comforting blues and greens of the pure water and sky. No discordant
music disturbs this idyllic vision; she hears only the natural sounds of
the water lapping the shore. "Nature's colors were so lovely and there
was no sound." This sequence offers no entrapping railings or
distancing windows, but ships are very significant, again embodying
mystery, fantasy, and human contact. "One morning a boat appeared.
Not one of the usual boats—a real sailing ship that braves the seas
and storms of this world. . . . From afar it looked splendid. As it
approached it became mysterious. She saw no one on board. It
stopped awhile, then sailed away silently as it had come. She was used
to the strange ways of people and was not surprised." This

description suggests a connection with Corrado, a stranger who constantly talks of travel, who has come to lure men to foreign lands, and who has sailed into her life; she reaches out to him but he is soon to leave. The ship brings with it high wind and waves, disrupting her idyllic serenity. Her initial response is fear. After the ship leaves, dark shadows and shrubs appear in the foreground, and the mysterious singing begins. "All right for one mystery, but not two." The siren's voice was "now near, now far." It seemed to come "from the sea, from the rocks" which she had "never realized looked like flesh. And the voice at that point was so sweet." This lone soprano is no longer the voice of the alienated woman (as in the opening), but of all creation. When Valerio asks, "Who was singing," Giuliana replies, "Everybody, everything." The girl realizes that she is not alone on the island; the rocks that call to her are like a wall of human flesh. This awareness parallels Giuliana's double response when, after fleeing from Corrado, she goes to the mysterious quarantined ship. Her initial panic is followed by contact with the sailor, with the realization that she's "not a woman alone," and by a movement toward acceptance of her life. The difference is that in the fantasy she responds to others as an undifferentiated presence; she is not required to love an individual human being or deal with the unknown, the experiences that are so frightening and so necessary to her survival.

In spite of Giuliana's limitations, the film does not allow us to dismiss her merely as a paranoid schizophrenic. More than anyone else in the film, she is sensitive to the emotional significance of the people and events around her and is capable of greater intensity of feeling. In the world of *Red Desert* this quality makes her extremely vulnerable and confused; however, it is also the source of her intuitive grasp of the truth and her continued sexual responsiveness. She emerges as a person who, despite the apparent chaos of her vision, constantly strives for greater access to her own experience.

For Antonioni, these qualities are linked to the fact that she is a woman. He once remarked that he believed that reality could be filtered better through women's psychologies "since they are more instinctive, more sincere."[7] Hence, he made a woman his central figure in the earlier films with a psychological focus—*L'Avventura*, *La Notte*, and *L'Eclisse*. In *Red Desert* only Giuliana and Linda hear the scream outside the shack. Linda's role-playing makes her willing to relinquish her perception when the men deny the existence of the scream, but Giuliana insists on it because denial of experience threatens her sanity. Yet from the outside, her persistence in challenging the men's perception seems further evidence of her abnormality. Another reason for the woman's value as the central consciousness in a world of social transformation is that her role is no longer defined by home and dependency; therefore, she is more alienated by the breakup of long term personal relationships and must experiment in order to find a new center of being. Corrado tries to lure men away to South America, leaving behind wives whose confusion will parallel Giuliana's. The extremity of this situation is rendered visually concrete in the deserted industrial town in *L'Avventura:* Claudia is frightened by the town and calls it a cemetery. Giuliana, too, is frightened by industry. Though she tries to open a shop, it is like a domestic enterprise where she is more concerned with decoration and mood than with commerce. Her husband is slightly embarrassed by her shop, as if it reflects upon his adequacy as a provider. His patronizing attitude toward what he perceives to be her child-like condition is also reflected in his suggestion that Linda stay with her during his business trip. Although he might seem justified because of Giuliana's previous accident, the film extends this situation to other women. The housewife in Ferrara confides that she "nearly went mad with fear" when her husband went away for only a week, implying that she too lacks an independent identity. The girl-friend of the factory worker who visits the shack conforms to another aspect of the stereotyped female role. A sex-object whom Max looks over approvingly (increasing his respect for the man who possesses her), she remarks archly: "I like to do certain things, not talk about them." Even Milli, the "lone woman" who seems independent and capable in a male dominated world, has her problems. Though she jokes about making love with men who earn less than she, Milli, too, is a potential victim and fears that Max, who preys on bankrupt businesses and single women, will get her yet.

Although Antonioni is sympathetic with women, he links them primarily to the old values and thereby dooms them to failure. If they cannot adapt, they are faced with madness and suicide. Yet the men are in danger, too. Those who adapt successfully risk a loss of sensitivity and humanity, exemplified in Ugo and Corrado. (In the later films, the men pay an even higher price.) For Antonioni, the new world is not only inevitable but full of beauty and power, particularly apparent in the factory sequence where a huge cloud of steam is released with terrific force, filling the screen and completely enveloping Ugo and Corrado, and in the profusion of strong geometric shapes and man-made objects like the rows of round blue bottles.

The conflict between the two worlds is developed with extraordinary subtlety and control in the sequence where Giuliana and
Corrado visit the radar towers. Arranged against the horizon like
visitors from another planet, these structures combine strength and
grace like the best of modern architecture. The vastness of their size is
revealed only when we see the tiny figure of a man crawling on the
grillwork. This is one of the few sequences where Giuliana's fear is
overcome by her pleasure and curiosity. Drawn by the beauty and
strangeness of these forms, she initiates a conversation with a worker
on the tower (as she is later able to do with the Turkish sailor).

> GIULIANA: Tell me please, who owns these things?
> WORKER: The University of Bologna.
> GIULIANA: Aren't you scared?
> WORKER: I'm used to it.
> GIULIANA: What's it for?
> WORKER: To listen to the stars.
> GIULIANA: Can I listen?
> WORKER:You have to climb up here.

Though the structures are owned by an institution, Giuliana relates
to them in terms of the individual worker who has personal contact
with them. Technology offers the possibility of listening to the stars,
but it demands the risk of climbing the tower. Realistically, Giuliana
balks at this danger. Undistracted by curiosity or beauty, Corrado
keeps his mind on business. The only thing that catches his eye is
Giuliana's brief exchange with the foreman he has come to hire. After
she finishes her conversation with the other worker on the tower,
Corrado comes over and asks her how she knew him. Fully involved
in her present experience, Giuliana at first thinks Corrado is
referring to the man on the tower. But Corrado, pursuing his
predetermined business, was referring to the foreman. Giuliana is
pleased to learn that he has turned down the offer. Corrado's single-
minded completion of his task, though efficient, precludes participation in the beauty or human contact which this moment of
experience evokes for Giuliana.

Red Desert presents a tragic vision of the world, not in terms of
what happens to Giuliana for whom there is some hope, but through
a conflict between two incompatible value systems, one of which
must inevitably be lost. Yet, it is possible to interpret the film quite
differently, depending on whether Giuliana's adaptation is seen
positively. Skinner and Laing provide the frameworks for coming to
opposite conclusions. Antonioni seems aware of the dichotomy they
represent.

I think that, in the years to come, there are going to be very
violent transformations, both in the world and in the individual's
interior.[8]

Many of Antonioni's comments about *Red Desert* seem to parallel
Skinner's world view:

> As for me, I hold that the sort of neurosis seen in *Red Desert* is
> above all a question of adaptation. There are people who adapt
> themselves, and others who haven't yet done this, for they are too
> tied to structures, or life-rhythms, that are now out of date. This
> is the case with Giuliana. The violence of the variation, the
> wedge between her sensitivity, intelligence and psychology and
> the cadence that is imposed on her, provoke the character's
> breakdown, contacts with the world, her perception of the
> noises, colors, cold personalities surrounding her, but also her
> system of values (education, morality, faith), which are no
> longer valuable and no longer sustain her. She finds herself,
> thus, in the position of needing to renew herself completely, as a
> woman. This is what the doctors advise and this is what she
> strives to do.[9]

If we adopted Skinner's view, we would see Giuliana's condition as
resulting from environmental influence. Her confusion and erratic
behavior would be attributed to improper conditioning that led her
to believe in freedom and dignity. In contrast, her son Valerio, being
trained in science and technology by his well-adapted father, would
emerge as a positive figure; the aberration of his feigned illness could
be explained by the unhealthy influence of his neurotic mother.
Skinner stresses the dangers and limitations of individualism by
arguing that children should be brought up by all the adults in a
community: "What the child imitates is a sort of essential happy
adult. He can avoid the idiosyncrasies of a single parent. Identification is easy and valuable."[10] A Skinnerian perspective on the ending
would see Giuliana learning to recognize the aversive features of her
surroundings, shifting her focus from her inner state of being to the
observable environment, and passing this adaptive information on to
her son. Skinner's ideas would emphasize Antonioni's focus on the
structures of industry and its effect on the physical universe. Giuliana
must learn to appreciate the beauty of the factory and her modern
apartment (already accessible to her in the radar towers) as she has
learned to shun pollution.

Yet to see *Red Desert* exclusively through Skinnerian eyes would
oversimplify it drastically; it would deny an essential element in the

film—the poignance with which the loss of old values is developed—and, hence would deny the central conflict and tragedy. Such a perspective would not give us access to Giuliana's feelings and could not explain her actions. For example, throughout the film she confides that she feels herself sinking down, that the floor is turning to quicksand and giving way beneath her feet. Skinner's comments on this very phenomenon would invalidate her experience and offer Giuliana no relief:

> A person's belief that a floor will hold him as he walks across it depends upon his past experience. If he has walked across it without incident many times, he will do so again readily, and his behavior will not create any of the aversive stimuli felt as anxiety. He may report that he has "faith" in the solidity of the floor or "confidence" that it will hold him, but the kinds of things which are felt as faith or confidence are not states of mind; they are at best byproducts of the behavior in its relation to antecedent events. and they do not explain why a person walks as he does.[11]

Laing is most helpful in the very areas of the film that are inaccessible to a Skinnerian view. The highly subjective point of view in *Red Desert* validates Laing's assumption that all reality is shaped by the unique perspective growing out of an individual's private experience. A Laingian would deal with Giuliana's fear of sinking floors, not by looking for events in her past, but by interpreting it as part of her present experience, and relating it to her fear of being alone with nothing or no one to hold on to. Laing's views would interpret all of Giuliana's behavior and experience as integrated behind this fear, a fear that is also experienced by others in our culture.

> We are living in an age in which the ground is shifting and the foundations are shaking. . . . In these circumstances, we have every reason to be insecure. When the ultimate basis of our world is in question, we run to different holes in the ground, we scurry into roles, statuses, identities, interpersonal relations. . . . We are afraid to approach the fathomless and bottomless groundlessness of everything. "There's nothing to be afraid of." The ultimate reassurance, and the ultimate terror.[12]

In her madness, the socially recognizable roles of mother, wife or shopkeeper do not provide Giuliana with an identity. Instead, she struggles to believe in her own existence by taking hold of inner experience. Laing's theories help to explain the contradictory desires for freedom and dependency in her fantasy of the girl on the island:

> The others have become installed in our hearts, and we call them ourselves. Each person, not being himself either to himself or the other, just as the other is not himself to himself or to us, in being another for another neither recognizes himself in the other, nor the other in himself. Hence being at least a double absence, haunted by the ghost of his own murdered self, no wonder modern man is addicted to other persons, and the more addicted, the less satisfied, the more lonely.[13]

Giuliana feels that Valerio could never have pretended illness if he needed her love as much as she needs his. Set adrift by this severed tie, she is frantic and rushes to Corrado, needing to locate herself in relation to another human being. This addiction to others has in fact been strengthened by her doctors who urged her to find identity by loving other individuals.

Laing would go further than Antonioni in defending Giuliana from the charge of madness. He sees schizophrenia as a label with political implications, which society imposes to control and victimize the psychotic as it does the child—the two kinds of people whom Skinner frequently chooses to show that institutional control is already possible

> In using the term schizophrenia, I am not referring to any condition that I suppose to be mental rather than physical, or to an illness, like pneumonia, but to a label that some people pin on other people under certain social circumstances. . . . The label is a social fact and the social fact a political event. . . . It is a social prescription that rationalizes a set of social actions whereby the labeled person is annexed by others, who are legally sanctioned, medically empowered and morally obliged, to become responsible for the person labeled. . . . A person, in being put in the role of patient, tends to become defined as a nonagent, as a nonresponsible object, to be treated accordingly, and even comes to regard himself in this light.[14]

Laing illustrates the extremes of invalidation and control by quoting E. Kraepelin's description of a situation where the patient's behavior is strikingly like Giuliana's and the behavior of the therapist emerges as far more bizarre and destructive than that of the schizophrenic.

> The patient is in continual movement, going a few steps forward, then back again; she plaits her hair, only to unloose it the next minute. *On attempting to stop her movement*, we meet with unexpectedly strong resistance; *if I place myself in front of her with my arms spread out* in order to stop her, if she cannot

push me on one side, she suddenly turns and slips through under my arms, so as to continue her way. *If one takes firm hold* of her, she distorts her usually rigid, expressionless features with deplorable weeping, that only ceases so soon as one lets her have her own way. We notice besides that she holds a crushed piece of bread spasmodically clasped in the fingers of the left hand, which she absolutely *will not allow to be forced from her.* . . . *If you prick her in the forehead with a needle,* she scarcely winces or turns away, and leaves the needle quietly sticking there without letting it disturb her restless, beast-of-prey-like wandering backwards and forwards.[15]

Laing's clinical work shows that if you examine the behavior of a schizophrenic from the point of view of his own experience, as Antonioni's film forces us to do, then invariably you will find it to be "a special strategy that a person invents in order to live in an unlivable situation."[16] He even recognizes the possibility that madness may be a form of progress—a way of resisting the pressures of an insane society and taking a step toward a better future.[17]

Psychotic experience goes beyond the horizons of our common, that is, our communal, sense. . . . Madness need not be all breakdown. It may also be breakthrough. It is potentially liberation and renewal as well as enslavement and existential death.[18]

In contrast to Skinner and possibly even Antonioni, Laing might interpret the ending of *Red Desert* entirely negatively. Along with her child who has already been successfully brainwashed by the society, Giuliana retreats from self exploration and is subdued by the harsh realities of her physical environment, which represents, not progress and beauty, but entrapment.

Une Femme Douce

Robert Bresson's *Une Femme Douce* (1969), based on Dostoevsky's story "A Gentle Spirit," is even more explicit in its exploration of a woman trapped in the limbo between experience and behavior. Like *Red Desert* it presents a tragic vision of a woman (Dominique Sanda) whose experience is not perceptible to those around her, particularly her husband (Guy Frangin), who is cold and insensitive, responding only to her outward appearance and behavior. Suicide is attractive to her, as it is to Giuliana, and, failing to adapt to the painful alienation of her life, she chooses that alternative. As in *Red Desert*, a subjective point of view controls the visuals; this time, however, it expresses the

husband's narrow perspective, not that of the woman whose experience, unlike Giuliana's, remains largely inaccessible even to the
audience.

As in the case of *Red Desert*, *Une Femme Douce* is closely related
thematically to Bresson's other works, which are all concerned with
the entrapment of the body and spirit. While present in his earliest
films—*Les Affaires Publiques* (1934), *Les Anges du Peche* (1943), and
Les Dames du Bois de Boulogne (1944), which are almost impossible
to see—this theme is developed with maturity in his next three works
(the prison cycle), where the protagonist strives toward spiritual
release. Paul Schrader describes the thematic pattern succinctly:

> In *Diary of a Country Priest (Le Journal d'un Cure de
> Compagne,*1950) this release occurs within the confines of a
> religious order, in *A Man Escaped (Un Condamné a Mort s'est
> Echappé,* 1956), it occurs with scape from prison, in *Pickpocket
> (Pickpocket,* 1956) it occurs with imprisonment, in *The Trial of
> Joan of Arc (Le Proces de Jeanne d'Arc,* 1961), it occurs both
> within the confines of religious belief and a physical prison. . . .
> Prison is the dominant metaphor of Bresson's films, but it is a
> two-faced metaphor: his characters are both escaping from a
> prison of one sort and surrendering to a prison of another. And
> the prison his protagonists ultimately escape is the most
> confining prison of all, the body.[19]

Au Hasard, Balthazar (1966), *Mouchette* (1966), and *Une Femme
Douce* (1969) all present a trapped female protagonist, as in *The
Trial of Joan of Arc*. But these later films are marked by the abject
helplessness of the victims and their masochistic suffering under the
cruelty of those around them. Although their escape into death may
still be a spiritual release from the body, it is not quite as uplifting.
Despite their peculiar tone, which almost verges on grotesque
humor, *Four Nights of a Dreamer* (1973), and *Lancelot du Lac* (1974),
continue to explore entrapment, but in the realm of idealism and
romantic love. Although the visual surfaces are brightly colored, the
only means of escape is still death, which now seems senseless rather
than transcendent. *Le Diable Probablement (Probably the Devil)*
(1977) is much darker in tone; in fact, it is probably the most
depressing film he ever made. His first work to be based entirely on
his own original script, it presents the trap in ecological terms and
drives its brilliant young protagonist to suicide, not because he wants
to die, but because he heroically refuses to be contaminated. In this
film, the austerity of Bresson's visual style is so severe and his
perspective on contemporary experience so grim, that it was attacked
in France for "inciting the young to suicide."

In *Une Femme Douce* the prison is the social context of marriage. The woman marries the man because she is looking for "something else . . . something wider." But instead, her vitality and hopes are stifled by the husband who controls and torments her until he finally screws down the lid on her narrow coffin. In Dostoevsky's story, the Russian husband wants to conquer this gentle spirit as a means of revenging himself for the humiliation of having been expelled from his regiment as a coward. In the film the husband is motivated more out of the compulsive greed and materialism of the French bourgeoisie, desiring to possess her as one of his valuable objects. Both men are attracted to her youth, gentleness, and fragility, qualities that make her a natural victim. Both exploit the inequities of a male-dominated culture where a woman without money or connections is an easy prey and where marriage can be used as an institutionalized form of enslavement approved by Church and State.

The film reinforces the focus on entrapment by allowing us to see the girl's development only through the flash-back structure, which the husband controls. Like *Red Desert*, the film begins and ends with parallel scenes. In *Red Desert* the parallel ending takes place considerably later in film time and reveals differences in Giuliana's behavior; we have seen some of these changes take place, but the open-ended structure could have included more incidents and implies that the future is unpredictable. But the suicide scene that opens *Une Femme Douce* is repeated at the end, locking the central characters and our experience of the film into a closed system. In an attempt to understand the suicide and justify himself, the husband tells Anna, the servant, the story of the marriage in a series of flashbacks that move between the room where the wife lies dead and the events of their relationship, many of which took place in the same room. As the flashbacks move forward in time, they increasingly narrow the gap between present and past, heightening our anticipation of the inevitable suicide. This effect is intensified whenever Bresson gives us a glimpse of the white shawl or the balcony and Thonet rocker that are important images in the suicide montage. Conventionally used to illuminate what has happened in the past, in this film, flashbacks work ironically. While they do explain her suicide by showing her husband's gross insensitivity, they do not reveal her inner feelings because he does not understand them. In this way, the flashbacks raise as many questions as they answer. The sense of entrapment is intensified by a circular structure based on tight parallels between scenes in the first and second halves of the film. This is most easily illustrated in the following chart:

BEGINNING

Free motion:
During the titles we see bright lights of Paris streets at
night shot from a moving car.

The suicide.

Their first encounter: She brings objects to pawn,
including the Christ on a gold cross; she takes his advice
on how to apply for a job; she leaves.

The entrapment: They go to the zoo where he proposes
and she tells him of her desire for "something wider;"
they visit her "sinister" home that she wants to escape;
their marriage is sealed by clasped hands.

Powerful expression of feeling: On their wedding night
they both laugh and appear to be happy, playful and
spontaneous. She jumps on the bed.

Their problems begin and they choose silence: They go to the
movies and see the garden scene from *Benjamin;*
she tells him of her visit to the Museum of Natural History;
they visit the art museum and respond differently to the nudes;
she rebels at their being a couple and they argue on the freeway;
they quarrel because he thinks she is paying too much to
the poor;
they respond differently to *Hamlet,* where the final line is, "The
rest is silence."

Her body: She lies seductively in a bathtub with one leg up on
the rim; they make love "as usual;" he says: "her attitude never
changed and I only wanted to possess her body."

CENTER "the real

They eat their soup in silence. They argue; she revolts and leaves
while he stays home and watches an air battle on TV in which
RAF underdogs are victorious.
When she comes home, they make love.

He catches her with the

ENDING

Final entrapment:
in the closing image the husband screws down the lid
on her coffin.

The suicide.

Their last encounter (while she's alive): She looks at the Christ
on a gold cross before committing suicide; she tells him, "I'll
be your faithful wife and I'll respect you"; he leaves.

The false vision of escape: He talks of going to a new place
where "everything will change . . ." and "all our sorrows will
vanish"; she reads from a book, "it is fairly certain that every
bird is predisposed to sing like its species;" it ends with her
in tears that express the loss of hope and the image of their
clasped hands.

Powerful expression of feeling: He hears her mournful song,
which at first angers him and then leads to his emotional
outburst on the bridge; later he makes a passionate
declaration of his love and she responds with tears. She lies
deathlike on the bed.

He tries to improve things and break the silence;
they walk in the park past the swan on the lake; they visit the
Museum of Natural History where he creates the impression
that they are talking;
they visit the Museum of Modern Art and respond differently
to a light machine;
he's pleased by their disparity as she moodily listens to music
while he works a puzzle;
he tries to please her by paying more money to the poor;
she reads while he watches horse races on TV and says: "She
seemed glad not to have to talk."

Her body: She lies ill in bed and he takes care of her haggard
body "regardless of the expense;" he buys a new bed,
rejecting her sexually.

torture begins."

They drink their coffee in silence.
She almost shoots him with the gun that he was earlier
planning to use to shoot her and her lover.
When they come home, for the first time she does not sleep
with him.

young boy in the car.

It is interesting to compare the film's structure with that of Dostoevsky's story, which is divided into two sections. As in the film, the central episode is the scene where the wife almost shoots her husband. The husband who narrates the story explains his structure to the reader: "I will simply tell it in order. (Order!)"[20] His disintegration into madness evokes this passion for chronological order, as he seeks to fit all the details and conflicting feelings into a single controlled explanation. The film introduces the circularity and parallels into the structure, shifting the emphasis from the narrator's fear of madness to the sense of entrapment. But neither structure provides a full understanding of the woman's experience; as Dostoevsky's narrator says at the end, "Why she died is still a question."[21]

Since the story is controlled by the narrator, its structure is one means of expressing his point of view. *Une Femme Douce* is one of the few films that succeeds in filtering events through the consciousness of an unreliable narrator, a strategy that has a rich tradition in prose fiction. In successfully adapting the story to cinema, Bresson sacrifices the mad intensity of the husband's sadomasochistic vision in order to emphasize his bourgeois deadness and ontological insecurity. The subjective point of view allows us to see the wife only through the husband's narrow perspective, and the distortions of his visions force us constantly to reinterpret her behavior, suggesting that her capacity for experience is far richer than his.

Desiring always that her emotions reflect his, he can tolerate disparity between them only when it reinforces his sense of superiority; if her feelings seem unexpected or more positive than his, he is threatened and destructive. On the morning of her suicide, he remarks: "I, so anxious, was struck by her calmness." He is extremely shocked by her first revolt, when she boldly declares "I forbid you to dominate me with money." Striving to remain an enigma himself, he needs to be absolutely certain of her feelings, sometimes even deluding himself to gain this security. After her first visit to the shop he asserts, "I knew she'd come back." After the flirtation in the movies, when she embraces him reassuringly, he says, "Then I was sure of her . . . she loved me . . . or wanted to love me." When she surprises him with knowledge of his firing from the bank, he is frantic about where she learned this, saying, "I had to know." When he spies on her in the parked car, he says, "There was no doubt. She had spurned his advances. I knew it. She had gone to see that boy just to hurt me." Equally certain that others cannot misunderstand the meaning of his behavior, after he buys the second bed he says: "That bed said I had seen . . . that I knew."

Several important scenes very subtly reveal the process by which the audience must reinterpret the husband's sense of what is going on between them. As we watch the husband in a close-up, intent upon a crossword puzzle, we hear loud popular music that is as distracting to us as it is to him. A moment later we see that the wife is playing the phonograph. The fluidity of her restless emotions is revealed as she suddenly lifts the needle, scraping it along the record, and puts on a calmer piece of classical music. The visuals show him out of focus in the extreme foreground but reveal her fully in depth focus. Ironically, at the very moment that we cease to share his irritation at the music and become interested and sympathetic to the wife, the husband, confident of his superiority, remarks smugly, "She looked so defeated. I felt a pity for her that gratified me . . . our disparity pleased me." In another sequence, surprised to hear her singing, he responds in fury: "What! In my house? Has she forgotten I exist?" After he learns that her song is melancholy, he wanders around distractedly and finally we see him standing behind the bars and railings of a bridge sobbing; later he observes: "No, it wasn't pity. I felt incredibly enthusiastic. No one could understand my feelings!" Having former-ly succeeded so well in his sadistic conquest of her that she has withdrawn into ignoring his very existence, he is at first shocked by this unexpected result. Now his fantasy reverses itself and he is overjoyed at the chance to play the victim, throwing himself at her feet, kissing her legs and ankles, and declaring his passionate adoration: "I'll give you whatever you want! I'll give you Paradise!" At first the wife is stunned and then breaks into hysterical weeping. Completely baffled by his reversal, she says: "And I thought you would desert me." As if he'd never given reason for such a thought, he says: "Her words pierced me like daggers. . . . But I could not help hoping and was fearfully happy." Later, when he praises her for how "cleverly" and "artlessly" she "snubbed that boy," he is baffled by her sobs, as if totally forgetting how he has made her suffer for her supposed infidelity. But we suspect that she weeps because her last faint hope is gone. He *will never* leave her; he will reinterpret everything to keep possession of her. Unable to act herself, she is both his victim and her own.

We experience the confinement of his perspective primarily through the film's visual techniques, which are so controlled that we never see the wife except in the husband's presence and only from his point of view. The camera focuses primarily on objects, almost caressing them in close-ups that reveal the rich colors and textures of his treasures—the polished surface of the finely grained table on which his customers display the objects they want to pawn, the smoothly curved bannister in the hallway, the oriental screen that separates the two beds, the Christ on the gold cross, the blue and white china, and the shiny toaster. In the scene where he throws himself at her feet, a book falls to the floor. As the husband picks it up, the camera dwells on the oriental rug for several seconds—the place where his wife's feet had stood, and where her book had fallen. This odd shot very subtly suggests the perversity of his new role as supplicant, gazing at the holy spot. When the camera looks at humans, it frequently omits their faces, making them seem more like objects and reinforcing the anonymity of these nameless people. In the wedding scene, for example, we see a close-up of his hand signing the official document, then hers. The film cuts to a restaurant table with a white cloth and four shiny glasses, and their hands putting on wedding rings. Not until they raise their wine glasses to drink do we finally see their faces. There are many shots through doorways, windows, curtains, fences, grillwork, railings, cages, and screens that fragment the cinematic space and enclose the people. As the wife reaches the low point of her vitality and passion, she lies close to death in a narrow bed with a nurse standing over her. Seen through the partially open doorway, this crowded corner of the room appears as a narrow strip in the center of the frame; the rest of the space is filled by the dark walls and doorway that seem to close in on her like her husband's oppressive being.

Expressing the silent power of his waiting game, the camera is frequently static, focusing single-mindedly on a space or object as people move in and out of its field of vision; although it seems passive (like the behavior of the husband), it controls what we see. This aspect of the point of view is a visual equivalent for the husband's admonishment against his wife's spontaneity on their wedding night: "Everything will remain as it is for the moment." As he doggedly seeks out his wife and her supposed lover, the camera focuses on the bannister in the hallway and he moves in and out of the frame. When the film cuts to an exterior, the camera shoots through the car window at the steering wheel. He gets in and drives off, but the camera remains fixed, now focusing on the building that was behind the car. When he arrives at his destination, the camera shoots through the car window at precisely the same angle as before and remains in this position even after he gets out of the car. The camera shows us, not *what* he sees, but *how* his perception works. All of these visual techniques express the baffling limitation of his vision, and provide a cinematic equivalent for the explicit statement of Dostoevsky's narrator: "I keep walking about, trying to explain it to myself . . . I can't think of it all as a whole."[22]

One of the unique qualities of the film is the mystification that surrounds the motives and experience of the characters. This mystery is partly a result of the way in which Bresson works with actors. Trying to avoid psychological acting, he is more concerned with "the physiology of existence."

> In order to reduce acting to physiology, Bresson carefully instructs his actors in nonexpressiveness. He forces the actor to sublimate his personality, to act in an automatic manner. He would not give the actor "hints" or explain the emotions that the actor should convey, but would give only precise, physical instructions: at what angle to hold the head, when and how far to turn the wrist, and so forth. He used repeated rehearsals to "wear down" any ingrained or intractable self-expression, gradually transforming fresh movement into rote action, expressive intonation into bland monotone.[23]

In *Une Femme Douce* Bresson focuses on the externals of behavior— their outbursts of joy and weeping, the obscure interactions in the movie theater, and the husband's proud interpretation of his wife's behavior in the parked car; the film deliberately avoids dialogue or business that would explain motive or effect, forcing the audience into interpretations that remain uncertain. The husband's controlled face, rigid posture and fastidious dress totally mask the wild intensity of his sado-masochistic desires and thus negate his wife's experience of his behavior.

Silence further obscures the human situations. It intensifies irrelevant sounds like his footsteps as he paces beside her body, or the maddening care with which he blows on his soup. We watch them eat and even embrace in total silence. It is one of the husband's most oppressive weapons, yet he pretends that the silence is mutual and the natural result of their emotions. He asks Anna rhetorically: "Why did we choose silence from the start?" As the wife recovers from her illness, he pretends that she prefers the silence and that it is for her own good, refusing to acknowledge that he is actually rejecting her: "She seemed glad not to have to talk . . . I thought I should give her time." He is pleased with his creative powers in manipulating the silence: "We didn't walk in absolute silence . . . I created the impression we were talking." The silence creates a pall that hangs over the film, oppressing us in the audience as well. Its association with death is made explicit in the theater sequence with Hamlet's dying line, "The rest is silence."

The film, however, necessarily cuts through the mystification at various points, providing subtle access to inner thoughts and feelings. The central episode offers some extraordinary clarification, along with the beginning of a new phase of the husband's self-conscious enigma. When they return home after the incident at the parked car, he reports that "She was deeply hit," presumably by guilt at his discovery. The next morning while he is still asleep, the camera cuts to a gun lying on a pile of books. The wife picks it up and walks toward him, the window curtains framing her, narrowing the space and intensifying the situation. One of the few times in the film when her face clearly reveals her inner state, it now seems filled with burning hatred. She puts the gun to his temple, in an agony of indecision she pauses, closes her eyes, and finally backs up and returns the gun to the table. The husband's behavior is very strange indeed. Pretending to be asleep, he lies back passively, feeling that he is proving his bravery and winning a great victory over her. He is completing his conquest of this "gentle creature" by bringing her to the verge of murder, burdening her with an overwhelming guilt and proving his moral superiority. Later, as the curtains are drawn to reveal the balcony from which she will jump to her death, he greets her with his customary silence as if nothing has happened and she submissively hands him a cup of coffee. Inwardly he relishes his triumph: "She could think I was actually asleep . . . it was unimaginable to her that I was awake. She could be held only by the feeling that I was expecting death." He is contemptuous of her because she cannot imagine what is in his convoluted mind, yet he is completely unaware of his own inability to understand her experience.

As another means of illuminating the mystification, Bresson uses many forms of art to provide access to the characters' experience. The only reference adopted from Dostoevsky's story is the line spoken by Mephistopheles when he first meets Faust: the man quotes it to the girl soon after their first meeting: "I am part of that force that does evil." "Or good," she adds, finishing the line and showing that she, too, is familiar with Goethe. Surprised that she is educated, he angrily projects his condescension onto her: "She was surprised to

find I was educated . . . I'm sure she thought that." Though the tone
is, of course, completely different, the girl is like Faust in that she
longs for knowledge and wider experience, but she has signed her
soul away to a husband who is, as Goethe describes Mephistopheles,
an eternal nay-sayer.

Her response to art is frequently contrasted with his, implying her
greater openness and sensitivity. He admits almost jealously: "She
had a passion for books and records." Throughout the film the music
expresses her range of emotions. As they pass a painting in the
museum, he remarks: "The nudes she used to admire made me think
of women as pleasure instruments." His tone implies that her
aesthetic admiration is silly, while his limited response is realistic. At
the museum of modern art, they look at a machine that makes light
paintings. He rejects it immediately, saying, "There's a break
between painting and this," and walks away. In one of her few
displays of impatience with his limitations, she replies curtly, "No,"
and continues to gaze in fascination. They go to the movies and the
theater; both forms of drama evoke parallels and contrasts with their
situation and generate action that is ambiguous. They go to see
Michel Deville's comedy *Benjamin* (1968) where the hero (Pierre
Clementi), an innocent young man, is initiated into the ways of love
as he arranges rendezvous at a garden party. During the flirtatious
dialogue, she begins to exchange glances with the young man seated
on her right; her husband, becoming jealous, changes seats with her.
His reaction seems excessive because we are not sure exactly what has
happened. When they go to see a performance of *Hamlet*, the violent
action of the duel, the richness of language, and the powerful
expression of feeling contrast sharply with the inertia and silence of
their lives. Yet the parallels of betrayal and imminent death are very
strong. Hamlet's abortive attempt to kill Claudius as he kneels in
prayer is strikingly parallel to the central episode where the wife is
unable to pull the trigger while the husband lies quietly, perhaps
awaiting death. Hamlet dies assured that Horatio can fulfill his
dying request: "Report me and my cause aright to the unsatisfied."
Although the husband feels compelled to tell her tale, it is impossible
for him to get it right. He also identifies with Hamlet and
soliloquizes: "To sleep, to sleep . . . if I could pray, but I only think."
When they return home from the theater, we know the wife has been
moved by the play, for she immediately runs to the bookcase to check
a passage that was omitted, and says triumphantly: "I was sure of it."
It is Hamlet's advice to the players:

> Speak the speach, I pray you, as I pronounc'd it to you,
> trippingly on the tongue; but if you mouth it, as many of your
> players do, I had as lief the town-crier had spoke my lines. Nor do
> not saw the air too much with your hand, thus, but use all gently;
> for in the very torrent, tempest, and, as I may say, the whirlwind
> of passion, you must acquire and beget a temperance that may
> give it smoothness. (III, ii, 11. 1-9)

The last line illuminates the gap between her experience and behavior—a tempest of passion beneath a gentle, smooth surface.

Television images also introduce dangerous action into their lives. At the touch of a button, auto races, horse races, and a terrific airplane battle suddenly appear in their small apartment; all of this motion and excitement, however, is domesticated by being contained within the narrow confines of the T. V. screen. These images also affect our interpretation of the strange scene on the freeway where the husband slams on his brakes, narrowly avoiding an accident. Instead of responding tensely in the context of the argument that's already going on, they surprise us by breaking into spontaneous laughter, echoing their only other outburst of laughter—on their wedding night when they were watching the auto races on television; in both cases, these static people apparently find motion and danger exhilarating. This missing element is established in the opening image behind the titles where the camera, situated in a moving car, races through the brightly lit boulevards of nighttime Paris.

The longing for freedom and motion is carried out in the bird imagery. The wife is associated with flight through the blue birds on her robe, her mournful singing, and the white shawl that suggests the poignance of lost freedom as it floats through the air just after she jumps off the balcony. The scene in which birds are most significant in relation to the question of freedom versus entrapment takes place as the husband offers his escape fantasy of going on a holiday where everything will be different. Significantly, the white shawl is draped over the chair where he sits, ironically linking his hopeful dialogue to lost freedom and to her suicide. The wife expresses her uncertainty by quoting from a book she happens to be reading: "It is fairly certain that every bird is predisposed to sing like its species." When he persists in seeing the trip as the "final solution" to their problems, she pursues her doubts: "But we ourselves won't be new. Can people change?" Without hesitation he answers: "Entirely." This scene is particularly effective in developing their role reversal not only in the sado-masochistic love relationship, but also in terms of their attitudes toward future possibilities. The husband formerly valued a static predictability; now he wildly argues for the possibility of change and growth. The wife began with greater hope that she could transcend the limitations of her blood and "sinister" background through her hard-won education and her marriage. One of the few experiences she tried to share with her husband is her delight in the discovery at the Museum of Natural History that men, mice, elephants and other animals are all made "from the same raw material, though differently arranged." This reinforces her belief that it is possible to "rearrange" the self, escaping the limitations of her present condition. The poignance of this sequence results from her relinquishing this open-ended vision and adopting the view that the individual is totally determined by genetic history and environment.

The triumph of entrapment over freedom is confirmed in the image of the model airplane (the mechanical bird, a sign of man's "progress") confined in the window of the travel agency where the husband goes, right before the suicide, to pursue his escape fantasy. The film cuts immediately to a shot of the wife's robe with the blue birds being laid out on the bed as she prepares for her final escape into death. Paradoxically, her suicide can be seen as an act of freedom. Although her death is predetermined in the opening scene of the film, we watch her choose it voluntarily, as she kisses the gold crucifix that first brought her into the pawnbroker's trap and smiles at her own reflection in the mirror as if to reassure herself that she has made the right decision and has God's grace.

Skinner and Laing could provide two quite contrary interpretations of the woman's suicide, just as they did for Giuliana's survival. While Laing would be far more useful in illuminating the pervasive mystification of her actions, a Skinnerian might argue that this very quality results from a muddled understanding of behavior inherent in the literature of freedom and dignity.

Though the mysteriousness of behavior is central to the film, Skinner would have to dismiss the husband's attempts to understand his wife's emotions. This effort would be useless to the behaviorist, who asserts that feelings do not cause actions:

> What is felt when a person protests is usually called resentment, significantly defined as "the expression of indignant displeasure," but we do not protest *because* we feel resentful. We both protest *and* feel resentful because we have been deprived of the chance to be admired or to receive credit.[24]

But, until her suicide, which indicates a massive rejection of her situation, the wife protests very little. Does this mean that she feels only a little resentful? Skinner argues that freedom is based on an avoidance or escape from the aversive features of the environment, yet these aversive qualities cannot be readily perceived in the film unless we acknowledge the existence of an interior reality. The husband gives her food, shelter, and material comfort that far exceeds that of her "sinister background." The silence in which they live is more oppressive than a prison cell and the inexplicable shifts in the husband's behavior are highly unsettling. We condemn the husband for the destruction wrought by his mysterious behavior, yet Skinner argues that, perversely, such behavior has traditionally been interpreted as a source of value: "The amount of credit we give is inversely proportional to the conspicuousness of the causes of his behavior."[25] A Skinnerian would probably conclude that we, who have been corrupted by the literature of freedom and dignity, value the wife more highly than the husband *because* her behavior is even more mysterious than his.

Skinner might direct us to the environment and past conditioning to explain the wife's suicide. The art that is so important in revealing her inner state throughout the film might be interpreted as the primary source of negative conditioning. Did misguided tragic heroes like Hamlet or Faust teach her the disfunctional alternative of suicide? Did her admiration for nude paintings somehow mislead her into thinking that she was more than a body? In the scene where the husband works on his puzzle while his wife moodily listens to music, Skinner's ideas could be used to support the husband's smug pleasure at their disparity, for he is involved in problem-solving and creativity while she is passively responding to someone else's creation. Like one of Skinner's cultural designers, the husband is the active manipulator who, in trying to control his wife's behavior, is also controlled by the environment he creates.

> The principle of making the controller a member of the group he controls should apply to the designer of a culture. A person who designs a piece of equipment for his own use presumably takes the interest of the user into account, and the person who designs a social environment in which he is to live will presumably do the same.[26]

Having designed his role as money lender to increase his power, he is trapped because his wife is disgusted by it. The morning after their joyous wedding night, in order to consolidate his control, he consciously throws "Cold water on that bliss;" but of course, he, too, must live in that dampened atmosphere. He creates an atmosphere of silence to manipulate her, but is also oppressed by it. Finally, he dreams of escaping his past conditioning and the world he has created by a simple change of environment. But by this time his wife believes that such escape and transformation are impossible. She has lost faith in the existential view that the individual can shape his own identity and accepts the Skinnerian assumption that a person is a member of a species shaped by evolutionary contingencies of survival and controlled by the environment in which he lives. This realization is intolerable to her, and she commits suicide, implying that survival itself is not the ultimate value. From a Skinnerian perspective, this is a far less progressive or "sane" adaptation than Giuliana's at the end of *Red Desert*. But in attacking the "meaning and scientific status of Skinner's claims," Noam Chomsky insists:

> It would be absurd to conclude merely from the fact that freedom is limited, that "autonomous man" is an illusion, or to overlook the distinction between a person who chooses to conform, in the face of threat or force or deprivation, and a person who "chooses" to obey Newtonian principles as he falls from a high tower.[27]

Again the issue is freedom. The woman in *Une Femme Douce*, instead of conforming, chooses her death and in this sense does achieve a kind of autonomy. By trying to explain a complex situation with self-consciously simplified terminology, Skinner's approach tends to ignore subtleties and acknowledge the existence of only those parts of a phenomenon that will work in his system, in much the same way that the husband restricts the experience of his wife.

> Skinnerian translation, which is easily employed by anyone, leads to a significant loss of precision, for the simple reason that the full range of terms for the description and evaluation of behavior, attitude, opinion, and so on, must be "translated" into the impoverished system of terminology borrowed from the laboratory (and deprived of its meaning in translation).[28]

The Politics of Experience is explicitly concerned with the processes that lead to the wife's suicide: the destruction of the potentialities of the child; the interdependency of individuals' experience; the ways that invalidation and mystification can be used to destroy someone else's experience.

> A man can estrange himself from himself by mystifying himself
> and others. He can also have what he does stolen from him by the
> agency of others. If we are stripped of experience, we are stripped
> of our deeds. . . . Men can and do destroy the humanity of other
> men, and the condition of this possibility is that we are
> interdependent.[29]

In longing to escape the material and emotional poverty of her
childhood, the wife is lured by the husband into a marriage that turns
out to be an extension of the same destructive trap. The husband is
also trapped into experiential poverty by his own self-mystification.
Distraught at his wife's singing (which seems to deny his existence),
he transforms his anger into joy without ever understanding his true
condition. He steals her experience, too, when he declares his love
and congratulates her on the "cleverness" with which he claims she
rejected the boy in the car, thus denying her rebellion, the guilt she
has been suffering, and her hope/fear that he would leave her for this
infidelity. Laing sees this kind of invalidation as one of our culture's
primary means of negation: "We are effectively destroying ourselves
by violence masquerading as love."[30] It is particularly damaging in
interpersonal relations between a man and woman:

> He may *invalidate* her experience. This can be done more or less
> radically. He can indicate merely that it is unimportant or
> trivial, whereas it is important and significant to her. Going
> further, he can shift the *modality* of her experience from memory
> to imagination: "It's all in your imagination." Further still, he
> can invalidate the *content:* "It never happened that way. . . ." In
> order for such transpersonal invalidation to work, however, it is
> advisable to overlay it with a thick patina of mystification.[31]

Even in his grossest distortions, the husband is totally dependent
upon the wife for a sense of identity and power. After the murder
attempt, as his wife lies overcome with illness, he breaks the silence,
crying urgently: "I'm here alive. That's me, look!" Most literally, he
is assuring her that she has not killed him, but he also tries to hold her
back from death by asserting his own continued existence, of which
she is a part.

We do not intend to take an excluding position that denies the
many clinical benefits of a behaviorist psychology. In fact, it is the
restrictive quality of Skinnerian theory that renders it less useful in
understanding complex persons and situations in both life and art.
Unlike Skinner, whose psychology is constructed only in terms of
behavior and the control of individuals, Laing's view of human

beings is inclusive. He wants to integrate behavior and experience, and argues for a science based on the relationship among persons:

> In a science of persons, I shall state as axiomatic that: behavior is a function of experience; and both experience and behavior are always in relation to someone or something other than the self. . . .[32]

This integrative view is crucial to illuminating the worlds of *Red Desert* and *Une Femme Douce*. Further, it is an essential element in transformalist criticism, which tries to incorporate two sets of apparent polarities: 1) the uniqueness of a work of art *and* its relations with other works and with the culture in which they exist; 2) attention to the work as an external artifact *and* to the experiential dimension of the film viewing process.

Footnotes to Chapter Three

1. R. D. Laing, *The Politics of Experience* (New York: Pantheon Books, 1967), p. 51.
2. B. F. Skinner, *Beyond Freedom and Dignity* (New York: Alfred A. Knopf, 1971), pp. 191, 200, 215.
3. Laing, p. 33.
4. Skinner, pp. 163-164.
5. Laing, p. 99.
6. Skinner, pp. 164-165.
7. In an interview, he said of Giuliana: "It is a character that participates in the story as a function of her femininity; her feminine aspect and character are the essential things for me." "Night, Eclipse, Dawn: An Interview with Michelangelo Antonioni by Jean-Luc Godard," *Cahiers du Cinema*, no. 1 (January 1966), p. 28.
8. Antonioni, p. 26.
9. Antonioni, p. 20.
10. B. F. Skinner, *Walden Two* (New York: Macmillan Co., 1962), p. 145.
11. Skinner, *Beyond Freedom and Dignity*, p. 193.
12. Laing, pp. 91, 20.
13. Laing, pp. 47-48.
14. Laing, pp. 70, 83-84.
15. E. Kraepelin, *Lectures on Clinical Psychology*, ed. T. Johnstone (London: Bailliere, Tindall and Cox, 1906), pp. 30-31, as quoted by Laing, p. 73. Italics are Laing's.
16. Laing, p. 79.
17. Doris Lessing's *Briefing for a Descent into Hell* (New York: Alfred A. Knopf, 1971), a brilliant novel that dramatizes many of Laing's theories, offers a fascinating extension of the basic situation in *Red Desert*. The central

character is a university professor experiencing a "psychotic break" that enables him to go beyond the restrictions imposed by conventional society. While confined in a mental hospital, he struggles to maintain his wakefulness and pursue his inner journey, but he is constantly drugged by the doctors who want to lull him back into the malleable condition first imposed upon him as an infant. The novel ends with the madman "cured" after agreeing to electro-shock therapy, but it is clear that Lessing sees this cure as a failure and a tragic return to the limitations and distortions of normality. On the final page, we find an "Afterword, or End-Paper: A Small, Relevant Reminiscence:"

> Some years ago I wrote a story for a film. This story was the result of a close friendship with a man whose senses were different from the normal person's.... The point of this film was that the hero's or protagonist's extra sensitivity and perception must be a handicap in a society organized as ours is, to favour the conforming, the average, the obedient. The script was shown to various filmmakers, several of whom toyed lengthily with the idea of doing it—as is the way of that industry, but they all asked the same question: What is wrong with the man in the film? (p. 307)

    18. Laing, pp. 92-93.
    19. Paul Schrader, *Transcendental Style in Film: Ozu, Bresson, Dreyer* (Berkeley: University of California Press, 1972), pp. 60,93.
    20. Fyodor Dostoevsky, "A Gentle Spirit," in *The Eternal Husband and Other Stories,* trans. Constance Garnett (New York: Macmillan Co., 1950), p. 285.
    21. Dostoevsky, p. 320.
    22. Dostoevsky, p. 285.
    23. Schrader, p. 66.
    24. Skinner, *Beyond Freedom and Dignity,* p. 54.
    25. Skinner, *Beyond Freedom and Dignity,* p. 58.
    26. Skinner, *Beyond Freedom and Dignity,* p. 172.
    27. Noam Chomsky, "The Case Against B. F. Skinner," *New York Review of Books,* XVII, no. 11 (Dec. 30, 1971), p. 23.
    28. Chomsky, p. 22.
    29. Laing, p. 13.
    30. Laing, p. 36.
    31. Laing, pp. 18-19.
    32. Laing, pp. 9-10.

RED DESERT. The powerful cloud of steam that rushes out of the factory dwarfs the figures of Corrado and Ugo, drowns out their conversation, and totally dominates the viewer's experience. Courtesy of Rizzoli Films.

RED DESERT. The tiny red shack crowds the people together into a forced intimacy that reveals the submerged sexual tensions and emotional dynamics and that separates the group from all outsiders. Courtesy of Rizzoli Films.

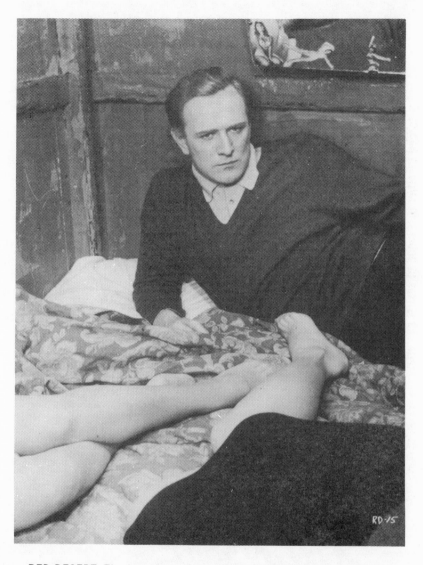

RED DESERT. The bare legs of the women push Corrado up against the wall, under a photograph of pinups in similar seductive poses.
Courtesy of Rizzoli Films.

RED DESERT. As inhibitions weaken and more flesh is exposed, Giuliana and Corrado are forced together in a mood of sexual hysteria. Courtesy of Rizzoli Films.

UNE FEMME DOUCE. The value of objects is magnified in the husband's perception. He appraises the Christ on a gold cross, which his future wife tries to pawn in their first encounter.
Courtesy of New Yorker Films.

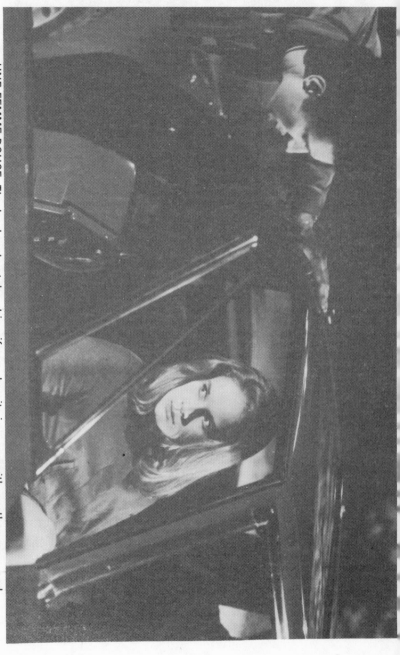

UNE FEMME DOUCE. The husband catches his wife as she sits in a car with another man, and the camera catches one of the rare expressions of anger on her face. The composition emphasizes her entrapment as her husband looms over her and blocks her escape from the confining car. Courtesy of New Yorker Films.

UNE FEMME DOUCE. When they visit the Museum of Natural History, her position reveals her fascination with the fossils while his posture reveals his indifference. As both the dangling bones and the couple are displayed behind the glass, we accept her discovery that "all animals are made from the same raw materials, though differently arranged."

Courtesy of New Yorker Films.

UNE FEMME DOUCE. He stands slightly above her on the stairway, his body framed by the doorway as if he were the official guardian, approving all comings and goings. Courtesy of New Yorker Films.

4

Subject and Object in *Last Year at Marienbad* and *The Exterminating Angel:* A Mutual Creation

> *Even if many objects are presented and are described with great care, there is always, and especially, the eye which sees them, the thought which reexamines them, the passions which distort them.*
>
> Alain Robbe-Grillet, "New Novel, New Man"

Last Year at Marienbad (1961) and *Exterminating Angel* (1962) are unconventional films presenting visual surfaces that are rich but extremely baffling. The situations and plots are so bizarre that they can hardly be taken literally. The characters are impersonal and unlikable, preventing the audience from slipping into an easy emotional identification. They are trapped in time and in the formalized patterns of a decadent society, as we in the audience are trapped in the intricacies of surface and structure. If we are to derive any meaning from the films, we cannot remain passive; we are forced into an active collaboration in which our response and interpretation are essential.

These films come together with phenomenological criticism in that they are all primarily concerned with the relation between consciousness and its objects. Phenomenology tries to reconcile the split between mind and matter, self and other, inner and outer reality, bi-polarities which express our ancient uncertainty about the existence of the external world. It transcends these dichotomies by defining reality as a subject perceiving an object. Thus the world as it is experienced exists for them in consciousness, which always has a subjective and an objective dimension.

In the context of aesthetics, we will be drawing on the work of the French literary phenomenologists, especially Georges Poulet, Jean-Paul Sartre, and Alain Robbe-Grillet (who wrote the screenplay for *Marienbad*). They place the locus of art, not in the object or work itself, but in the coincidence of the reader/critic's consciousness and that of the artist as manifest in the work. The experience of art is unique in that the work (an object) is the means by which two subjects—the consciousness of the artist and that of the reader/viewer— are united in a "conjoint effort—the synthesis of perception and creation."[1] Words and images incarnate the artist's consciousness and make it available to others. Poulet describes the process:

> The work forms the temporary mental substance which fills my consciousness. . . . Such is the characteristic condition of every work which I summon back into existence by placing my consciousness at its disposal. I give it not only existence, but awareness of existence. . . . So long as it is animated by this vital inbreathing inspired by the act of reading, a work of literature becomes (at the expense of the reader whose own life it suspends) a sort of human being.[2]

Thus criticism itself is a work of art. The critic participates in creating the work by embodying in a new form the themes which are already present in it. The phenomenologists define criticism as "consciousness of consciousness" or literature about art.

But while it gains creative status, phenomenological criticism must sacrifice certain traditional assumptions: the humanistic search for anthropomorphism and ulterior meaning, and the security of a linear view of history. Distinguishing between cosmic time (that of science and public reference) and subjective time (that of the individual's experience of the world), Husserl affirms that time is accessible only through the present moment of consciousness. Memory and imagination, rather than constituting other tenses or modes, exist only as components of present consciousness. But the mind is not wholly absorbed in the moment; it becomes aware that the present is now, that there have been other "nows," and that time is a continuous flow. Duration, then, is made up of variations in the contents of the consciousness, which may include anticipations of the future and memories of the past. Robbe-Grillet realizes that cinema is particularly well-suited to express this view of time:

> Whereas literature has a whole gamut of grammatical tenses which makes it possible to narrate events in relation to each other, one might say that on the screen verbs are always in the present tense ... by its nature, what we see on the screen *is in the act of happening*, we are given the gesture itself, not an account of it. ... The total cinema of our mind admits both in alternation and to the same degree the present fragments of reality proposed by sight and hearing, and past fragments, or future fragments, or fragments that are completely phantasmagoric.[3]

The very act of examining consciousness liberates perception from historical custom, prejudice, assumption, and tradition. Poulet focuses on the creative potential of this attitude:

> Each instant appears as the instant of a choice, that is to say of an act; and the root of this act is a creative decision. ... The mind ... must recognize in its act of creation an act of annihilation; it must create its very nothingness in order to give itself a being.[4]

Most phenomenological artists and critics focus on the surface of things, the sensory data (particularly visual) provided by objects since, they argue, only this is known. This approach results in an emphasis on showing rather than telling, on description rather than explanation.

> To describe things, as a matter of fact, is deliberately to place oneself outside them, confronting them. It is no longer a matter of appropriating them to oneself, or projecting anything onto them. ... To limit oneself to description is obviously to reject all the other modes of approaching the object: sympathy as unrealistic, tragedy as alienating, comprehension as answerable to the realm of science exclusively.[5]

Robbe-Grillet implies that a person can most fully realize the potentialities of life by seeing himself as separate from the objects around him—as only one inhabitant of the universe he perceives.

> Objects will gradually lose their instability and their secrets, will renounce their pseudo-mystery, that suspect interiority which Roland Barthes has called "the romantic heart of things." No longer will objects be merely the vague reflection of the hero's vague soul, the image of his torments, the shadow of his desires.[6]

Free from the burdens and confusions of illusory relationships, with which we try to bridge the void between self and other, we accept things as they are and find the world adequate to our needs.

> To reject our so-called "nature" and the vocabulary which perpetuates its myth, to propose objects as purely external and superficial, is not—as has been claimed—to deny man; but it is to reject the "pananthropic" notion contained in traditional humanism, and probably in all humanism. It is no more in the last analysis than to lay claim, quite logically, to my freedom.[7]

This freedom, which is one of the most important values in French literary phenomenology, is interpreted differently by Robbe-Grillet and Sartre, particularly concerning how the artist uses it. Sartre identifies social freedom as an essential part of the creative process, involving both artist and audience.

> The appearance of the work of art is a new event which cannot *be explained* by anterior data. And since this directed creation is an absolute beginning, it is therefore brought about by the freedom of the reader, and by what is purest in that freedom. Thus, the writer appeals to the reader's freedom to collaborate in the production of his work. . . . The more we experience our freedom, the more we recognize that of the other; the more he demands of us, the more we demand of him.[8]

Although he acknowledges that art "is one thing and morality a quite different one," he nevertheless insists that "at the heart of the aesthetic imperative we discern the moral imperative."[9] Thus, freedom becomes a political issue and is prescribed as an essential theme for all good art.

> It would be inconceivable that this unleashing of generosity provoked by the writer could be used to authorize an injustice, and that the reader could enjoy his freedom while reading a work which approves or accepts or simply abstains from condemning the subjection of man by man.[10]

Robbe-Grillet rejects this view of freedom because it prescribes themes to the artist and restricts innovation.

> Sartre, who had seen the danger of this moralizing literature, advocated a *moral* literature, which claimed only to awaken political awareness by stating the problems of our society, but which would escape the spirit of propaganda by returning the reader to his liberty. Experience has shown that this too was a utopia: once there appears the concern to signify something (something external to art), literature begins to retreat, to disappear.[11]

Instead, he argues for a purely aesthetic freedom that is manifested in a perpetual experimentation in form. He insists that in all media and historical periods, forms have lived and died and must be continually renewed.

> The discovery of reality will continue only if we abandon outworn forms. Unless we suppose that the world is henceforth entirely discovered . . . we can only attempt to go farther. It is not a question of "doing better," but of advancing in ways as yet unknown, in which a new kind of writing becomes necessary. . . . Nothing, in art, is ever won *for good.* Art cannot exist without this permanent condition of being *put in question.* But the movement of these evolutions and revolutions constitutes its perpetual renaissance.[12]

In exploring *Last Year at Marienbad* and *Exterminating Angel,* we will focus on four concerns central to phenomenology: the relationship between subject and object, subjective time, surface textures, and freedom. Though we will attend carefully to the surfaces of both films, we will also explore their implications and how they embody statements about the nature of both aesthetic and social freedom. Consciously created from a phenomenological perspective, *Marienbad* grew out of a collaboration between Alain Resnais, an important director in the French New Wave, and Alain Robbe-Grillet, the phenomenological critic and leader of the French New Novel who was making his debut in cinema. *Exterminating Angel* was directed by Luis Buñuel, who began in the twenties making films embodying the surrealist aesthetic, which bears certain similarities to that of literary phenomenology. In describing *Un Chien Andalou,* Buñuel rejected anterior significance of objects and events, insisting that "nothing in this film symbolizes anything." He explained that he and Salvador Dali, his collaborator, purposely chose images that could be separated from memory and cultural associations. Also an *avant-garde* movement struggling against the prevailing conventions, surrealism tried to create a new consciousness by the surprising integration of a highly realistic surface texture and the irrational world of the subconscious. The camera could be used to record the appearance of objects and events with an accuracy far surpassing what was possible in any other medium. But through its capacity for discontinuities of time and space, and its various illusionary devices, the cinema was "the superior way of expressing the world of dreams, emotions and instincts."[13] Echoing Buñuel's statement, Robbe-

Grillet acknowledges that cinema is uniquely suited to the goals of artists working within a phenomenological aesthetic.

> They do not conceive of cinema as a means of expression, but of exploration, and what most captures their attention is, quite naturally, what has most escaped the powers of literature . . . the possibility of presenting with all the appearance of incontestable objectivity what is, also, only dreams or memory—in a word, what is only imagination.[14]

Last Year at Marienbad (1961)

The basic situation in *Marienbad* concerns a man (X, played by Giorgio Albertazzi) who is trying to persuade a woman (A, played by Delphine Seyrig) that they met and perhaps had a romance last year at the resort hotel at Marienbad. He insists that she promised to leave M (perhaps her husband, played by Sacha Pitoeff) and go away with him in a year's time (the present of the film). The setting is an enormous baroque hotel, surrounded by formal gardens, where the anonymous idle rich follow the strict patterns of their lives.

One of the most fascinating elements of this film is its attempt to embody concretely the phenomenological concept of the relationship between subject and object. On the one hand, the film is extremely subjective, consisting entirely of images in a consciousness, which may be perceived, remembered, or imagined, which may belong to one or several persons, and which may be expressed in conversation or interior monologue. Yet, on the other hand, the surface of the film is extraordinarily objective; the contents of consciousness are tangible percepts rather than abstract concepts or feelings—specific phrases, people arranged like objects, statues, furniture, ornaments, sounds like running water and crunching gravel. This double quality is expressed in the opening sequence, particularly in the way the narrator, X, is introduced. We hear him describing highly concrete images at the same time that the camera moves through the luxurious corridors of the hotel. Yet the visual images and his description do not coincide. We in the audience experience through both sight and sound a catalogue of fragmented percepts—"silent deserted corridors overloaded with a dim, cold ornamentation or woodwork, stucco, moldings, marble, black mirrors, dark paintings, columns, heavy hangings, sculptured door frames."[15] The man's rambling monologue and the freely moving camera suggest the unpredictable quality of an individual consciousness, but belonging to someone we have not yet seen. Then the camera moves inside a room where a play is being performed. Although both actors and audience are frozen like statues, the moving camera seems to be linked with the narrator who presumably has just entered the scene. His monologue is interrupted by the voice of a woman while the camera pans the audience. At first we don't know who is talking, but then we realize it is the actress speaking her lines in the play, only for that moment X assumes the role of the actor—the boundary between external conversation and interior monologue breaks down. From the perspective of the entire movie, we realize that this conversation between the actor and actress is a variation of X's interaction with A, whom he is trying to persuade to leave with him at the end of the film and whom we first see in this scene as a member of the frozen audience. When we finally see X for the first time, he is standing in the left foreground and in the right background is a mirror, in which we see at some distance the reflection of a couple talking.

> MAN: The others? Who are the others? Don't be so worried about what they are thinking.
> WOMAN: You know perfectly well. . . .
> MAN: I know you said you would listen to no one but me.
> WOMAN: I am listening to you.
>
> (p. 30)

Despite the fact that we both see and hear the couple talking, it becomes clear that *they* are the "others" to X, the man silent beside them who is the subject, the consciousness in which this conversation is taking place. In fact, this conversation (in which a man tries to persuade a woman) is a variation of his interaction with A, whom he is trying to convince he met last year at Marienbad. Throughout the film, the dialogue of the minor characters echoes that of X and A.

> Really, that seems incredible. . . .
> We've already met, long ago. . . .
> I don't remember very well. It must have been in '28 or '29.
>
> (p. 32)

Perhaps this dialogue reflects X's subjective distortion of phenomena around him, or expresses the idea that everything—characters, setting, dialogue—is the creation of his imagination and memory. The unconventional opening establishes the fact that nothing in the film has autonomous existence apart from the perceiving consciousness. The reflective quality of the dialogue suggests that consciousness (where self and other coexist) may be at every moment creating "other" in the image of self.

This fusion of subject and object is exemplified in the statues that are important throughout the film. Fixed and frozen in marble like the characters who often seem frozen in space, the statues also lend themselves to interpretation or recreation by each consciousness that encounters them. As we see a stone grouping of a man, woman, and dog in a sequence of stationary shots taken from a great variety of angles, X tells A of a past encounter:

> To say something, I talked about the statue. I told you that the man wanted to keep the young woman from venturing any farther: he had noticed something—no doubt a danger—and he stopped his companion with a gesture of his hand. You answered that it was actually the woman who seemed to have seen something—but something marvelous—in front of them, which she was pointing to. But this was not incompatible: the man and the woman have left their country, journeying on for days. They have just reached the top of a steep cliff. He is holding back his companion so that she doesn't go near the edge, while she points to the sea, at their feet, stretching to the horizon.
>
> (p. 63)

Their interpretations of the statues are analogous to their different visions of their own relationship—while X offers her protection and freedom, A fears he is leading her into another form of entrapment. The shifting camera angles, the movement from indirect reportage to direct dialogue, and the changes in their clothing reinforce the fluidity of their interpretations. Later, M, her impassive companion whose subjective consciousness we never penetrate, offers an historical interpretation of the statues, presenting it in a manner that suggests it is the objective truth:

> I think I can supply you with some more precise information: this statue represents Charles III and his wife, but it does not date from that period, of course. The scene is that of the oath before the Diet, at the moment of the trial for treason. The classical costumes are purely conventional. . . .
>
> (p. 69)

Both Resnais and Robbe-Grillet deny the fixed, pseudo-objective quality of M's vision and both emphasize the emblematic power of this sequence for the entire film.

> RESNAIS: We wanted to feel ourselves in the presence of a sculpture which one studies first from one angle, then from another, from near or farther away.[16]

> ROBBE-GRILLET: One can think of *Marienbad* as a documentary about a statue: with "interpretative" glimpses of gestures and constant returns to the gestures as they endure, "frozen," by the sculpture. Imagine a documentary which centered on a statue with two people, and succeeded in combining a series of shots, taken from different angles and by various camera-movements, so as to tell a complete story. And in the end we realize that we have returned to our starting point, the statue itself.[17]

This sculptured quality is expressed throughout the film in composition, in the omnipresence of marble and plaster statuary and ornament, and in X's comments (particularly significant in the opening and closing) that are repeated throughout the film:

> Forever in a marble past, like these statues, this garden carved out of stone, this hotel itself . . . its motionless characters . . .
>
> (p. 95)

Like the statues, the hotel setting and the obsessive efforts of the narrator are fixed in patterns—object and subject mutually reflecting the frozen, trapped quality of consciousness that pervades the film. The labyrinthine nature of X's perceptions, memory, and imagination is reflected in the patterned gardens that appear to be orderly and predictable, but that are slightly altered in different shots. In his final speech, X acknowledges this:

> Gravel, stone, marble and straight lines marked out rigid spaces, surfaces without mystery. It seemed, at first glance, impossible to get lost here . . . at first glance . . . down straight paths, between the statues with frozen gestures and the granite slabs, where you were now already getting lost, forever, in the calm night, alone with me.
>
> (p. 165)

The sense of entrapment is heightened by the physical characteristics of the hotel, and by the fragmented, ritualistic behavior of its inhabitants as perceived by X:

> There were always walls—everywhere, around me—smooth, even, glazed, without the slightest relief, there were always walls . . . and silence too. I have never heard anyone raise his voice in this hotel—no one. . . . The conversations developed in the void, as if the sentences meant nothing, were intended to mean nothing in any case. And a sentence, once begun, suddenly remained in suspension, as though frozen by the frost. . . . But

starting over afterwards, no doubt, at the same point, or
elsewhere. It didn't matter. It was always the same conversations
that recurred, the same absent voices.

(pp. 89-90)

Just as we have seen experience frozen within the hotel by other
forms of art (the statues, gardens, maps, paintings), the film also
traps consciousness into a circular structure. *Marienbad* opens with a
"Romantic, passionate, violent burst of music, the kind used at the
end of films with powerfully emotional climaxes." (p. 17). X enters a
theater, just as a play is ending:

> ACTRESS: This whole story is already over now. It came to an
> end—a few seconds . . . more—it has come to a close.
> ACTOR: . . . forever—in a past of marble, like these statues, this
> garden carved out of stone—this hotel itself with its halls
> deserted now, its motionless, mute servants long since dead no
> doubt, who still stand guard at the corners of the corridors, along
> the galleries, in the deserted salons, through which I walked to
> meet you, as if I were passing between two hedges of motionless
> faces, frozen, watchful, indifferent, while I was already waiting
> for you, forever, and while I am still staring at the door to this
> garden . . .
> ACTRESS: Very well. Now I am yours. . . .

(pp. 24-26)

The actor's long speech is strikingly similar to the final speech by X
already quoted; but the opening and closing sequences offer even
more exact parallels.

> **Opening**
> ACTRESS: We must still wait—a few minutes—more—no more
> than a minute, a few seconds.
> X: A few seconds more, as if you yourself were still hesitating
> before separating from him . . . from yourself . . . as if his
> silhouette . . .

(p. 24)

> **Closing**
> A: A few hours is all I'm asking you for.
> X: a few months, a few hours, a few minutes. (A pause) A few
> seconds more . . . as if you were still hesitating before separating
> from him . . . from youself . . . as if his silhouette. . .

(p. 151)

At the end of the film, as they are waiting to leave, the play from the
opening is being performed (again? still?), enclosing the film in an

endless circle, implying that they never really escape from the frozen pattern. Whereas in the play it is very clear that the woman has agreed to go off with the man, the ending of the film creates greater ambiguity by returning to the opening. Rejecting the conventional dramatic structure of the well-made play with its beginning, middle, and end, this film adopts a phenomenological structure with a series. of successive "nows." Robbe-Grillet acknowledges that we can never be certain of the future:

> It is impossible for the author to reassure a spectator concerned about the fate of the hero after the words "The End." After the words "The End" nothing at all happens, by definition. The only future which the work can accept is a new identical performance: by putting the reels back in the projection camera.[18]

The repetitive circularity of the film's structure is also manifest in the game played by X and M. Objects are arranged in rows of 7, 5, 3, and 1; the person forced to remove the last object is the loser. According to Resnais:

> Apparently it is very ancient; the Chinese played it three thousand years before Jesus Christ. It was the game of Nim, of which Robbe-Grillet has invented a variation without even knowing it existed. . . . My personal impression is that when Albertazzi [X] loses it is consciously and deliberately. Perhaps through sheer unconcern.[19]

In the original game, the player who makes the first move must lose; but Robbe-Grillet changes the rules and makes X the loser no matter who moves first. M tells X: "I can lose . . . but I always win" (p. 39). Thus the game ironically combines the possibility of freedom with the actuality of entrapment. The symmetrical pattern within the game controls much of the visual imagery throughout the film: we frequently see objects and characters arranged in parallel rows. In one striking shot, two men play checkers in the extreme foreground while the background is devoted to the large squares of a black and white checkered floor, and parallel rows of columns, growing smaller as they recede into the extreme depth of the background. In another shot X and A are seated side by side in the foreground; M walks into the background, forming the point of a triangle, while servants move in and out between them as if to fill in the other rows of the game pattern. In many scenes the manicured hedges of the formal gardens are similarly arranged. In the final image of the film we see the dark expanse of the hotel façade and its reflection in a pool; eight windows, grouped in three rows, are lighted asymmetrically, as if they are objects left on the table in the middle of the game.

Like the statues, the game is emblematic of the whole film and its central situation. Allusions to games and other forms of conventionalized amusement are frequent—checkers, the pistol range, the concert, and the theater performance—as if suggesting that in the world of Marienbad life is a game involving control, risk, rules, and competition. Resnais sees the game and the film as related in that both require

> the necessity of making a decision. Of course, the charcters, while playing, may be allowing themselves a few moments' reflection while arriving at their decisions. In any case, the whole thing is possibly a part of the woman's stream of consciousness, as, on the point of deciding what to do, she recalls all the various factors in a few seconds.[20]

The game puts a new perspective on the love triangle. Since the person who is forced to take the last object is the loser, and since the photographs of A are arranged in rows as in the game, we begin to wonder whether this means that whoever winds up with the woman is really the loser. Both X and M constantly tell her it is too late for her to change her mind. In describing their past encounter in her bedroom, X tells A: "Why always try to escape? It's too late. . . . It was already too late" (p. 125). When A urges M, "Don't let me go," he replies simply: "You know it's too late. Tomorrow I'll be alone" (p. 157). At what point in the game or in the love triangle is it determined who will win? Within the game, the usual sign is the situation where three objects are left, each in a separate row. Within the love triangle, there is a shot in which we see three images of A (two of which are reflected in a mirror), like three objects in separate rows; then the film cuts suddenly to the image of broken columns, as if suggesting that the moment of decision has been reached. At the end of the film she is left with X, who, as Resnais suggests, deliberately loses.

The same paradoxical combination of freedom and entrapment can be seen in X's attempts to persuade A that they actually met last year at Marienbad. On the one hand, in much of the film it appears that X is trying to impose his fantasy on A and deny her experience. If last year at Marienbad did *not* happen, then her uncertainty and vulnerability imply that she has a weak hold on her own experience and is susceptible to entrapment in his consciousness. Robbe-Grillet sees the film in this way:

> The whole film, as a matter of fact, is the story of a persuasion: it
> deals with a reality which the hero creates out of his own vision,
> out of his own words.[21]

A makes this point explicit.

> You are like a shadow—and you're waiting for me to come
> closer.—Oh, let me alone . . . let me alone!
>
> (p. 105)

On the other hand, if last year at Marienbad *did* take place, then A has
forgotten or repressed the experience in some way, which also renders
her extremely vulnerable to X's persuasion. But if this were the case,
X would actually be offering her a kind of freedom—a repossession of
her own experience and the ability to move outside the frozen
patterns of her life:

> You weren't waiting for anything any more. It was as if you were
> dead. . . . That's not true! You are still alive. . . . You're on the
> point of leaving. The door of your room is still open. . . .
>
> (p. 106)

Robbe-Grillet, too, sees X as offering A an important gift: "He offers
her a past, a future, and freedom."[22] The final speech does not resolve
the paradox of freedom and entrapment. X tells her that they are
already lost within the straight paths and rigid spaces, where getting
lost had seemed impossible. On the one hand, being lost might imply
freedom from pattern and control; on the other, it might suggest
eternal entrapment within the labyrinth.

This paradox applies not only to A, who has been subjected to X's
consciousness, but also to the audience, who has gotten lost within
the labyrinthine structure of the film. Throughout *Marienbad*, A
functions like an audience for X (we first see her in the audience at the
play). He is telling a story and trying to make her believe it has
actually happened. He accepts the phenomenological assumption
that his story will come to life only if she participates by lending her
consciousness to its creation. This is precisely what must happen
between a film-maker and his viewers:

> The only important "character" is the spectator; in his *mind*
> unfolds the whole story, which is precisely *imagined* by him.[23]

Like A, the spectator has the choice of how to interpret the film's
mode of reality:

SELF AND CINEMA

Two attitudes are then possible: either the spectator will try to reconstitute some "Cartesian" schema—the most linear, the most rational he can devise and this spectator will certainly find the film difficult, if not incomprehensible; or else the spectator will let himself be carried along by the extraordinary images in front of him, by the actors' voices, by the sound track, by the music, by the rhythm of the cutting, by the passion of the characters . . . and to this spectator the film will seem the "easiest" he has ever seen: a film addressed exclusively to his sensibility, to his faculties of sight, hearing, feeling. The story told will seem the most realistic, the truest, the one that best coresponds to his daily emotional life, as soon as he agrees to abandon ready-made ideas, psychological analysis, more or less clumsy systems of interpretation which machine-made fiction or films grind out for him *ad nauseam*, and which are the worst kinds of abstractions.[24]

Marienbad has consistently evoked questions of the first type, in which the spectator examines data as if they will yield logical structures of meaning. As Robbe-Grillet complains, frequently these questions try to establish what has happened *in-itself*.

The questions most often asked were: Have this man and this woman really met before? Did they love each other last year at Marienbad? Does the young woman remember and is she only pretending not to récognize the handsome stranger? Or has she really forgotten everything that has happened between them? etc. Matters must be put clearly: such questions have no meaning.[25]

Even if the spectator is unable to determine whether the encounter at Marienbad had existence apart from a perceiving consciousness, "last year" dominates everything.

At first we think that *Marienbad* did not exist, only to realize that we have been there from the beginning. The event which the girl repudiates has, by the end of the film, contaminated everything. So much so that she has never ceased to struggle against it, to believe that she was winning, since she has always rejected everything, and, in the end, she realizes it is all too late, she has, ˙after all, accepted everything. As if everything were true— although probably it isn't. But *true* or *false* have been emptied of meaning.[26]

It is equally impossible to answer the related question: through whose consciousness do we perceive the phenomena? Resnais asserts:

> We never really know if the scenes are occurring in the man's
> mind or the woman's. There is a perpetual oscillation between
> the two. You could even maintain that everything is told from
> her viewpoint.[27]

The bedroom sequence effectively illustrates the techniques by which
Resnais and Robbe-Grillet insist that reality has no autonomous
definition. Shots of the bar and bedroom alternate with each other
perhaps a dozen times until the various versions of what happened in
the bedroom come to dominate the cross-cutting. Within these shots,
there are many variations: A is dressed in black, she is dressed in
white; she is raped, she is murdered; she welcomes X, she rejects him.
Scenes are shot from every possible angle and at different exposures;
at least one version contains a loop. Frequently, the images on the
screen do not match X's verbal description, reinforcing the suggestion that some of the scenes are seen through A's consciousness
(memory or imagination?). In one version as X describes walking
along a mirror toward a closed door, we in the audience see that the
door is open. Even X's confidence is undermined as the various
discrepancies appear and A accuses him of madness. He finally says:

> He had come in. . . . You had been surprised by his visit. . . . He
> referred to the concert of the night before, I think . . . or else it was
> you who began talking first . . . No . . . No . . . I don't remember
> any more. Don't remember any more myself. I don't remember
> any more.
>
>   (p. 130)

Thus, X, A, and the audience are forced to choose among various
alternatives, reaffirming what may be an uncomfortable freedom.

In the bedroom sequences, as in the entire film, there is also a
fusion of many tenses: past, present, future, conditional. One can try
to sort out these layers of time, using the changes of costume and
setting as clues, or even try to reconstruct the film in chronological
order, as Resnais insists is possible:

> In the editing, this scene follows such and such a scene, but, in
> actual chronology it follows another scene, which will appear
> much later in the film. I frequently recorded a fragment of the
> preceding scene, so as to work from the continuity rather than
> from the cue. This chronological chart was drawn up after the
> scenario was finished. Obviously, all the changes of costume
> correspond to different "layers" of time. That isn't the "key" to
> the film, assuming there is one. But one could edit the film so as

to restore the chronological order of the scenes. One might see
the film as extending over a week, or with all that is shown in the
present tense as taking place from Sunday to Sunday inclusive.
This doesn't stop Robbe-Grillet from saying: "Maybe it all
happens in five minutes."[28]

Yet such an attempt to create a linear structure reflects the very
attitude that Robbe-Grillet has rejected:

> The universe in which the entire film occurs is, characteristically,
> that of a perpetual present which makes all recourse to memory
> impossible. This is a world without a past, a world which is
> self-sufficient at every moment and which obliterates itself as it
> proceeds. . . . The duration of the modern work is in no way a
> summary, a condensed version, of a more extended and more
> "real" duration which would be that of the anecdote, of the
> narrated story. There is, on the contrary, an absolute identity
> between the two durations. The entire story of *Marienbad*
> happens neither in two years nor in three days, but exactly in one
> hour and a half.[29]

The experience of the film supports Robbe-Grillet's approach more
effectively than Resnais'. Frequently, X describes an event that
presumably took place in the past (such as A breaking the heel of her
shoe), and the visuals show us either a different action or later reveal
the same action with A dressed in clothes from the "present." Thus it
is impossible for the spectator to determine whether these scenes take
place in the past, present, or imagination.

Just as the images and events are created for us by both X and A, the
film itself grows out of a collaboration between Robbe-Grillet and
Resnais. Some critics have emphasized the differences between their
conceptions of the film. Stoltzfus goes so far as to assert:

> The meaning of this film is almost diametrically opposed to the
> meaning of Robbe-Grillet's script. What comes through most
> forcefully in the film is a sense of A's final liberation. This
> conincides not only with Resnais' idea that the two had met the
> year before but with his interpretation of the script and
> consequently its filming. For Resnais, A is a young woman
> imprisoned among the bored guests of a luxurious hotel. She is
> like a fairy princess caught in an enchanted castle. The young
> man X rescues her and leads her to something unknown in an
> alive outside world. The final lines of the script, however, negate
> this liberation and Resnais, to be consistent, should have left
> them out. These lines are a capsule summary of Robbe-Grillet's
> philosophic purpose. *Marienbad* like his previous novels, is a
> demonstration, an example of what can happen to those who
> humanize the world about them.[30]

In order to reach such a conclusion, Stoltzfus is forced to rigidify their respective attitudes and to define a single purpose or message for each. Yet one difference is essential: Resnais assumes that the past meeting was real while Robbe-Grillet says it probably was not. Nevertheless, their collaboration achieved an amazing degree of harmony that allowed room for their differences:

> When Resnais and I had our first discussion, we found we had both conceived a cinematic "form" of the same kind. I knew that all my ideas on the Cinema would somehow suit whatever Resnais would set out to achieve from then on. It so happened that he wanted to make the kind of film I had been thinking of. . . . That doesn't stop us from having different ideas about all his films or my novels. But we do seem to have a world in common, which we can both inhabit. There was never any question of compromise between Resnais and myself, but of a common "form" which functioned in the same way for us both, although it's not certain that we both give the same importance to the details. . . . It is quite possible that *Marienbad* isn't exactly the same film for Resnais as it is for me. We must see the world around us rather different, although it's the same world.[31]

From a phenomenological perspective, these different perceptions, far from weakening the film, actually enrich it. Like A's and X's interpretations of the statues, Resnais' and Robbe-Grillet's perceptions of the film ("a documentary about a statue") are different "but not incompatible." The spectator, as creative perceiver, is also involved in the collaboration with the filmmakers. Our discussion of this creative interplay of consciousness is further complicated since it too is a collaboration, recreating some elements of our individual experiences of the film in the medium of verbal criticism.

Marienbad is frequently accused of being a cold film, which fails to evoke an emotional response in its audience. This raises a variety of questions. Does the film intend to arouse such a response? If not, what does it offer instead? What aesthetic or emotional values does it sacrifice, and what new ones does it develop? The film emphasizes not the possibility of emotional identification, but a sharing of consciousness itself. *Marienbad* focuses on perception of objects and events as the primary source of information about states of being; it does not imbue them with qualities analogous to the emotions of the perceiver. But frequently, the unimpassioned and sometimes puzzled witnesses to the film find they experience a belated reaction. The film itself offers an example of this delayed emotionality. In the opening sequence, we see a frozen, impassive audience watching the play. As it ends (when the shared process of creating the play is over), the audience suddenly rises and applauds, the only time in the film when anyone other than A and X displays any emotion whatsoever. The clapping is highly conventional behavior, but the audience uses it to express enthusiasm and approval, and at that moment, they seem to come alive. If this delayed reaction exists (as Robbe-Grillet has asserted and audiences have agreed), and it depends on creative perception, rather than identification, there still must be sources of emotion in the film to give rise to these effects. Robbe-Grillet sees emotionality as the center of the film, however difficult of access:

> The theme is of a passionate love affair and it is precisely these relationships which comprise the highest proportion of inconsistencies, doubts, and phantasms. *Marienbad* is as opaque as the moments we live through in the climaxes of our feeling, in our loves, in our whole emotional life. So to reproach the film for its lack of clarity is really to reproach human feelings for their obscurity.[32]

As the film develops, we understand that like the protagonists of Robbe-Grillet's novels, X is obsessed with last year's encounter and with his need to convince A that it actually took place. He is willing to do violence to her memory and perception to serve his obsession. Robbe-Grillet describes his protagonist as:

> The least neutral, the least impartial of men: *always* engaged, on the contrary, in an emotional adventure of the most obsessive kind, to the point of often distorting his vision and of producing imaginings close to delerium.[33]

X's emotionality is most apparent when he is trying to construct the bedroom sequence, desperately clinging to the details of his vision, and urgently requiring A's agreement:

> A: I'm sure you're making it up . . . I've never had a white robe. You can see it must be someone else. . . . (with a kind of terror): No! Be still. Please. You're completely mad. (A short silence) X: (Gently) No, no, please . . . I hear your voice the way it sounded then. You were afraid, You were already afraid. . . . You've always been afraid. But I loved your fear that evening. (Without losing its softness, his tone gradually becomes more excited.) I watched you, letting you struggle a little . . . I loved you. There was something in your eyes, you were alive . . . finally . . . I took you, half by force.
>
> (p. 115)

This intensity is heightened by the visuals in the bedroom sequence. The camera suddenly pulls back very rapidly and the image of A and X in the bedroom becomes a small rectangle surrounded by blackness, as if reduced to a still photograph. Then there is a sudden cut to a long, deserted corridor in a strange overexposed white lighting; the camera races down the hallway as we hear loud, emotional organ music and X's voice desperately pleading: "No, no, no! (violently): That's wrong. . . . (calmer): It wasn't by force . . ." (p. 147). The camera cuts to an over-exposed shot of A, in her white peignoir, smiling and opening her arms to welcome X who is not visible; this shot is repeated over and over, each time accelerating in pace and drawing closer to her face. Throughout the film the repetition of images in both the visuals and the dialogue (e.g., the garden, the broken shoe, the crunching gravel) convey the obsessive quality of his agitated state.

> If the mind is forced to return over and over again like this to the same mental image, then it must eventually become apparent that this image is of a different epistemological order from the explanations provided for it. Robbe-Grillet's heroes keep on having to return to facts, which will come to transmit a more and more potent emotional charge as the [work] proceeds. Thus the successive appearances of a particular object or image constitute a barometer, a consultation of which allows the reader to measure off the intensity of the imaginative efforts which the narrator is making to finalize his fiction to his own satisfaction.[34]

A's emotional condition is expressed in her impassive voice and gestures; she reveals her agitation through her behavior, such as breaking the glass in the bar. Certain objects become "contaminated" analogues for the breaking down of her emotional control and resistance to X's pressure—the shattered glass, the broken shoe, and the disintegrating columns. The strongest displays of emotion take place when she is trying to resist X's story and finds herself involved. In one scene, as he says, "I loved you, I loved you," she walks backwards toward him, as if his words have a magical power to draw them together. The emotional force is so intense that she staggers and almost falls, but suddenly walks away and then runs forward, the camera racing ahead as if eager to restore her serenity by reaching the peaceful view of the orderly garden.

In this film there is no intense emotional identification as in *Red Desert*, which creates in us a sympathetic attitude toward Giuliana and her perceptual distortions. As a component of the work of art, she becomes a kind of contaminated object for the viewer, who imbues her with his own pain in the same way that the attitude of tragic humanism anthropomorphizes objects. In contrast, *Marienbad's* focus on perception rather than emotion enables us to share the consciousness of the protagonists while maintaining a distance that allows us to be aware of their distortions. Thus, while relinquishing certain customary sources of aesthetic power, it offers a different kind of possibility for audience interest and, indeed, for self development. At the heart of the difference between these aesthetic approaches lies the concept of tragedy, which is the mode Antonioni adopts in *Red Desert*, and which is consciously rejected by Robbe-Grillet, who defines it as:

> An attempt to "recover" the distance which exists between man and things as a new value; it would be then a test, an ordeal in which victory would consist in being vanquished. Tragedy therefore appears as the last invention of humanism to permit nothing to escape: since the correspondence between man and things has finally been denounced, the humanist saves his empire by immediately instituting a new form of solidarity, the divorce itself becoming a major path to redemption.[35]

Like Skinner, Robbe-Grillet sees tragedy as a dangerous reactionary tendency that prevents man from progressing toward a better life.

> Wherever there is distance, separation, doubling, cleavage, there is the possibility of experiencing them as suffering, then of raising this suffering to the height of a sublime necessity. A path toward a metaphysical Beyond, this pseudo-necessity is at the same time the closed door to a realistic future. Tragedy, if it consoles us today, forbids any solider conquest tomorrow. Under the appearance of a perpetual motion, it actually petrifies the universe in a sonorous malediction. There can no longer be any question of seeking some remedy for our misfortune, once tragedy convinces us to love it.[36]

Robbe-Grillet locates the potential for development, not in science of behavior or political reform, but in the free play of individual consciousness (especially the formal experimentation of the artist). But one question persists—are we really able to escape tragedy?

> Today its rule extends to all my feelings and all my thoughts, it conditions me utterly. My body can be satisfied, my heart content, my consciousness remains unhappy. I assert this

> unhappiness is *situated* in space and time, like every unhappi-
> ness, like everything in this world. I assert that man, some day,
> will free himself from it. But of this future I possess no proof....
> This struggle, I shall be told, is precisely the tragic illusion par
> excellence: if I seek to combat the idea of tragedy, I have already
> succumbed to it; and it is so natural to take objects as a refuge ...
> perhaps. But perhaps not.[37]

While it is clear that *Marienbad* does not exhibit the tragic world
view of *Red Desert* (which laments the passing of old values), we also
realize that X and A do not escape the contamination of a "neo-tragic
complicity." With X trapped in his need to affirm the existence and
significance of "reality," *Marienbad* manifests the phenomenological struggle toward freedom of consciousness.

> Does reality have a meaning? The contemporary artist cannot
> answer this question: he knows nothing about it. All he can say
> is that this reality will perhaps have a meaning after he has
> existed, that is, once the work is brought to its conclusion. Why
> regard this as a pessimism? In any case, it is the contrary of a
> reunuciation. We no longer believe in the fixed significations,
> the ready-made meanings which afforded man the old divine
> order and subsequently the rationalist order of the nineteenth
> century, but we project onto man all our hopes: it is the forms
> man creates which can attach significations to the world.[38]

The Exterminating Angel (1962)

In *Exterminating Angel* a group of aristocrats attends a dinner party
in which they find themselves trapped, mysteriously unable to leave
the room in which they spend an indefinite period of time. The
events at the party are interwoven with shots of the outside world,
where a group of spectators (including servants who have inex-
plicably left the mansion) are similarly unable to enter. The trapped
guests abandon civilized forms and behave like savages until they are
suddenly able to leave. After their miraculous escape, they go to the
Church to give proper thanks to the Virgin. Once again, they are
unable to leave, and outside people riot in the streets.

The bizarre nature of the basic situation invites an allegorical
interpretation where we might see the film as depicting the inevitable
breakdown of a civilization based on a corrupt church and class
system. But no matter what symbolic interpretation we may construct, we cannot explain away the perverse tone and the absurd

existential situation. We don't know how or why it happened, but the
fact is, they are trapped in the room. Robbe-Grillet's description of
the basic situation in Beckett's *Waiting for Godot* could also apply to
Exterminating Angel.

> They *are there;* they must explain themselves. . . . Their
> conversation, which no plot sustains, is reduced to ridiculous
> fragments. . . . They try a little bit of everything, at random. The
> only thing they are not free to do is to leave, to cease *being there.* .
> . . They will still be there the next day, the day after that, and so
> on . . . *tomorrow and tomorrow and tomorrow . . . from day to
> day . . .* alone on stage, standing there, futile, without past or
> future, irremediably present.[39]

Like *Marienbad, Exterminating Angel* not only centers on the
theme of entrapment, but implies that the way the guests perceive the
trap shapes their experience within it. The same is true for the
audience as they view this baffling film. The opening images of a
street sign reading, "Calle de la Providence," and an iron gate being
shut immediately inform us that the fates of the characters have been
sealed. *Exterminating Angel* also shares the quality of unpredictability, but instead of being located in discontinuities of time and
perception as in *Marienbad,* here it is expressed through a surprising
absence of causality or motive for the bizarre events.

The most literal trap is spatial—the room that they are unable to
leave. The opening into the next room becomes an invisible wall that
Buñuel and the actors handle with great cleverness. Draped with
black curtains, the doorway between the drawing room and the
darkened space beyond draws our attention like a proscenium arch.
The camera is frequently positioned at the far end of the empty salon,
exaggerating the lonely distance to the crowded drawing room, the
focal point of light and movement in the house where the guests mill
about like souls lost in limbo. The power of the invisible barrier is
emphasized as Buñuel frequently has the camera pan along a row of
guests lined up across the arch. Mysteriously it can be penetrated by
the trash, which is thrown into the next room, transforming the rest
of the house into uninhabitable territory. Determined to walk
through, characters go to the doorway and are distracted, look up to
examine the ceiling, or turn to talk to someone just before they must
confront the barrier. When Blanca, Roc and his wife declare they are
going to leave "right now," they get sidetracked into conversation. As
they talk in the foreground, we see Julio the butler making

preparations in the background space. Then with renewed determination the three guests line themselves in the archway as if ready to
step through. Suddenly Julio appears pushing the laden breakfast
cart in front of him as if it were that and not the barrier that prevented
their exit. After Julio's entrance into the drawing room, the barrier is
sealed to all human passage.

The trapped guests retreat to the even smaller enclosure of the
closets for the basic functions of life such as lovemaking and
excretion. The closets also function as a kind of underworld (or
unconscious, though Buñuel rejects Freudian symbolism) where the
guests receive visions or hallucinations and where they encounter
death:

> SILVIA: I lifted the lid and saw a huge precipice, and at the
> bottom the clear waters of a torrent.
> ANA: Yes, and before I sat down, an eagle flew past a few yards
> below me.
> RITA: And as for me, the wind blew a great whirl of dead leaves
> in my face.[40]

When the Doctor and the Colonel hide the body of Russell (the first
guest to die), they find the lovers Beatrice and Eduardo in the closet;
their strange conversation links lovemaking and death within their
private ritual:

> EDUARDO: This is where the sea flows in . . .
> BEATRICE: I can't . . .
> EDUARDO: Lower . . . There, already . . . the rictus . . . It's
> horrible!
> BEATRICE: My love!
> EDUARDO: My death! Oh, my refuge!
>
>   (p. 150)

The mysterious closets are so dark that we can see little of their
interior; like the guests, the camera is confined primarily to the
drawing room.

The trap also extends outward to include the entire mansion.
When the camera occasionally cuts to outside scenes, we find similar
spatial limitations, this time created by the gates that encircle the
mansion and reinforce the invisible barrier. We frequently see the
bystanders positioned in a horizontal line like the guests inside. At
the end of the film, the trap is extended to the cathedral which, with
all its loftiness, is just as confining as the room. The simultaneous
riots in the streets outside imply that the people are exploding under

the pressure of a trap that includes the entire world of the film. The centrifugal movement extends even to the audience. When we watch a movie, we are always temporarily confined to the theater and the images that appear on the two dimensional screen. But when we go outside we sometimes find that our consciousness has been altered by these new percepts. We now perceive that we too are trapped within a society dominated by corrupt institutions. The very act of creating such a structure of meaning out of the chaotic phenomena is another kind of trap into which we, like the guests, are driven by our rage for order; Buñuel mocks the guests (and us?) for offering such escapist explanations, which are as irrational as the baffling events:

> RAUL: I really don't understand. There must be a solution. Look at me closely. We haven't gone crazy, have we? . . .
> ROC: The attitude of the people outside worries me more than our own situation. What's happened to them? They should have tried something.
> COLONEL: Unless everyone in town has died and we are the last survivors. . . .
> ROC: It's concerned with the servants' leaving. Why did they go?
> NOBILE: Please, gentlemen. You mustn't jump to such alarming conclusions. Er . . . the servants . . . er . . . had their reasons for leaving.
> RAUL: Yes, like rats when the ship is sinking.
> BUTLER: With these gentlemen's permission, I think the servants left without knowing why. (He removes his white gloves.) They were quite happy fifteen minutes before these gentlemen arrived.
> CHRISTIAN: So in the end, nothing explains anything.
> (pp. 145-156)

In all of their behavior, the guests, like those at *Marienbad,* are ultimately trapped in time. *Exterminating Angel* also rejects cosmic (public) time through an almost abstract imprecision. As in most Buñuel films, the time setting is indefinite; in *Exterminating Angel* the period of entrapment is purposely vague. At the beginning, however, the guests try to cling to clock time as a way of maintaining order: Christian comments that "I have an appointment early tomorrow morning . . . (Looks at his watch.) That is to say, in four hours" (p. 132); Eduardo and Beatrice remind each other that they have only five days before their marriage; Raul remarks that "This isn't the first time I've stayed till eight in the morning at a party like this one" (p. 142); Blanca laments that "we've already been here twenty-four hours and nobody has come" (p. 145); the Doctor predicts how long Leonora and Russell have before their hair falls out and they drop dead;

while Ana has an hallucination in which she is pursued by a detached human hand, she hears the exaggerated ticking of a clock that helps to increase the tension. By linking these precise time markings to absurd statements and events, Buñuel mocks the false security of clocks and calendars. The disintegration of the guests' civilized behavior is partly reflected in their relinquishing the precision of clock time and replacing it with subjective, phenomenological time.

> EDUARDO: How long have we been here? More than a month, haven't we?
> BEATRICE: No, not that long. (pause) We wouldn't have survived without eating.
> EDUARDO: I feel as though I've been here forever.
> BEATRICE: Me too.
> EDUARDO: And that we'll be here forever!
>
> (p. 167)

Ultimately, the trap is forever; it encloses the entire film in repetition and circularity, creating a sense of timelessness that can be measured only as the experience of the film's duration.

The characters are also restricted by their cultural patterns, one of the most powerful of which is religion; Buñuel has been attacking this institution for decades. Like Robbe-Grillet's view of tragic humanism, Buñuel sees religion as dangerous because it tantalizes human beings with the false hope that they can escape their animal nature and the finality of death. It promises them an impossible transcendence and prevents them from making the best of what they have. Its deceptive nature is revealed in the scene outside the mansion where a priest urges a child to go through the gates and enter the house. The church official seeks as a scapegoat the one with the greatest innocence and potentiality, a choice he has learned well from Christian mythology. The camera looks down from behind the dark crowd, emphasizing the isolation of the lone child standing in the bright, open, no-man's land. When the boy is unable to break through the barrier, the priest pretends that he has willfully refused and fabricates a perverted moral for the spectators: "Don't ever trust a child" (p. 174). Religion encloses the characters, the society, and the film itself. Opening and closing with shots of the cathedral, *Exterminating Angel* offers many examples of characters blindly putting their faith in religious symbols like the Te Deum, the Shrine at Lourdes, Masonic distress signals, and a "washable rubber virgin." When they have finally escaped from the mansion, the guests, like the flock of sheep that precedes them, risk slaughter by willingly reentering their trap, this time the ornate cathedral.

Buñuel also explores the trapped consciousness created by class distinction, which he sees as inextricably fused with the lessons of religion. People are clearly divided into masters (who are trapped at the party) and servants (who leave before it begins). There is no middle class, and Julio the butler (the head servant), because of his authoritatian position, takes his place among the masters. Though limited to the aristocracy, the guests represent a moral cross section of society—the best and the worst. The leader who seems to emerge is a Virgin, who appears in a trinity of forms: the flesh and blood Virgin, who leads the guests out of the room by a clever ritual of reversal; the holy symbolic virgin, who leads them back into the larger trap of the Church; and the "washable rubber virgin," who deflates the whole trinity, and renders her power as laughable as that of a rubber shark or head-swiveling demonic doll.

Buñuel mocks the naive assumption that it is possible for an individual hero or heroine to save a corrupt society. Even the noble host, the perceptive virgin, and the rational doctor, who struggle to preserve human dignity, are instruments of the corrupt social structure in which they hold privileged positions. They lead the guests back to Christian values, reinforcing their entrapment within a perverted hierarchy based on a false myth of individual nobility. Buñuel exposes this myth as the basis of social evil. One of the guests compares their situation to a train wreck she had once witnessed.

> The third-class compartment, full of common people, had been squashed like a huge accordion. And inside . . . what carnage! I must be insensitive, because the suffering of those poor people didn't move me at all.
>
> (p. 135)

A lifetime of class identification has ludicrously distorted and limited her consciousness, her experience of the world. Ironically, the same woman faints away with grief at the "lying-in-state of Prince Luttar." When confronted with this contradiction, she explains.

> Oh! How could you make such a comparison? How could one be insensitive, before the grandeur of the death . . . of that admirable prince, who was our friend . . . and such a noble profile!
>
> (p. 135)

The Passion of Christ, the noble Prince of Peace who sacrifices himself for his inferiors, has trained us to have this kind of elitist response. This tradition teaches us to focus on the fates of stars with noble profiles while keeping us insensitive to the flocks of extras who anonymously succumb to death. As another of the trapped aristocrats explains:

> I think that the common people, the lower classes, are less sensitive to pain. Have you ever seen a wounded bull? Quite impassive!
>
> (p. 137)

By assigning dignity only to a small elite and regarding the others as animals, these aristocrats deny their own humanity.

Exterminating Angel devotes considerable attention to surface manners, which are an outward manifestation of class structure. The aristocrats are trapped in forms that control their consciousness and behavior down to such details as the order in which the dinner courses are served, the proper time to leave a dinner party, and the appropriate dress for all situations. Even in the middle of a life-and-death crisis, their attention is fixated on trivia.

> LEANDRO: These stiff clothes are fine for statues but not for men . . . especially at five in the morning.
> LUCIA: They're taking off their dinner jackets! Don't you think that's a bit much?
> NOBILE: Don't forget that Leandro lived in the United States. And at such a late hour bodies reach the limits of exhaustion. (Pause) And the temperature in here is so pleasant.
> LUCIA: I'm sure they'll feel ashamed when they remember their behavior.
> NOBILE: So am I, I'd hate them to feel embarrassed. (He takes off his own jacket.) Let's come down to their level so as to mitigate their bad manners.
>
> (p. 133)

We witness a comical breach of etiquette turn into the total disintegration of civilization. The situation forces the nobility (and the audience) to confront the human condition, which their privileged position within society ordinarily allows them to ignore. The growing desperation of the guests makes them relinquish private property, strips them of their false refinement, and ultimately leads them to question the value of survival. Nobile, the humanistic host, understands the true horror of their situation.

> This is what I've most hated since my childhood. Vulgarity, violence, and filth have become our inseparable companions. Death would be preferable to living on top of each other in this despicable way.
>
> (p. 164-165)

Yet, these are precisely the conditions under which so many are forced to live in most societies of the world. We soon realize that the real disaster is the way our civilization has willfully organized its population into an unjust class system, which denies human instincts and traps people in perpetual misery.

When social conventions are codified in art, they form the basis of genres. In this context, *Exterminating Angel* can be seen as an ironic parody of the disaster film (which had a long history before it became such a fad). The guests feel compelled to interpret their irrational situation with logical explanations. Hence they compare their predicament to a shipwreck, as if it were a natural disaster. They accuse the servants of leaving "like rats when the ship is sinking;" as they break open the water pipes to quench their thirst, the men shout "Women first!" The host uses the shipwreck metaphor in an attempt to restore order: "We're all in the same boat and we'd all benefit . . . if we showed a little consideration" (p. 159). This analogy allows the guests to label and hence cope with their crisis, just as it enables us in the audience to see the film in the context of the disaster genre and recognize its ironic deviation from those conventions. While the typical disaster film offers false assurance that we can escape any holocaust if only we follow the right heroic leader—whether he be an engineer, architect, policeman, fireman, doctor, or priest—Buñuel forces us to see the real threat and to question whether, in fact, we deserve to survive. By presenting the inexplicable disaster as a matter of will, he makes us see that our mind-forged order is the true source of the trap. Clinging to their culture, the guests resort to paranoia, superstition, violence, and nonsensical formulae. Like the creators of *Jaws* and *The Exorcist*, they try to kill a scapegoat—to sacrifice a child, a lamb, and a host. It is our Christian heritage that leads us to this absurd sado-masochistic solution. Ironically, the reconstruction of society (which follows the Christian prototype) is as terrifying as its disintegration, perhaps even more so.

From the very beginning of *Exterminating Angel* it is apparent that beneath the surface of elegant refinement and extreme predictability, the irrational forces of bestiality and surprise operate with equal power. In an environment marked by delicately beautiful objects like an ice swan and a crystal chandelier, violence, racism or insanity may surface at any moment. As she stands alone at the dinner table, the Valkyrie suddenly flings an ashtray out the window. Leandro, unaware that something was thrown, suggests that the window broke because a wandering Jew was passing outside. During a piano recital, Ana opens her purse and takes out two chicken claws. At the mercy of irrational forces in their personal lives, the guests frantically seek escape in sexuality. Beatrice and Eduardo rush into a passionate affair before their marriage. Leonora, who is dying of cancer, makes sexual advances to her doctor. Roc, faced with old age and the decline of his powers, engages in a desperate, senile sexuality. Lucia, Nobile, and the Colonel are involved in an adulterous triangle. Francisco and Juana turn to incest, homosexuality, and drugs. Perhaps to escape some of these traps, Letitia has remained the "wild virgin," though this is interpreted as a perversion by one of the other characters.

The guests and the audience are confronted with the problem of how to reconcile these contradictions in what is perceived. Sometimes, the guests seem to accept phenomena on their own terms, without acknowledging their strangeness or trying to fabricate explanations. The betrothed Beatrice and Eduardo pretend that they are strangers. Raul introduces Christian and Leandro, who behave as if they've never met; a few moments later Christian exclaims, "Leandro!" and Leandro responds with open arms, "My dear friend! Christian" (p. 126). Perhaps five minutes later they are reintroduced and once again respond as strangers. Throughout the film, conversations reveal only the most superficial engagement with experience and seem to exist without the body of significance and emotion that usually accompanies human interaction.

> LUCIA: It's your fourth child, isn't it?
> CHRISTIAN: I don't know. I can't keep count any more.
> JUANA: Are you sure you know who the father is? I mean. . . .
> CHRISTIAN: You'd better ask her.
> RITA: Science will tell.

Verbal repartee is full of contradictions and non-sequiturs, creating a humorous tone even when the subject is death.

> LEONORA: I feel marvelously well. My appetite was very good tonight, doctor. Your treatment has really changed me.
> DOCTOR: I don't desire any credit . . . there was nothing seriously wrong with you.
> LEONORA: Do you dance, doctor?
> RAUL: (To the doctor, in a low voice) Why did she kiss you so passionately? Poor Leonora. And how is the cancer progressing? Is there any hope?
> DOCTOR: None whatsoever. I give her just three months to lose all her hair and drop dead.
> RAUL: Oh, but she's in top condition!

> (pp. 124-126)

Buñuel seems to suggest that when consciousness relates only to the surface of phenomena, there may be dangerous consequences. It prevents one from dealing with death, passion and one's own destructive potential. This is powerfully demonstrated in Ana's vision of the disembodied hand. Having earlier been startled by the sight of Russell's dead hand falling out of a closet, she now perceives herself to be attacked by the hand and in a fusion of perception, memory, and imagination, she stabs it with a dagger. However, in failing to acknowledge the irrationality of her selective perception, she becomes a destructive force because, in fact, the hand belongs to another guest.

Another solution practiced by both Buñuel and the characters is to acknowledge the contradictions with a charming sophistication that tames the irrational and unpredictable forces through acceptance. Lucia, the hostess, arranges for her butler to perform a comic fall, splattering food all over the floor. We never learn what tricks she planned for the bear and sheep, which then become instruments for Buñuel's surreal trickery. Although they have some symbolic function (suggesting the latent bestiality of the guests and the sacrifice of the lamb), their main quality is a kind of phenomenological playfulness: What are these sheep doing under the kitchen table? Is the bear dangerous as he wanders through the palatial mansion and clambers up a column to juxtapose his clumsiness against the elegant fragility of a chandelier? The ability to tolerate these surprises temporarily alleviates the terror of the unknown.

> NOBILE: I like the unpredictable quality of this situation. If you'd like to spend the night here, we can make beds for you all. I'm glad to see that the good old spirit of improvisation is still alive. (p. 132)
> COLONEL: Do you think it's normal to have spent the night here in this drawing room without showing any elementary signs of good manners? Or to have turned the room into the most unbelievable gypsy camp?
> ANA: Well, I found it all very original. I love anything that's an escape from routine.
>
> (p. 140)

However, this radical chic acceptance is also destructive, because it lulls the characters into a passivity that prevents them from doing anything about their predicament, just as it allows them to tolerate the injustice of their society.

Since neither of these solutions will work by itself, escape from the room seems to require a synthesis of acute sensory perception and a theoretical construct. When Letitia, the virgin, suddenly notices that all the guests are positioned exactly as they were at the beginning of the party, she sees this as the "key" to a ritual reenactment that will release them:

> I don't know . . . or rather, I do . . . It's so extraordinary. . . . Think how each of us has changed places during this awful eternity. (Insisting) Think of the thousands of combinations, like pawns in a chess game, which is what we were. Even the furniture: we've moved it around hundreds of times. . . . Well, at the moment we're all, both people and furniture, in the same place and in the exact position that we were in that night . . . or is it another hallucination?
>
> (p. 188)

She urges them to "make an effort" and "try to remember"; our memories, too, are tested as they struggle to reenact the earlier scene.

Just as the guests have been trained by their culture to pursue ritual and explanation, we have been trained by earlier sequences that repetition is the key. Some scenes, like the toast to Silvia and the arrival of the guests, are repeated as if on a loop; but careful scrutiny reveals minor variations, challenging the audience's perception and making us wonder if there has been some mistake in the editing. The first time the guests enter, the camera looks up at Nobile who is seen beneath the glittering chandelier. In the repetition the camera looks down at him standing on the patterned floor. The first entry of the group blocks two women servants who are about to leave the mansion. Then the camera returns to the servants as if they are going to try again after the guests enter the dining room. But instead of this linear progression, the guests' entrance is repeated. This time the maids succeed, assuring both the characters and the audience that repetition is the key to escape. Sartre argues that it is precisely this kind of assurance that is provided by art, but not by nature. When we perceive a pattern in nature, it may be of our own making. "The idea of a universal providence is no guarantee of any particular intention."[41] But when we perceive a pattern in a novel or film, we can assume it has been freely chosen and created by the artist. Yet, Buñuel's intention may be ironic. Within the world of *Exterminating Angel*, why should reenactment lead to freedom? On the one hand, the characters' entrapment may be seen as a matter of consciousness or will; they are trapped so long as they believe they are, and are free to leave the room as soon as they believe it is possible. On the other hand, the escape is as irrational as the entrapment, and repetition merely provides them the security of an explanation. Indeed, their escape is an hallucination; it offers only a temporary release, and finally traps them in a larger pattern that is equally confining. In fact, this mode of thought, this humanistic passion for logic and anterior significance, is the ultimate trap into which our own critical exegesis unfortunately falls.

Buñuel's omnipotence is everywhere apparent as he intentionally baffles us and manipulates our flight from one impossible alternative to another. The visual style is perversely unselfconscious. There is almost no self-reflexive camera work, composition, or cutting (as in *Marienbad*) to remind us that we are watching a film and should suspend our expectations for verisimilitude. Rather, its style is surrealistic, presenting the most irrational content through a surface texture of realism. Characteristic camera work consists of conventional pans and slow tracking shots, which focus our attention on objects of narrative importance (e.g., a knife lying on the table, a drug box, the face of a character about to have a dramatic outburst). The realistic texture parallels the "plain style" or low mimetic tone that is conventional for literary satire, and provides a visual context that heightens the ironic power of the film. The only deviation is the nightmare sequence where style changes dramatically: cutting pace is accelerated; lighting is more expressionistic; the focus is softened; composition is highly stylized; special effects like superimposition, cross dissolves and misted images appear. As the camera pans from dreamer to dreamer, we hear the voices and see the images of their inner reality. This montage combines perception, memory, and imagination from the various dreamers, creating a kind of collective unconscious that also eludes logical explanation. Like the retreat to the inner closets, the dream offers an inward route to escape, yet the guests confront and are blocked by images that have been programmed by their culture.

Whereas *Marienbad*, with its highly innovative visual style, presents the kind of formal freedom advocated by Robbe-Grillet, Buñuel's use of an unselfconscious visual style to present a radical political vision is more compatible with Sartre's conception of artistic freedom. Buñuel rejects *Marienbad's* emphasis on "the way in" as a meaningful alternative and instead chooses to focus on "the way out."

The narrative structure is Buñuel's primary means of moving outward; it appears to be breaking through barriers while, in fact, it is merely expanding the circumference of the trap. Encircled by the images of the cathedral, the film is neatly divided into five acts, each beginning with a scene from the outside world, and each showing a further stage of the breakdown of civilization within the drawing room. The outside scenes increase in length and complexity, culminating in the epilogue inside the Cathedral where the entrapment and anarchy are extended to the entire society. As in *Marienbad*, there is no linear progression to events, and it is possible to become lost within a highly patterned, repetitive structure.

All five acts maintain a tension between the impulse toward anarchy and the rational desire for order. In the first act, the hosts, Nobile and Lucia, try to control the inexplicable force that prevents the guests from leaving by explaining it as a breach of good manners and behaving as if they chose to go along with it. Act II ends with the first death and is largely concerned with the hopeless task of finding reasons for the irrational situation and a scapegoat to blame it on. Just before Russell dies, he prophesies: "Happy . . . I won't see the extermination" (p. 148). In Act III, the primitive conditions intensify with a greater emphasis on violence. Ana stabs Alicia's hand; the lovers commit suicide; Raul throws away Christian's pills, covertly threatening his life; Christian challenges the Colonel to a duel; Roc goes about in the dark, sexually assaulting the women. Violence is imminent outside the mansion, too, where the police try to restrain the crowd as someone shouts: "We're not dogs! Let us through! Death to the police!" (p. 152). By now the guests are hungry, thirsty and ill-tempered; their clothes are rumpled, the room is littered with debris and the vestiges of civilization seem out of place. Disregarding private property, the guests break through the wall to reach a water pipe. As they jostle each other, Beatrice says: "Oh! You stepped on my foot! What's this habit of walking around with your shoes on!" (p. 153). In the midst of the filth, the Colonel tries to maintain decorum:

> FRANCISCO: You smell like a hyena.
> BLANCA: What did you say?
> FRANCISCO: I said that you smell like a hyena, madam.
> BLANCA: How dare you! Why do you insult me?
> COLONEL: You should be ashamed to talk of such unfortunate things when we are trying to behave like gentlemen and ignore them.

FRANCISCO: Why are you afraid of the truth? She smells bad
. . . like you . . . like me . . . like all of us. We're living in a pigsty.
Like real pigs! You disgust me! All of you! I hate you!

(p. 164)

The elements of violence, survival, and ritual begin to come
together when the sheep suddenly appear. In the midst of a heated
argument, we hear the sound of bleating and then the film cuts to a
shot of three sheep climbing the stairs. Next the camera pans along
the faces of the guests lined up expectantly in the archway anticipating the slaughter. Then the huge shadow of a bear looms against the
wall as it lumbers upstairs after the sheep, rendering visually concrete
the guests' emerging bestiality. As the sheep meekly pass through the
barrier, they are encircled by the hungry guests and we hear the
savage growls of the bear. To get their first food in days, they must
commit their first act of killing.

Act IV is largely concerned with the extension of ritual to create a
new order. Succumbing to the religious habit of mind, the guests
imbue various objects with significance or power—the closet, the
painting of the exterminating angel, the masonic words and gestures,
the sheep, and Ana's chicken claws. Ana leads the group in a call for
sacrifice. "We must have innocent blood. . . . We must wait for the
sacrifice of the last sheep" (p. 179). This ritualistic act is prepared for
by the Valkyrie (the Virgin) and Nobile (the human scapegoat), no
longer to assuage hunger, but to appease by magic the forces which
hold them captive and are reducing them to a primitive state. The
cloth that formerly bound Nobile's aching head is now used to
blindfold the sheep awaiting slaughter, which pathetically rubs its
muzzle along Nobile's cheek. The outside activities (introduced by
the image of a cluster of balloons that parodies the elegant chandelier
inside the mansion) parallel the sacrifice as the Priest, himself afraid
to enter, urges the child to risk the danger. These ritualistic attempts
to restore order result, not in a return to civilized behavior, but in the
establishment of a primitve collective unconscious expressed in the
group nightmare.   In Act V the rituals are more closely identified
with Christianity; therefore, they become more violent. The guests
demand human sacrifice; Nobile, the Host, must atone for their
situation. Instead of being rescued by the Doctor who represents
Reason and Science, Nobile is saved from martyrdom by the interces-
sion of the Virgin. The curtains of a small stage open, revealing the
calm, imposing figures (in a traditional pose evoking religious
paintings) of Nobile and Letitia (who has perhaps sacrificed

her virginity, preserved for this occasion). Suddenly she is inspired to reenact the significant moment. Her act of salvation fulfills an earlier prophecy:

> LEONORA: We will prostrate ourselves at the Virgin's feet, for she is the only one who can get us out of here.
>
> (p. 161)

The epilogue renders literal the return to Christianity. The power structure is held captive in the Church. As the masses riot outside (fulfilling the earlier cries for "Death to the police"), the flock of sheep quietly return to the fold. Buñuel presents these two kinds of behavior in surrealistically different modes. The bear is translated into the realistic street-fighting, while the sheep remain the familiar Christian symbol rendered comically literal. As in all of his films, civilization, at best, offers only a flimsy disguise for man's animal nature, be it sheep or bear.

A fascist society with strict government controls, sharply divided social classes, and an omnipotent hierarchy has the greatest potential for anarchy and violence. But, if rigid order is the other side of anarchy, then what positive alternatives exist for human beings? This film suggests that personal self-realization or heroism is not an answer. We have seen individuality lead to selfishness, and the unique elements of personality become grotesque. By assigning dignity only to a small elite, the guests cut themselves off from their fellow species members. This is precisely the vision developed in Jonathan Swift's "A Modest Proposal," where the rational man (full of human sympathy) advocates the eating of Irish children, thereby inviting us to regard *him* as an animal. As in Swift's satire, the primary value in Buñuel's films lies not in a program for reforming human society, but in honestly facing man as he is—not educable toward freedom, as Robbe-Grillet sees him, but a creature of limited potential, always affected by his animal nature.

Exterminating Angel deals with these limitations and the decline of civilization not in the tragic mode like *Red Desert*, but with an irony that denies the value of tragedy for reasons very different from those of Robbe-Grillet. Tragedy grows out of a positive view of humanism; individualism, and civilization, in which their failure would be seen as a serious loss. As in *Marienbad*, Buñuel's characters are trapped in a no-exit universe, held there by conventional modes of thinking condemned by the film. Traditional humanistic values cause man to strive for things he cannot attain, for a vision of himself created partly in fantasy, and partly by those who wish to maintain power and control. Therefore, from Buñuel's perspective, the failure of these values is not tragic but absurd.

Footnotes to Chapter Four

1. Jean-Paul Sartre, "Why Write?" in *Critical Theory Since Plato*, ed. Hazard Adams (New York: Harcourt Brace Jovanovich, 1971), p. 1062.

2. Georges Poulet, "The Phenomenology of Reading," *New Literary History: A Journal of Theory and Interpretation*, I, no. 1 (October, 1969). Unlike other phenomenological critics or members of the Geneva School, Poulet insists that subjectivity can exist in itself and that there can be consciousness without an object, thereby supporting Cartesian dualism.

3. Alain Robbe-Grillet, "Introduction," *Last Year at Marienbad*, trans. Richard Howard (New York: Grove Press, 1962), pp. 12-13.

4. Georges Poulet, *Studies in Human Time* (Baltimore: Johns Hopkins University Press, 1956), pp. 35-36.

5. Robbe-Grillet, "Nature, Humanism, Tragedy," in *For a New Novel: Essays on Fiction*, trans. Richard Howard (New York: Grove Press, 1965), p. 70.

6. Robbe-Grillet, "A Future for the Novel," *For a New Novel*, p. 21.

7. Robbe-Grillet, "Nature, Humanism, Tragedy," p. 57.

8. Sartre, pp. 1061, 1063.

9. Sartre, p. 1067.

10. Sartre, p. 1067.

11. Robbe-Grillet, "On Several Obsolete Notions," *For a New Novel*, p. 41.

12. Robbe-Grillet, "From Realism to Reality," *For a New Novel*, pp. 158-159.

13. Luis Buñuel, "A Statement," *Film Makers on Film Making*, ed. Harry M. Geduld (Bloomington: Indiana University Press, 1967), p. 175.

14. Robbe-Grillet, "Time and Description," *For a New Novel*, p. 149.

15. Robbe-Grillet, *Last Year at Marienbad*, trans. Richard Howard (New York: Grove Press, 1962), p. 18. Subsequent references to this screenplay will appear in the text.

16. Alain Resnais, *Film Makers on Film Making*, p. 157.

17. Alain Robbe-Grillet, *Film Makers on Film Making*, pp. 172-173.

18. "Time and Description," p. 154.

19. Resnais, *Film Makers on Film Making*, p. 155.

20. Resnais, *Film Makers on Film Making*, p. 156.

21. "Introduction," *Marienbad*, p. 10.

22. "Introduction," *Marienbad*, p. 11.

23. "Time and Description," p. 153.

24. "Introduction," *Marienbad*, p. 14.

25. "Time and Description," p. 152.

26. Robbe-Grillet, *Film Makers on Film Making*, p. 173.

27. Resnais, *Film Makers on Film Making*, p. 159.

28. Resnais, *Film Makers on Film Making*, p. 162.

29. "Time and Description," pp. 152-153.

30. Ben F. Stoltzfus, *Alain Robbe-Grillet: And the New French Novel* (Carbondale: So. Illinois University Press, 1964), p. 107.

31. Robbe-Grillet, *Film Makers on Film Making*, p. 169.

32. Robbe-Grillet, *Film Makers on Film Making*, p. 167.

33. "New Novel, New Man," p. 138.

34. John Sturrock, *The French New Novel: Claude Simon, Michel Butor, Alain Robbe-Grillet* (London: Oxford University Press, 1969), p. 217.

35. "Nature, Humanism, Tragedy," p. 59.

36. "Nature, Humanism, Tragedy," p. 61.

37. "Nature, Humanism, Tragedy," p. 75.

38. "New Novel, New Man," p. 141.

39. Robbe-Grillet, "Samuel Beckett, or Presence on the Stage," in *For a New Novel*, p. 121.

40. Luis Buñuel, *Three Screenplays: Viridiana, the Exterminating Angel, Simon of the Desert* (New York: Orion Press, 1969), p. 149. Subsequent references to the screenplay of *Exterminating Angel* will appear in the text.

41. Sartre, pp. 1063-1064.

LAST YEAR AT MARIENBAD. As they stand fixed and frozen like the statues, the fluid thoughts of X and A lend themselves to interpretation or recreation by each consciousness that encounters them. Courtesy of Audio-Brandon Films.

LAST YEAR AT MARIENBAD. X and M face each other from opposite sides of the frame as they play the match game. The spectators encircle the round table, symmetrically arranged like statues in the elegant baroque hotel. Courtesy of Audio-Brandon Films.

LAST YEAR AT MARIENBAD. Image and object, viewer and viewed, memory-imagination-perception, past-present-future all fuse in the multiple "realities" of the mirror sequence. Courtesy of Audio-Brandon Films.

LAST YEAR AT MARIENBAD. This archetypal image of A as dying swan suggests a combination of glamour and assault, reflecting the ambiguity of last year's encounter at Marienbad; what, if anything, happened the previous year or the previous moment. Courtesy of Audio-Brandon Films.

THE EXTERMINATING ANGEL. The first death occurs before the guests realize the full extent of their entrapment. The men have not yet removed their jackets; they still look toward their noble host to provide a civilized solution. Courtesy of Audio-Brandon Films.

THE EXTERMINATING ANGEL. The actions of the trapped guests display the tension between the impulse toward anarchy and the rational desire for order and control.

Courtesy of Audio-Brandon Films.

THE EXTERMINATING ANGEL. Revealing the uplifted eyes and transcendental aura of the Holy Virgin, the Valkyrie, who will finally save the guests, is also a flesh and blood member of her social class, as glittering as the ornate piano before which she strikes her power pose. Courtesy of Audio-Brandon Films.

5

The One and the Many in *El Topo*, *2001: A Space Odyssey*, and *Zardoz*: Archetypal Journeys Beyond the Self

*The possession of originality cannot make an artist uncon-
ventional; it drives him further into convention, obeying the law
of the art itself, which seeks constantly to reshape itself from its
own depths, and which works through geniuses for its metamorphoses, as it works through minor talents for mutation.*
Northrop Frye, Anatomy of Criticism

*The most complete, individual feeling is also the most complete,
collective feeling. Because you must go inside you, inside you,
inside you through the door; and when you open the door, the
collective unconscious comes out through your individuality.
You open the door, but the world comes through the door.*
Alexandro Jodorowsky, Interview, Los Angeles Free Press

El Topo, 2001: A Space Odyssey, and *Zardoz* present an archetypal
quest, pursued by an individual and the species, moving into the past
and the future in search of survival and progress. In all three films,
the hero breaks through the ego barrier, using individuality in the

service of transcending itself, so that the one can embody the many. On a formal level, these films make analogous use of artistic tradition, self consciously incorporating a large body of material from various genres, media, and myths with great transformational power.

These films come together with Northrop Frye's system of archetypal criticism in a number of shared polarities. Frye's *Anatomy of Criticism* combines circular (synchronic) and linear (diachronic) views of the history of art. He divides all of Western literature into five chronological historical modes that form a circle, one phase moving into another; the mythic (pre-Medieval) in which a divine hero has powers "superior in degree to those of other humans and the environment"; the romantic (Medieval) in which a human hero sometimes has the same superiority of powers; the high mimetic (Renaissance) in which the hero's powers are superior only to other men but not to his natural environment; the low mimetic (18th and 19th centuries) in which the hero is "superior neither to other men nor to his environment, the hero is one of us"; and the ironic (20th century) in which the hero is "inferior in power or intelligence to ourselves, so that we have the sense of looking down on a scene of bondage, frustration, or absurdity...."[1] All three films move between the ironic and mythic modes. At some stages of their quest, the heroes seem inferior, but at other times, they seem infused with divine power.

Frye also points out that the meaning of any work of art moves simultaneously in two directions—inward and outward. He defines the centrifugal/centripetal polarity in literature:

> One direction is outward or centrifugal, in which we keep going outside our reading, from the individual words to the things they mean, or, in practice to our memory of the conventional association between them. The other direction is inward or centripetal, in which we try to develop from the words a sense of the larger verbal pattern they make.[2]

The images in all three films move in both directions, to comment on the history and future of the human species, and to call attention to the cinematic medium and its conventions. Frye argues that this centripetal, self-reflexive movement is especially characteristic of the ironic art of the twentieth century. In both dimensions, the films, like Frye's approach, incorporate the one and the many. They are autonomous works, yet at the same time, they are part of a structure that includes all works of art in Western civilization. Analogously, the central figures are both individual characters and representatives of the human race.

Frye's elaboration of the archetypal quest of Romance illuminates the narrative structures that lie at the center of all three films. Indeed, the full cycle of the quest is central to Frye's entire system of narrative categories. Based on his conception of an Ur-myth of decline and renewal, it is linked to the cycle of the seasons and the stages of human life. Frye divides the quest into four stages:

> There are . . . four distinguishable aspects to the quest-myth. First, the *agon* or conflict itself. Second, the pathos or death, often the mutual death of hero and monster. Third, the disappearance of the hero, a theme which often takes the form of *sparagomos* or tearing to pieces . . . Fourth, the reappearance and recognition of the hero. . . .[3]

He also delineates four poles of characterization: the hero; the antagonist, or deceitful challenger; the nature spirits, who may aid the hero; and the rustic clown, who provides humor and contact with practical reality. All three films incorporate the four character poles and four aspects of the quest. They develop the Romance in what is, according to Frye, two of its most popular generic variations—the western and science fiction.

Frye explicitly rejects evaluation as a goal of criticism, yet implicitly he suggests that the better a work of art is, the more easily and fully his system can be applied. Thus richness, complexity, and density are primary aesthetic values.[4] We will apply the archetypal approach to *El Topo, 2001,* and *Zardoz* not merely to see whether the films fit into Frye's system, but to locate the special ways in which a large body of mythic material is absorbed and transformed into the three quests.

El Topo (1971)

El Topo is an extraordinarily fascinating film because of its imaginative power, yet at the same time it is highly derivative. We are not using this word in a negative sense, for one of Jodorowsky's unique values is in absorbing everything he has experienced, including other works of art, Eastern and Western mythology, and making it peculiarly his own.

> I think there are multiple influences in the film—I have them
> all: the influence of all the books I've read and all the films I've
> seen, of all the winds that have blown against my skin, of all the
> stars that have exploded during my lifetime, of each manifesta-
> tion of the non-manifested, of each flea that's shit on me.
> Especially a flea I met in 1945. It shit on me in such an incredible
> way that it changed my life. I'm sure that flea's in my film.[5]

What is unique is the way the film combines the various elements of
Jodorowsky's experience. At the same time that we are horrified at the
violence, we laugh unexpectedly, never able to predict what out-
rageousness will follow (which is also true of Jodorowsky's commentary on the film). We are acutely aware that this film is making us
and the rest of the audience nervous, unsettling us by moving from
obscene farce to spiritual enlightenment. Like Makavejev's Reichian
cinema, Jodorowsky's bold extremes of grotesquery and playfulness
engage us both intellectually and emotionally, keeping us always at a
high level of excitement.

Of all the films discussed in this book, *El Topo* is the most
personal, the one that is most expressive of a single personality.
Alexandro Jodorowsky directed, wrote, starred in, composed music,
designed costumes and sets for this movie. As in Bergman's films, all
characters are aspects of himself, seen in a mythic rather than a
psychological context. Jodorowsky attributes this theory to Otto
Weininger, the philosopher who wrote *Sex and Character*.

> He [Weininger] says that a genius is identified as one who lives
> all lives, one who has many people within him. A genius can be
> many people and they live within him. So, the less genius a
> person has, the fewer people he can be. . . . An artist cannot
> express what he doesn't live. Right? And the greater his state of
> sainthood, the greater and more horrible is the devil who
> appears to him.[6]

He identifies the individual with the collective unconscious,
which enables him to create a film in which a personal vision
expresses an archetypal pattern of experience. As Frye suggests "in
the archetypal phase the work . . . is a world of total metaphor, in
which everything is potentially identical with everything else, as
though it were all inside a single infinite body."[7] Since the mythic
presents a collective dream, everything is charged with symbolic
significance; hence this view of the world is completely antithetical
to that of the phenomenological approach and similar to Reich's
notion of functional identity.

> When you put a body in a film, you don't put the body; you put
> an image. Everybody in a picture is a symbol; it's not a real body,
> it's a picture. . . . We are symbols—unrealistic things. A symbol is
> always a spiritual event. So I don't use human bodies in a
> picture; I use symbols.[8]

In the mythic mode there is no contradiction between exploring the
inner self and turning attention outward to the corruptions of society
(or in Frye's terms, between the confession and the anatomy) because
external evil is a painful violation of the mythic dream. The
microcosm/macrocosm relationship of the mythic vision implies
that the evil without will inevitably be reflected in the evil within;
hence total innocence is impossible.

In *El Topo*, the mythic quest is for self-realization and spiritual
illumination.

> I think that the journey of Alexander the Great is a psychedelic
> trip. Many say that Alexander the Great was an idiot because his
> conquest was so great, so complete, that as he progressed in
> conquering the entire world, he was actually progressing toward
> his ultimate failure. I think that Alexander the Great was
> journeying into the depths of his being. I think that Odysseus
> was another great traveler. I want to travel the route of the
> Odyssey. I want to travel the route of Alexander the Great. I want
> to travel into the deepest areas of my being in order to reach
> enlightenment.[9]

The hero (played by Alexander Jodorowsky the Great), journeys
from pride to humility, reaches sainthood and self-immolation, and
thereby begins a new cycle.

The plot is abundant and unpredictable, to say the least. It begins
with El topo and his son riding through the desert. After his son's
initiation into manhood, they ride into a village littered with corpses.
Next they encounter three of the killers, whom El Topo executes. He
seeks out and castrates their leader. He rides off with one of the
prisoners he has freed; in her place, he leaves his son with the
liberated priests. Goaded on by this woman, he next challenges and
defeats Four Masters in the desert. His woman is captivated by a
lesbian who shoots El Topo. A group of dwarves takes him to their
cave where they revive him. He undergoes an epiphany, shaves his
head, and re-emerges with a pretty dwarf to clown for money in a
nearby sinful city. In the course of marrying the dwarf, El Topo
encounters his son, who is grown up and wants to kill him. The son
agrees to delay his vengeance and joins the couple in tunneling the

dwarves to freedom. When the liberated freaks enter the city, they are massacred by the citizens. In retribution, El Topo kills them all, liberates the Indians, and commits suicide. Meanwhile, his wife is giving birth. In the end, mother, infant, and El Topo II ride off into the sunset.

The title *El Topo* (the mole) introduces the central metaphor, suggesting the route taken by the quest. While drawings show hands digging through dirt, a man's voice tells us: "The mole is an animal that digs tunnels underground searching for the sun. Sometimes his journey leads him to the surface. When he looks at the sun, he is blinded."[10] This parable of apparent hopelessness is reminiscent of the Myth of Sisyphus, which also implies that whatever value life may have is not to be found in a single goal or final stage, but through engagement in an ongoing process. Digging imagery recurs through- out the film (frequently shot from overhead camera angles), particular- ly in sequences that include the passage from one stage of experience to another: the child Brontis becomes a man as he buries his first toy and a picture of his mother; after rejecting the child, El Topo affirms the significance of sensuality in this phase of his life by burrowing into the sand to make love to the woman; he passes into deceit by digging a trick pit to kill the First Master; digging symbolizes his redemption as he tunnels the dwarves to freedom.

El Topo's quest moves through four stages, each one including a designation from the Bible and paralleling the traditional four-part structure of the Romance as described by Frye. The four poles of characterization—the hero, the antagonist, the nature spirits, and the rustic clown—are manifested in El Topo himself, and emerge in different phases of the journey as he moves from pride (stages one and two) to humility (stages three and four).

The first stage (or *agon*) reveals El Topo as hero, associated with the innocence of the naked child although, as ironic hero, he wears black. In these preliminary adventures, he is the winner who champions the underdog and saves the heroine from the bestiality and sadism of the Colonel and his obscene pack of cohorts, who threaten the heroine, brandishing huge lizards like phalluses. To prove the full martial power of his machismo, El Topo castrates the decadent old king (the Colonel) in a ritualistic *mano a mano*. When the Colonel asks, "Who are you to judge me?" El Topo replies, "I am God."[11] These victories, however, are ironically undercut by the parody of the Western that dominates this section. This irony is further developed through the section's title, "Genesis," which has several possible implications. It could suggest the beginning of the film, the child's initiation into manhood, the beginning of a new social phase with the killing of the old king, or an ironic conception of innocence with El Topo as the Adam of the Western. This section appears to end with the hero and heroine enjoying their brief stay in an Eden-like garden, where he baptizes her Mara, which means "bitter water."

In the second phase El Topo becomes the *alazon* or deceitful challenger—his own antagonist. He is moved further into pride by Mara who urges him to kill the "Four Master Sharpshooters," thus proving that he's the best and winning her love. As soon as she has convinced him to cheat in his battle with the First Master, they are joined by a Woman in Black, who embodies the beautiful witch of the traditional Romance and the negative *anima* figure of Jungian psychology. Instead of standing in contrast to the virtuous heroine, she enhances the evil which Mara has already shown and liberates her narcissism. Dressed almost exactly like El Topo, the lesbian also functions as a feminine parody of him, whom she is able to challenge and defeat at this point of his development. This stage of the archetypal quest involves pathos or catastrophe, a death struggle which can end in victory or defeat for the hero. Although El Topo succeeds in killing the Four Masters, their final words reveal that he is really the loser:

> You shoot to find yourself, I do it to vanish. You loath yourself,
> you now desire to play by the law. You lost.

El Topo realizes that "Even if I won, I would lose."[12] Not until he loses everything (his gun, his woman, nearly his life) in the final battle with the women, is he able to begin the process of winning enlightenment. In this final sequence his outstretched arms and stigmata, as well as his plea, "My God, my God, why hast Thou forsaken me?"[13] link him to Christ and the Four Masters—the "Prophets" who give this section its Biblical designation. Ironically the negative act of killing the Masters has led to his positive growth. El Topo's experience has broadened as well as deepened; no longer merely the Western hero, he is also embarked on the Eastern journey to enlightenment. The Masters are not only the fastest guns in the West, but the humblest gurus in the East.

The third stage of the Romance involves the disappearance of the hero, who, in this case, is rescued and taken underground by the cave people, "the nature spirits . . . who can be brought to serve the hero."[14] El Topo is physically transformed—shaven, shorn and reclothed so radically that he says: "This isn't me! This isn't my face!"[15] By completely losing his old self, he wins a new life. His rebirth prepares him for the final stage of the quest, experienced in a mountain cave.

> The Lower world . . . is often inhabited by a prophetic sibyl, [who in this case gives El Topo the sacred scarab] and is a place of oracles and secrets [like the bizarre foetus in a bottle] . . . the reward of the quest usually is or includes a bride. . . . She is often to be found in a perilous, forbidden, or tabooed place. . . . The "black but comely" bride of the Song of Songs belongs in the same complex [as does the beautiful dwarf].[16]

The Biblical designation "Psalms" comes at the beginning of the section (rather than in the middle as in other sections) because it separates the two halves of the film as El Topo moves from pride, ("I am God")[17] to humility ("I'm not a god. I'm a man.").[18] Called on by the sibyl to release her people from the cave, as Moses led the Jews out of Egypt, and as Christ invited the meek and lame to follow him, El Topo now loses himself in the service of others. In contrast to the *femmes fatales* in phase two, the two women (the sibyl and the dwarf) are now positive *anima* figures who help him on the spiritual path.

The fourth stage of the Romance is the reappearance and recognition of the hero. El Topo reappears as the *argoikos* or rustic clown, the character who represents the "practical reality" (clowning for money and doing the physical labor) within the dream world of Romance. He is recognized by his son, who seeks revenge for his abandonment and yet is now in a stage of development similar to El Topo's at the beginning of the film. This is reinforced by the costumes; El Topo now wears the homespun cassock of the humble monk, while his son's priest garb covers the shiny black "El Topo" costume.

The Biblical designation is the "Apocalypse," which traditionally evokes images of the heavenly city. but in this section the revelation is of a demonic society, and the focus is on bitter social satire. For Jodorowsky, society is a context that renders its people ugly. Appropriately he develops a beauty parlor scene in which hideous women prepare themselves for "the ugly reality" with cosmetics and sacrifice—they try to rape and eventually lynch a young black man. After their first contact with the townspeople, the dwarf asks El Topo whether "it's worth it for my people to leave the cave for this? This is worse!"[19] Her doubts are justified when her people are exterminated like vermin. This genocide renders El Topo's life work futile, and he returns to the gun and slaughters the town, leaving a litter of corpses like the one he found at the beginning of the film. But he also releases a flock of horses and white clad Indians who run freely through the town, suggesting rebirth and revolution. The centrifugal connection with contemporary events like the war in Viet Nam and American racism is further strengthened by El Topo's self-immolation. The film ends with the son of El Topo riding off with the dwarf and her baby behind him, suggesting that the film does not end but returns to its beginning. The final shot is of El Topo's grave, swarming with bees, reminding us of the First Master.

The Four Masters are nature spirits, each associated with a particular animal that is emblematic of his special virtue. El Topo's final actions and his death reveal that he, the mole, has incorporated each of these qualities into himself. As Jodorowsky observes,

> So when El Topo kills the Masters, he has the Masters within him. But he doesn't know that. He doesn't know he's suffering from introjection . . . introjection from the Masters. And when he realizes it, he becomes the Four Masters.[20]

The development of the First Master most clearly mixes Christian symbolism and values with the other mythologies of the film. He is associated with two animals—the lamb and the white horse, both symbolically linked to Christ, the former traditionally (although Jodorowsky denies it), and the latter idiosyncratically (to say the least).

> The white horse is Christ. Christ is a white horse. A white horse has four horseshoes. Christ has four horseshoes: four wounds. And the fifth shoe, the wound on his side, are the spurs you kick the horse with. . . . In the same sequence, there is a sheep. Everyone knows the meaning of a sheep. I'm not going to say it, but everyone knows that a sheep is a shoe. Sometimes I feel like running with a pair of sheep on my feet—live sheep-shoes. Maybe the First Master is the sheep.[21]

The First Master represents enlightenment; his blindness suggests that he can see spiritual truths (like the mole who will be blinded by the sun but can reach true vision). Like Christ, true vision enables him to accept the beauty of the armless and legless grotesques who serve him, as El Topo can see the beauty of the deformed cave people. Enlightenment also enables mind to transcend matter. He says to El Topo, "Killing you doesn't bother me because I know that death does not exist."[22] He can withstand bullets because his flesh offers no resistance, a lesson which El Topo learns in the final shootout with the townspeople. Both this Master and El Topo die with their people and both of their graves are filled with honey and alive with bees—the paradoxical bee-ing of death.

The Second Master stands by a chained lion, which represents the power of love to transform brute force so that it can coexist with the lamb, as ego can be subdued and lose itself in unity of being. At first he projects a bearish strength (reinforced by his Persian lamb coat), but his pouty mouth and playfulness make him seem babyish. He is so infused with love of his mother, whom he serves, that his powerful fingers can play with delicate forms and leave them unharmed. He defines perfection as "Losing yourself. And to lose yourself, you have to love."[23] El Topo's transformation of self in the service of the cave people and in his love of the dwarf reveal his internalization of this Master's lesson.

The Third Master, clad in the humble white of the Mexican Indian, is surrounded by hundreds of rabbits who begin to die with the approach of the profane El Topo. Gentle and trusting, this Master is associated with purity, a quality of the heart. His one shot at El Topo is aimed directly at his heart which, ironically, is protected by the copper ashtray which the Second Master has given him. After killing him, El Topo cynically observes: "Too much perfection is a mistake."[24] But, by the end of the film, he has incorporated these qualities, suggested by his self-immolation, reminiscent of the funeral pyre's purifying flames that earlier consumed the Third Master and his rabbits, and by his identification with the Indians.

The Fourth Master, associated with the butterfly who represents immortality through metamorphosis, says: "My life? It means nothing to me. I'll show you."[25] Whereupon, he shoots himself in the "liv-er" with El Topo's own gun. This comical figure (suggestive of Don Juan, Carlos Castaneda's brujo) teaches El Topo how to be the rustic clown, which enables him to serve the cave people. Being the only Master whom El Topo cannot kill, the old man's suicide teaches him that death is merely another experience. Later, when the son of El Topo decides that "I can't kill my Master," El Topo (now the Master), commits suicide, too. A great Master lives on in his disciples who incorporate him.

The pattern of the Four Masters also develops El Topo's movement from pride to humility, which is emphasized by Jodorowsky's description of their possessions:

> Through the Masters I show El Topo progressing from every-
> thing to nothingness. The house of the First Master is brick, very
> strong; the Second Master's house is wooden; the Third's is of
> straw; and the fourth has no house. . . . The First Master has a
> large animal; the Second, a smaller animal—a lion is smaller
> than a horse; the Third has a rabbit; and the Fourth, an invisible
> butterfly.[26]

> The possessions of the Masters have been diminishing. The first
> lived in a tall tower, the Second Master in a wagon, the Third
> Master in a lean-to. The Fourth Master has only a pole in the
> desert and a sheet covering his body. The First Master has two
> revolvers, the Second Master one revolver that fired several shots,
> the Third Master one revolver that fired a single shot. The
> Fourth Master has no revolver, only a butterfly net. The First
> Master has a large oasis, the Second Master a small stream, the
> Third Master an oval pool. The Fourth Master has only the sand
> in the desert.[27]

Although the lessons of the Masters and the reappearance of the
second El Topo suggest a cyclical development in the film, the
description of the possessions of the Masters also suggests a linear
movement or progress toward change. This combination of synchronic and diachronic patterns ultimately implies a spiral, which is
the form Jodorowsky uses to describe the film's movement.

> It's a spiral, not a circle. . . . Your mind is a circle, but you break
> the circle and then begin a spiral. The energy is there, but if you
> interrupt it—break it—it becomes a fantastic spiral. But you
> must break it upwards, not downwards. If you break it down-
> wards, you go to Hell. You must break it upwards to go toward
> Heaven.[28]

The film's circle imagery (round bloody pools, bandits circling the
girl, the monks encircling the child, the townspeople enclosing the
victimized performers and boxers) usually suggests entrapment. But
the significant movements downward (El Topo into the cave, the
diminishing possessions of the Masters) break the circle and paradoxically imply movement inward and upward toward greater spiritual
realization. When El Topo begins his search for the Masters and is
confronted with the labyrinthine desert, he draws a circle in the sand,
his finger continuing toward the center to form a spiral. He says:
"The desert is circular. To find the Four Masters, we'll have to travel
in a spiral."[29]

This pattern of simultaneous movement is also reflected in the
transitions between major sections of the film. Instead of being four

clearly separable units, the sections usually flow into each other. This helps to explain why the Biblical designations come in the center of each section, rather than at the beginning or end, except in the case of "Psalms," which marks the epiphany of rebirth. The scene with El Topo and Mara in the garden oasis could either conclude "Genesis," the period of innocence before El Topo becomes a trickster in his confrontation with the Prophets, or it could begin his Fall, as it follows his rejection of the child, marking his new sexuality and the beginning of his wanderings in the desert. Another example is the shootout on the bridge between El Topo and the two women. This scene could merely be another of the duels which have characterized section two, or it could be a reversal of them in which El Topo is now the true prophet being defeated by a deceitful challenger, or his near death could mark the beginning of his transformation ("In my end is My beginning") and the "bridge" to his first stage of enlightenment.

While El Topo is moving upward, the world through which he travels lies in the lowest circle of the spiral. Since both Heaven and Hell are extensions of the same circle, in a mythic sense, they are mirror images of each other. As Frye says, the demonic universe is an ironic parody of the Christian apocalypse, "Opposed to apocalyptic symbolism is the presentation of the world that desire totally rejects: the world of the nightmare and the scapegoat, of bondage and pain and confusion. . . ."[30]

The apocalyptic world of heavenly vision presents the categories of reality in the forms they assume under the work of human civilization. Frye diagrams the components of the apocalyptic universe (all of which are unified in the single identity of Christ) in the following way:

divine world	society of gods	One God
human world	society of men	One Man
animal world	sheepfold	One Lamb
vegetable world	garden or park	One Tree (of Life)
mineral world	city	One Building, Temple or Stone[31]

The universe of *El Topo*, which is thoroughly demonic, is composed of the same elements, all of which are parodied and made threatening to human life.

"The demonic divine world largely personifies the vast, menacing, stupid powers. . . ."[32] Instead of acting with benign watchfulness, the

Divine powers are either cruelly ironic, coldly indifferent, or conspicuously absent.

> Dostoevsky said, "If God doesn't exist, everything is permitted."
> But I say, "If God doesn't exist, every human value is permitted."
> Saints are people who give up possessions, adornments, petty
> egos, selfishness . . . and they make love very well, they have
> tremendous orgasms . . with God. . . . When Literature was born,
> the written word and the spoken word were inseparable. The
> same thing happens now with the concept of sainthood. The
> concept of sainthood was born inseparable from God. We must
> take the step of separating it from God and discover sainthood
> apart from God. Without the concept of God . . . the limited
> concept of God.[33]

After an arduous struggle to reach "the light," no God protects the cave people; they are massacred with comic dispatch. As Frye says, in the demonic universe, the sky is inaccessible; in *El Topo* the parable of the mole is extended to the cave people. The church sequence in part four emphasizes the corruption of religion in this world. In front of an ancient symbol—the pyramid containing an eye—which Jodorowsky points out can now be found on dollar bills, the worshippers act out rituals, not of immortality, but of death. When the priest tries to expose the dishonesty in their game of Russian roulette by substituting a bullet for the blank, a small child (traditionally the symbol of innocence and renewal of life) blows his brains out. As if to underscore the demonic parody, it is at this moment that Jodorowsky offers us the Biblical designation of "Apocalypse."

In the human world of the Apocalypse, there are three kinds of fulfillment: individual, sexual, and social. "In the sinister human world one individual pole is the tyrant-leader, inscrutable, ruthless, melancholy, and with an insatiable will, who commands loyalty only if he is egocentric enough to represent the collective ego of his followers. The other pole is represented by the *pharmakos* or sacrificed victim, who has to be killed to strengthen the others. In the most concentrated form of the demonic parody, the two become the same."[34] As is clearly apparent, there is surprisingly precise correspondence between Frye's theoretical description and the concrete reality of *El Topo*. In the first half of the film the hero overthrows the despotic Colonel and proves himself the stronger tyrant; in the second half he and the cave people with whom he is identified are hounded and sacrificed. In the area of sexual fulfillment, "the

demonic erotic relation becomes a fierce destructive passion [Mara
and the lesbian whip and claw each other] that works against loyalty
[El Topo rejects the child to possess Mara] or frustrates the one who
possesses it [Mara rejects El Topo for the lesbian] . . . . The demonic
parody of marriage, or the union of two souls in one flesh, may take
the form of hermaphroditism, incest [among the cave people], or
homosexuality [the pair of sheriffs in the town as well as Mara and
the Woman in Black]."[35] Even El Topo and the dwarf are forced into
perverted sex by a leering audience in corrupt surroundings (an
underground "playboy" club.). In the demonic world, social fulfillment is "that of the mob . . . essentially human society looking for a
pharmakos. . . ."[36] We see the workings of the mob most clearly in
part four: in the branding and rodeo massacre of the Indians, in the
lynching of the black man, in the bloody spectacle of the boxing
match, and in the mindless killing of the cave people.

Although traditionally in the demonic universe "the animal world
is portrayed in terms of monsters or beasts of prey,"[37] the animals in
El Topo are usually victims of monstrous humans: the gutted burros
in the first massacre, the crucified lamb, and the twitching rabbits. A
common form of torture is to rope, brand, and slaughter men like
cattle. In one scene, a carrion crow pecks at the bloody ears of a dead
rabbit, but in general it is as if the strength of the animal world is
overshadowed by the evil forces of man.

In the demonic vision the vegetable world is the desert wasteland or
the "sinister enchanted garden."[38] El Topo moves between the oasis,
where he is corrupted by the two women, through deserts devoid of
vegetation. "Coming out of the desert, El Topo and Brontis ride past
a green tree, the first sign of the desert's end. El Topo crosses the
threshold marked by the tree as if he were entering the vegetal door to
the human world."[39] But instead they encounter only death—
including a child impaled on a stake, a hundred brides who have been
raped and murdered, and the corpses of their bridegrooms hanging in
the church.

> In the Bible, the waste land appears in its concrete universal
> form in the tree of death, the tree of forbidden knowledge in
> Genesis, the barren figtree of the Gospels, and the cross. The
> stake with the hooded heretic, the black man or the witch
> attached to it, is the burning tree and body of the infernal world.
> Scaffolds, gallows, stocks, pillories, whips, and birch are or
> could be modulations.[40]

In *El Topo* the leafy trees become the barren poles marking the little boy's initiation rite and the Masters' dwellings. Stakes are conveniently placed everywhere—to tie a horse, impale a man, slice a banana, support an umbrella, or mark time as a sundial. We are first made aware of the dwarves as a walking stick appears in the frame. They carry El Topo away on a stretcher made of leafy branches—one of the few times other than in the sinister oasis that we see vegetation. The Tree of Life is the emblem embroidered on the outer vestment of the old sibyl who guides El Topo through his rebirth.

The environments of *El Topo* are predominantly mineral—the desert, the cave, and the town. The heavenly city is transformed into "cities of destruction and dreadful night." "Corresponding to the temple or One Building of the apocalypse, we have the prison or dungeon. . . ."[41] The effeminate sheriffs have made the jail resemble a brothel where they humiliate the prisoners to the strains of organ music. The desert wasteland is made more ominous by its labyrinthine paths.

> Corresponding to the apocalyptic way or straight road, the highway in the desert for God prophesied by Isaiah, we have in this world the labyrinth or maze, the image of lost direction, often with a monster at its heart like the Minotaur. The labyrinthine wanderings of Israel in the desert, repeated by Jesus when in the company of the devil (or "wild beasts," according to Mark), fit the same pattern.[42]

The primordial elements of fire and water are also symbolically significant. "The world of water is the water of death, often identified with spilled blood."[43] In the parodic spirit of the demonic universe, whenever someone is being murdered in *El Topo*, he is dragged to a nearby pool so that he can bloody its waters. Mara, the woman who leads El Topo astray, is named after the bitter water that Moses found in the desert. When El Topo recognizes his own evil, he cries, "I've been spilled like water. . . ."[44]

The demonic vision even affects the choice of shots and angles. For the most part, Jodorowsky avoids close-ups and instead reveals the grotesque and incongruous in medium and long shots, implying that to see the outrageous elements requires no special perspective; the demonic pervades the universe and is to be found wherever the eye falls.

Every detail announces its symbolic significance or mythic origin, even when we cannot locate its traditional roots or implications. In his commentary on the film, Jodorowsky is eager to identify the Eastern, Western, or privately imaginative sources of these details, and urges us toward a liberated iconography in which everything signifies everything else. The ways in which Jodorowsky makes connections between specific phenomena and their symbolic implications are dazzling. When El Topo rapes Mara, "He opens her legs and forces his penis into her like a bullet—with the same power the Dove forced himself into Mary's ear at the Annunciation."[45] Regarding the rabbit that leads El Topo to the Third Master, Jodorowsky notes the parallel between the string tied to the rabbit and the thread with which Ariadne led Theseus through the labyrinth.[46] His acknowledged sources and connections include: Grimm's Fairy Tales, Zen Buddhism, Classical mythology, Medieval Romance, Tarot cards, Don Quixote, Sufi literature, Persian engravings, Brancusi, Dali, Magritte, Breughel, Goya, Jung, Egyptian mythology, Alexander the Great, Karate, vaudeville, Kurosawa, Tod Browning, Mondo Cane, Nietzshe, and "all the books I love."[47] He hopes some day to collaborate with Frank Zappa, Robert Crumb, Buckminister Fuller, Jerry Rubin, and Dennis Hopper.

> There are moments in the picture when I pay small homages. Homages. For example, when the bandit sucks on the shoe, that's homage to Buñuel. When Mara circles El Topo in the desert saying, "Nothing,nothing nothing. . ." to Godard, especially to a part of his film Pierrot Le Fou. The duel scene between El Topo and the Colonel in the circular space: Leone. When the camera is stationary and the action takes place in a single frame, I pay homage to Buster Keaton.[48]

This self-conscious, playful freedom transcends any conventional definition of eclecticism; rather, it is the most fluid expression of the transformational habit of mind that pervades the film.

This mixing of myths and modes creates a complex and fascinating tone that is one of the film's primary sources of power, particularly in its sleight of hand in manipulating the genre of the Western. In the very first image we see a long shot of El Topo, dressed elegantly in sinister black; seated on the horse behind him is a naked little boy. Western buffs will probably be reminded of Jack Palance's incarnate evil and the theme of the innocent child in Shane. Here it is no blond and reforming Alan Ladd who takes the child in hand, but the sinister gunfighter who leads him to a parody of initiation in which the child must bury his teddy bear and a picture of Momma, and later must kill his first man. Neither children nor women (as we later learn) are innocent in this film.[49]

After this comic episode, we are completely horrified as El Topo and Brontis encounter the bloody massacre in which scores of people and animals have been ripped open, impaled, shot, and hung. From this grim scene the film cuts to the hilarious shot of a bandit sucking and licking a pink shoe, accompanied by the familiar strains of a brassy Mexican trumpet. The other two bandits are acting out equally outrageous fetishes: one carefully peels a banana, impales it on a pole, slices it neatly with his sword, and delicately takes a slice with a toothpick; the other outlines the form of a woman on the ground with little beans, and leaps upon it to make love. El Topo and Brontis ride into the scene and the bandits reach new heights of craziness, encircling them, poking at them, stroking El Topo's beard, spitting at the horse and patting the naked boy; El Topo and his manchild remain impassive and aloof, secure in their Aryan dignity. All the while, the bandits are shrieking and dancing with laughter, leering at them and parodying the classic Hollywood stereotype of the Mexican bandit, known to every movie-goer from *Treasure of Sierra Madre* ("I don't need no stinkin' badge").[50] The shoot-out that follows continues the hilarity. In ritual preparation for simultaneous first shots, the bandits blow up a red balloon. In this conventional period of tension before the duel, accompanied by the incongruous whine of the deflating balloon, Jodorowsky uses the traditional Western technique of cross cutting between close-ups of the combatants' faces. Lest we take it seriously, however, he includes a comical shot of the child's bare arms, encircling El Topo from behind as if these little arms were his and crossing on his chest like an absurd parody of criss-crossed ammunition belts. When the silly red balloon finally goes limp, El Topo shoots; the film suddenly cuts to the bandit's bloody face and again horror replaces comedy. The parody of the Western provides other mixtures of the comic and grotesque.

> The two men: the one with no arms, and the other with no legs. I designed their costume from one I saw in the Encyclopedia of Film: a John Wayne costume. It was one costume, which I cut into two parts. I put the upper half on the man with no legs and the pants on the man with no arms. Two cripples make one John Wayne.[51]

Several elements in the film specifically bring to mind Peckinpah's *The Wild Bunch*. Perhaps the most striking connection is the profusion of blood. *The Wild Bunch* celebrated the fascination with blood, taking it beyond realism with its crimson richness and flowing

abundance. Jodorowsky used over five thousand liters of artificial
blood and learned his technique from Peckinpah.

> I used Mexican technicians who had worked with Peckinpah in
> *The Wild Bunch*, and they taught me how to do the tricks. They
> told me that Peckinpah was very bloody, but when I made my
> effects, they were astonished. I actually used a very classic tech-
> nique. But as I became more familiar with the technique, I began
> to fall in love with it and wanted to use it more and more. I
> started out with five liters of American blood, which is very
> expensive in Mexico. It tasted very good. . .like strawberries.[52]

Both *El Topo* and *The Wild Bunch* parody the conventional innocence of women and children as presented in the romanticized western like *Shane*. Both films contrast the corrupt perverted Mexican
stereotype from *Treasure of Sierra Madre* (the bandits from *El Topo*,
the soldiers from *Wild Bunch*) with the noble, white-clad revolutionary Indians, who represent the hope for the future and the radical
political vision of both movies. Both films use the conventional
figure of the half-mad old man with the demonic laugh (Freddy
Sykes, Edmund O'Brien in *The Wild Bunch* and the Fourth Master
in *El Topo*), based on the Walter Huston figure in *Treasure of Sierra
Madre*. This character combines humor, wisdom, and power of survival, and represents the Jungian archetype of the wise old man. Both
films are framed by two massacres in which women and children are
also victims. At first it seems that both sides are equally murderous,
but by the end we are making a kind of moral distinction; we agree
that the victims of the final massacres deserve killing and that violence serves morality in coping with a totally corrupt society. In both
films the heroes enter the battle willing to die for their vision; this is
the price exacted by violence and the archetypal ending of tragedy.
But there are survivors (Sykes and Deke Thornton [Robert Ryan] in
The Wild Bunch and the dwarf and the two sons of *El Topo*) who ride
off to the possibility of starting a new society, the archetypal ending
of comedy.

Despite the several similarities between *El Topo* and *The Wild
Bunch*, they are extraordinarily different in tone. *El Topo* does not
parody *The Wild Bunch*, but adapts many of its conventions and
attitudes, transforming them from romantic realism to irony and
myth. In a sense, Jodorowsky is like the Indian would-be filmmaker
in Dennis Hopper's *Last Movie* who tries to make a Western after the
Hollywood company has gone home. Jodorowsky uses not only

native technicians left over from *The Wild Bunch*, but the abandoned set from a Glenn Ford movie *(The Law of Tombstone)*. Hopper explored what happens when Hollywood imports its myths, media, and settings into another culture, which has a different understanding of the relationship between art and reality and which creates a new myth around the magical power of the camera. Jodorowsky, born in Chile of a Russian father and Argentinian mother, interprets the conventions of the American Western in terms of his own sense of reality. "When you live the picture, when you are not acting, there is no dichotomy . . . no alienation. What you are doing is real."[53] Thus, Jodorowsky shoots the film in sequence. When there is a rape scene, he *really* rapes the girl (so he says). El Topo's son is played by Jodorowsky's own child, Brontis, who buries his actual mother's picture. Supposedly, Jodorowsky risked his own life many times—in shooting the scene on the rotting bridge, and every time he got on a horse.

> The first time I touched a horse was in this movie. It threw me three times. I couldn't direct the horse. But when the cameras started rolling, I had complete control over the horse. When the camera stopped, I'd fall off. When the cameras were on, I could have done anything. I was invulnerable, I was invulnerable. I even threw myself down a mountain.[54]

As hero and creator of *El Topo*, Jodorowsky moves between the extremes of ironic impotence and mythic invulnerability.

El Topo has a truly transformational structure that is analogous to the metamorphosis of its hero. It starts out parodying the western and presenting a mock quest, which then grows into an exploration of serious political and philosophical questions. One could never predict from the opening where the various eipsodes would lead; the film begins as one thing and ends up as another species. This transformational structure can be traced back to *Don Quixote*, which begins by parodying the Romance and invents the mixed form of the novel along the way. In both works the epiphany or moment of truth is experienced in a cave, evoking Plato's allegory of transcending sensory vision to reach ideal forms. In both works, breaking the ego barrier is translated into breaking the genre barrier; they begin in irony and move to myth. In the end, the quixotic hero may die, and his ideals may be defeated by the material world, but his myth survives.

2001: A Space Odyssey (1968)

2001 presents a quest for knowledge that will transform the individual and the human species, and guarantee their survival. It raises the question of whether this change will result in progress—technologically, aesthetically, and psychologically. Unlike El Topo, the film is not primarily ironic and its universe is not demonic. Kubrick as creator rejects the stance of impotent antihero and is purely godlike in his total control. He is an impersonal director in that he does not see himself as drawing upon the events and emotions of his own life as an individual; yet his aesthetic vision is unique, incorporating a wide range of cultural elements and expanding the technical possibilities of the medium. The double movement into past and future is central to the journey in 2001.

The very title 2001: A Space Odyssey immediately creates a number of expectations, introducing bipolarities that will control the structure and themes of the film: science and myth, past and future, space and time. The title is expressed in two forms linked by a colon—numbers and words. The fact of the numbers evokes the language most trusted by science, and the particular choice of 2001 suggests the binary system of computers; there are 2 units—0 and 1. These numbers also signify a date, moving us forward in time to the second millenium and implying that the film is not on the boundary, but one step inward. The two key words on the other side of the colon set up an ironic opposition. At the far end, the word Odyssey designates the archetype of the mythic journey, carrying us back in time to Homer. Space moves the old archetype into the future, and occupies the linking space between the two time polarities. In oppostion to 2001, it stresses space rather than time. The second part of the title identifies the roots of the narrative structure, since Odyssey implies movement through space and time. The choice of A rather than The implies that this is merely one of the possible imaginative routes into the future.

Based on a story by Arthur C. Clarke, the narrative line of 2001 is minimal. In a prologue—"The Dawn of Man"—a group of apes defends a waterhole against another group. Mysteriously, a black monolith appears, which they approach with fear and curiosity. After this encounter, one of the apes handles a bone in a new way, transforming it into a weapon, which enables his group to kill. In the second part, an American scientist travels through space on a mission to investigate mysterious happenings on a distant planet, which may involve the black monolith. Part three begins in a spaceship that is part of the Jupiter Project, manned by two astronauts and HAL, the computer, who is the only one with knowledge of the Project's goals, and its possible connection with the monolith. HAL has a breakdown and kills the sleeping crew members and one of the astronauts; the other dismantles him. The lone survivor continues the journey and sees the black monolith moving through the cosmos. He enters a special pocket in space called the Stargate Corridor, has a spectacular visual experience, and is mysteriously transported into a strange room where he watches himself age and die. The final image is of an embryo floating through space. The black monolith is the one constant linking the disparate narrative units. As an embodiment of the unknown, it can be seen in all three parts as both a threat and a source of radical invention.

In *2001* the quest for knowledge does not depend on a single central figure as in *El Topo;* rather, the hero is the species itself, which, throughout the film, is embodied in a number of individuals. After the prologue with the apes, the animal and vegetable worlds disappear and we are left with a universe dominated by the human species and its extensions. Frye suggests that science fiction is a form of Romance that is mythic rather than ironic.

> Science fiction frequently tries to imagine what life would be like on a plane as far above us as we are above savagery; its setting is often of a kind that appears to us as technologically miraculous. It is thus a mode of romance with a strong inherent tendency to myth.[55]

The film clearly offers the four parts of the quest as described by Frye, but they do not control the narrative structure as in *El Topo.* The first phase, the *agon,* involves the hero in his earliest stage of existence. One ingenious ape, through his invention of a weapon, advances his group in its struggle for territory and the water of life. After this conflict, the hero must travel before he encounters the unknown, as the scientist, young in knowledge journeys toward information in part two of the film. The second phase, or *pathos,* involving the mutual death of the hero and monster, is acted out by HAL (the mechanical dragon) and the surviving astronaut. The third stage focuses on the disappearance or tearing to pieces of the hero. Since the species hero is embodied in many forms, this phase has two manifestations in the film. The dismantling of HAL represents the tearing down of human intellect, with which it is analogous. The

surviving astronaut is then split in two: the one who undergoes the
physical transformation of aging and death, and the one who
watches. The death of both HAL and the astronaut is necessary to free
humanity from its present state of intellectual and biological
development, so that it may evolve toward a new identity. The fourth
stage, the reappearance and recognition of the hero, is embodied in
the embryo, which may represent a new evolutionary stage for the
species.

  2001 also includes the four poles of characterization traditionally
found in the Romance. As we have seen, the hero is the species, and its
individual manifestations—the inventive ape, the American scientist,
HAL, the surviving astronaut, and the embryo. The antagonist or
"deceitful challenger" is the fearful unknown, manifest in the black
monolith, and man's own destructive nature, embodied in HAL.
These exterior and interior antagonists also double as the nature
spirits, who are unpredictable, but have the potential of serving
humans in their quest. The rustic clown is also present in HAL, the
nuts and bolts brain, who makes all the systems go. His name
provides one of the film's few jokes—a humanized acronym one
alphabet letter back from IBM.[56] The fact that HAL embodies all four
elements of character helps to explain why he arouses such a strong
emotional response from the audience. The presentation of typical
characters and phases in multiple forms represents a transformation
of the archetype itself. In a world where the population has grown
huge and individual heroism is no longer the only source of progress,
the storytelling forms themselves must change to accommodate the
future.

  Striving for the apocalyptic vision that includes all of time, *2001*,
like Frye's system for classifying art, moves in both circular and
linear patterns, and both backwards and forwards. This structure
characterizes several other recent works of science fiction, which fuse
past and future into a new unity: e.g., *Zardoz, A Boy and His Dog,
Lucifer Rising, Chariot of the Gods, Memoirs of a Survivor*. In *2001*,
the quest moves from the prehistoric past into the next millenium.
This diachronic movement traces the advancement of technology,
both in space exploration and film techniques. The strongest
argument for this progressive view is the technical achievement of the
film itself, which also becomes evidence for the implicit movement
toward a utopia for the species. The film also looks at phenomena
synchronically as having a simultaneous, ahistorical existence. From

this perspective, everything exists in a single system with set parameters; elements are reshuffled to create transformational changes, like music growing out of a limited number of notes, sentences out of a fixed language, and images out of a kaleidoscope. There is a paradox in the opposition between the diachronic and the synchronic views of change. Although the synchronic approach is essentially static, there is perpetual flux and transformation within the system. The diachronic, though it stresses linear movement and progress, usually posits a static goal at the end of the journey—a utopia that is never really attained.

The synchronic notion that man is basically unchanged is reinforced by the static spatial forms—particularly the circle—that dominate *2001*. Repeatedly we see round images—planets, satellites, the giant centrifuge, the wheel-like Space Station 5, globular space vehicles, the human eye, and the embryo enclosed in its sac. The overall structure is also circular. The film begins with the newly born human species; it ends with an embryo awaiting birth. Whether this infant merely suggests repetition of our present life cycle or the emergence of a new species, the imminent birth moves the narrative structure back around toward its starting point. In the space travel between the beginning and the end of the film, there are two phone calls back to earth, both to acknowledge the ritual importance of birthdays. Within the circle of the whole, the film has a three-part structure, another externally imposed static spatial arrangement. Kubrick rejects traditional linear plot development by moving erratically in time. There is a gigantic leap between parts one and two—from four million years ago to *2001*, and then a brief time lapse between parts two and three. Kubrick is obviously more concerned with exploring space than time, perhaps implying that cinema is primarily a visual rather than a narrative medium. This emphasis also has implications about progress. Time is not a singular linear development but a recurring cyclical pattern—a model which, like the spiral in *El Topo*, combines a static pattern with progressive development. In the end the spaceman watches himself go through the life cycle; we witness a similar technological cycle for the species. The ape creates a tool out of the bone of another animal, which he may use either creatively or destructively. We have created sophisticated spacecrafts, weaponry, and thinking machines based on our big brain, which may either conquer the unknown or destroy us. Despite the technological advance, in all three parts of the film humans are still curious and fearful of the black monolith; the same conflicts and choices remain from the time of Homer and the dawn of man.

In the realm of art, this synchronic/diachronic distinction is expressed in T. S. Eliot's essay "Tradition and the Individual Talent," which is an important source for Frye's conception of aesthetic change. Eliot argues that art has a temporal (diachronic) and universal (synchronic) dimension. Works may reveal specific historical meanings, but all works are part of a single structure of art that perpetually absorbs and is transformed by the new. Not only do old works influence new ones, but the genuinely new transforms the identity of the old.[57] This is vividly demonstrated in Kubrick's choice of Johann Strauss's "Blue Danube Waltz" instead of futuristic electronic music to accompany the space station as it floats through the heavens. He moves backward for the music and forward for the visuals. After seeing this sequence, one cannot hear this music again without associating it with the joyful, gliding weightlessness of movement through space. In a display of aesthetic wit and power, Kubrick turns to the other Strauss for the Dawn of Man and provides an image grand enough to be linked forever with the opening bars of "Also Sprach Zarathustra." He uses the same technique in *A Clockwork Orange,* but there "Singing in the Rain" and Beethoven's Ninth symphony are ironically transformed by their association with violence.

Like *El Topo, 2001* consciously draws on other art from a great variety of periods and media, exhibiting a high degree of self-reflexiveness. On the centripetal and diachronic levels, *2001* seems to be about the development of the film medium. Part one starts with still photography (the roots of cinema) and moves into silent film. Part two suggests the early days of talkies, specifically the corny science fiction film and its conventions. Part three draws on the futuristic independent film with its emphasis on opticals and its goal of expanding our perception. At the same time, within each section, we find a recurring combination of the strange and the familiar, the old and the new, qualifying the emphasis on technological advancement and reaffirming the centrifugal and synchronic perspectives.

In the "Dawn of Man" prologue, the cinematic technique seems to parallel the subject. The sequence opens with a series of still shots of the primitive landscape, which are presented in marvelous visual compositions with a subtle use of color, just as still photography represents the dawn of cinema (Kubrick began his career in still photography before going into moving pictures). As we move into the live action sequence with the apes, it is as if we have entered the era of silent cinema, emphasizing the physicality of movement with exaggerated gestures to communicate underlying feelings. There is no language—only grunts and music. This is the appearance and the illusion, but the underlying reality is quite different. Actually, this is one of the most technically innovative sequences in the film. Kubrick selected the southwest African setting as the perfect primitive terrain, yet to film such a sequence on location would have presented tremendous financial and technical problems. Instead he used front-projection of 8 x 10 transparencies to create the background. Since it is basically a desert scene, nothing had to move; thus one is not likely to realize that the sequence is shot on a sound stage against a background composed of still photographs. Kubrick had to build a special projector because, though front projection was not new, it had never before been used on this scale.

The transition between parts one and two is a matched cut from the bone to an orbiting bomb. Continuing Kubrick's emphasis on the visual power of the medium, the similarity between the two images strikes our eyes before we realize the narrative link—both weapons are products of human technology, the most primitive and the most advanced. Once we enter the space station, we move from the silent cinema into the talkies, but the conversations are trivial and uninteresting: What is happening on that distant planet? What is the nature of the threat to civilization? Does the American scientist *really* know what is going on? Kubrick parodies the science fiction genre, which, as Susan Sontag has perceptively observed, frequently expresses "the imagination of disaster."[58] Frye sees this concern as one of the archetypal components of science fiction.

> From Wagner's *Ring* to science fiction, we may notice an increasing popularity of the flood archetype. This usually takes the form of some cosmic disaster destroying the whole fictional society except a small group, which begins life anew in some sheltered spot.[59]

Like the disaster genre, science fiction is frequently concerned with survival. Both genres rely heavily on special effects, which persuasively demonstrate human ingenuity. If filmmakers can figure out how to make the illusion of an earthquake, towering inferno, or space travel convincing, then humans are probably resourceful enough to survive any holocaust. The narrative lines of these genres, however, are not quite so persuasive about human progress in morality.

Yet, in part two of *2001*, what engages our curiosity is not the conventional plot concerning survival and morality developed through dialogue, but the conception of space developed through the visuals. The futuristic vision is repeatedly juxtaposed with something familiar. The giant centrifuge floats to the strains of the "Blue Danube." The spaceship clearly belongs to the same genre as the commercial airline with its arrangement of seats, stewardess and pilots, and dozing passengers. But mixed with these recognizable cues are the incongruous touches of a pen floating in the nongravitational air and the stewardess walking upside down into the space kitchen. The concept of a space station is exotic, yet its concrete forms are mundane: the names Hilton and Howard Johnson, the attractive yet sterile modern furniture, the conventional clothes, the interactions of the people. When the American scientist makes a telephone call, the great distance of space and the video aspects are strange; yet the instructions, the instruments, the behavior of his daughter back on earth, and the content of their conversation are all familiar.

Our visual education is accelerated in the spaceship, which is full of inner recesses constantly intersected by new angles. Kubrick invites us to explore its space and understand its motion. The effect of the stewardess walking upside down in a weightless chamber was created by fastening the camera to the front of the set, which rotated 180 degrees while the actress paced upright on a treadmill. Like the "Dawn of Man" prologue, this technically sophisticated sequence alludes to the basic illusion of cinema—motion from the series of still images. The overall composition of the shot, moreover, looks like a human eye, stressing that our perception is beginning to be expanded. The interiors of the spacecrafts have multiple dials and screens on the instrument panels, which look amazingly authentic, each projecting a separate moving picture on a different scale. The view, through the windows, of the stars and planets in the distance introduces an additional dimension. To create an illusion of such complexity, Kubrick had to combine many separate images on one negative, probably the dominant technique of the film. While we are watching *2001*, we are never really sure whether the scale is accurate, whether the moon is a model or a photograph, whether the action is live or animated, whether the setting is an actual landscape or a front-projected transparency, whether an object is moving or stationary. But do we really care? What matters is that these disparate elements are masterfully combined into a single convincing image, which parallels Kubrick's synthesis of a wide range of cultural and temporal elements in the film's vision of the quest. Never before in the history of movies has a film employed so many of these complex special-effects shots while using the huge scale of 70mm and achieving such marvelous clarity of image. The successful design and operation of this technical system is almost as impressive an accomplishment as the Jupiter Project. It is the film's strongest argument in favor of human progress.

In part three, the self-reflexiveness is developed on a psychological level, which had been latent in the earlier sections. In part one, we see the creative roots of man in fear, affection, aggresion, and curiosity. In part two, these same emotions are present in familiar human beings, but we have no emotional engagement whatsoever with these characters. In part three, which considers the self and its future possibilities, we begin to explore inner space. Frye describes this movement inward as typical of the quest in its mythic or anagogic phase, in which art tries to "imitate the total dream of man."

> Nature is now inside the mind of an infinite man who builds his cities out of the Milky Way. This is not reality, but it is the conceivable or imaginative limit of desire, which is infinite, eternal, and hence apocalyptic.[60]

In part three we meet three new characters: the two astronauts and HAL, the computer that has never made a mistake. Yet HAL is subject to pride and madness. Only he knows the purpose of the Jupiter Project—to contact the advanced civilization that has made the black monolith: presumably, this knowledge contributes to his breakdown. He is as frightened by the unknown as the primitive apes. The inward journey is rendered literal when the astronaut gets inside of HAL and starts to disconnect his wiring. Although we should identify with the human, we actually empathize more with the murderous machine who, ironically, is the most sympathetic character in the film; he delivers the only dialogue in the film that has any emotional power.

> Stop, Dave.
> I'm afraid.
> I'm afraid, Dave.
> Dave. My mind is going.
> I can feel it. I can feel it.
> My mind is going. There is
> no question about it.
> I can feel it. I can feel it. I can feel it.
> I'm afraid.

The exploration of inner space is continued with Dave, the surviving astronaut. When he enters the Stargate Corridor, its images suggest the double quality of psychic pioneering; they are at once gorgeous and terrifying. We don't know whether they exist in inner or outer space. At first they are abstract—flashing columns of light, optical warpings created by a computerized slit-scan device. But then we begin to recognize negative shots of landscapes reminiscent of the muted-tone stills in the opening sequence but now transformed into wildly colored, flashing kaleidoscopic images. We have moved from the dawn of cinema to the outer edge of visual experimentation usually found in independent films using the optical printer. The recurring shots of the multitinted semiabstract human eye stress the primacy of perception. We are reminded that the basic illusion of moving pictures is dependent not only on the projection of a series of still photographs but also on persistence of vision. Cinema itself combines inner and outer space. This fusion continues in the environment of the final sequence. The capsule, and later the black monolith, appear, not in outer space, but within the confines of a strange, green tinted room with traditional furniture and a futuristic, luminescent floor. We are puzzled as to how Dave got there, and whether this room exists in space, on a strange new planet, or inside his own mind. As he moves through his aging process, he eats his "last supper" and drops a glass of wine, evoking the death of Christ and the ancient glass breaking ceremony of the Jewish wedding. The one ritual marks the end of a life cycle, and the other the birth of a new society. The camera focuses on the glass as it splinters into countless pieces, transforming the event into a fascinating visual experience in pure phenomenological terms. In the context of the narrative, these acts shatter Dave's identity, and prepare him for the rebirth to follow. In Frye's description of the archetypical ending of the science fiction quest, a small group survives, shutting out the rest of the world, and beginning life anew with "the image of the mysterious newborn infant floating on the sea."[61] In this truly futuristic version, the sea as a source of death and life and metaphor for the unconscious is transformed into cosmic space where myth and technology are united. The circular embryonic child is a world unto itself, a microcosm ready to explore the macrocosm. If one goes far enough and deep enough into the self, one breaks through to the universal, to the collective unconscious and its archetypes. In this final powerful image there is a mystical fusion between the individual and the cosmos, between inner and outer space, between verisimilitude and fantasy, between familiar images of the past and strange discoveries of the future, between diachronic linear progress and synchronic cyclical repetition.

Both *El Topo* and *2001* draw their strength from this synthesis of a great variety of elements from the culture and from filmmaking, giving them a resonance that cannot be exhausted by a single interpretation. But the two films differ greatly in tone. Like *Barry Lyndon*, *2001* is characterized by a sense of grandeur in its music, pace, narrative structure, and, especially, its visual impact. Thus more than *El Topo*, it represents the quest myth in its fully developed anagogic phase, as defined by Frye:

> It unites total ritual, or unlimited social action, with total dream, or unlimited individual thought. Its universe is infinite and boundless hypothesis; it cannot be contained within any actual civilization or set of moral values, for the same reason that no structure of imagery can be restricted to one allegorical interpretation. . . . The *ethos* of art is no longer a group of characters within a natural setting, but a universal man who is also a divine being, or a divine being conceived in anthropomorphic terms.[62]

Zardoz (1974)[63]

Zardoz presents an ironic quest in which an "exterminating angel," a stylized western hero from the Outlands, seeks a Holy Grail, a crystal enshrined in a Tabernacle, in order to bring death and fertility to an advanced but sterile utopia. Like *El Topo* and *2001*, it is highly allusive, unifying past and future, inner and outer experience, and combining many media and genres. In particular, it fuses the western with science fiction, literature with film. *Zardoz* is liberated and experimental in form, yet, like John Boorman's earlier films (e.g., *Point Blank* and *Deliverance*), its sexual and political attitudes are reactionary. It deals with the struggle for survival in a late phase of Romance where the species is in an advanced stage of decline. Like *El Topo*, it is ironic rather than mythic. It assumes that in order for humans to survive, they must resolve certain paradoxes, giving up some values for the renewal of others.

The title sets the tone. Extracted from *The Wizard* of *Oz*, it identifies its "Holy Book" as a literary and cinematic classic. While the god-head is a transformation of the cowardly lion, there is a dark incongruity in drawing the name of a violent god from a work of kiddie literature. In both versions, however, a funny little man hides behind the threatening mask. The joke is intensified by the word *Zardoz* itself; surrounded by Z's, it suggests the circular repetition of a palindrome.

The plot is complicated. In a prologue, Zed, a rebellious mortal, kills Arthur Frane, the wizard Eternal who created the god-head Zardoz to control the primitive Outlands. Then the brutish Zed invades the Vortex, the highly refined culture of Eternals who have mastered art and science and banished aggression and death. In this nonrepressive, nonsexist world, life unfortunately is sterile and dull. Zed is captured and studied as a freak, his mind and body probed to discover how he got into the Vortex. Although he is treated as a slavish beast of burden, he has the power to give life and take it away. He appears to be a lower form than these Eternals, but he turns out to be a mutant who is superior to them in every way. Eventually he conquers them and becomes their god-head. He absorbs their knowledge and destroys their civilization. He takes a wife, Consuela, and in an epilogue, they reestablish the nuclear family. He also impregnates May, the leading scientist of the Vortex, and all of her female followers, who ride off into the sunset to build a new society. All of the other Eternals are killed off by Zed's fellow exterminators; the final massacre is relished by both killers and victims. The film develops a series of polarities: Is humanity dominated by the mind or the body? Is the primary form of human creativity aesthetic or sexual? Is religion wizardry or paganism? Should society aim for a peaceful, static utopia or constant, violent flux? *Zardoz* reaffirms one of the basic assumptions of the Eternals: the unity of opposites is the fundamental law of nature. Life/death, male/female, love/violence, pleasure/pain are merely different facets of the same experience; each side is essential to the other.

In *Zardoz* the goal of the quest is to reconcile these opposites in order to insure the survival of the species. The central conflict is between an individual and a society—the one and the many—who must reabsorb each other. The species is closer to extinction than in *El Topo* and *2001*. Hence, the film begins in the second stage of the quest—the mutual death of hero and monster, but there is confusion as to which is which and ironically the death is not final. Zed, a mutant, kills the eccentric Frane, who poses as a lion god. Being an Eternal, he doesn't really die; Arthur is merely reconstructed and is still willing to use Zed to bring about his own end and that of his culture. Both of them can also be seen as a *deus ex machina;* Zed is a savior who has been dreamed up and programmed by the wizard, who also likes to descend from the sky. Like Frankenstein, Frane loses control of his monster. Later, when the Eternals are deciding whether to kill Zed because he threatens their stability, one of them argues that it would be self-destructive: "The monster is a mirror and when we look at him we look at our own hidden faces." The first stage of the quest—the conflict—is told in flashback, as in Homer's *Odyssey*. The civilization has already exhausted itself through eons of perpetual war. In the distant past, a "small group" sought "some sheltered spot"—the Vortex—where they could create a peaceful utopia; this "cosy group . . . managed to shut the rest of the world out"[64] but at the price of separating mind and body and widening the gulf between a privileged elite at the center and the suffering masses in the Outlands. This division was futile, however, for two reasons. When man's animal nature is isolated from reason and culture, aggression and violence run rampant; shouting "Kill, kill, kill," the Outlanders continue their internecine wars and rebel when their god tries to bring peace. When animal nature is excluded, the species turns sterile and apathetic; the Eternals greet their own brutal death with joy. The violence and flux persist until the serene images of the epilogue.

The disappearance or physical transformation of the hero—the third phase—occurs when Zed enters the Tabernacle, and sees the myriad reflections of himself and others. He shoots his own image, breaks through his ego barriers, and becomes the crystal. The transformation of the human species also requires the sacrificial death of a group—the dwarves in *El Topo*, the sleeping spacemen in *2001*, and the Eternals in *Zardoz*. In the rebirth phase, Zed finds his "comely bride" and revives the patriarchal nuclear family. On a larger scale, he launches a new society of Amazons, all carrying Zed's seed.

The four character poles of Romance are developed with a high degree of self-reflexiveness, which, as in *2001*, has both an aesthetic and psychological dimension. Again as in *2001*, all four facets are embodied in a single individual, this time in the central figure Zed, another means of reconciling the one and the many. The hero is played by Sean Connery, Agent 007, veteran of the James Bond series. No one could be better qualified to perform this fascist coup of a non-sexist society. His primary antagonists take three forms— Zardoz, his god; Consuela, his woman; and the Vortex society, his conquest. In becoming the god-head, he absorbs the trinity. The nature spirit is represented by the ancient scientist who originally discovered immortality and founded the Vortex. According to Frye, this "old man in a tower, the lonely hermit absorbed in occult or magical studies," is typical of the last phase of Romance, which moves from action to contemplation.[65] As he lies in his bed reviewing his past deeds with regret, he reaffirms Zed's purpose and identifies him as a force of nature: "The Vortex is an offence against nature; she had to find a way to destroy this, so she made you. We forced the hand of evolution."

The rustic clown is the comical Arthur Frane, who has aided the hero by training and arming him, and launching him on his quest into the Vortex. In this film, his role is considerably expanded; he is used by Boorman as the deflating trickster who self-consciously plays with the idea of creation. He addresses us directly in the prologue, implying that he is the controlling consciousness of the film. Introducing himself as god, magician, and puppet master, he brags about his ability to manipulate his characters. Yet, he admits that he has also been invented—presumably by Boorman—and then mockingly asks us: "And you poor creatures, who conjured you out of the clay? Is God in show business, too?"

The multiple identity of the creative mind is developed visually in the prologue through the appearance of three giant faces linking the clown and the hero, the creator and his monster as alter-egos or shadow figures who share the lion persona. The film opens on Arthur's face, with theatrical mustache, floating through space, gradually getting larger until it dominates the entire screen. The next head we see is a stone spaceship flying over worshippers wearing matching leonine masks. The Zardoz god-head flies away, leaving the camera to focus on a huge close-up of a rebellious brutal; instead of the mask we see Zed's face. He shoots his gun directly at the camera displaying his sexual and lethal power; the screen turns to flames and then fades. With the titles in the background, we see the stone god-head gliding through space to the strains of Beethoven's Seventh Symphony, evoking the first image of the centrifuge in *2001*, and following the path across the screen charted by Arthur's face. It, too, moves forward, grows larger, and gradually takes over the entire screen. Thus, the prologue reveals that like the Christian god, the creator has three personae: Arthur, the Eternal Magical Father; Zed, the Active Mortal Son; and Zardoz, the Holy Leonine Spirit.

The animal and vegetable worlds in which Zed fulfills his quest display polarities that must be reconciled for the health of the species.

While the Eternals live in a lush, green pseudo-Eden, the Outlanders live in a barren desert and are identified with the wild horses they ride. Yet they also live near the ocean, suggesting their access to the life force. In their rejection of animality, the Eternals cage Zed with an eagle and a camel, other specimens for study. One of them mocks Zed's "obscenely decaying flesh," using him to draw his carriage and beating him for information. Zed sarcastically licks his hand like a dog. In their science the Eternals have found ways to deny their animality altogether, eliminating sex and sleep; they hang upside down from the trees, rejuvenating themselves as if they were fruit.

Boorman uses the crystal image as the primary means of reconciling the polarities that dominate the film. It is a receiver and a transmitter, a medium of communication between the inner and the outer, the individual and the culture, the body and the mind, the yin and the yang, nature and art. As an emblem of creativity, it has aesthetic, sexual and religious associations. As object and place of worship, it is a thing of beauty, but not necessarily a joy forever, a fragile form incapable of radical change. On the one hand, the crystal represents the utopian society; it is the concrete embodiment of all humanistic values as well as the means of transmitting them. As it informs Zed, "I am the sum of these people." It is a decorative ring on their fingers, which also functions as television, radio, telephone, teaching machine, encyclopedia, university, ballot box, and computer. Zed is told by the Eternals: "The crystal shall join us each to each and all to the Tabernacle." On the other hand, since it insures that all members of society are on the same wave length, it is also a source of conformity and sterile aestheticism, inhibiting change. The crystal, like the society, is waiting to be entered and violated. Zed enters the Vortex (as sexual an entry as we find in *Alice in Wonderland*) and also "penetrates" the crystal ball. The crystal has the power to reaffirm the marriage of Yin and Yang. After one of the Eternals (Friend) has been declared a Renegade, he drops his crystal ring and lays his face down on a mirrored table; we see a huge close-up of his head and its reflection. Later, after Zed has acquired the knowledge of the crystal, there is a similar shot as he lays his head down on the same table. When they finally join forces in the rebellion, Zed is brought to Friend in bridal drag. This relationship is parallel to the one between Zed and Consuela. At first she actively seeks his destruction. Attracted by the force of opposites, he is turned on by her coldness, and his desire arouses hers. Finally, she admits: "In hunting you, I have become you." Their fusion further reflects Zed's interaction with the crystal. When Arthur drops the crystal ball into the palm of Zed's hand, he gives him the key to power and survival. As in his sexual conquest of Consuela, Zed is able to conquer the Tabernacle only when he can look into it and see its multifaceted nature, including his own reflection. Once inside, he destroys his old self image and becomes an omnipotent reincarnation of the crystal. As the ring of eternity, the crystal speaks with the voice of paradox: "I am everywhere and nowhere."

The crystal also helps control the structure of the film in its simultaneous movement inward and outward. From the prologue onward, Boorman repeatedly raises the question of who is getting inside of whose head. This is most apparent in five parallel sequences, where the Eternals, led by May the scientist, probe Zed's mind. The visuals obscure the distinction between inner and outer boundaries, and the actions reveal shifting power relationships, explicitly linking sexuality with knowledge. These sequences imply that learning must be sensual as well as rational, and that knowledge is power.

In the first sequence, the screen is totally dominated by images of rape and murder as we hear Zed's narration before establishing the context: Zed is lying spread eagle on a table in a pyramid room while his memories are flashed on one wall. The other two walls are fluid and contain floating bodies of reconstructed Eternals. Within the room, Eternals watch this "terribly exciting" footage, but with aesthetic distance. One viewer observes: "You can't equate their feelings with ours. It's just entertainment." In contrast, Zed watches his own images with complete involvement and actually re-experiences his own adventures: "I love to see the memory, I love the moment of their death, when I am one with Zardoz." Presumably, Boorman hopes we in the outer theater will respond like Zed and become one with Boorman.

The second sequence takes place in the same environment, but this time the brute stands in front of the screen, watching pornographic movies that are supposed to arouse him while Consuela lectures on penal erection in a coolly rational tone. The important lesson learned by the pale aesthetes is that Zed is turned on, not by art, but by Consuela in the flesh. In the third sequence, May leads Zed inside a pyramid where his internal genetic structure is projected on the walls that enclose them. Discovering his superiority and capacity for destruction, she forces him to obey her. Zed seeks out May in the fourth sequence, penetrating the flimsy material that encapsulates her as she meditates. Once he enters her space, she encloses him and probes his mind, demanding to see how Arthur led him to commit murder and lose his innocence. His desire for revenge sexually arouses her; they are observed by Consuela, who accuses them of bestiality. Immediately turned on, Zed tries to rape Consuela while May, frustrated and jealous, temporarily blinds him. Consuela vows to hunt him down. Zed's power struggle with the two women mirrors the conflict he previously had with Arthur.

Finally, in the fifth sequence Zed trades his sexual seed for all the knowledge stored within the crystal. Images of paintings, words, numbers, and symbols are projected onto parts of the body (mainly close-ups of heads), creating a visual collage; words, songs, and music construct an analogous effect in sound. As the camera pans across a chain of images (like the kissing chain where Apathetics are awakened and aroused by a drop of Zed's perspiration and nearly rape him), the pace accelerates until it reaches a sexual climax. Zed's first "loss of innocence" came with knowledge of the Holy Book of Oz; now he is gang banged by the entire culture. As in the Bible, "knowing" has a sexual meaning. At the end of the sequence, Zed is told, "Now you know all that we know."

Perhaps we are also being raped. Just as the crystal is implanted in everyone's brain and activated by a laser beam of coherent light, the film itself is a crystal, which allows us to see into the mind of John Boorman. Yet it is also a means by which he projects his fantasies into our consciousness through the medium of light. This process, of course, has been dramatized in the scene where the Eternals watch Zed's memories, which look very much like westerns, war movies, and other popular adventure films. Here, Boorman is identified with his potent hero and we with the passive audience waiting to be turned on and ravished by art.

The idea that film is a crystal is reinforced by many formal aspects of Boorman's style. The structure is kaleidoscopic rather than linear, providing us with a multifaceted view of reality. Like the spiral in *El Topo* and the circle in *2001*, the crystal offers a synchronic view of experience. Claude Lévi-Strauss claims that this kind of structure is basic to myth.

> Myth grows spiral-wise until the intellectual impulse which has originated it is exhausted. Its growth is a continuous process whereas its structure remains discontinuous. . . . It closely corresponds, in the realm of the spoken word, to the kind of being a crystal is in the realm of physical matter.[66]

Many of the sequences reflect each other (as we have seen); many shots contain photographic images projected on other surfaces, splintering the light in various planes and creating density and simultaneity. We understand the whole by going back and forth among the parts as each is illuminated. The splintering effect is intensified once the Eternals begin to hunt down Zed, mirroring his behavior. The film cuts abruptly among a variety of brief scenes, whose time connections are unclear. For example, we see the Eternals (led by Consuela) trying to break into a plastic bubble that encloses Zed. The camera cross cuts between interior and exerior views, then in slow motion reveals Zed breaking out of the capsule. Similarly, the continuity of space and time is broken as we cut to Zed signalling his warriors from the Outlands. Later when the film cuts back to the attack, we don't know whether it has been suspended or whether the action has continued while we were gone. The scene where liberated Renegades, Apathetics, and Eternals smash the statues is interrupted by Zed's encounter with the crystal; when we cut back to the destruction, we see it in reverse as vases are restored. Then Zed leads his friends out of the Vortex and the violence resumes a forward motion.

The structure makes it very difficult to tell where the film begins and ends. The prologue provides no context: a head suspended in space. When we cut to a long shot of a landscape with the date 2293 superimposed, we think this must be the opening: Zardoz giving commands to his killers. But then we see the titles and realize that this has been another prologue, and we have no way of knowing how much time has elapsed before the next scene where Zed kills Arthur. The film provides earlier flashbacks before Zed's entry into the Vortex—the begetting of the mutants (is that Zed we see, or his ancestor?), and the founding of the utopia. The ambiguity concerning the beginning is related to the confusion over who is the ultimate Maker.

Similarly, it is hard to tell where the film ends. From the final massacre, the film cuts abruptly forward to Consuela giving birth as Zed looks on and then further telescopes time in a montage of family portraits. In contrast to the rich visuals of the earlier sequences, this final scene has an almost abstract cartoon simplicity—two or three figures dressed modestly in natural green, posed against the blank walls of an empty cave. Like the editing techniques, the changes within the scene create a pattern of condensation. The son matures and leaves his parents. The couple ages and is reduced to hand-holding skeletons, then cobwebs, and finally handprints on the wall.

Is this the origin of primitive cave paintings? We had thought of the Vortex as far in the future. Was it actually deep in the past? The crystal refracts the diachronic illusion, allowing us to see the lines of infinity moving in both directions.

This fusion of past and future is also reflected in the costumes and settings. When Zed enters Arthur's quaint dwelling, we see a sign on the wall that reads: "In this secret room from the past, I seek the future." Zed comes from a culture that is living in a new dark age; it looks medieval, with a few modern touches (e.g., abandoned automobiles). His appearance (braided pony tail, mustache, boots, red bikini, crossed ammunition belts, and Zardoz mask) is primitive, yet it could easily be the costume for a modern guerrilla with a theatrical flair. The advanced society of the Eternals has a similar mixture. The bakery is primitive, yet it has an ultra-modern oven. The decor juxtaposes classical statuary, contemporary boutique fabrics, Renaissance architecture, and plastic bubbles. The Eternals wear unisex costumes including Egyptian headdresses, chic low-cut midriffs, wrap-around skirts, and loose trousers of varying lengths, all becoming to the fashionably slender. The Zardoz spacecraft (a Sphinxlike head) is whimsically comical, offering an earlier conception of science fantasy in the mode of Flash Gordon serials and *Barbarella*.

The film's complex network of allusions transforms it into a crystal—a storehouse of archetypal imagery and ideas from our literary and cinematic past. As he is about to give Zed the crystal ball, Arthur quotes T. S. Eliot, the poet who has relied most heavily on allusions to provide a unifying framework for the fragmented experience of the twentieth century. In fact, the passage quoted from "The Love Song of J. Alfred Prufrock" builds on lines from Marvell's "To His Coy Mistress," where a pair of lovers (like Zed and Consuela) use violent sexuality to fight against Time and Death.

> Let us roll all our strength and all
> Our sweetness up into one ball.

Eliot's version is even more immediately relevant to the situation in *Zardoz*.

> Would it have been worth while,
> To have bitten off the matter with a smile,
> To have squeezed the universe into a ball
> To roll it toward some overwhelming question,
> To say: "I am Lazarus, come from the dead,

Arthur asks Zed to quote the next line, as if testing his literary knowledge.

Come back to tell you all, I shall tell you all.

Returned from the dead, Arthur won't tell Zed the secrets of the Tabernacle until he can see into the crystal ball. When he squeezes it in his hand, Zed penetrates the crystal and is transformed. In all three contexts, the unifying archetypal image is the ball—a condensed form or microcosm that fights off meaninglessness and death by crystallizing experience. In "Tradition and the Individual Talent," Eliot provides the synchronic assumptions that underlie the aesthetic used by Boorman in this film (and also in *El Topo* and *2001*).

> No poet, no artist of any art, has his complete meaning alone. . . . You must set him, for contrast and comparison, among the dead. I mean this as a principle of aesthetic, not merely historical, criticism. . . . What happens when a new work of art is created is something that happens simultaneously to all the works of art which preceded it. The existing monuments form an ideal order among themselves, which is modified by the introduction of the new (the really new) work of art among them. Whoever has approved this idea of order . . . will not find it preposterous that the past should be altered by the present as much as the present is directed by the past.[67]

The basic situation in *Zardoz* is adopted from Book 3 of *Gulliver's Travels* by Jonathan Swift. (Other filmmakers had already succeeded with material from Book 4 in the *Planet of the Apes* and its sequels.) The most anti-utopian of the four voyages, Book 3 attacks three temporal visions of human perfection: a visit to the Moderns' Academy ridicules the attempt to exalt the present through scientific experimentation (here Swift mocks the Royal Society, which was trying to establish Bacon's "New Atlantis"); conversation with spirits from the past reveals that humans have degenerated rather than progressed and that all historical knowledge has been hopelessly distorted; an encounter with the immortal Struldbruggs destroys all illusions about a future without death. Recognized by a black spot on their forehead (rather than an implanted crystal), Swift's immortals are the mutants rather than their visitor. When Gulliver hears of them, he naively has great expectations. Swift's satire always moves inward against Gulliver, his narrator, as well as outward toward the society he encounters. Despite the fact that he has just received direct evidence of human degeneracy, Gulliver muses that if he were to become a Struldbrugg, "I should be a living treasury of knowledge and wisdom, and certainly become oracle of the nation." But the catch is age—the immortals must suffer "a perpetual life under all the usual disadvantages which old age brings along with it." Although Boorman grants his immortals Gulliver's fantasy, he uses age as the medium of punishment within utopia. Swift's description of the pathetic Struldbruggs applies perfectly to the Renegades in *Zardoz*, who have been condemned to decrepitude.

> They were not only opinionative, covetous, morose, vain, talkative; but incapable of friendship, and dead to all natural affection. Envy and impotent desires, are their prevailing passions. But those objects against which their envy seems principally directed, are the vices of the younger sort, and the deaths of the old.[68]

The Eternals who retain their youth are still miserable because of boredom, the same reason suggested by Samuel Johnson in *Rasselas,* another 18th century anti-utopia. This form is well established in English literature as a sub-genre combining satire and science fiction (e.g., *Erehwon, 1984, Brave New World*), but Swift seems the one who is most sensitively aware that when one rejects all utopian ideals, one runs the risk of an equally dangerous extreme. After Gulliver has been sadly disillusioned, he falls into despair and becomes susceptible to death at the hands of a fascist. "I grew heartily ashamed of the pleasing visions I had formed; and thought no tyrant could invent a death, into which I would not run with pleasure from such a life." Boorman makes this tyrant the hero and this pleasurable death the climax of his film.

Zardoz is also based, as we learn explicitly from Arthur Frane, on the *Wizard of Oz.* The leonine god-head is a transformation of the cowardly lion, who ultimately proves courageous and becomes the model for Boorman's killers. Arthur, the Wizard behind the mask, leads his courageous brute along the yellow brick road to power. This source is also very important because, unlike *Gulliver,* it doubles as a literary *and* movie classic, and this verbal-visual fusion is precisely what Boorman is attempting. He is trying to use his medium in its broadest sense, exploiting its potential for incorporating other art forms. Thus the allusion to the source is both visual (in the god-head) and verbal (the name); both dimensions are present in the concrete image of the "Holy Book," hovering in space like the stone head, which leads Zed, our red bullet-crossed knight, into his mission. His quest is to restore fertility to the Wasteland, another connection with Eliot.

The allusions to film are more subtle but more extensive. Like *2001, Zardoz* presents a panoramic history of the cinema, with special emphasis on science fiction. The opening image of Arthur's head floating through space evokes Georges Méliès, the magician who first explored the medium's potential for visual illusion and who launched the science fiction genre with *A Trip to the Moon* (1902). As the spaceship reminds us of *Flash Gordon* and *Barbarella*, the masks suggest *Judex*. Several key scenes in *Zardoz* seem to be variations of key sequences from other movies. When the brute is attacked by the aged with impotent rage, we recall the scene from *A Clockwork Orange* where Alex is beaten up by the vengeful old derelicts. Both films see the future as a conflict between sterile socialism and brutal fascism, seeming to prefer the latter. When Zed enters the crystal and is confronted with multiple reflections, culminating in the shooting of his own image, we remember the powerful climax to Welles's *Lady from Shanghai*, one of the most dazzling shootouts in cinematic history. There, too, a vital young man is drawn into an adventure by a manipulative old man named Arthur; but the tables are turned and the young rogue (played by Welles himself) helps to destroy the old man and his corrupt circle of friends.

The lion's head is also associated with the scene from *El Topo* where the brutish hero challenges the Second Master. Playful and effeminate like Arthur, and identified with the lion chained beside him, he is indifferent to death. He tries to give El Topo the secret to his power by showing him a pyramid made out of toothpicks, which (like the crystal) combines delicacy and strength. El Topo defeats the Master, incorporating them as Zed incorporates the crystal.

The most extensive network of allusions is to Kubrick's *2001*. The conversation with the crystal ball and the entry into the Tabernacle suggest the scene where one of the astronauts gets inside HAL in order to disconnect his power and take over his functions. The extraordinary visual flashes that occur within the crystal are reminis- of the Stargate Corridor sequence, where the fusion of inner and outer space is most intense. Like the stone god-head, the mysterious black monolith functions as a spaceship from an advanced race, which elicits a primitive response. Both films end with the birth of a child, marking the beginning of a new society. Both films explore the idea of whether human beings, in a state of advanced technology, have really progressed psychologically. Both develop this polarity by combining the strange and the familiar, the new and the old, in decor, costumes, and music. Both juxtapose our animal origins with our future. But whereas Kubrick keeps the brutes and the astronauts in distinct sections, marking the division with a weapon, Boorman fuses them in combat. As Arthur points out, Zed is a bomb which can advance or destroy the civilization that created it. Both films self-reflexively offer an analogue for human development in their style, which surveys cinematic history. Yet Kubrick begins with stills and advances the medium, ending with the sophisticated opticals of *avant-garde* cinema, whereas Boorman concludes with family portraits.

For all its allusive richness and successful combination of the western and science fiction genres, *Zardoz* does not really make a breakthrough toward expanded consciousness, for its lacks the transformational power. Rather, it accumulates its sources almost mechanically, lining up conservative heavyweights like Swift and Eliot, as if building a case for a return to the past. The rejection of the utopian society of the Vortex is unconvincing; we believe it is sterile and depressing only because characters tell us so, not because we experience it that way. It is true that in forming an elite society totally cut off from the misery and violence experienced by the masses, the Eternals have hardened their hearts and lost their sexual and imaginative energy. Since their egalitarian society is based on the enslavement of others, they are bound to reap the consequences. But are these limitations necessarily inherent in all movements toward social change, as the film implies? The Eternals live in a nonsexist, classless, communal society. Why should these characteristics nec-essarily be associated with sterility and loss of humanity? Only because that is Boorman's vision. Significantly, when Friend releases the "monster" within himself and rebels against the androgynous group, he shouts: "The Vortex is an obscenity! I hate all women!" In some ways, *Zardoz* seems to offer a polemical answer to the arguments of the women's movement, particularly certain ideas articulated by Susan Sontag:

> To create a nonrepressive relation between women and men means to erase as far as possible the conventional demarcation lines that have been set up between the two sexes, to reduce the tension between women and men that arises from "otherness" . .
> . . As "otherness" is reduced, some of the energy of sexual attraction between the sexes will decline. Women and men will certainly continue to make love and to pair off in couples. But

women and men will no longer *primarily* define each other as
potential sexual partners. In a nonrepressive nonsexist society,
sexuality will in one sense have a more important role than it has
today—because it will be more diffused. Homosexual choices
will be as valid and respectable as heterosexual choices; both will
grow out of a genuine bisexuality. . . . In such a society, sexual
relations will no longer be hysterically craved as a substitute for
genuine freedom and for so many other pleasures (intimacy,
intensity, feeling of belonging, blasphemy) which this society
frustrates.[69]

Boorman destroys the Vortex to restore, not only fertility, but also
sexual opposition, masculine dominance, violence, and the nuclear
family.

In creating an anti-utopia, Boorman also seems to argue against a
closed society like Skinner's *Walden Two*, which, in trying to control
behavior and minimize risk and pain, actually eliminates the
possibilities for intensity and change. No mutation like Zed would be
possible in Skinner's utopia. Yet ironically, the reactionary world of
Zardoz is equally closed. The crystal image, with its futuristic
connections to lasers and its potential for infinite variety, is actually
used to crystallize repression. In the end we discover that hiding
behind the surface wizardry is a conservative little vision. The return
to the nuclear family shuts off all new, imaginative possibilities for
human life. In this way, it is like Frye's cyclical view of art, where the
present returns to the past, allowing no room for an unknown future.
But all cyclical views do not necessarily involve such a dead end.
Despite their circular structure, both *El Topo* and *2001* incorporate a
diachronic view of history in their spiral structure and backward/
forward movement. The unpredictability of El Topo's adventures
and the genetic ambiguity of the embryo and the visual expansiveness in *2001* leave the future open; we cannot predict the exact course
to be followed by the new society in either film.

Archetypal criticism enables us to see the individual artifact in
relation to the whole body of art and to identify both the unique and
conventional aspects; truly transformational works like *El Topo* and
2001 invent new possibilities. Our own transformalist approach to
criticism shares with these films an openness to new experience. In
the final analysis, *Zardoz* does not. Like its hero, it is a mutant, not a
true metamorphosis.

Footnotes to Chapter Five

1. Northrop Frye, *Anatomy of Criticism* (New York: Atheneum Press, 1969), pp. 33-34.
2. Frye, p. 73.
3. Frye, p. 192.
4. T. S. Eliot's critical perspective shares a similar assumption regarding the relationship between present and past works: "We do not quite say that the new is more valuable because it fits in; but its fitting in is a test of its value." "Tradition and the Individual Talent," *Selected Essays* (New York: Harcourt Barce Jovanovich, 1932), p. 5.
5. "Conversations with Jodorowsky," in *El Topo*, ed. Ross Firestone (New York: Douglas Book Corp., 1971), p. 130. Odd as the flea may be in this context, he is metamorphosed by Jodorowsky in a later interview; "I am influenced by everything I did in my life. I am influenced by every object I see, every movie I see, every person I know, every play I read, every fly. In 1955 a fly sat on my shoulder; and this fly is in my picture." Chris Van Ness, "An Interview with Alexandro Jodorowsky," *Los Angeles Free Press* (December 17, 1971). Part Two, p. 5.
6. Conversations with Jodorowsky," p. 97.
7. Frye, p. 36.
8. "Interview," p. 4.
9. "Conversations with Jodorowsky," p. 97.
10. *El Topo*, p. 11.
11. *El Topo*, p. 20.
12. *El Topo*, p. 32.
13. *El Topo*, p. 52.
14. Frye, pp. 196-197.
15. *El Topo*, p. 58.
16. Frye, p. 193.
17. *El Topo*, p. 20.
18. *El Topo*, p. 54.
19. *El Topo*, p. 64.
20. "Conversations with Jodorowsky," p. 146.
21. "Conversations with Jodorowsky," p. 109.
22. *El Topo*, p. 32.
23. *El Topo*, p. 41.
24. *El Topo*, p. 47.
25. *El Topo*, p. 49.
26. "Conversations with Jodorowsky," p. 114.
27. *El Topo*, p. 48.
28. "Interview," p. 5.
29. *El Topo*, p. 27.
30. Frye, p. 147.
31. Frye, p. 141.
32. Frye, p. 148.
33. "Conversations with Jodorowsky," p. 171.
34. Frye, p. 148.
35. Frye, p. 149.

36. Frye, p. 149.

37. Frye, p. 149.

38. Frye, p. 149.

39. *El Topo*, p. 11.

40. Frye, p. 149.

41. Frye, p. 150.

42. Frye, p. 150.

43. Frye, p. 150.

44. *El Topo*, p. 51.

45. *El Topo*, p. 26.

46. *El Topo*, p. 44.

47. "Conversations with Jodorowsky," p. 102.

48. "Conversations with Jodorowsky," p. 129.

49. Andre Bazin notes that "in the world of the western, it is the women who are good and the men who are bad, so bad that the best of them must redeem themselves from the original sin of their sex by undergoing various trials. In the Garden of Eden, Eve led Adam into temptation. Paradoxically Anglo-Saxon puritanism, under the pressure of historical circumstances, reverses the Biblical situation. The downfall of the woman only comes about as a result of the concupiscence of men." *What is Cinema*, Vol. II (Berkeley: University of California Press, 1971), p. 144.

50. Jodorowsky is very conscious of this stereotype, and offers a corrective. "The Third Master is a Mexican Master. In every Western ever made, the Mexican is always the outlaw, the bad guy. In my picture, the Mexican is a very powerful man, because Mexico has a very wonderful culture." "Conversations with Jodorowsky," p. 112. ·

51. "Conversations with Jodorowsky," p. 99.

52. "Conversations with Jodorowsky," p. 103.

53. "Conversations with Jodorowsky," p. 105.

54. "Conversations with Jodorowsky," p. 105.

55. Frye, p. 49.

56. This word puzzle was decoded for us by Richard Reath, Professor of Political Studies ot Occidental College in Los Angeles.

57. Eliot, "Tradition and the Individual Talent," p. 6.

58. Susan Sontag, "The Imagination of Disaster," *Against Interpretation* (New York: Dell Publishing Co., 1966).

59. Frye, p. 203.

60. Frye, p. 119.

61. Frye, p. 203.

62. Frye, p. 120.

63. This discussion of *Zardoz* was originally published in a different form as an essay by Marsha Kinder entitled, "Zardoz crystallized," *Film Quarterly* (Summer 1974). Some of the material on *2001* is drawn from our treatment of that film in *Close-up: A Critical Perspective on Film* (Harcourt Brace Jovanovich, 1972).

64. Frye, p. 203.

65. Frye, p. 202.

66. Claude Lévi-Strauss, "The Structural Study of Myth," *The Structuralists from Marx to Lévi-Strauss*, ed. Richard and Fernande De George (New York: Doubleday and Co., 1972), pp. 193-194.

67. Eliot, "Tradition and the Individual Talent," p. 6.

68. Jonathan Swift, *Gulliver's Travels* (New York: Rinehart and Co., 1958), p. 204.

69. Susan Sontag, "The Third World of Women," *Partisan Review, II* (1973), 389.

2001: A SPACE ODYSSEY. This convincing shot of the moon bus suggests how the film's technical virtuosity in combining many different kinds of images is itself a good non-discursive argument for the film's optimistic transformational plot.

Courtesy of MGM.

2001: A SPACE ODYSSEY. Playfully providing both elements necessary for establishing scale in a film frame, this image celebrates a technology that has become erotic in its forms and motions.
Courtesy of MGM.

2001: A SPACE ODYSSEY. Delivering recognizably mundane plastic dinners, the stewardess on the passenger spaceship is rendered visually and technologically exotic as she walks up the "walls" in the gravity-free chamber that seems to be looking back at us.

Courtesy of MGM.

EL TOPO. The beautiful blind prophet and his armless and legless disciples are stacked to form a totem pole trinity sharing one John Wayne costume. Courtesy of Abkco Films Inc.

EL TOPO. Kneeling like a little lamb, El Topo is shorn by the comely dwarf under the watchful gaze of the mother Sybil, who directs his transformation. Courtesy of Abkco Films Inc.

EL TOPO. The Colonel is carefully coiffed, costumed, and painted for his performance as macho tyrant. Courtesy of Abkco Films Inc.

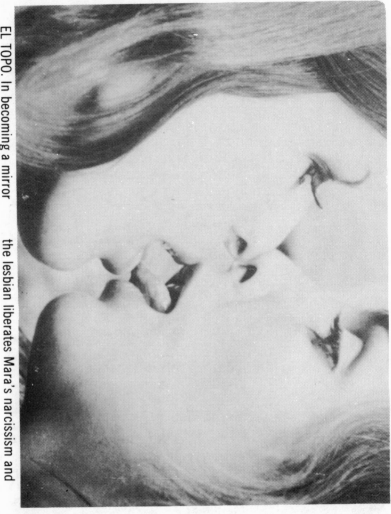

EL TOPO. In becoming a mirror the lesbian liberates Mara's narcissism and takes her away from El Topo. Courtesy of Abkco Films Inc.

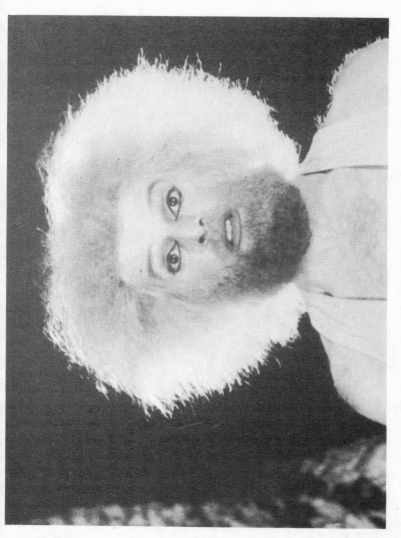

EL TOPO. El Topo on the point of epiphany! Courtesy of Abkco Films Inc.

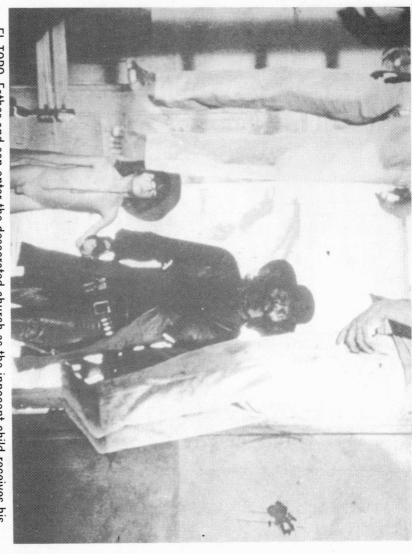

EL TOPO. Father and son enter the desecrated church as the innocent child receives his demonic First Communion of bodies and blood in the massacred town. Courtesy of Abkco Films Inc.

EL TOPO. Turning their back on mama, El Topo and his naked manchild ride off into the surreal, shimmering space of their mutual quest, directed by the shadow of the phallic pole. Courtesy of Abkco Films Inc.

ZARDOZ. The whimsical but ominous Zardoz god-head, representing the Holy Leonine Spirit, is hailed by its worshippers as it lands on the barren outlands. Courtesy of 20th Century Fox.

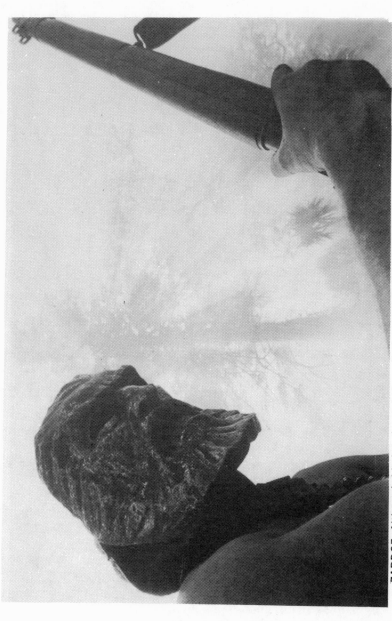

ZARDOZ. Although his leonine mask and rifle foreground his destructive power, this Exterminating Angel is on a holy quest for enlightenment, which is glimpsed in the background. Courtesy of 20th Century Fox.

ZARDOZ. As Zed lies spread-eagled on a table in a pyramid structure, he projects on one wall his memory.   The other walls of the room contain fluid compartments with young naked bodies waiting to be reconstructed.

Courtesy of 20th Century Fox.

ZARDOZ. Some of the action footage from Zed's memory bank includes a brutal rape, but it is ambiguous whether the star performer is Zed or one of his ancestors. Courtesy of 20th Century Fox.

ZARDOZ. Zed, as the rebellious, well-fleshed Brutal, wears his modern guerilla costume with great theatrical flair, particularly in contrast with the sterile, futuristic Eternals who are packaged in plastic.

Courtesy of 20th Century Fox.

6

Cultural and Cinematic Codes in *The Man Who Fell to Earth* and *Walkabout:* Insiders and Outsiders in the Films of Nicolas Roeg

It is because man originally felt himself identical to all those like him . . . that he came to acquire the capacity to distinguish himself as he distinguishes them, i. e., to use the diversity of species as conceptual support for social differentiation.
                    Claude Lévi-Strauss, Totemism

BROTHER: I think he might take us to the moon.
SISTER: I wish we had proper crayons.
BROTHER: Why did you say we were the first white people he's ever seen?
SISTER: I thought you had crayons in your satchel. Please have a look.
BROTHER: I think he's going to take us to the moon.
                                        Walkabout

MARY LOU: You know this is a very unhealthy place, the water is all polluted, . . . they put chemicals in it to keep people from getting sick, it's a very unhealthy place.
NEWTON: I think it just takes getting used to, that's all.
MARY LOU: It sure does.
                            The Man Who Fell to Earth

Walkabout (1971) and *The Man Who Fell to Earth* (1976), both directed by Nicolas Roeg, center on the confrontation between outsiders and insiders—alien visitors from a culture that is sick or dying who enter a foreign culture seeking survival and a way to get back home. The encounter contrasts the two cultures and the codes they use for creating meaning. The ultimate question is: What will result from the meeting—growth, transformation, or death? Through the unusual visual and emotional power of their cinematic choices, both films demand a parallel growth and transformation from their audience.

These films come together with structuralism, particularly as developed by anthropologist Lévi-Strauss, and cinesemiology, particularly as defined by film theoretician Christian Metz, in their focus on the relationship between the individual and the group and the processes by which they create meaning. Roland Barthes, whose application of structural analysis to literature and social patterns provides a valuable model for practical criticism, defines structuralism as:

> The strictly human process by which men give meaning to things. . . . What is new is a mode of thought (or a "poetics") which seeks less to asign completed meanings to the objects it discovers than to know how meaning is possible, at what cost and by what means.[1]

Seeing films like *Walkabout* and *The Man Who Fell to Earth* that contain so many mysterious images, signs and events is somewhat like encountering an alien culture. We are forced to dissect and reconstruct in order to gain access to meaning; we provide the consciousness in which the perception of opposition and integration must take place. Barthes describes the process:

> We see, then, why we must speak of a structuralist *activity:* creation or reflection are not, here, an original "impression" of the world, but a veritable fabrication of a world which resembles the first one, not in order to copy it but to render it intelligible. . . . The structuralist activity involves two typical operations: dissection and articulation. To dissect the first object [the film] . . . is to find in it certain mobile fragments whose differential situation engenders a certain meaning. . . . Once the units are posited, structural man must discover in them or establish for them certain rules of association: this is the activity of articulation, which succeeds the summoning activity.[2]

In this chapter we intend to dissect these films in order to discover the codes by which cinematic and cultural meaning is created. We will apply only those ideas and procedures from structuralism and cinesemiology, which we find particularly illuminating for these works and for our transformalist goals.

Lévi-Strauss's structural analysis provides a means of defining the deep structure of a group of related stories, which together comprise a single myth. Not only does his approach show how meaning is created and how elements are transformed in various versions; it also reveals the bipolarity that lies at the center of the myth and the implicit means of resolving it. Despite the fact that he works with myths of anonymous authorship, his method is particularly well suited to discovering an *auteur* code and has, in fact, provided the basis for the work of several British cinestructuralists.[3] Lévi-Strauss proceeds by creating for each version of the myth a chart that is structured diachronically along one axis—that of the narrative itself—and synchronically along the other axis, which, when read vertically reveals simultaneously all the elements of one constituent unit of the myth. This unit expresses not one isolated set of relations, but a bundle of relations among a character, event, theme, or object that have been combined to produce meaning. The charts must be read like dissected musical scores:

> The myth will be treated as would be an orchestra score perversely presented as a unilinear series and where our task is to re-establish the correct disposition.[4]

In fact, in his "overture" to *The Raw and the Cooked,* he claims that Richard Wagner is "the undeniable originator of the structural analysis of myths." Lévi-Strauss suggests that music makes individuals conscious of their psychological rootedness (by appealing to their heartbeats and breathing rhythms) while mythology makes them aware of their roots in society. Like Wagnerian opera, cinema combines the two, appealing to physiology through brain waves, persistence of vision, and cutting rhythms as well as to social awareness through the myths contained in the diegesis. Thus Lévi-Strauss's approach to myth is particularly well suited to analysis of Roeg's films with their pronounced rhythms of montage and movement interphased with complex sound tracks, their powerful rituals of song and dance, and their strong reliance on myths well known in our culture.

The Deep Structure of Roeg's Myth

Thus far, Roeg has directed four films: *Performance* (co-directed with Donald Cammell), 1970; *Walkabout,* 1971; *Don't Look Now,* 1973; *The Man Who Fell to Earth,* 1976. In *Performance,* based on an original screenplay by Donald Cammell, Chas (James Fox), a small time gangster, murders his pal Joey against the orders of his boss Harry Flowers, who decides to kill him. He hides out in the Chelsea underground retreat of a declining rock star named Turner (Mick Jagger). Turner and his two women alter Chas's identity visually, sexually, and psychedelically. When the killers finally catch up with Chas, he shoots Turner and their identities merge. In the final scene it is Turner who is taken away by the killers.

Based on a popular adolescent novel by James Vance Marshall, *Walkabout* focuses on an adolescent girl (Jenny Agutter) and her younger brother (Lucien John, Roeg's son) who are lost in the Australian outback, having run away from their father who tried to kill them and then committed suicide. Hungry, thirsty, and exhausted, they encounter a young Aborigine boy (David Gumpilil, who is referred to in credits of later films as Gulpilil), who is on his Walkabout, a rite of passage in which a boy must prove his manhood by surviving off the land, "even if it means killing his fellow creatures." The Aborigine provides the English children with food and water and finally takes them to a road that will lead back to white civilization. Then he does a strange dance that the white children do not understand, but which the girl interprets as a sexual threat. Later, they find him dead, hanging in a tree. He fails his Walkabout, but they succeed in staying alive. They find a mining settlement and are finally restored to their culture. Once back home in safety, the girl has an idyllic fantasy about their experience with the Aborigine.

Based on a story by Daphne du Maurier, *Don't Look Now* follows a modern couple, John (Donald Sutherland) and Laura Baxter (Julie Christie) to Venice after the death of their daughter. In Venice, where John is working on restoring a church, they meet two middle-aged sisters, one of whom claims to have established contact with the Baxters' dead daughter Christine, who is trying to warn her parents to leave Venice. Laura wants to follow their advice but John ignores it, though the sisters claim that he, too, has second sight. When they learn that their son has been hurt in an accident, Laura returns to England and John continues his work in the church, where he experiences a near-fatal fall. He then has a vision of Laura in a funeral boat with the two sisters. Misreading this warning, he concludes that Laura is in danger, and asks the police to investigate the seer. When he learns that Laura is safe and on her way back to Venice, he takes the psychic sister back to her hotel and is stabbed to death by a killer dwarf, whom he mistakes for the ghost of his daughter or a child in need. The final image is of the funeral boat, which John had earlier misinterpreted.

The Man Who Fell to Earth is Thomas Jerome Newton (David Bowie), a visitor from another planet who has learned about earth from monitoring our radio and television transmission. Based on a novel by Walter Tevis, the film follows Newton who has come to find water for his family on the home planet, which is suffering a drought. He contacts Oliver Farnsworth (Buck Henry), a patent lawyer, who helps him build World Enterprises, an advanced electronic company that he hopes will finance the building of a spaceship for his return home. While on earth, he lives with Mary Lou (Candy Clark), to whom he reveals his true identity. Nathan Bryce (Rip Torn), a disillusioned chemistry professor, joins World Enterprises and discovers Newton's secret. As W. E. prepares to send Newton back to his planet, a CIA type organization kills Farnsworth, and causes Bryce and Newton's chauffeur to betray him. They kidnap him, do medical experiments, which result in his getting "stuck" in his earth cover, and finally let him go since he is no longer a threat. Later, Bryce finds Newton, who has cut an album called "The Visitor" that he hopes his wife will some day hear. The American distributors have cut twenty-two minutes from Roeg's version of the film. Although Lévi-Strauss asserts:

> It cannot be too strongly emphasized that all available variants should be taken into account. . . . There is no one true version of which all the others are but copies or distortions. Every version belongs to the myth.[6]

we will base our analysis on Roeg's original version.

Despite the apparent diversity of these plots, they follow the same patterns with surprising consistency. In the following chart, we have isolated the bundles of meaning that recur in all four versions of the myth, using repetition as a guide to significance as Lévi-Strauss advises.

> A myth exhibits a "slated" structure which seeps to the surface, if one may say so, through the repetition process.[7]

We have reversed the axes, placing the diachronic vertically, and the synchronic horizontally because of the limitations of the full process:

> A variant of average length needs several hundred cards . . . to discover a suitable pattern of rows and columns, special devices are needed, consisting of vertical boards . . . where cards can be pigeon-holed and moved at will; in order to . . . compare the variants, several such boards are necessary, and this in turn requires a spacious workshop . . . as the frame of reference becomes multi-dimensional . . . the board-system has to be replaced by perforated cards which in turn require I.B.M. equipment, etc.[8]

We offer a shortened version of the combined results of charting the four films separately.

UNIT OF MEANING	PERFORMANCE	WALKABOUT
VISITOR (outsider) leaves a declining or deathly place.	Chas flees from gunmen in gangster/business world after killing Joey.	English brother and sister from sterile Australian city flee their father, who tries to shoot them and then commits suicide.
Visitor has potential to transcend cultural limits.	Chas has strong individuality, enabling him to rebel against the power structure.	Children have the potentiality of youth, which is not yet entirely culture bound.
Visitor's sexual identity affects potential growth.	Chas begins with macho persona and repressed female side; ends up integrating his *anima* and merging with the androgynous Turner.	The *male* begins as weak pre-pubescent; but is less shaped by culture and thus more accepting of the Aborigine and his values and more capable of growth. The adolescent *female* at first plays wise, strong mother; but is stuck in her ethnocentricism and becomes the frightened virgin.

	−	+	Male	−	+
	Male	Androgyny	Female	+	−

UNIT OF MEANING	PERFORMANCE	WALKABOUT
Visitor accepts (+) or rejects (−) an endangered family in the old world.	Chas, a "lone ranger," rejects mafia family which is on trial; he kills his boyhood mate.	Siblings are victims of a failed family—almost killed by father.

− |
| Visitor accepts (+) or rejects (−) new kind of group in new world. | He accepts integration into extended Turner household. | Brother accepts the family tie offered by Aborigine, mistaking him for father.

Sister rejects family tie with Aborigine. |

		Male	+
	+	Female	−

UNIT OF MEANING	PERFORMANCE	WALKABOUT
Visitor's main goal is to save self or family.	Self	Themselves

DON'T LOOK NOW

John and Laura Baxter leave their home in England after their daughter drowns.

Baxters have love and sensitivity, enabling them to transcend their grief and have another child.

The *male* begins as strong restorer with second sight who gets over grief; but he denies his powers and the supernatural and is murdered.
The *female* at first seems weak, incapable of recovering from grief; but she accepts the supernatural and survives.

Male   +   –
Female   –   +

Couple belongs to and accepts strong family, which is threatened by death and injury of its members.
+

Father rejects weird sisters and daughter's ghost.

Mother accepts weird sisters and family tie beyond death.

Male   –
Female   +

Family, including themselves.

MAN WHO FELL TO EARTH

Tommy Newton leaves his drought-ridden planet.

Newton has superior vision and knowledge, enabling him to travel through space.

Newton begins with an alien sexuality, which appears *androgynous;* as he declines and becomes more imprinted by earth, he becomes more explicitly bisexual.

Androgyny   +   –

Newton is a "family man" trying to save his wife and children.

+

Family man is partially integrated into modern liaison and an industrial family, but later there is mutual rejection.

–

Family and planet, including himself.

UNIT OF MEANING	PERFORMANCE	WALKABOUT
JOURNEY taken by visitor moves in three directions:		
downward	Chas goes underground and lives in a Chelsea basement; during a psychedelic trip, he falls down.	English children are in Australia, the land "down under"; in the outback, they fall to the ground to escape their father's bullets.
outward	Chas moves "further out" through mind expansion— out of the conventional world and out of his persona; he tries to get out of danger and out of the country.	"Outback" is the location. The children strive to get out of the city; later, they strive to get out of nature.
backward	Chas is taken "further back" to his archetypal roots in lone ranger, assassin, juggler; he considers going back in time to Persia or back to the gangster business world in the USA. In the end, he is taken back by the gangsters as we see a child walking backwards.	The "Outback" takes the children back to a more primitive society. They want to get back to the road and the city. In the end, they go back to the city and to the beginning of the film; she imagines a return to the outback.
HOST (insider) helps (+) or endangers (–) the visitor.	Turner and his androgynous "foreign birds" Lucy and Pherber help expand Chas's identity, but Chas may suspect they informed on him to the gangsters.	Adolescent Aborigine enables children to survive, but the girl is frightened of him sexually.
Host's sexual identity affects how he/she treats the visitor.	+Androgynous Males and Females primarily help.	+Adolescent Male primarily helps.

DON'T LOOK NOW	MAN WHO FELL TO EARTH
English couple goes to Venice where they contact underworld of ghosts; she falls in restaurant, he falls in church.	Alien falls to earth; in New Mexico, he falls in an elevator.
Laura reads "Beyond the Fragile Geometry of Space"; they move out of their familiar home territory and out beyond the realm of nature and reason.	Newton travels through outer space and lands in the wide open spaces of New Mexico.
Venice takes them back in time as he tries to restore old buildings. She goes back to England, then back to Venice. He plays back his life as he dies.	Newton wants to go back home, which looks primitive. He goes backwards mentally and sends back his image on TV and his voice on radio.
In the end, the film goes back to the funeral scene.	In the end, the song "Stardust" returns to nostalgic musical past and earlier Bowie persona.
The Venice hosts (the Bishop and police inspector) don't believe and can't help prevent death. The hosts to the underworld (the seer and the daughter's ghost) believe and try to help visitors escape or transcend death. The androgynous killer dwarf succeeds in ushering John into death.	Institutional power (represented by supermasculine Peters) obstructs and maims Newton. Nate joins and helps Newton, then betrays him for personal ambition. Mary Lou helps lift him up, then betrays him out of love. Oliver, a homosexual, helps him and stays loyal.
+Adult female seer and pre-puberty female ghost primarily help. −Androgynous dwarf hinders. −Adult male Bishop and inspector neither help nor hinder.	+Androgynous male helps + −Adult female helps more than hinders. − +Adult male hinders more than helps. −Adult super male hinders.

UNIT OF MEANING	PERFORMANCE	WALKABOUT
Host benefits or suffers from the encounter.	Turner is shot by Chas, but reemerges with an expanded identity incorporating Chas. +	Aborigine dies after being rejected by girl and having vision of white hunters. –
ENCOUNTER between outsider/insider includes several key elements, which have both positive and negative aspects. WATER traditionally marks the border or passage between worlds of the living and the dead.		
+Water is a means of loving fusion between people.	Bathtub scene with Turner, Pherber and Lucy occurs before they accept Chas into their house. Bathtub scene between Chas and Lucy occurs before fusion of Chas and Turner.	"Water" is the first word the insider and outsiders learn in each other's language. Girl teaches brother how to swim. Aborigine sees her beauty as she swims. She has beautiful fantasy of swimming with brother and Aborigine in lagoon.
Water is necessary for survival.		Aborigine shows them how to get water from dried up billabong.
–Water is used as a means of subjugation or restriction.	Flowers orders his houseboy to draw his bath.	Girl forces Aborigine to say "water" in English and to fetch it, turning him into a servant. Children bathe for their return, conforming to city standards of cleanliness. Sprinklers mechanically move back and forth as the mining official commands the children to respect private property. Children swim in private pool right next to huge ocean.

DON'T LOOK NOW	MAN WHO FELL TO EARTH
Seer is arrested as a result of John's suspiciousness, but then released.	Peters and Nate get more powerful and rich, but also more co-opted and corrupted.
	Mary Lou gets rich and unhappy; she is deceived into betraying Newton.
−+	Oliver at first gets rich and powerful, but is then murdered for his loyalty.
	+−
Bathtub scene occurs before John and Laura make love.	Mary Lou bathes before she and Newton agree "she'll do for now" and before she gets him to go to church.
	Newton bathes and stays wet before positive love scene with Mary Lou.
	Newton fantasizes about wet sex at home.
	Newton drinks water thirstily; he has come for water; his name for earth is "planet with water."
	Mary Lou and Tommy become addicted to Beefeater gin.
	Peter displays his wife as a sexual possession as they sit beside pool and tells his followers to drink less alcohol.

UNIT OF MEANING	PERFORMANCE	WALKABOUT
Water is linked with death.	Chas kills Joey in a bathtub scene. Flowers orders Chas's death as his bath is drawn.	Children nearly die when billabong dries up. Father's suicide is linked with drinking problem.
CHILDREN are closest to birth and have the greatest potential for transformation before death.		
+ Children are wise.	Precocious girl informs Chas about Turner and Pherber.	English boy quickly learns how to communicate with the Aborigine.
Children are innocent victims.	As Chas kills Joey, he sees childhood photograph when he and Joey were still innocent.	Boy in inset story dies trying to contact mother. Children almost shot by father.
Children are deceptive.	Precocious girl hustles Chas out of money and wears mustache drag.	English children lie.
RITUAL song or dance marks passage into a new stage of knowing or being.		
+ Ritual has potential for fusion and fertility.	Turner's 3 songs fuse him with Chas and Flowers, and lead Chas to dance with Lucy.	Aborigine's feather dance can be seen as a courtship ritual.
− Ritual is linked with violence or failure.	The 3 songs also prepare for Chas putting a bullet in Turner's head.	The ritual also functions as a death dance.

DON'T LOOK NOW

Daughter drowns.
Girl's body is dragged out of
canal.
Venice canals are polluted.
Fluid spills when Laura falls
and daughter drowns.
Rain falls when daughter
drowns and at John's
funeral.

Daughter's ghost warns her
father of his danger.

Daughter drowns.
Young girl murdered.   .
Child relative of seer dies
young.
Baxter son is injured in
accident.

Child turns out to be tiny
wolfish killer in red-riding-
hood drag.

The agility and rhythm of
the lovemaking turn it into a
fertility dance, marking the
end of the couple's grief.

Violence and death rather
than birth follow the lovemaking.

MAN WHO FELL TO EARTH

Peters dives into pool as
Oliver and Trevor are mur-
dered.
Water on earth is polluted.
Children on home planet
are dying of thirst.

Nate's daughter sends him
book with poem and paint-
ing about Icarus.

Newton's children are dying
of thirst.
Peter's hybrid children are
potential victims of his co-
option and the society's
racism.

Sexually precocious college
girls act out incestuous
daughter role with Nate.

Japanese dance ritual is
linked with sex scene be-
tween Nate and student and
introduces Newton to live
theatre.
Church singing is supposed
to integrate Newton.
Newton's record album may
some day reach his wife at
home.

Japanese swordplay reaches
climax of death as violent
sex play between Nate and
girl reaches orgasm.
Church singing leads New-
ton to withdraw into first
vision of home.
In Mary Lou and Newton's
country rock sexual reunion,
the gun and the banana
transform failed love into
mock violence.

UNIT OF MEANING	PERFORMANCE	WALKABOUT
MEDIA in a technologically advanced society function as corrupted oracles, linking present and future.		
+ Media expose the truth about society.	Pornographic film reveals connections among various performers and audiences.	English children cling to their radio as a lifeline to their culture.
− Media are controlled by evil forces and imprint their audience with perverted images.	But its subject is sado-masochism.	But it brings messages about superheroes and doomsday and frightens the Aborigines.
TRANSFORMATIONS OF MENTAL STATE (mind) and PHYSICAL APPEARANCE (body) enable humans to transcend DEATH, changing it into a rebirth or renewal —the ultimate transformation.		
MENTAL STATE (mind) +	Chas's psychedelic trip enables him to see beauty and expand his identity; his "mind is blown."	Girl's fantasy life is enriched by experience in outback.
−	Chas blows Turner's mind with a bullet.	Father drinks and goes crazy. Aborigine has vision of death while hunting and then wills his own death.
PHYSICAL APPEARANCE (body) +	Using wigs, paint, costumes, mirrors, photographs, Chas gets to look like Turner. Turner becomes Chas. Lucy and Turner change identities as Chas's bed partner.	Aborigine paints boy's body. Children remove their clothes when they are most open to the outback. Aborigine dresses for dance. In final lagoon fantasy, city clothes are hung on poles like tribal banners.
−	Chas rejects lawyer's persona. Turner rejects persona of Flowers and faggy leather boy.	Boy gets sunburned. Children redress for city.

DON'T LOOK NOW	MAN WHO FELL TO EARTH
	Newton's album is the one faint hope to offset his failure to return.
Red stain on the slide accurately tells the future.	Radio and television teach Newton about earth and make his visit possible.
But it predicts death.	But they corrupt and weaken him once he's here.
John has two flashes of second sight. The blind seer has two visions of the future which she uses to warn John. Bishop has a prophetic dream.	Newton has many visions of home planet in the past, future, and conditional. He sees pioneers from past. Nate sees Newton's dream image.
John misinterprets his visions. His life flashes before him at death. John drinks and Laura takes pills to dull their senses.	Newton is freaked out by TV images. Mary Lou, Bryce, and Newton get drunk. Newton's and Oliver's special eyes are destroyed.
John and Laura dress up after lovemaking, as if they are over their grief.	Newton and Mary Lou look alike after successful lovemaking. Newton reveals his true identity to her.
Red raincoat disguises dwarf. Police drawing distorts seer's face.	All hosts age, but Nate and Mary Lou become grotesque. Mary Lou gets increasingly artificial with wigs, makeup, clothes. Newton gets stuck in his earth costume.

UNIT OF MEANING	PERFORMANCE	WALKABOUT
	Gangsters "redecorate" businesses, "drop acid" on a Rolls Royce, shave the chauffeur, and mess up Chas's face.	
DEATH occurs in several forms and is frequently caused by a loved one.		
Someone is "stuck" which leads to death.	Turner is "stuck" in old identity; he must be shot in order to acquire a new demon and get unstuck.	Boy in story gets "stuck" on ledge before falling and breaking his neck.
Two parallel deaths frame the film, with others unseen.		
− Some deaths seem final.	Opening death of Joey, murdered with a gun by childhood mate.	Opening suicide of father with a gun after trying to kill children; then burned, and later hanged in tree by Aborigines, like a crucifixion. Closing death of Aborigine after trying to communicate with girl; hangs in tree like a crucifixion. Unseen death of boy in story who accidentally falls and breaks his neck while trying to contact mother.
+ Other deaths seem transcendent.	Closing death of Turner, mind is blown with a bullet and becomes Chas. Unseen death of Chas/Turner; earlier foreshadowed by Turner's song: "I might take ya down to the riverside, I might drown ya, I might shoot ya."	Although all 3 deaths are clearly negative, the dead are evoked in the minds of the surviving children: the boy sees his father and tells the story about the falling boy; the girl sees the Aborigine in a fantasy.
SEX integrates. male and female, love and violence, birth and death.		
+ Right couples with limitations.	Turner/Pherber ("Their love story's famous.")	Girl/Husband
physically	They are united, but want a third person (Lucy and/or Chas). +	They are suited. +

DON'T LOOK NOW	MAN WHO FELL TO EARTH
	Nate Bryce dresses up like Santa Claus, but really is more like the demonic Old Nick.
John gets "stuck" in throat by murderer's knife.	Newton's fake earth eyes get "stuck," implying that he's stuck on earth; he tells Mary Lou that if he stays here he'll die.
Closing death of John, throat cut by dwarf, who reminds him of his daughter and a child in need. Unseen death of young girl, murdered in canal. Unseen death of bishop's father who accidentally falls.	Inset death of Icarus in painting and poem, falls out of sky into water. Inset death of Billy Budd in film on TV, hanged and thrown in sea. Death of children on home planet, of thirst. Death of Oliver and Trevor, thrown out of high building as man who ordered killing dives into pool.
Opening death of daughter, who accidentally drowns; her ghost returns. Unseen death of seer's child relative with whom she's in contact.	Although all these deaths seem negative, they are somewhat transcended in mental life. Death of children is only imagined—what may happen if Newton doesn't return. All others are controlled by Icarus myth—a fall and a splash in the service of aspiration; that is why they recur throughout film rather than framing it.
John/Laura	Newton/Wife
Before his death, they are suited; after his death, they are separated. + –	They are suited but separated in time and space. + –

UNIT OF MEANING	PERFORMANCE	WALKABOUT
mentally	They are united, but want a third person. +	They are separate because of her outback experience. −
Their match is further weakened by the absence or injury of children.	They have no child of their own, but live with the house-keeper's daughter.	They have no children.
⁻Wrong couples who have a loving relationship but little chance for birth or renewal.		
inbreeding (endogamy) homosexuality	Chas and Joey Chas and Turner Pherber and Lucy Flowers and houseboy	
incest		The father eyes his daughter's legs before trying to kill her.
outbreeding (exogamy) racially		Aborigine and girl
cross-species		
Sex or courtship scenes	Stresses triplets as an expansion of the couple—3 versions of a positive 3-way, 3 versions of violent sex.	Never presents an actual sex scene, suggesting cut off potential in failed rite of passage.
+Scenes leading to loving fusion and expanding vision or identity.	3 way between Turner, Pherber, Lucy, filmed by Pherber. Chas and Pherber with Turner waiting in the wings. Chas with Turner/Lucy.	Aborigine's hunting is linked with girl swimming in the lagoon, both acts reveal their beauty.
+−		

DON'T LOOK NOW	MAN WHO FELL TO EARTH
Before his death, there's a "world" of difference in their vision and belief; after his death, they may make contact. −+	They are suited and remain in contact. +
They have one dead child and another injured.	They have two dying children.
	Oliver and Trevor
	Nate and fake daughters Newton and Mary Lou, (in later scenes where she plays mother to Tommy)
	Peters and wife
	Newton and Mary Lou (especially in scenes where he removes his earth cover)
Retains the clear polarity between sex and death, good and evil.	Has the fullest integration of most possibilities from earlier films in new combinations.
John and Laura make love, which is fused with their dressing; both acts enhance their beauty.	Newton and Mary Lou make love, which is linked with his giving her a telescope and her looking through a microscope; afterwards, they look alike.
	As Newton has a mental image of joyfully making love to his wife, Mary Lou rejects him as an alien.

UNIT OF MEANING	PERFORMANCE	WALKABOUT
⁻Scenes linked with rejection or violence.	Chas has a one-night stand with a singer, linked with car that later gets vandalized. Joey's beating of Chas is linked with his earlier sex scene with the singer. A pornographic film of sado-masochistic sex is linked with trial of a gangster.	Aborigine's courtship or death dance is rejected by girl.

DON'T LOOK NOW	MAN WHO FELL TO EARTH
When John is murdered, he recalls earlier lovemaking scene.	The staged incest between Nate and his student is linked with a Japanese performance of ritualized violence; the girl films the sex while Newton watches the violence; Nate makes love to a series of young girls, who are interchangeable, who play his daughter, and whom he dominates. Final lovemaking scene between Newton and Mary Lou is punctuated by gunshots.

In all of these charts, the basic polarity is clearly between life and death. Lévi-Strauss suggests the next step for integration:

> If we keep in mind that mythical thought always works from the awareness of opposition towards their progressive mediation, the reason for those choices becomes clearer. We need only to assume that two opposite terms with no intermediary always tend to be replaced by two equivalent terms which allow a third one as a mediator; then one of the polar terms and the mediator becomes replaced by a new triad and so on.[9]

+ **LIFE**		− **DEATH**
Advanced Culture It dominates and survives but wastes its resources: the criminal world of business in P; the city in W; England in DLN; Earth in MWFE.		**Primitive Culture** It is arid and declining, but has greater spiritual potential for life: Chelsea underground in P; outback in W; underworld in DLN; home planet in MWFE.

Mediating Location

	LIFE		Mediating Location		DEATH
P:	USA/west, future Last Poets Bonnie & Clyde poster Morrison poster Electronic music	◄─►	Turner's house, where decor and art move back and forward, east and west, in and out.	◄─►	Persia/east, past Arabian nights Moroccan decor Persian 3-D post cards Indian Music
W:	city future	◄─►	Deserted house in the outback, that contains only desert creatures and photographs and that is close to the mining settlement and the "real" road.	◄─►	country past
DLN:	west present the living material world	◄─►	Venice, historically the seaport between East and West, a city built on polluted water, fuses past and present, declining both physically and spiritually.	◄─►	east past the dead spiritual world
MWFE:	west/L.A. home of Nate, who betrays Newton and survives.	◄─►	New Mexico home of Mary Lou, who morally mediates between Nate & Oliver.	◄─►	east/N.Y. home of Oliver, who is loyal and dies.
	TV and far-out phonograph.		Newton's New Mexico house, which he shares with Mary Lou.		Japanese decor
			Multi-roomed halfway house where Newton is imprisoned and from which he escapes, combines decors, of different periods and countries, indoors and outdoors; in desert oasis town called "Artesia."		

+
LIFE

−
DEATH

Insiders (host culture)

Outsiders (visitors)

Male
Mediators
(outside insiders & inside outsiders)

Hosts: In P&W, the mediators are isolated insiders who seek fusion with the outsider. **Visitors:** In DLN & MWFE, the mediators are outsider family men who become insiders against their will. In DLN, the visitor brings part of his family along. An outsider in Venice, he becomes an underworld insider after his death. In MWFE, the visitor is without his family. On earth, he's an outsider who becomes an insider financially and physically.

Female
Mediators

Hostesses: In P and MWFE, Pherber and Mary Lou help integrate the visitor into their culture; Pherber, like Turner, is an isolated insider, but Mary Lou is an insider in every sense.
Visitors: In W, when the girl returns to the city, she brings the outback with her in fantasy, making her an outsider.

DLN has three mediators:

Hostess
Christine's ghost belongs to world of dead, but tries to contact and affect the world of the living.

Double Mediator
The blind seer with second sight who mediates between Christine and Laura, hostess and visitor, dead and living; she's not a Venetian, but an insider in contrast to John and Laura.

Visitor
Laura remains in world of living, but through belief in second sight keeps contact with the dead.

FEMALE
Predominantly survive.

MALE
Predominantly succumb.

Mediating Sex
Androgyny

Sex is an essential vehicle of mediation, whereby the opposition between male and female leads to the birth of a new form and the death of the male. Roeg uses the sex act as a microcosm for his entire myth: a male alien enters a female body, trying to impregnate her but risking sterility and decline. Although the male will eventually be maimed or killed in a ritual sacrifice, he imprints the surviving female, expanding her vision and increasing the chances, however slender, for the positive transformation of her culture.

The final integration of the basic opposition between life and death and the intermediary polarities occurs in one act, which is the climax of all four films: the ritual sacrifice in the mediating location of the male mediator—who has supernatural powers, who is somewhat androgynous, and who moves between the two worlds. The mythic resonance of this sacrifice is heightened by Roeg's magical casting of the scapegoat: Mick Jagger's androgynous sexuality and performing talents provide a strong basis for Turner's transformational power; David Gumpilil is an authentic royal Aborigine, whose extraordinary grace, beauty, and purity intensify the tragic dimension of the character's failure; the protean nature of David Bowie, enabling him to move so fluidly and convincingly from one exotic persona to another, makes the idea of his getting "stuck" in one disguise extremely painful. In *Don't Look Now*, the sacrificial victim John Baxter denies his supernatural powers of vision and restoration and represses his androgyny. As a result, his death fails to achieve mythic status. Hence, Roeg quite correctly casts Donald Sutherland, a highly competent actor in the ordinary sense of the term, who lacks the magic that Jagger, Gumpilil, and Bowie bring to their performances. *Don't Look Now* consequently lacks the emotional impact of the other films. As Turner tells Chas, "The only performance that makes it is the one that achieves madness," the one that goes all the way and breaks through the boundaries of ego and culture. Like the fisher king, the sacrificial figures played by Jagger, Gumpilil, and Bowie lie at the center of Roeg's myth of limited renewal. They emerge as a powerful life source, not only for the women who survive but also for us in the audience. Their performing powers draw on all their personae, enriching the emotional resonance of these extraordinary films.

Like all myths, Roeg's films contain rules about how to deal with the basic opposition—in this case, between life and death.

Life

When a surviving individual or culture is declining spiritually, contact with an alien person or culture may bring:

+mind expansion that enables one to transform one's life and accept death as a form of growth (Chas in *Performance*, Laura in *Don't Look Now*).

−mind expansion that enables one to see the sterility of life in which one is stuck (Girl in *Walkabout*, Mary Lou in *The Man Who Fell to Earth*).

Death

When an individual or culture is declining physically and moving toward death, contact with an alien person or culture may bring:

+mind expansion that enables one to welcome death as a life-giving transformation (Turner in *Performance*).

−mind pollution that leads one to get stuck in sterility (Newton in *Man Who Fell to Earth*) and to accept a nontranscendent death (Aborigine in *Walkabout*, John in *Don't Look Now*).

+In *Performance*, the characters succeed and grow whether they live or die.

+−In *Don't Look Now*, the surviving character grows and the dying character gets stuck.

−In *Walkabout* and *The Man Who Fell to Earth*, the characters fail and get stuck whether they live or die.

This pattern formed by the four films can be illuminated by Lévi-Strauss's essay "How Myths Die," where he describes three stages of transformation followed by the later versions of a myth as they vary from the original.[10] The first stage is *romantic elaboration (Don't Look Now)*, which is characterized by a movement from myth to romance, various inversions, self-reflexiveness, and the substitution of metaphorical equivalents for literal expression. In two other stages, the myth is adapted to the interpretation of history for political goals.

> We wish to stress an evident organic continuity between mythology, legendary tradition, and what must certainly be called politics.[11]

This process of historical legitimization takes two forms: the *retrospective (Walkabout)*, where myth is transformed into fake history in order to justify a traditional order; and the *prospective (The Man Who Fell to Earth)*, where the same myth is adapted to recent history in order to treat this past as the beginning of a future that is in the process of taking shape. Within Roeg's myth, these two films have the heaviest political emphasis, which helps explain why they are the most pessimistic.

As the original and most optimistic version of Roeg's myth, *Performance* has the strongest emphasis on the individual pursuing self-realization and transcending the social corruption around him. Both visitor and host are "lone rangers" who rebel against their culture and successfully fuse. In the "Memo from T" ritual, Turner's personal powers of transformation succeed even with the criminal world of Harry Flowers. On the level of genre, Roeg and Cammell fuse the gangster film and the trip movie; through a process of dialectic transformation they create a new genre. The literary sources for the film—Borges' "The South" (which is explicitly alluded to both verbally and visually), "The Arabian Nights" (which is quoted), and Hesse's "Steppenwolf" (which provides the basic plot)—also center on individuals who expand their identity and transcend death by drawing on their mythic roots.

As a *romantic elaboration, Don't Look Now* adapts the myth to an ironic DuMaurier story, creating a sophisticated gothic romance. Incorporating conflicting alternatives from the earlier films (*Performance* and *Walkabout*), it provides inverted fates for the husband and wife. One form of recurring inversion is the literal rendering of the basic polarities, which now work as double metaphors—e. g., John gets "stuck" with a knife, the killer dwarf is actually mistaken for an innocent child, the dead contact the living, a sign informs us that "Venice is in peril." Despite the visible pollution of Venice, its corruption seems more symbolic than literal. Of all Roeg's films, *Don't Look Now* has the least to say about politics. Instead, it draws our attention inward to the self-reflexive issue of perception, which is underscored by lines like, "Nothing is what it seems," and "Seeing is believing." The fascination of the visual surface is the film's primary source of value, reaffirming the validity of second sight. On the level of genre, Roeg integrates narrative action from a gothic horror movie with the stylistic surface beauty of the abstract "visual" film. This particular combination draws on the basic polarities in the film's primary literary sources—the conflict between perception and action in *Macbeth* (Roeg uses "weird sisters" from Scotland, whose self-fulfilling prophecies both foretell and insure the fate of the hero, and who win the support of his believing wife), and the opposition between sensuous and ideal form, perversion, and beauty in *Death in Venice*.

In several ways, *Walkabout* is a complete inversion of *Performance*, offering the most pessimistic version of the myth, where failure occurs in both worlds and in all aspects of the encounter for both visitors and hosts. As a *retrospective historical legitimization*, it offers a mythic version of past history—the imperialist take-over and destruction of so-called primitive cultures by technologically advanced societies. Like the father's attempted murder and suicide, this action is self-destructive for the aggressor as well. On the level of genre, Roeg stays with the adventure film, using powerful visuals to heighten the emotional intensity of the loss; just as the children fail to transcend their cultural limitations and the Aborigine fails to survive his Walkabout, the film does not transform its genre. The primary literary sources for the film take different attitudes toward the conquest of the primitive. Roeg offers an ironic inversion of *Robinson Crusoe*, the classic myth celebrating western imperialism. As Ian Watt perceptively observes:

> The programme of action of Empire: and it includes, as we have seen, temporary submission to primitivism, or at least to the lure of the wide open places. . . . This is the ultimate message of Defoe's story. The most desolate island cannot retain its natural order; wherever the white man brings his rational technology there can only be man-made order, and the jungle itself must succumb to the irresistible teleology of capitalism.[12]

Walkabout 'ends with a quotation from A. E. Housman's "A Shropshire Lad," which takes a position diametrically opposed to Defoe's: it romanticizes the primitive society and mourns its loss.

> Into my heart an air that kills from yon' far
>   country blows,
> What are those blue remembered hills, what
>   spires, what farms are those?
> That is the land of lost content, I see its
>   shining plain,
> The happy highways where I went and cannot
>   come again.

Like the poem, the film transforms the lost culture into an imaginative ideal, which lives on in the girl's fantasies and in the minds of the audience.

As the latest variant, *The Man Who Fell to Earth* offers a complex inversion of both *Performance* (the visitor declines rather than grows, rejects and is rejected by the extended group in the new world, and longs for his family back home) and of *Walkabout* (reversing the roles of visitors and hosts while retaining the pessimism and political focus). Despite his desire for privacy, the alien becomes a public figure, whose program for self and communal development is impeded by corrupt forces in the power structure. As a *prospective historical legitimization,* it reinterprets the myth in light of recent historical events—the investigations of the FBI and CIA, the Kennedy assassinations, Watergate, the destruction and co-opting of black power leaders, the death of Howard Hughes, the growing power of the media, the landings on the moon and on Mars—and raises questions about the future: how will our corrupt leaders use our increasing technological capabilities? what will happen when we contact life from other planets? The prognosis is not optimistic. On the level of genre, the film combines futuristic science fiction with many traditional genres popular in the west—the gangster film as in *Performance,* the rock melodrama like *Stardust,* the love story like *Love in the Afternoon,* political allegory like *Billy Budd,* political intrigue like *The Third Man,* and the western. In this film, Roeg makes the most complex transformation of his literary source. He chooses Icarus, which was originally a Greek myth about human pride. Wearing artificial wings, a young man flies too close to the sun, which melts the wax, causing him to fall into the sea and drown. Brueghel's painting "The Fall of Icarus" and Auden's poem "Musée des Beaux Arts" (both included in the film) reinterpret the myth, focusing not on Icarus' over-estimation of his powers, but on the way others ignore his failure.

> In Brueghel's Icarus, for instance: how everything turns away
> Quite leisurely from the disaster; the ploughman may
> Have heard the splash, the forsaken cry,
> But for him it was not an important failure; the sun shone
> As it had to on the white legs disappearing into the green
> Water; and the expensive delicate ship that must have seen
> Something amazing, a boy falling out of the sky,
> Had somewhere to get to and sailed calmly on.

Roeg incorporates these earlier meanings and adds a new dimension. Not only is Icarus unaware of his own personality and the limits of his knowledge, not only do others ignore his suffering, but they also take an active role in destroying his powers and insuring his failure. Hence, the myth is politicized; it becomes an allegory for the way entrenched power crushes the potential of anyone who refuses to conform and who pursues what it deems to be alien goals.

Lévi-Strauss's own methodology works against such oppression. Since structuralism assumes that codes emanate from the human mind, which is "ever the same," there can be no real aliens. Rejecting ethnocentrism, he sees a unity of the species that integrates the most extreme polarities such as primitive and modern, magic and science.

> Magical thought . . . forms a well-articulated system. . . . . It is
> therefore better, instead of contrasting magic and science, to
> compare them as two parallel modes of acquiring knowledge.[13]

He suggests that his own method of bipolar analysis is rooted in
totemism, which he defines as "a particular fashion of formulating a
general problem, viz. how to make opposition, instead of being an
obstacle to integration, serve rather to provide it."[14] As Susan Sontag
observes in her brilliant essay on Lévi-Strauss, "The Anthropologist
as Hero," this mode of thinking has shaped our current understanding of the relationship between self and other; she develops this
polarity in terms that evoke Roeg's films.

> Modern thought is pledged to a kind of applied Hegelianism:
> seeking its Self in its Other. Europe seeks itself in the exotic—in
> Asia, in the Middle East, among pre-literate peoples, in a mythic
> America; a fatigued rationality seeks itself in the impersonal
> energies of sexual ecstasy or drugs; consciousness seeks its
> meaning in unconsciousness; humanistic problems seek their
> oblivion in scientific "value neutrality" and quantification. The
> "other" is experienced as a harsh purification of "self." But at
> the same time the "self" is busily colonizing all strange domains
> of experience. Modern sensibility moves between two seemingly
> contradictory but actually related impulses: surrender to the
> exotic, the strange, the other; and the domestication of the
> exotic, chiefly through science.[15]

This double impulse has led Lévi-Strauss to regard his own work,
The Raw and the Cooked, as a myth.

> It would not be wrong to consider this book itself a myth: it is, as
> it were, the myth of mythology. . . . However, this code, like the
> others, has neither been invented nor brought in from without.
> It is inherent in mythology itself, where we simply discover its
> presence.[16]

Just as Lévi-Strauss sees Freud's writings on the Oedipus complex as
one more variant of the Oedipal myth, his own structural analyses,
like Roeg's films, are variations of the mythic encounter between self
and other. Lévi-Strauss is the visiting anthropologist who enters an
alien culture, where he interacts with a friendly host or informant,
gathering data to take home and enlighten his own culture. Sontag
describes him in terms that make him sound very similar to Roeg's
heroes.

> The man who submits himself to the exotic to confirm his own
> inner alienation as an urban intellectual ends by aiming to
> vanquish his subject by translating it into a purely formal code.

> The ambivalence toward the exotic, the primitive, is not overcome after all, but only given a complex restatement. The anthropologist, as a man, is engaged in saving his own soul. But he is also committed to recording and understanding his subject by a very high-powered mode of formal analysis—what Lévi-Strauss calls "structural" anthropology—which obliterates all traces of his personal experience and truly effaces the human features of his subject, a given primitive society.[17]

Although Lévi-Strauss' life work and methodology bear such strong connections with the deep myth in the films, they in no way illumnate the uniqueness of Roeg's cinematic style. Lévi-Strauss would be the first to acknowledge this limitation. Distinguishing between myth and poetry, he suggests that myth can easily be translated from one language to another because its primary meaning resides in the narrative, whereas in poetry it lies in the contextual value of particular images.

> Poetry is a kind of speech which cannot be translated except at the cost of serious distortions; whereas the mythical value of the myth remains preserved, even through the worst translation. Whatever our ignorance of the language and the culture of the people where it originated, a myth is still felt as a myth by any reader throughout the world. Its substance does not lie in its style, its original music, or its syntax, but in the *story* which it tells.[18]

Since he works with myths of anonymous authorship, he is never concerned with the way in which they are transformed by an individual artist into particular visual and auditory images; he never asks whether the myth is enriched or impoverished. But these are precisely the questions that are essential if we are to define Roeg's style.

To accomplish this part of our analysis, we will turn to cine-semiology. We will also shift our attention from Roeg's entire canon to a more specific focus on two individual films. While structuralism traces one code in its transformations through various texts, semiology is more useful in tracing a network of intersecting codes through a single work.

Cinesemiology

The primary goal of cinesemiology is to discover and define the system of codes that control the meaning of an individual film text and of the cinematic language that is drawn upon by all films but which is never fully expressed in any single work. A code is a system of rules governing the choices by which a specific message is arranged and interpreted by a sender and a receiver. In verbal language, this system is defined as *langue* (system of signs), which must precede *parole* (specific message or text); no utterance can be made without an underlying code understood by both sender and receiver. In the context of film language, there is no single code or *langue*, but a system of possibilities or choices by which the sender (those making the film) organizes or creates the message (the film) and by which the receiver (the audience) interprets the message. Metz defines film as a language based on a multiplicity of intersecting codes and subcodes. These codes are both arbitrary (like the word "water" and the formula "H_2O") and analogous to the outside world (a film image of water looks like water in the real world). They are both cultural (water is associated with fertility and the unconscious—these meanings are included in Roeg's films, but are not specific to the nature of the film medium and its modes of expression) and cinematic (flat cuts between a pond and girl's dead body or a pond and birds happily fluttering their wings as they drink would create different meanings for water through the montage code specific to the medium). Codes may be linked to a genre (water is traditionally a source of life and power in the western) or to the style of an auteur (in all of Roeg's film, water is a central image associated with both life and death).

In order to be a code analogous to that of verbal language, the system must control both paradigmatic and syntagmatic relations among its elements. Syntagmatic rules govern the horizontal or diachronic arrangement of elements in a message (for example, the order of parts of speech such as subject and predicate in a sentence); the syntagmatic combination of parts in a sentence embodies the basic structure of narrative. Syntagms are structurally different from each other and are not in competition for the same position. There are certain general cinematic codes like editing, lighting, and camerawork, which are common to all films and which bear a syntagmatic relation to each other; these elements cannot be substituted for each other, but must all function in every film. Although not found in all films, narrative is one of the general cinematic codes that offers the richest source of syntagmatic relationships. It is not surprising, then, that Metz has focused on narrative codes, tentatively defining the "Grand Syntagmatique" as eight possible kinds of syntagms that can be used to create a narrative structure in film.[19] Of autonomous segments which are parts of the whole film and not parts of parts, there are Autonomous Shots and Syntagms (groupings of shots); of

1) Autonomous Shots, there are five kinds: sequence shots, non-diegetic inserts, subjective inserts, displaced diegetic inserts, and explanatory inserts. Syntagms are either chronological elements of narrative: 2) Alternate Syntagms, 3) Scenes, 4) Episodic Sequences, and 5) Ordinary Sequences, or achronological: 6) Parallel, 7) Bracket, and 8) Descriptive Syntagms. This system should be helpful in illuminating Roeg's highly unconventional form of narrative.

Paradigms are vertical or synchronic groups or categories of elements that can be substituted for each other in a given syntagmatic position (*boy* and *girl* both belong to the category of nouns, and either can be chosen for the subject, just as *grow* or *die* can be chosen for the predicate). Particular subcodes that belong to the same general cinematic code (e.g., close-up and long-shot both belong to the camerawork code, dissolve and fade belong to the code of cinematic transition) have a paradigmatic relation and are in competition with each other; they cannot both be chosen for the same shot. In discovering or defining the codes, the critic looks for consistent paradigmatic choices. For example, Roeg's films consistently rely on complex montage of visual image and sound, and on disorienting camera movement. Though Metz is suspicious of a style relying heavily on montage, which he sees as "dismantling the immanent perception of things in order to reel it off in slices,"[20] this is precisely what is needed to explore the perceptions of an alien in a strange culture.

As Metz is certainly aware, the analogy between film and verbal language has many limitations. Film syntagms lack the clarity, exhaustiveness, and reliability of their verbal equivalents; further, Metz's syntagms apply only to narrative film. There are no real image paradigms in film; that is, images cannot be grouped into categories like nouns and verbs where it is possible to choose one item from a category to fill a grammatical slot. Rather, each image is like a neologism—a new word inventing a new category. Film images also have no double articulation; that is, the image cannot be broken down into smaller units without signifieds like the morphemes and phonemes of verbal language. Finally, cinema language is not a *langue*— "a system of *signs* for the purpose of *intercommunication*":[21] 1) it's only partly a system in that there are no image paradigms and no double articulation; 2) it has few signs that are arbitrarily coded, but relies more heavily on visual analogy; 3) it is a one-way communication in that the audience has no return channel of communication.[22]

The issue of what kind of signs are operating in cinema remains unresolved. Whereas in verbal language the relationship between signifier and signified is almost always arbitrary, in cinema the images or signs are based primarily on an analogical relationship with the objects they signify. This discussion of signs is rooted in the early semiological work of Charles Sanders Peirce, whose general theory of signification enumerated three basic categories of signs: 1) *indexical*, a sign in which meaning is based on an existential bond between itself and its object (signifier and signified); 2) *iconic*, a sign that represents its object (signified) mainly by analogy or similarity to it; and 3) *symbolic*, a sign that is arbitrary and coded, demanding neither resemblance to its signified nor any existential bond (contemporary semiotics uses the word "sign" only for this third category). It is possible to see all three types operating within the film medium.[23] The indexical sign is basic to photography; the camera is a machine that records light waves being broken by an object (signified) in the real world. This particular image cannot be created except in the presence of the signified. For example, a photograph of David Bowie (or his potential footprints at Grauman's Chinese) bear an existential bond with the actual person they signify. The iconic sign is dominant in painting, sculpture, and animated film. For example, a drawing of David Bowie or of an androgynous groupie with red and gold hair both use resemblance to evoke the signified. The symbolic sign prevails in literature and film dialogue. In *The Man Who Fell to Earth*, the song "Stardust" and the name "Tom" evoke David Bowie in his earlier personae of Ziggy Stardust and Major Tom. In current usage, some cinesemiologists collapse the indexical and iconic into what they call "analogous images," arguing that they dominate film signification, making it uncoded and uncodable. Umberto Eco, however, argues that even analogous images can be coded, offering ten codes for the image, ranging from those of perception and recognition to those of cultural values. Influenced by Eco, Metz has accepted the idea that images can be coded in specific texts while still functioning analogically at more general levels of coding. This is particularly important for Roeg's use of montage, which creates new coded meanings for analogical elements through patterns of juxtaposition. Thus Roeg gives structural expression to his narrative encounter, between two cultures, where old codes are necessarily inadequate and new ones must be created that can be mutually understood by insiders and outsiders, characters and audience.

Roeg's functional interweaving of these three kinds of signs is most effective in the sequence from *Walkabout* where the children find a weather balloon. The white girl interprets the balloon indexically. It signifies that the civilization that produced it is nearby; hence, she has her brother ask the Aborigine how much longer before they reach the white settlement. The Aborigine responds to the balloon iconically, associating it with the sun. The red, round ball of the sun is an image that occurs throughout the film and appears just before we see the red balloon for the first time. The Aborigine offers the balloon to the girl as a gift, as if he were offering her the sun, but she misperceives his gesture. Then the balloon suddenly bursts, suggesting metaphorically the Aborigine's bursting hopes and foreshadowing that he will be the one to suffer as a result of the misunderstanding. The exchange is reversed in the scene where the Aborigine rejects the toy soldier offered to him as a gift by the white boy. Failing to discover any indexical or iconic meaning and not knowing the code by which it might be a symbolic sign, he tosses it away as a worthless object. Yet the toy has considerable iconic value for the white boy; it is a visual representation of a man who fights with strength and prowess. In offering the gift, he attempts to repay the Aborigine for teaching him some of the skills of manhood within the "primitive" culture. The girl interprets it indexically, seeing the toy as a product of a technologically advanced society; the "poor" Aborigine doesn't have any proper toys of his own and she encourages her brother to offer the gift in a spirit of *noblesse oblige*. Unfortunately, the children are isolated in their separate codes, but Roeg's innovative visual style moves beyond them, creating for the audience the possibility of expansion and integration. The psychologist Jean Piaget sees the ability to invent new codes as one of the definitive characteristics of the human species in its evolutionary development; it is a source of freedom and creativity:

> Whereas other animals cannot alter themselves except by changing their species, man can transform himself by transforming the world and can structure himself by constructing structures: and these structures are his own, for they are not eternally predestined either from within or from without. So, then, the history of intelligence is not simply an "inventory of elements"; it is a bundle of transformations. . . .[24]

In the rest of this chapter, we will define the textual system of Roeg's *The Man Who Fell to Earth* and *Walkabout*—the particular combination of cinematic and cultural codes that control their meaning. We have selected these particular films because we have dealt at length elsewhere with *Performance* and *Don't Look Now*.[25] In trying to apply this particular theory, we have combined elements from various sources, developing a procedure to serve our own transformalist goals and the special qualities of the films under examination; we have relied most heavily on Metz's *Grand Syntagmatique* for the basic identification of structural units and on Barthes' erratic but insightful performance in *S/Z*. We will dissect *The Man Who Fell to Earth* into its thirty-one syntagms; within each, we will trace the ten codes that dominate the creation of connotative meaning within the film:

1) Narrative (based on Metz's events and Barthes' proairetic code)—what happens, what actions are performed by which characters along the horizontal axis.

2) Adaptation—how the film transforms its literary source, resulting in changes within the other codes.

3) Montage—how the structural units (the syntagms and their components) are articulated; it applies to both image and sound tracks.

4) Music (recorded musical sound is one of Metz's five matters of cinematic expression)—Roeg relies so heavily on music to create meaning that it functions as a separate code in his films.

5) Hermeneutics (based on Barthes' code)—units that raise questions in the audience, and then delay, equivocate, mislead, or provide answers.

6) Time—the various ways in which time is organized to convey meaning.

7) Space—the various ways in which space is organized to convey meaning.

8) Perception (based on Metz)—how point of view differs among characters and cultures, as it is based on various kinds of sense data.

9) Self-reflexiveness—units that call attention to this film as an artifact, to the cinematic medium, to earlier films by Roeg and others, and to the functions of the filmmaker and audience.

10) Culture (from Barthes)—in one sense, all the codes are cultural, yet while the other nine stress signification within the text (centripetal), this final code emphasizes referential meanings that point to the world outside the film (centrifugal).

In the next stage, we will draw general inferences about how the codes work in themselves and in relation to each other in order to articulate Roeg's cinematic style. We will test these inferences against *Walkabout*, using selected material and summary statements about its codes since space does not allow a detailed dissection of this film.

The Man Who Fell to Earth

1. The Arrival (Behind the Titles)

Narrative

Plot:
A spaceship falls to earth. Observed by an unknown watcher, an alien figure stumbles down a hill, crosses a highway near Haneyville, New Mexico, and enters a pawn shop where he sells a gold wedding ring.

Commentary:
Establishes Thomas Jerome Newton as central character of the film. This syntagm presents a simple narrative line with complex visuals, suggesting the combination of naivete and perceptual superiority in Newton's character.

Adaptation

Adds:
a) The descent of the ship (Time, Perception).[26]
b) The mysterious observer (Perception, Culture).
c) The gun in the drawer of the pawn shop (Culture).

Omits:
a) The section title "1895: Icarus Descending" (Narrative, Time).
b) Anthea, the name of the home planet, and a comparative analysis of the alien's physical similarities to and differences from human man (Hermeneutics).

Substitutes:
a) A woman wearing Indian jewelry for a male shopkeeper (Culture).
b) Wedding ring for man's diamond ring (Culture—sexual coupling).

Montage

Ordinary
Sequence:
$(1-2= cut)$[27]
Edits together documentary footage of actual moon landing, opticals and live action, transforming them into components of a single story.

Music

Home-planet theme:
Haunting music (which sounds like whale songs) is associated with space travel.

Oriental music and wind chimes:
associated with splashdown, wooden shack, and alien's coming into this world (a kind of birth). This association helps to explain why Newton will later develop a taste for oriental decor in his environments.

Co-option theme:
Louis Armstrong's "Blueberry Hill" being played inside a New Mexico pawnshop introduces theme of co-opting blacks in America, to be continued in the figure of Peters, the black government agent.

Hermeneutics

The Alien:
Who is landing, from where, and for what purpose? The visuals give us partial answers—we watch him take off his hood and coat, we see his face in close-up—but these clues are misleading,

because he is wearing a cover. The dialogue also misleads us by telling us that he is British and that his name is Thomas Jerome Newton; it also reveals one truth that will become central in the narrative—he has a wife.

The Observer: Who is observing the alien, for what purpose?

Time

Narrative time: NASA documentary footage of past moon landing is used to portray futuristic space travel, implying that this science fiction film is about the present and recent past.

Economic time: Woman opens shop and sounds the alarm bell, indicating it is morning and time for work and business.

Space

This syntagm introduces a wide variety of spatial contexts: from outer space travel, to open landscape, to a small town in New Mexico, to the interior of the pawnshop, to exploration of smaller cases, drawers, and mirror. The order suggests spatial diminishment, from the large to the small, accentuating the fall and foreshadowing what is to happen to the alien's potentialities in his new environment.

Perception

Establishes an alien perspective on familiar phenomenon: the NASA footage that we have already seen is made to represent a strange kind of space travel; our home planet appears ominous with its dangerous highways, grotesque plastic clowns, and drunks; when the alien enters the pawnshop, the moving camera represents his subjective point of view, unsure of what to focus on. These techniques lead us to identify with the alien's perspective as he is bombarded with a complex network of unfamiliar signs that are visual, auditory, and verbal; we have all had this experience in our infancy and in our travels. We recapture the mysteriousness of the familiar. At the same time, there is also a broader perspective—that of the unknown observer. The camera cuts from the feet of the observer to an overhead shot of Newton as if from the observer's p.o.v.; then the camera suddenly pulls back behind the observer, showing that he, too, is being watched by us, establishing a complex chain of multiple perspectives.

Self-reflexiveness

The use of documentary footage to portray events comments on the double nature of the film medium. The self-conscious camera movements stressing multiple perspectives lead the audience to reflect on their own role as observers. Just as the alien is bombarded with signs from a strange culture, we are bombarded with signs from the new world of this film; this syntagm introduces most of the codes for the entire film. We have probably seen the NASA footage on TV, a medium which has shaped our image of space travel. By incorporating this footage, this syntagm introduces the comparison between the two media, which recurs throughout the film. Like the alien and the characters from earth, we have been imprinted by both media; this film attempts to alter the imprinting.

Culture

Science: NASA footage establishes the historical context of the space program and the American emphasis on technological progress. The name Newton evokes Isaac Newton, the scientific genius who altered our conception of the universe.

Icarus myth: The alien's fall through space and splashdown introduce the Icarus theme.

Biblical myth: The landing suggests the Creation and the Fall of Man. The alien appears to be praying by the river.

Power: The observer presents first the indication of a power group, whose identity and connections (CIA, FBI, Mafia, Mars?) are unknown (as in the real world).

Water: Associated with birth in the splashdown.

Alcohol: A drunk offers the alien a beer, introducing the cheapest, least powerful, most low-brow form of a dominant corrupting influence.

Train: When we see the alien's face for the first time, we hear the faint sound of a train, which we see in the background. The train is an important structural image, frequently introducing the alien's subjective train of thought.

Clothing: The hooded car coat worn by the alien is the first cover he discards. Since it is associated with his entry into this world, it will function like a security blanket. The Indian jewelry worn by the shopkeeper visually develops the theme of economic co-option; she lives off the Indians.

Gun: The gun in the shopkeeper's drawer is a sign of widespread danger and distrust; physical power is necessary to maintain economic exploitation.

Sexual coupling: The alien uses rings as a convenient way to sell gold while appearing needy and exploitable. Ironically, he is in fact sacrificing his family ties to gain resources from the new planet, and he will in fact be exploited by those who claim to be his friends. Though he doesn't know it yet, the exchange of love for money is common on our planet.

2. Counting Money by the River

Narrative

Plot: Newton sits by a river drinking water in a strange manner. He counts a huge roll of hundred dollar bills, sees a passing truck carrying caged sheep, and counts a huge number of gold wedding rings.

Commentary: Continues the focus on the lone alien and his rise to power.

Montage

Ordinary sequence: (2–3 = musical sound bridge, cut) Visually this sequence is linked with the previous syntagm, but then we learn there has been a leap in time; it is fused with the following syntagm by means of a musical fade-in. We learn that visuals, sound, and time will be the three main factors governing the relationship between adjoining syntagms.

Hermeneutics

The Alien: Once we see the money, we wonder where he got it? Once we see the rings, we wonder why he lied in the pawnshop? Why is he amassing money? Why is he drinking so strangely?

Time

Narrative time: The visuals at first give no indication of time passing—he is wearing the same clothes and is in the same setting. But when we see the roll of bills, we wonder whether that was the first pawnshop he visited or the last. Duration of ellipses may be hours, days, or weeks.

Economic time: We wonder how long it has taken him to amass that much money. In our culture, time is money; both must be counted.

Perception

We observe Newton's alien gestures, particularly the way he moves his mouth when he drinks; he looks more like a frog or infant than a civilized human. Although he is associated here with animals (frogs and sheep), he has money and gold, signifying power and knowledge. We are unsure whether to perceive him as primitive or advanced.

Culture

Water: Identified as a valuable resource along with money and gold.
Train: The train whistle is identified with the pleasure of drinking water; the alien is probably thinking of his home planet, which he left to search for water, but we are not yet able to perceive his subjective train of thought.

Biblical myth: The sheep evoke the Christian symbolism of Christ as the sacrificed lamb. They are caged, foreshadowing the entrapment and economic exploitation to which Newton will be subjected.

3. Hiring a Lawyer

Narrative

Plot: Newton visits Oliver Farnsworth, whom he hires as a patent lawyer and as a front to control World Enterprises. While waiting for Oliver to read his nine basic patents, he looks at the New York skyline and has a flashback to his space travel. When he leaves and drives off in his waiting limousine, Newton gets dizzy and tells his chauffeur Arthur to slow down. Meanwhile, Oliver tells Trevor that he won't follow his father's advice ("Always look a gift-horse in the mouth!"); instead, he will trust Newton.

Commentary: As soon as Newton establishes his first real contact by seeking out Oliver, the narrative begins to get more complicated—with various kinds of inserts, disjunctions of sound and image, and media images (stereo and television). Oliver's narrative line begins *with* Newton; he will function as the alien's human alter ego.

Adaptation

Adds:

a) Views outside the window and subjective thoughts they inspire (Perception).

b) Farnsworth's offered handshake, which Newton fails to respond to (Perception, Culture).

c) Farnsworth's glasses, magnifying his eyes (Perception).

Substitutes:

a) Indeterminate time ellipses between this scene and previous events for a specified period of two months (Time).

b) Trevor, Farnsworth's male lover, for female maid (Culture—sexual coupling).

Montage

Ordinary
sequence
with Inserts:

(3-4 = cut)

3A Explanatory Insert: New York skyline at twilight; romantic music begins.

3B Subjective Insert: Lights that become fireworks or starburst against a black sky: home-planet musical theme. This image resembles the opening flight sequence and hence suggests Newton's memory or association.

3C Episodic Sequence: Moving from late night to early morning through a series of dissolves of New York City. Midway through the sequence, there is a voice-over dialogue between Oliver and newton concerning the patents. This sequence is incorporated into the basic syntagm where it also functions like a series of Explanatory Inserts (magnified details occupying "the abstract space of a mental operation").[28] Yet, as point of view shots, they also suggest Subjective Inserts ("an absent moment experienced by the hero of the film") in that Newton has left the present of Farnsworth's apartment and the patents folder and gone into his own mind and perception. The fluidity and ambiguity are increased when the first shot of the return to the apartment is a TV image of street violence.

Music from Oliver's stereo began in previous syntagm. Disjunction between sound and image track continues when camera follows Newton as he leaves the apartment while Oliver continues speaking to him in voice-over dialogue.

Music

Music is established as a means of linking adjoining syntagms and as making associative links between visual images widely separated in the narrative. Oliver is associated with sound systems (that will improve) and a wide variety of music, both of which help define his character. The home-planet theme accompanies first subjective insert.

Hermeneutics

The Alien:

His money, his mispronunciation of the word *patents* indicates he's probably not English, his unfamiliarity with handshakes and glasses indicates he may be from a totally alien culture. New questions are introduced: why does he need so much money (explicitly asked in the dialogue), what thoughts are occurring in his mind (suggested by the visuals and music).

Oliver Farnsworth:

What is his relationship with Trevor—lovers? friends? master/servant? Is he trusting and trust-worthy, or will he betray Newton? Visuals (his glasses) and dialogue (Oliver: "Perhaps you're not so different after all") give us clues that Oliver and Newton will be allies or alter-egos.

Time

Narrative time:

Temporal connections are varied and ambiguous; Does the montage of New York images indicate the natural time that it takes Oliver to read the patents, or does it reflect Newton's special powers of seeing into the past and future? Is the fireworks or starburst shot a flashback or a wishful flashforward?

Economic time:

Newton buys Oliver's time at the rate of $1,000 per hour.

Time and motion:

Going 40 miles per hour in an automobile makes Newton dizzy, yet he has travelled at much faster rate from one planet to another; time and motion are relative.

Space

The contrast between inner and outer space is introduced, signalled by both image and sound tracks.

Perception

Just as in the previous syntagm we observed Newton's alien gestures, now we see him react to Oliver's, which are just as alien from his point of view. Oliver's glasses magnify what he sees; they are false eyes like Newton's, but we are unsure whether they indicate that his vision is weaker or stronger than normal. Similar questions are raised about Newton's perceptive powers as he looks out the window.

Oliver transcends his father's point of view by rejecting his advice—always look a gift horse in the mouth; this raises for us the question of whether it is possible to perceive signs of deception and betrayal in Oliver, Newton, and other characters.

Self-reflexiveness

The audience's memory is tested by the first subjective insert—do we remember the music and visual image from the opening syntagm? By moving from the New York street montage to the television image of street violence, this syntagm explicitly compares the two media and the way they shape our view of violence and power.

Culture

Water and alcohol:

Established as a polarity (the good and bad drink). When Newton is asked if he wants a drink, he takes the water, and Oliver takes the scotch, the more potent, expensive drink.

Power:

Dialogue establishes the connections between knowledge, money, and power, raising the question of whether science controls money or money controls science.

Howard Hughes myth:	The image of Newton as the strange, eccentric founder of a technological empire who keeps a limousine on 24-hour service suggests a connection with Howard Hughes; perhaps he was also an alien.
"Gift-horse" dialogue interweaves several cultural codes:	a) Cliches that dominate the dialogue and imprint us with stock attitudes. b) Horse will function as a key image like train. c) Trust as a key moral theme; when Newton explains that he can't leave the patents with Oliver overnight, the camera moves into a close-up of Oliver's eyes, visually linking trust with perception. Later, when we see a close-up of Arthur's shifty eyes in the rear-view mirror, we have a clue that he will not turn out to be trustworthy. d) Gifts that will be accepted or rejected, and prove illuminating or deceptive.
Sexual coupling:	Introduces Oliver and Trevor as first of a number of odd couples, through which the film will explore the problem of finding a mate or a family group within a corrupt society.

4. Incestuous Sex and Oriental Violence

Narrative

Plot:	Nathan Bryce, a college professor, eyes a pretty student on the campus. At home, he receives a gift from his daughter and has sex with the student, who reminds him of his daughter. Meanwhile, Newton watches theatrical swordplay in a Japanese restaurant. He leaves the restaurant and phones Oliver about World Enterprise business—he is going to New Mexico. The student photographs their lovemaking with an amazing new film, which instantaneously develops the whole roll; Bryce notices that it is a World Enterprise product. The gift from his daughter is a book published by the same firm and contains Brueghel's painting and Auden's poem about Icarus.
Commentary:	It begins as an ordinary sequence introducing Bryce, a new character in a separate narrative line. At first he seems to be a simple, trustworthy character, but then as the syntagm becomes more complex we see his deviousness, which will eventually threaten Newton. His association with the probing, voyeuristic camera is established.

Adaptation

Adds:	a) Lovemaking between Bryce and his young girlfriend (Culture—sexual coupling). b) Newton watching Japanese theater (Culture, Narrative, Space).
Omits:	a) Bryce's original discovery of World Enterprise film in a movie theater (Self-reflexiveness). b) Bryce's suspicion that the film comes from an alien planet (Hermeneutics).
Substitutes:	The gift book from Bryce's daughter for a print of Brueghel's painting on Bryce's wall (Culture—sexual coupling, Self-reflexiveness).

Montage

Parallel syntagm with Inserts:	(4-5 = cut) Fluidly combines three groups of intercut parallel events: Newton in the theater/restaurant and Nathan in his apartment with his co-ed lover; Newton in the car and Oliver in his office; Nathan looking at the book and Newton speaking with Oliver.

4A Explanatory Insert: Picture of Nathan's daughter.

4B Explanatory Insert: Icarus painting by Breughel.

4C Explanatory Insert: Pan up the skyscraper.

4D Explanatory Insert: Oliver's name on office door.

The greatest editing complexity occurs in the intercutting between Nate in the bedroom and Newton in the restaurant where visuals, sounds, and themes interweave many meanings: sexplay and swordplay, orgasm and kill, sexual and violent thrusts, penis and sword, sex and food, fake incest and fake murder, an observer watching a performance and a lover photographing a sexual performance. Sounds from both scenes are integrated with various kinds of music into a dense rhythm, which counterpoints the visual montage. This intercutting suggests not only the deceptiveness of both Bryce and Newton (neither is what he appears to be on the surface), but also the inventiveness of Nicolas Roeg as filmmaker.

Sound disjunction between image of Newton getting into car and Oliver's voice-over talking to Trevor or directly addressing the audience before starting his phone conversation with Newton introduces another plane of reality where characters function like narrators.

Music

In the intercutting between the restaurant and the bedroom, the music takes a more active role by coupling Eastern and Western themes and establishing the rhythm for the editing pace.

The rock music that introduces Bryce on the college campus helps imply that his tastes bridge the generation gap.

Hermeneutics

Nathan Bryce:	Is he reliable? How is he related to Newton and Oliver? We get an important clue we do not yet understand: when he receives the book as a gift, he is more interested in who published it than in the mythic figure of Icarus.
The Alien:	He is again linked with Icarus.
Oliver Farnsworth:	We get evidence concerning his reliability. He questions Newton's decisions, but remains loyal. He is concerned about his loss of freedom, yet he has been able to change and begin a new life.

Time

Narrative
time:

We are unsure of the time relationship among the intercut scenes. Newton's reactions to the theatrical violence also seem appropriate to the sex scene, introducing lateral time. Oliver's monologue·about his changes and the phone conversation with Newton seem continuous although their time relationship is obscure. Ellipses have various durations ranging from seconds to hours and perhaps days, weeks, or years. The introduction of Bryce suggests a conceptual future time when he will be relevant to Newton. The complex rhythms of image and sound create an artistic timing found in dance, theater, poetry, sex, and other performances.

Economic
time:

We watch Oliver and World Enterprises growing in wealth and power through external signs—buildings, clothes, logos, products. The emphasis is on fast development both in the specific product (the film) and in the corporation.

Biological
time:

Nathan receives a birthday gift and makes love with a very young girl—two signs that he is getting older. Oliver makes the theme explicit: "I didn't think a man could change at my age."

Space

As the story moves from one narrative to another, Newton moves westward to New Mexico; Oliver moves upward economically to the top of a skyscraper; and Nathan moves in and out between home and school, daughter and coed, sex and World Enterprise logos. This syntagm introduces the recurring pattern of a phone call transcending the distance between Newton, who is in a moving car, and Oliver, who is stationary in a room.

Perception

The emphasis is on observation—Newton watching the performance in the restaurant, learning that oriental culture feeds on ritualistic violence, learning how Western lovers need fake violence and incest to turn them on. Voyeurism may also be sexually arousing—for Newton, for the girl who photographs the lovemaking, for Bryce who examines the pictures, and for us in the audience.

Self-reflexiveness

This syntagm compares various media combined in film—theater, dance, photography, painting, poetry, music—thereby commenting on the integrating power of cinema. The shot of the co-ed photographing her mirror image and then her lover refers back to a similar shot of Pherber doing the same thing in *Performance*. Oliver's monologue about changing his life is delivered like an informal speech about his own development to an audience, summarizing the time between the syntagms. This same kind of self-reflexive monologue will be delivered by Mary Lou in syntagm 6 and by Nathan Bryce in syntagm 8. The suggestion of the future through Bryce parallels the early flash forward to Jagger in *Performance*.

Culture

Icarus myth: Elaborated by painting and poem and identified as the central myth in the narrative. It is associated with birds and water, freedom and life.

Biblical myth: Oliver says to Newton: "If I owned a copyright on the Bible, I wouldn't sell it to Random House." Reinforces the mythic subtext of the Fall of Man.

Sexual coupling: In our culture, it is dominated by violence and incest taboos.

Gift: Like the "gift horse" mentioned in the previous syntagm, the gift book must be looked into as a means of foreshadowing future events and recognizing the mythic level of the story. In *Performance*, Borges' story "The South" played a similar role, as it alluded back to the magic book of the *Arabian Nights*.

Oriental theme: The oriental musical theme linked with Newton's landing is now deepened to include imprinting of association between food and violence, which will shape his taste for oriental motifs.

Academia: The academic world is introduced in terms of the familiar cliché—the burned-out middle-aged professor preying on female students. This syntagm also suggests the connection between the university and business.

World Enterprises Logo interweaves several cultural codes: The Logo is a verbal symbol representing products, people, and corporations, fusing scientific knowledge and economic power. The plural form *Logos* literally means the Word, and suggests the polarity between Logos/Eros. The male-dominated rational Western mind definitely prefers Logos to Eros.

5. An Academic Argument

Narrative

Plot: Nathan Bryce argues with Professor Canutti at the college where he teachers; he intends to quit his job and get a position with World Enterprises.

Commentary: Continuing the separate development of Bryce, this simple scene makes him appear heroic but proves misleading. He begins to compete with Newton for control of the narrative. Roeg makes us distrust simplicity.

Adaptation

Adds: Bryce's sexual pursuit of "young things" as an issue in the argument (Culture—sexual coupling).

Montage

Scene: (5-6 = cut)
There are no time ellipses in this unit, a pattern that will be associated with entrapment.

Music

There is no music, an omission that undermines the emotional level of the argument.

Hermeneutics

Nathan Bryce:

We are given a helpful clue about how he will be linked with Newton, but we are misled about his reliability.

Time

Biological time:

Age is relative. Bryce claims it depends on what you know, how open you are to change, rather than how many years you have lived. Canutti argues that those trying to bridge the generation gap are doomed to decadence and deviance, and implies that people become obsolete. In contrast, Bryce links progress with mutation and insists that ideas go out of date rather than human beings.

Space

Although physical space is confined to one room, the cosmic photograph on the wall reminds us of the larger context of the entire narrative into which this scene fits. The spatial reversal (the whole being inserted into the part) is a visual sign of the pomposity and co-optive power of both characters. The largeness of the office also implies that Canutti is Bryce's superior within the academic hierarchy.

Perception

This scene emphasizes the relative nature of interpretation: the two men disagree about politics, education, time, human nature; they perceive the world differently. The double meaning of the word "pursuit" (Canutti accuses Nate of pursuing young things instead of knowledge) reinforces the relativity.

Self-reflexiveness

The warning about relativity applies to the audience's interpretation of the scene. We can easily be misled by their words, particularly those with multiple meanings. We are unsure whether to take the scene straight or satirically, or whether Roeg's awareness of the misleading simplicity and clichéd dialogue prevents this scene from failing.

Culture

Academia:

The academic world is faced with the same problems of power and corruption as found in business and government. Like the mass media, it provides another means of imprinting and co-opting.

Clichés:

This highly verbal scene introduces the familiar jargon of various stereotypes—the profane vocabulary of the radical professor who flourished in the sixties, and the complacent administrator defending decency and tradition with genteel phrases. The issues are all familiar: man vs. machines, progress vs. decadence, freedom vs. control, the young vs. the old.

6. Meeting Mary Lou

Narrative

Plot:
Newton checks into a New Mexico hotel where he meets Mary Lou, a chambermaid. When he faints in an elevator, she carries him to his room, stays with him till he recovers, then returns to spend the evening. Their evening is intercut with scenes of Nate Bryce having sex with a series of interchangeable young girls, who act out the daughter role. Mary Lou talks and drinks steadily and tries to interest Newton in gin; he finally asks her to leave and to bring a TV set the next day. She leaves the hotel and delivers a monologue.

Commentary:
Like the introduction of Nate's narrative, this accidental encounter with Mary Lou begins as an ordinary syntagm but then is complicated by being linked with a series of sex scenes involving Nate, comprised of a highly complex mixture of shots, girls, and time periods, foreshadowing Bryce's sexual and moral co-opting of Mary Lou. When we return to Mary Lou and Newton, their relationship may seem innocent by contrast, but it begins to become more complicated. The incestuous overtones carried over from Nate's scenes makes us reinterpret as maternal behavior Mary Lou's act of lifting up Newton, carrying him to his room, and telling him he's too thin. The alternation between fusion and separation begins to characterize their relationship.

Adaptation

Adds:
a) Nate's sexual encounters (Culture—sexual coupling).
b) Newton's asking Mary Lou to bring him a TV set.

Omits:
Newton's opinion that humans are vulgar, self-absorbed apes (Culture).

Substitutes:
a) Artesia, New Mexico for Louisville, Kentucky (Space).
b) A young, attractive Mary Lou for a 40-year-old, heavy, deteriorating Betty Jo, who passes for a housekeeper (Culture—sexual coupling).

Montage

Parallel
syntagm
with Inserts:
(6-7 = Sound dissolve, cut)
Throughout the syntagm, there is simple intercutting between interior and exterior shots of the hotel, which are taken to be simultaneous, and complex intercutting of sex scenes involving Nate, which contrast with the diegetic action.

6A   Displaced diegetic insert: Cut to the hotel exterior after Newton is already in the lobby, showing signs reading: *FREE ICE, TOURIST INFORMATION.*

6B   Explanatory insert: An Impressionistic landscape painting. Complex montage of Nate's sexual encounters implies he treats women as interchangeable bodies. Back in the room with Mary

Lou and Newton, the sound track grows more complex, mixing outside noises (a cat or baby crying), talk, music, and static from a radio. The fluidity of the sound track undermines the separate identity of the whole syntagm and parts within it: Mary Lou's monologue with street noises in the background begins as we watch her walking home from the hotel; Oliver's voice-over from a telephone conversation with Newton fades in as we still see Mary Lou.

Music

Sentimental country western songs and commercials ("It's the real thing. . . .") have imprinted Mary Lou with clichéd ideas of love and morality.

Hermeneutics

The Alien:

As he faints in the elevator, we learn that he reacts differently to gravity changes than we do. We learn a new name—Sussex—which he uses in the hotel. Why is he so secretive?

Nathan Bryce:

Confirms that he is obsessed with incestuous fantasies about his daughter.

Mary Lou:

What kind of relationship will she have with Newton? Will it be the "real thing?"

Time

Narrative time:

The intercutting between interior and exterior shots of the hotel implies simultaneity, whereas Nate's intercut sex scenes have an ambiguous time relationship with the diegetic actions. Within Nate's sexual encounters, the time is also ambiguous—we do not know how many different girls he is making love to, in what order, or at what intervals. This method of handling time implies a repetition compulsion.

Biological time:

Nate actively fills the generation gap.

Romantic time:

Mary Lou expects to have sex right away whereas Newton does not. Their slow-developing romance is contrasted with the frenetic pace of Nate's sexual encounters. Sex depends on timing.

Space

Spatial contrasts dominate the syntagm. The opening shot reveals a static "Hotel Artesia" sign in the left foreground with a Santa Fe train moving from left to right in the background. Throughout the syntagm there is intercutting between interior and exterior shots of the hotel. In one insert, the two-dimensional space of a painting takes over the illusion of three dimensional space within the hotel room. The dialogue introduces another spatial contrast between the city and the country.

Perception

Perception depends on breadth. New Mexico locals are narrow minded in what they see: the cops treat New Yorkers as foreigners, the hotel clerk is impressed with Newton's pen, Mary Lou considers any out-of-state traveller exciting.

Self-reflexiveness

Mary Lou is consistently identified with media—pop songs, radio, and television. She has a monologue about her own ordinariness: "They always seem to lead such interesting lives—people who travel. People who write stories must lead interesting lives, too.... I'll never get to travel. Maybe some day." Ironically, it is precisely her ordinariness—the small town, low-class, uneducated American woman imprinted by the media—that makes her a perfect character for the story.

Culture

Sexual coupling:

Nate chooses interchangeable girls whom he casts in his own incestuous fantasy; as a rational westerner, his sex is highly verbal: "You're a lecherous little girl . . . no one would ever believe it." The young girls deliver their lines: "You know, you're not at all like my father." The whole experience is like a dramatic performance. This view of sex is contrasted with the unusual romance developing between Newton and Mary Lou. While she expects him to make a pass and then starts mothering him, he resists the aroles she tries to impose on him. Sex depends on expectations.

Water and alcohol:

He has come to the "Artesia Hotel," which advertises "Free Ice;" when he faints, he asks for something to drink and Mary Lou tries to give him gin rather than water. At this stage, he is still pure but she warns him that the water here is "all polluted . . . they put chemicals in it to keep people from getting sick." He over-estimates his powers and thinks he can "adapt" without being similarly polluted, but ultimately he will become an alcoholic like her. In contrast to Oliver who drinks scotçh, Mary Lou appropriately drinks gin, which is cheaper, less potent, and more lowbrow.

Xenophobia:

Expands the idea that America is made up of a series of subcultures, all of whom consider the others alien: west vs. east, naive vs. sophisticated, country vs. city, families vs. strangers, locals vs. travellers.

Train:

The image of the train in the opening shot suggests it will be used as a transition to introduce a new syntagm, a new location, and a new significant character.

Censorship:

An economic power elite has deleted from the American version the scenes of Nathan Bryce having sex with a series of young girls. They may have felt that the American public was not ready for this kind of explicit reference to the incestuous nature of his behavior.

7. Invasion of Privacy

Narrative

Plot:
As Mary Lou silently irons, Newton watches television and talks to Oliver on the telephone about privacy. Oliver mentions a chemistry professor named Bryce who keeps writing to Newton.

Commentary:
For the first time, the four main characters are brought together in one syntagm. Newton and Oliver are both seen and heard, Nate is mentioned but not seen, Mary Lou is seen but not heard.

Montage

Alternate
syntagm
with Inserts:
(7-8 = cut)
Begins with Oliver's voice, fading in, which began in previous syntagm, and close-up of Newton's eyes before revealing context of Newton's room, which he shares with Mary Lou. This scene is intercut with Oliver's office, which is also introduced with a disorienting shot—the construction seen through the office window—before establishing the context.

7A   Explanatory Insert: Newton's eyes.

7B   Explanatory Insert: Construction through window.

Hermeneutics

The Alien:
We get a visual clue when the editing implies a connection between Newton and the cat, who both watch television; we may suspect that they have similar eyes and multiple lives.

Mary Lou:
We get visual clues that her relationship with Newton is developing and that they are now probably living together.

Time

Economic
time:
The progress of World Enterprises begins to be measured by the construction going on outside of Oliver's window; this image will recur periodically.

Space

Oliver has followed Newton in his westward movement, from New York to New Mexico, from the city to the country, from vertical skyscrapers to wide open spaces.

Perception

Emphasis on observation—Newton and the cat watching and being imprinted by television; like Oliver, we watch the construction going on outside his window. These parallel inserts imply a comparison between two rectangular devices (TV set and window) that frame art and life. Oliver's dialogue informs us that people are beginning to observe Newton and to be suspicious about his privacy; Nathan Bryce is trying to reach him.

Self-reflexiveness

Like the TV and window, the movie screen is another rectangular device that frames moving images of art and life, attracts the eyes of an audience, and imprints their minds.

Culture

Howard
Hughes myth:
Suggested by Oliver's comment about Newton's extreme privacy attracting attention.

Sexual
coupling:
Newton has established a new family group that reflects traditional sex roles: she silently does domestic chores while he changes the world. The narrative reinforces her subordinate role: she has no narrative identity separate from Newton's (for different reasons than Farnsworth).

8. Bryce Joins World Enterprises

Narrative

Plot:
Nate leaves the campus and his pursuit of 18-year-olds for a French car and a job with World Enterprises. He flies to New Mexico where he meets Oliver Farnsworth, who describes the new job.

Commentary:
Nate's and Oliver's narrative lines are finally joined, with Nate starting to rise and Oliver beginning to decline. Nate dominates both the sound and image tracks of the syntagm.

Montage

Episodic
sequence:
(8-9 = music bridge, cut)
Bryce's direct address on the sound track unifies the passing of a year, which is fragmented by the visual ellipses of time. The music from the TV film in the next syntagm fades into the end of this sequence. Both of these effects continue the disjuncture between sound and image. Intercutting between Nate and Oliver in the final scene stresses the narrative competition between them.

Hermeneutics

Nathan
Bryce:
As we watch him rise in power, we get more clues about his character—the foreign car and his focus on his salary make him seem more materialistic than in earlier syntagms. He has faith in himself and in some greater power ("What I didn't know then was that someone else had faith in me as well"); we now wonder who is that power? God, Newton, or some other established power group?

Time

Narrative
time:
The dialogue compresses at least a year of narrative time while the visuals present four selected scenes: Nate on the campus, a plane taking off, a limousine with New Mexico plates, and Oliver's office.

Economic
time:
The construction outside Oliver's window continues to grow.

Biological
time:
Oliver shows the first signs of aging, which is linked with his decline in the narrative structure.

Space

Oliver explicitly comments on his move from New York to New Mexico: "I keep an apartment there. . . . I've come to like it out here. It has a lot of space—that means freedom. You know what I mean?" As if to answer his question, the camera moves to the window where we see the construction and its sign of growth.

Perception

In the process of intercutting between Nate and Oliver, the camera moves into a close-up of Oliver's glasses and magnified eyes, as if he were trying to perceive whether Nate is trustworthy. A very similar shot was used to link trust with perception in syntagm 3. Hence, the film tests our memories and the effectiveness of its own imprinting.

Self-reflexiveness

Nate's monologue makes him function as a narrator—a pattern that has already occurred with Oliver (in syntagm 4) and Mary Lou (in syntagm 6).

Culture

Sexual coupling:
In Western culture, mind and body, work and sex function as bipolarities. Nate tells us that for a year he was obsessed with two things—fucking 18-year-olds and getting a job with World Enterprises; when he gets the work, he gives up the sex: "My conscious mind had developed a libido of its own." As a substitute for the young girl, he takes the sexy French car. Similarly, when Oliver's job takes him to New Mexico, he leaves his lover Trevor to maintain the apartment in New York.

Biblical theme:
Nate sees himself as one of God's elite, carrying out His Manifest Destiny—"Someone else had faith in me." In the West, this is a common method of justifying questionable causes—God is on our side.

Censorship:
The French car is deleted from the American version, perhaps for economic reasons.

9. Love, Faith, & TV

Narrative

Plot:
Mary Lou and Newton discuss their relationship as he watches several television sets, one of which features Gary Cooper and Audrey Hepburn in *Love in the Afternoon*. Mary Lou suggests they have a drink, she takes a bath, and they go to church the next day. They continue their conversation while she bathes.

Commentary:
As their relationship develops, the narrative becomes complex, comparing the romantic film on television with the closeness growing between Mary Lou and Newton. Not only is there a thematic comparison, but the television seems partially to control what happens in the room. There are also ambiguous inserts, which relate to what is going on in Newton's mind.

Adaptation

Adds:
The specific parallel content of the TV images (Perception, Self-reflexiveness, Culture).

Montage

Alternate syntagm with inserts:

(9-10 = music bridge, cut) Intercuts between Mary Lou and Newton's conversation and the film on TV.

9A Subjective or Explanatory Insert: Construction site.

9B Subjective or Explanatory Insert: Santa Fe train moving from left to right.

These inserts follow Mary Lou's comments about everyone needing a meaning for life or something to believe in, as if Roeg is explaining what Newton believes in—building a vehicle to get back home. Immediately following the second insert, he says: "They're so strange here, the trains."
Church music again introduces the next syntagm before its visual identity is established.

Music

"Fascination," the theme song from *Love in the Afternoon*, imprints us with romantic ideas and triggers certain emotions, as a bell affects one of Pavlov's hungry dogs. After the violinists have performed this function in the film, they tiptoe out of the love nest, leaving Gary Cooper and Audrey Hepburn to their own devices and Mary Lou and Newton to their own thoughts of love.

Hermeneutics

The Alien:

Certain information is confirmed—Sussex is a false name; he is married; he needs Mary Lou. New questions are raised about what is going on in his mind—why are trains so significant to him? What is he thinking of?

Mary Lou:

She is not so "innocent" as she first appeared—she is willing to be the mistress of a married man, she dyes her hair; yet, she believes in God and Love and is a church-goer.

Time

Romantic time:

The modern temporary liaison is explained by Gary Cooper in *Love in the Afternoon*. Two lovers have a regular appointment at a certain hour (as in business) and act as if they're between trains. Ironically, this applies to Newton, who actually is between trains (and spaceships). Having been trained by the movies, Mary Lou is willing to accept the arrangement: "Guess I'll do for now."

Space

Develops much further the interaction between inner and outer space—what's happening within the TV screen and the mental space of the inserts affects and is affected by the external behavior in the room. Modern liaisons depend on keeping one's distance. Cooper says: "The trouble is, people get too attached."

Perception

We watch Newton watching television and being imprinted; Mary Lou has long ago been imprinted with a belief in romantic love and god. This process helps explain the differences in point of view on most topics. From Newton's perspective, earth trains are "so strange"; this anticipates our own reaction when we see trains from his home planet. Mary Lou considers Newton a freak, even with his earth cover, because of her provincial perspective; this anticipates her reaction when she sees him as he really is.

Self-reflexiveness

Romantic films influence Newton and Mary Lou, while Roeg's film tries to counteract the conventional programming. The bathtub scene in which Mary Lou is dyeing her hair suggests a similar scene in *Performance*.

Mary Lou drops the name Sussex and starts to call the alien Tommy; both names evoke films that follow the rise and fall of a rock star. David Essex stars in *Stardust* and *Tommy* is the title of the rock opera by the Who, adapted by Ken Russell to the screen, which features a mother/son relationship.

Culture

Sexual coupling:

Mary Lou and Newton move closer to forming another odd couple. She says: "Tommy, you're really a freak. . . . I like freaks, that's why I like you." This exogamous desire will lead her across the species barrier; another sexual taboo (like incest) creates the turn-on. In Western culture, romantic love has become a religion; at the moment that Mary Lou praises religion as a source of meaning in life and looks to the heavens with uplifted face, the camera cuts to Gary Cooper kissing Audrey Hepburn to the strains of "Fascination." Religion brings the concept of sin and guilt, which helps explain why forbidden love is so exciting.

Water and alcohol:

Mary Lou suggests a ritualistic series—having a drink, taking a bath, and going to church, implying that cleanliness and drunkenness are next to godliness.

Media:

With their monkeys (or evolutionary precursors), mandalas (an archetypal image), and movies (collective dreams), the media have co-opted the syntagm and the direction of our evolutionary development.

Train:

The centrality of this image is reaffirmed, as it introduces a train of thought, an associative train of images from two cultures, and a process of training in cultural assumption.

Clothing:

Mary Lou's yellow outfit with black rick-rack locates her in the heartland of polyester country—western chic.

10. Church Singing

Narrative

Plot:

Mary Lou and Newton are in church; he tries to sing for the first time.

Commentary:

A simple scene for a simple, ordinary experience that delights Mary Lou; Newton is trying to please her and to adapt to his surroundings. Although the church is supposed to make him feel that he belongs, it evokes images and sounds that lead him back to his home planet in the next syntagm.

Adaptation

Substitutes:

Newton's visit to Church for his refusal to go to Church (Music, Self-reflexiveness)

Montage

Scene:
(10-11 = music bridge, cross dissolve)
One of the few syntagms with no time ellipses, suggesting its entrapping quality for Newton, whose mental life has begun to move among various planes in the other syntagms. The scene ends with a cross-dissolve to a galloping horse and music fading in from the next syntagm (the only time a dissolve occurs simultaneously in the sound and image tracks), breaking its autonomy and suggesting that Newton's mind has escaped at last.

Music

This syntagm implies that music has tremendous spiritual power (whether it be a church hymn or a sentimental pop song like "Try to Remember") to transport one through time and space and affect the emotions. Most religions rely heavily on the power of music to express transcendental experience and spiritual unity.

Hermeneutics

The Alien:
Why doesn't he know how to sing?

Time

Narrative time:
The real time in this scene is confining.

Space

The restriction to the church is confining: the camera begins to pan along the faces of the congregation as if it, too, wants to escape.

Perception

Pleasure or discomfort is a matter of perspective—the same external stimuli arouse delight in Mary Lou and feelings of entrapment in Newton.

Self-reflexiveness

Roeg creates an ironic situation by giving David Bowie, a famous rock star, only one scene where he actually sings and having him pretend he doesn't know how.

Culture

Xenophobia:
The church as an institution presents itself as a unifying force (here it incorporates two aliens—Newton and the lone black man sitting behind him), but actually it co-opts other cultures and fosters a conforming adaptation.

11. Old Trains and Pioneers

Narrative

Plot:
As Newton and Mary Lou drive through the country, they see a white horse galloping, which reminds him of his home planet and his departure on a train. Newton and Mary Lou cross the

railroad tracks, and Mary Lou recounts nostalgic memories regarding trains. As they drive to the site where he originally landed, he sees pioneers from the past and they see the limousine. When Mary Lou and Newton reach the lake where he splashed down, they decide to build a house on that spot. Then he mentally returns home, but Mary Lou calls him back to earth, thiking he is ill. Once in the car, Newton phones Oliver, who is in his New York apartment, and tells him that he wants to begin a space program, presumably so that he can get back home. Trevor warns Oliver not to trust Newton because he's a freak.

Commentary: Immediately following his attempt to adapt to Mary Lou's narrow world, Newton breaks away from her and develops one of the most highly complex narrative structures, integrating many kinds of subjective experience and various conceptions of time, space, and motion. His desire for a return home is so strong that it takes over the syntagm and is reflected in many other returns— back to earlier scenes in the narrative, back to the historical past, back to subjective memories, and Oliver's return to Trevor in New York. When Newton's subjective visions break through, his family enters the narrative.

Adaptation
Adds: The entire event of the ride through the country and all of Newton's subjective and visionary material (Time, Perception).

Montage
Alternate   (11-12 = bridge, cut)
syntagm with   The intercutting is basically between the ride in the country and
inserts: Newton's mental images concerning his home planet; then, between Newton and Mary Lou in the car and Oliver and Trevor at home in New York. Yet the editing is so varied and fluid, that it challenges all boundaries, blurring the identities of the syntagms and its units and making them very difficult to categorize. Having previously been used to show Newton incorporating new experience and new people into his human identity, the integrative editing now reveals the alien trying to reinterpret this data by reference to his home planet. Ironically, even the beauty and lushness of earth increase his alienation and his yearning for his old identity. The editing reveals that the longer Newton is on earth, the less unified he is in his new identity, foreshadowing his instability and decline. The fluidity and fragmentation are achieved in several ways:
1)   The ambitious beginning: The syntagm opens with a cross-dissolve to a galloping horse and a fade-in of the song "Try to Remember." We are not sure whether this is a Subjective Insert occurring while Newton is still in church, or an actual image he sees through the window and a song he hears on the radio while driving through the country. ·
2)   The heavy use of dissolves to show associations between varied experiences and to integrate material we have never previously seen:
a)   Dissolve to first view of the home planet when it was green and fertile.

      b)   Dissolve to an Impressionist painting with similar colors—does the painting remind him of his home as it used to be, or has he recolored his memories in order to suit his desires, borrowing the shades from Western art?

      c)   Dissolve to home planet after the drought—does the dissolve refer literally to the loss of the water?

      d)   Dissolve from image of train on home planet to image of Santa Fe train, allowing us momentarily to see them both on the screen at the same time.

      e)   Dissolve from Mary Lou telling story about old trains to Newton getting on home planet train as he leaves his family.

      f)   Dissolves between empty landscape seen by Mary Lou and images of pioneers seen by Newton.

      g)   Dissolves between Newton looking in water, visions of his home planet, and a close-up of his eyes covered by dark sunglasses.

3)   The use of cuts to introduce subjective inserts based on narrative flashbacks or flashforwards:

11A Subjective insert: Flashback to Newton walking down the hill from syntagm 1.

11B Subjective insert: Reversal of splashdown in lake from syntagm 1.

11C Subjective insert: Reversal of Newton's body springing out of the lake from syntagm 1.

11D Subjective insert: Flashforward to alien floating and spinning through space, which will be elaborated in syntagm 20.

4)   The pioneers are treated with sepia tinting of the image and a final flash cut, both suggesting that we are getting a photographic glimpse into the past. We wonder if this is the way Newton is actually seeing them, or is his vision based on old photographs he has seen.

Music

The power of music is exploited in many ways that help advance the narrative:

a) To introduce the theme and tone of romantic nostalgia with the sentimental pop song, "Try to
Remember."

b) To test the memory of the audience—do we recognize the sad home planet theme from the opening syntagm?

c) To help identify the pioneers and the culture they belong to; the vision flashes out with the last strum of the bluegrass banjo theme.

d) To change the mood and scene when the limousine pulls up at the lake and we hear steel guitar striving to achieve cosmic grandeur.

e) To help suggest that Oliver and Trevor are, indeed, lovers by means of romantic music playing in the background.

f) To introduce the next syntagm with a dramatic shift in tone and mood.

Hermeneutics

The Alien: At last, we learn where he is from, what his family and planet look like, why trains are significant, and what he has been thinking of. A new set of questions are initiated. What will happen to him in the future? Will he get back home, or build a house with Mary Lou and settle down?

Mary Lou: We learn that she will try to prevent him from going back home. Her role shifts from raising him up to keeping him down; this is the conventional dual role of the parent.

Oliver: He defends Newton against Trevor, maintaining his trust and trustworthiness.

Time

Narrative time: It is greatly expanded as we see multiple ways of expressing both the past and the future, making the temporal relationship among elements central in the syntagm. The past is evoked through song lyrics, visual memories of the home planet in two time periods, Impressionist painting from an earlier era, Mary Lou's verbal memories of trains in her childhood, photographs taken for a scrapbook, flashbacks of the landing, images (the shack, the lake, the strange way he moves his mouth) and sounds (the home-planet theme) we may recall from earlier syntagms, shots moving in reverse, the pioneers shot in an old-fashioned photographic style. Since most of the questions concerning the past are answered in this syntagm, it now focuses our attention on ways to see the future: Mary Lou and Newton discuss building a house, which we later will see; the pioneers from the past see the limousine in the present, which for them is the future, implying that all tenses are relative; Trevor reads the cards but sees nothing in the future, which may foreshadow his own death; Newton plans a space program to get back home.

Time and motion: We are presented with a linear progression of vehicles—from the horse in the distant past, to trains in the recent past, to cars in the immediate present, to a futuristic space program. Technological progress implies obsolescence; loss is built into the system.

Space

Space is expanded on all levels—Newton's mental space, which at last externalizes its images for the film audience; the space of the frame, which now shows two different images simultaneously, representing inner and outer space; the launching of a new space program in order to link the two planets physically as well as visually and narratively.

Perception

The ordinary perception of Mary Lou and Trevor is contrasted with the xpanded vision of Newton and Oliver, who both wear glasses. Perception is the basis of trust and love. Mary Lou values Newton for his freakiness th ough she underestimates it; Trevor distrusts and dislkes Newton for the same reason; Oliver who has a broader vision, remains loyal to both Trevor and Newton although he may distrust them in different ways; Newton, whose vision is the broadest, trusts and likes everyone he encounters. We wonder about Newton's sensory capabilities—can he actually see images of the past both here and from his home planet; is he capable of teleportation; can he see into the future? Ironically, the

answers to these questions must be based on our own perception—what we see rather than what we are told. When Mary Lou
forces Newton back to earth, the camera moves unsteadily from
water, to sky, to hills, as if representing his unstable point of view.
This subjective perspective is similar to the one he had in the
pawnshop in syntagm 1; he temporarily regains his alien point of
view on phenomena that have started to become familiar.

Self-reflexiveness

Our perceptions are tested—do we belong with ordinary Ameri-
cans like Mary Lou and Trevor, or can we develop the expanded
vision of Oliver or Newton? The complexity of the cinematic style
and the theme of expanded perception demonstrate that Roeg is
clearly on the side of Newton and Oliver and is trying to train us
as members of this elite. The image of the Impressionist painting
points to an artistic movement that succeeded in what Roeg is
trying to accomplish with this film—expanding the vision of its
viewers. Roeg's use of earlier forms of art is linked with the idea of
progress and obsolescence, developed through the image of the
scrapbook. Newton wants a photograph of the shack for his
"scrapbook" —a place where we keep traces of things we have
scrapped. Ironically, books as a medium are now being scrapped
and replaced by television and movies (just as planes have
replaced trains); in making this film, Roeg has recovered books—
Tevis' novel and the gift book containing Auden's poem and
Brueghel's painting.

Culture

Biblical
myth:

The home planet is presented first as an Edenesque garden, and
then plagued by drought as if after a Fall. Within this myth,
Newton plays the dual roles of Adam and Christ.

Clichés:

Mary Lou functions in this syntagm as a walking cliché—her
ordinary vision, her patriotism ("I never knew America was so
beautiful—this is beau-ti-ful!"), her green synthetic pants and
black western shirt, her maternal concern for her Tommy.

Train:

The associative powers of this image are now fully revealed—it
links horses and spaceships, past and future, earth and the home
planet, external and inner space, Mary Lou and Newton, and
most important, Newton and his family.

Birds and
Horses:

They are identified with freedom, motion, escape, and the return
home. Apparently, they also have horses (or a similar creature) on
the home planet.

Xenophobia:

Ironically, Trevor, a homosexual defined as a deviant by the
straight world, considers Newton a "freak" and therefore rejects
him. Frequently in our culture, one minority group will actively
persecute another.

12. Helicopter in New Mexico

Narrative

Plot:

Nate Bryce takes pictures from a helicopter as it passes over a
canyon; he meets Arthur, Newton's chauffeur, and is driven to the
lake.

| Commentary: | After a highly complex syntagm dominated by Newton, we return to Bryce's separate narrative line. In his pursuit of World Enterprises, he is linked with Arthur, foreshadowing their common betrayal of Newton. |

Adaptation

| Omits: | The section title "1988: Rumplestiltskin" (Narrative; Time). |

Montage

| Episodic | (12-13 = cut) |
| sequence: | The editing condenses brief elements preceding the meeting between Newton and Bryce, heightening the significance of their encounter through the delay. The musical bridge between syntagms 11 and 12 also accentuates the contrast between the two men and what they represent. |

Hermeneutics

| Nathan | We get conflicting clues concerning his trustworthiness. The |
| Bryce: | simplicity of the syntagm is deceptive, since by now simplicity has been linked with entrapment. His demonic laughter and encapsulation in the helicopter may associate him with the ominous plastic clown from the opening syntagm. |

Perception

Bryce is consistently linked with photography, either as a voyeur or as a probing scientist. He uses technology to expand his vision in contrast to Newton's "natural" range.

Self-reflexiveness

As Bryce is taken to World Enterprises, the car passes a printed sign that reads: ALL PASSES MUST BE SHOWN. This verbal message comments on Roeg's style, which relies more on showing than telling what is important. We should follow this advice in evaluation of Bryce's character: while his dialogue and monologues are misleading, the film graphically shows us all his "passes."

13. Sex and Seeing

Narrative

| Plot: | After a bath, Newton gives Mary Lou a telescope, and they make love. |

| Commentary: | This is the moment of peak fusion between Mary Lou and Newton, the high point of their relationship. Later, Mary Lou, Newton, and the audience will return to images from this syntagm with nostalgic yearning. |

Adaptation

| Adds: | a) The entire event of lovemaking intercut with the telescope (Culture—sexual coupling; Perception). |
| | b) The Oriental motif of decor and music (Space; Culture). |

Montage

**Parallel
syntagm
with inserts:**

(13-14 = cut)

The intercutting moves between Newton and Mary Lou making love, and the two of them playing with a telescope outside on the balcony, a microscope, and a strip of reflective mylar inside the apartment before or after the lovemaking. The intercutting presents no dominant experience with other elements intercut into it as in other syntagms, and in no way suggests a movement *out* of present experience as in syntagm 11. Instead, the events, spaces, and times are harmoniously integrated into a loving, positive experience, suggesting that Newton may be able to unify his identities after all.

The inserts present either expanded vision (A and B) or slightly abstracted images surrounded by white fades (C and D) so that they will be strongly imprinted in their memories and ours and frozen like photographs for a scrapbook, as if already being prepared for future flashbacks.

13A   Explanatory Insert: A view through Mary Lou's microscope showing a circle with moving microscopic organisms; the colors have been solarized.

13B   Explanatory Insert: A crescent of light with tiny sparks that look like spermatozoa. This could be a view of the cosmos through the telescope or a microscopic view of sex. The point of view could belong to Mary Lou (her passion for microscopes and telescopes), Newton (his expanded powers of perception), or to Roeg (his self-reflexive choice, showing how sex unites the microcosm and the macrocosm).

13C   Non-Diegetic Insert: Huge close-up of Mary Lou and Newton (who for the first time look alike) facing each other in profile, shot against the same white background in overexposed light; the image fades to white.

13D   Non-Diegetic Insert: Immediately following 13C, another huge close-up of Mary Lou and Newton, this time facing the camera and looking even more alike, shot against the same white background in overexposed light; the image fades to white.

Although after 13D we return to the diegesis, the last two shots in the syntagm are visually similar to inserts C and D, furthering the fusion and reinforcing the coupling on a structural level. The first shot is an overhead view of their intertwined bodies curled in the bed, as if forming a single organism; the image fades. Then we are presented with another shot of the couple from another angle.

Music

The music also stresses fusion, integrating western and oriental motifs. The blending of romantic music with lovemaking sounds enriches the emotional tonality of the event.

Hermeneutics

Mary Lou:

We now *see* for ourselves that it is possible for them to have a sexual relationship that crosses the species barrier.

The Alien:	We begin to wonder whether he will still want to go back home after experiencing such unity with Mary Lou; but we do get a verbal clue that he is still keenly aware of the difference between them. When Mary Lou lovingly says, "You're such a *nice* man," he replies: "No, I'm not." While she thinks he is challenging the appropriateness of the word "nice," we know that he is questioning whether he can accurately be called a "man." This foreshadows that the real test of their unity must come when his true alien nature is revealed.

Time

Narrative time:	Distinctions between past, present, and future are obscured. Certain shots in the present are clearly set up for future flashbacks.
Romantic time:	Love implies an expanded moment, which embraces all tenses and unifies past, present, and future. Sex is dominated by subjective and lateral time.

Space

There is a recurring circle motif—in the globular Japanese light shade, the cell under the microscope, the heavenly bodies in the sky, the entwined bodies of the lovers. As in Marvell's "To His Coy Mistress," the lovers wrap themselves up into a ball, becoming their own world that transcends biological time. Love fuses the microcosm and the macrocosm, inner and outer space, the yin and the yang; like the circle, it is a ring of eternity.

Perception

Expanded perception is the means of loving fusion and good sex. Mary Lou may need advanced technology (the microscope and the telescope) to catch up with Newton's perceptive power, but Roeg also uses advanced cinematic technology (special lenses, microscopic photography, solarization, optics) to expand our vision. We actually experience a perceptual shift when Mary Lou and Newton, who have formerly been such opposites, appear to be visually similar. The paradox is that beneath the surface, he is still more alien than she or we realize. Yet, if one had a microscopic view, they might appear similar after all. Similarity and difference are relativistic concepts, like time and space.

Self-reflexiveness

The visual apparatus calls our attention to the way technology enables us to discover new worlds and ideas; Roeg fully exploits this dimension of the film medium.
The insert shots that make Mary Lou and Newton look alike allude to similar shots in Bergman's *Persona*, which also influenced certain shots in *Performance*. The experimental use of intercutting alludes to a similar positive lovemaking sequence in *Don't Look Now*.

Culture

Sexual coupling:	They succeed in crossing the species barrier through expanded vision.

Water:	For the first time, water is linked with sexuality. The sex play begins when Newton enters the room after a bath and says: "I'm still wet, I can't seem to get dry." But we don't yet realize what an important role the wetness plays in sex on the home planet.
Oriental theme:	Formerly connected with birth, sex, and violence, this theme is now associated with love. It is expressed visually in the decor as well as in the music.
Gifts:	Like the Trojan horse and the book the telescope is a gift well worth looking into. It is not deceptive like the horse, but is given as a token of love and expands vision like the book. Newton also calls it a "prize," a term he probably learned on TV game shows.

14. TV Freakout

Narrative

Plot:	Newton and Mary Lou argue as he gets drunk. He rejects a suit she has ordered, complains about his records, and asks to hear singing. As he watches a panel of twelve television sets and gets drunker, she stands in front of him, tearfully demanding that they talk. Then she withdraws. He continues watching television and screams at the images, telling them to get out of his mind and leave him alone. Meanwhile, Oliver is in his office with two unidentified men.
Commentary:	After the loving fusion in the previous syntagm, this one reveals a separation growing between Mary Lou and Newton, as they both decline. Just as Newton is beginning to be harmed by television and alcohol, Oliver is beginning to be pressured by outside forces. Newton's decline necessarily implies a similar weakening of Mary Lou and Oliver, both of whom are subordinate characters within his narrative line and part of his new identity (his mate and his alter-ego).

Adaptation

Adds:	a) The specific content of the television images (Culture). b) The sorrow over their failing romance as part of Mary Lou's reaction (Culture—sexual coupling).
Substitutes:	The bank of twelve television sets for a single TV set (Perception).

Montage

Scene with Insert:	(14-15 = cut) The conversation between Mary Lou and Newton takes place in front of television sets with various significant images. 14A Displaced diegetic insert: Oliver in his office with two unidentified men. The integration of the television images as a constant presence rather than cutting to them for specific symbolic relationship (as in syntagm 7) undermines the unity of the uninterrupted scene and expands their range of influence; they affect Newton's experience as a whole and, in fact, substitute for other forms of interaction (e.g., a live conversation with Mary Lou). Another kind of complexity is introduced in the form of layering rather than lateral fragmentation or integration. By analogy, mysterious insert suggests a new form of imprinting or control entering Oliver's life.

Music

Music is very important as a means of expressing decline and depression as well as joy, as was already hinted in syntagm 1 by Louis Armstrong's "Blueberry Hill." Newton wants to hear "singing" rather than instruments playing or Mary Lou talking. The song lyrics ("I feel so bad . . . ") establish the emotional tonality of the scene. In the various television images, we see how music is co-opted in the commercial and how the tonal quality is flattened out by the medium; even Elvis Presley's visuals are more expressive than his voice when he's on TV. The music industry is linked with technology and economics; the futuristic record player implies the same kind of technological advancement and obsolescence that we found with vehicles and other media. We may recall from syntagm 3 that Newton promised Oliver that if he joined World Enterprises, he could upgrade his sound system. This new kind of globular change has apparently replaced the old rectangular phonograph just as David Bowie has replaced Elvis Presley as the reigning rock star.

Hermeneutics

The Alien: Why is he so unhappy? We begin to see clear signs of his weakening.

Mary Lou: What caused the distance between her and Newton? Will she be condemned to a future of misery?

Oliver: Who are these strange men in his office? Will they harm him or lead him to betray Newton?

Time

Narrative time: We wonder how much time has elapsed between syntagms 13 and 14 since we go directly from a moment of peak fusion to the decline. This appears to be a new fall. Everything is speeded up.

Space

There is a pattern of spatial co-option. The circle image, which formerly signalled loving fusion and infinity, is now a trendy design for a phonograph. Newton's mental space is dominated by television images, which help destroy the fragile unity he had previously achieved within his new identity. The screen is splintered into twelve separate images, which may allude to past diegetic events (e.g., the school girls evoke Nate's sexual escapades, the copulating lions contrast with the lovemaking in the previous syntagm) or foreshadow future violence (e.g., a snake devouring an insect, the hanging of Billy Budd, and the karate fight from *End of the Road*).

Perception

Newton's powers of expanded perception, formerly a source of strength, now contribute to his corruption; his capacity to watch twelve television images simultaneously speeds up the imprinting process and accelerates his breakdown.

Self-reflexiveness

All of the television images are Roeg's choices, commenting on the main narrative situation through selected parallels, particularly with other movies. Like *The Man Who Fell to Earth, Billy*

Budd is a political allegory in which the superior hero is destroyed by those in power because he poses a threat to the culture's more limited conception of morality and stability. In the existential adventure film, *End of the Road*, the hero undergoes "myth therapy" because he has no personal identity and his doctor is trying to force him to accept one from the common cultural mythology. This scene both parallels the influence that television has on Newton and foreshadows his later encounters with dangerous doctors. Like Roeg's movie, both films are based on earlier literary works, making their adaptation to television three media deep. The Elvis Presley movie suggests a precedent for a rock star succeeding in cinema, which Mick Jagger acomplished in Roeg's first film *Performance* and which David Bowie now does as well.

Culture

Biblical myth:

The TV image of the snake devouring the insect implies that evil has entered the garden; the media will be the Satanic force that corrupts Adam's innocence, working through the weak woman Mary Lou, who brought him his first TV set. Yet, like the forbidden fruit, television also brings knowledge. Billy Budd, like Newton, is a Christ figure whose last line before he is hanged is "God bless Captain Vere." Newton is also incapable of bitterness.

Icarus myth:

Billy Budd dies with a fall (from the yard-arm as he is hanged) and a splash (his body is dumped in the ocean).

Sexual coupling:

Mary Lou becomes increasingly the nagging mother. Although she brought TV and alcohol, she now preaches against them as harmful influences. She is the provider—ordering his clothes and his records. She tries to make contact by running her hand through his hair or getting him to talk or even argue, but he withdraws like a sullen adolescent. Newton's new family unit is beginning to disintegrate.

Alcohol:

Although it was a strong latent threat from the opening syntagm, alcohol now emerges as a serious destructive force on Newton's character.

Media:

The very medium which enabled him to come to earth seeking water now becomes another destructive force like alcohol, undermining his vision, his sanity, and his morality.

Horses:

In contrast to the wild, free horse in syntagm 11, the animated laughing horse on TV appears demonic. It exposes its teeth, inviting us to look in its mouth (like the deceptive Trojan horse). Its laughter links it with Nate Bryce, who will later be developed as the deceptive western hero.

15. Insects and Dreams

Narrative

Plot:

Nate is in the office at the New Mexico construction site talking on the phone with Oliver. He learns that he will meet Newton day after tomorrow. Later, he fishes off a pier and sees an image of Newton.

Commentary:	After the other three characters have started their decline in the previous syntagm, Newton and Nate move closer to their meeting, which is signalled verbally.

Adaptation

Adds:	The appearance/apparition of Newton as Nate is fishing (Perception).

Montage

	(15-16 = cut)
Episodic sequence with inserts:	Compresses the day and night before Newton and Oliver finally meet.

15A   Displaced Diegetic Insert: Oliver in his office.

15B: Displaced Diegetic Insert: Newton and Mary Lou sleeping.

15C: Displaced Diegetic Insert: Newton and Mary Lou sleeping. Insert A contrasts Oliver's (earth people's) powers of communication with Newton's. The inserts of Newton and Mary Lou sleeping explain that he cannot be appearing to Bryce in the flesh.

Hermeneutics

The Alien:	How did he cause his image to appear to Nate?
Nathan Bryce:	We get a visual clue concerning his reliability. He toys with the insect like the snake in the previous syntagm, implying that he is a Satanic figure.

Time

Narrative time:	Nathan relies on verbal time signals that are very specific: He will meet Newton day after tomorrow. Yet the ellipses are unclear, and seem to indicate that only one day has passed.
Economic time:	Construction is progressing.
Biological time:	Oliver is getting older; Newton is not.

Space

Newton is capable of some form of teleportation.

Perception

Expanded perception through the dream image. Newton can project his image in some way that Bryce can receive. Mental and physical planes can merge.

Culture

Biblical myth: Nate is identified with snake from Genesis.

16. The Meeting of Newton and Nate

Narrative

Plot:	The two men finally meet and visit the space capsule.

Commentary:	At this point—the central syntagm—Bryce begins to take over the narrative, and will play a bigger role than Oliver or Mary Lou. He begins to collaborate with Newton on a new project, and they form a friendship. The beginning of the second half of the film is underscored by a series of birth images. This syntagm and the two elements of the previous one are linked by a refrain of "to-morrows" when he will meet Newton; now we actually see the meeting. Up to this point, the visuals have preceded the verbals— we see something before it is made explicit through dialogue; now the pattern is reversed and verbals take over the visuals as the Western hero begins to take over the Alien—Nate will eventually replace Newt.

Adaptation

Adds:	The entire visit to the space capsule (Space, Self-reflexiveness).

Montage

Ordinary sequence:	(16-17 = cut) The image of Newton's family that appears in the glo e functions like an insert, but we don't know whether it's subjective (projected from Newton's mind) or transmitted through space.

Music

Harp music:	As they enter the tunnel, this music suggests entry into a new (heavenly) realm of experience.
Oriental music:	These faint sounds refer back to the first intercutting between Newton and Nate in syntagm 4 and the first birth when Newton enters this world in syntagm 1.

Hermeneutics

The Alien:	What are his transmitting powers? He lies, claiming to be English; Nate catches him at it because Newton never heard of Latin (which has never been mentioned on TV).
Nathan Bryce:	Is he reliable? He presents himself as a man of integrity who won't work on the capsule if it's a weapon.

Time

Time and motion:	Nathan's precision limits him. He couldn't last "twenty minutes" in the capsule, even though he would travel astronomical distances in such a short period. Is the image of Newton's family delayed or simultaneous with its transmission, or is it a vision of the future, as in a crystal ball? Time and distance are relative.

Space

The space capsule continues the circle imagery from the fusion scene; its walls look like an egg carton, creating birth associations earlier suggested by the movement through the long tunnel and emergence into space.

Perception

Newton has never accepted the earth gesture of handshaking; when he pulls down the arm rest to avoid it, this startles Bryce, who doesn't know what to expect after the long delay; he is rattled and bumps his head in the car. Nate says their common interest is photography (scientific perception), but Newton says his interest is transference of energy, involving unknown capacities of the mind such as teleportation; these are two different views of a similar problem—the rational, mechanistic western scientific view vs. the unknown, expanded, synchronic alien view. In the capsule, Newton reads Bryce's mind, telling him to ask the question in his thoughts.

Self-reflexiveness

Newton's comments about TV—"A strange thing about television—it doesn't tell you everything . . . it shows you everything about life on earth. Perhaps it's the nature of television—just waves in space"—are also comments about the unique qualities of this film; it shows a great deal without telling or explaining it, a visual rather than narrative emphasis. It's also a comment on the film medium—the interruption of light waves in space. Bryce gives a self-conscious description of his own persona and generic identity, suggesting what other western "heroes" he is connected with: "I'm kind of a cliché. I'm the disillusioned scientist. It goes with the cynical actor and the spaced-out spaceman." But his self-designation is actually unreliable.

Culture

Xenophobia:

Bryce's question, "Are you a Lithuanian?" is a comical version of the questions usually asked to identify someone's subculture; it mocks the common fear of the alien and masks Nate's real suspicions about Newton's extraterrestrial origins.

Cliché:

The Royal Air Force motto "Through difficulties to the stars" links the military to stereotyped thinking; it's always a matter of "us vs. them." Bryce thinks in terms of weapons—what is the war? who is the enemy?—and simple bipolarities—good vs. bad; true vs. false; reality vs. hallucination. Newton's mind transcends these earthly patterns of thought.

17. Peters' Pressure

Narrative

Plot:

Peters, a black CIA type, tries unsuccessfully to pressure Oliver into some form of cooperation; he then confers with his white colleague.

Commentary:

Introduces Peters and his power group. We have only glimpsed these people previously (the observer when Newton lands, the two men in Oliver's office in syntagm 14). Now they intrude into the narrative and will ultimately control it. Peters tries to take over Oliver as Newton did in syntagm 3.

Adaptation

Adds:

Peters as a character. (Narrative, Culture).

Montage

Ordinary
Sequence:

(17-18 = cut)
One of the several brief, simple syntagms in which Oliver fronts for Newton, dealing with people who will ultimately force their way into Newton's reality, to be interwoven with complex editing.

Hermeneutics

Oliver Farnsworth:	Reveals himself as loyal to Newton and courageous in standing up to pressure.
Peters:	Who is he? What group does he represent—the government (CIA, FBI), crime (Mafia), business (IT&T)?

Time

Economic time:	Progress and keeping up with a changing world is defined in terms of financial power, which will be controlled by Peters' group.
Narrative time:	Farnsworth calls World Enterprises a "pioneer," referring us laterally to Newton's vision of the pioneer family.

Perception

Peters says the world is always changing "like the solar system." He has the language of cosmic range, but not the true vision; he wants planetary control and uses the phrase to try to limit Farnsworth's vision. The question of who is behind or "way ahead" depends on the point of view, on whose interests are foremost.

Self-reflexiveness

Peters' group and their desire for control refers back to the criminal/ business/government complex central to *Performance*.

Culture

Power:	The issue of control by the American power complex is now made explicit as an important theme. Peters, like the Indians and black musicians, has been co-opted to serve this group to increase his own status and power.
Clichés:	They trade back and forth the stock phrases that dominate the conversation. Social/economic control depends upon/results in limited, controlled language.
Xenophobia:	Farnsworth calls World Enterprises a "loner;" the power complex cannot tolerate this.

18. No Recovery Program

Narrative

Plot:	Riding through the desert in the limousine, Newton and Bryce discuss the recovery program for the capsule.
Commentary:	This scene parallels the previous one between Farnsworth and Peters. Bryce has limited vision of the space program like Peters; Newton has pioneering vision like Farnsworth's. The parallels strengthen the identification between Newton and Farnsworth, and suggests the one between Peters and Bryce, which will be developed later.

Montage

Scene with Insert:	(18-19 = cut) Simple, linear progression that usually accompanies Bryce's false appearance marks the brief event (conversation).

18A Explanatory Insert: panning, spiralling shot of canyons, desert and sky. The free, expansive camera work contrasts Newton's vision with that of Bryce visually, conceptually, and in terms of the syntagm structure.

Music

The banjo music was first used with Newton's vision of the pioneers, suggesting the bold spirit of Oliver and Newton, which is linked with expanded vision. The radio station is like the interference associated with Peters and Bryce, which ultimately limits World Enterprises and keeps Newton from achieving his goal. Thus the music suggests the conflict between two points of view.

Hermeneutics

The Alien: The fact that he doesn't need a recovery program clarifies his goal—to get back to his home planet.

Nathan Bryce: His parallel with Peters strengthens the suspicion that he will not prove trustworthy.

Space

Camera moves from enclosed space of the car to wide open spaces, which Farnsworth has already defined as freedom; the link, is here reinforced with birds, camera movement, music, and the insert shot's independence from narrative association.

Perception

The basic contrast is developed through the above codes.

Self-reflexiveness

The sweeping pan (an important camera move in *Walkabout*) reflects Roeg's omniscient point of view.

19. X-Raying the Alien

Narrative

Plot: While Mary Lou paces alone on the dock, Bryce prepares for Newton's visit by planting a hidden X-ray camera. When he arrives, they watch a WE commercial (starring Newton), which his wife receives on the home planet. As a storm begins outside, they discuss family life. Elsewhere, Peters confers with his boss concerning what to do about World Enterprises. Newton leaves Bryce's house drunk and anxious to know how long it will take to complete the project. Bryce eagerly develops the film, which reveals that Newton is an alien.

Commentary: The power group (Peters and his boss) begins to close in on Newton and WE, unwittingly aided by Bryce and his camera. The intercutting between Bryce and Peters foreshadows their alliance as similar intercutting between Bryce and Newton had done in syntagm 4. This is the first time we have seen Mary Lou alone since her walk home from the hotel (syntagm 6), but merely in a brief insert; she waits for Newton just as his wife waits for him on the home planet.

Adaptation

Adds:

The TV commercial as a means of communication with Newton's wife on the home planet (Perception).

Omits:

a) A meeting between Bryce and Mary Lou, where he tries to get information about Newton (Narrative, Hermeneutics).
b) Bryce's feelings of guilt regarding the X-raying of Newton (Narrative).

Montage

Ordinary
Sequence
with Inserts:

(19-20 = cut)
The controlling event is Newton's visit in Bryce's house.

19A   Displaced Diegetic Insert: Mary Lou on the dock.

19B   Displaced Diegetic or Subjective Insert: Newton's space wife receiving TV commercial message. The designation of the Insert depends on whether he actually did send the message or whether he's set up something for the future, like the recording in the last syntagm, and is now imagining the result.

19C   Displaced Diegetic Insert: Mary lou on the dock.

19D   Displaced Diegetic Insert: Lightning and rain on the lake.

19E   Explanatory Insert: The American flag.

19F   Displaced Diegetic Insert: Peters and his boss.

19G   Displaced Diegetic Insert: Arthur outside Bryce's house.

19H   Explanatory Insert: X-ray photo of Newton. The editing of this syntagm comments on various views of Newton's identity. It is one of the freest and most unpredictable units of the film in timing and range of inserts. Bryce's idea of Newton's identity (photographic/scientific) is extremely simplistic. The different inserts (and closeups) bring in all the elements that are, in fact, a part of his new and changing identity: sexual coupling, memories and desires, media, the planet itself, the power group, and science. The position of Arthur's insert between the power group and Newton foreshadows structurally his negative mediation between Newton and his enemies. Although the closeup of Kelly Laing doing a weather report on television may be part of the diegesis, it functions like an insert, obscuring the boundaries; this function of media images is common to several syntagms.

Music

World Enterprises has a jingle: "We'll do it for you. . . ." The emotional and mnemonic power of music has been co-opted to sell products.

Hermeneutics

The Alien:

Bryce and the audience now know for sure that he is an alien with false cover. But having seen only the "skeleton," we still do not know what he looks like under the cover.

Nathan Bryce:	We learn that he is both clever and deceptive, and that his family has broken up.
Peters:	He is more clearly linked with some agency of the American government.

Time

Narrative time:	Lateral time is expanded as we realize that many events in various times must be comprehended simultaneously to complete one concept (Newton's identity) or one event (the visit with Bryce). Some predictions about the future are fulfilled: Bryce's hypothesis about Newton's identity proves true; the future goal of the TV commercial is realized as the wife (and the audience) receive the message; the storm follows the TV weather forecast. The conversation between Peters and his boss increases the probability that Farnsworth and Newton will be harmed.
Biological time:	Newton's prediction that 15 months will be too long for completion of the project is linked to his ability to survive in the new environment.
Economic time:	When Peters' boss says "This is modern America and we're going to keep it that way," modern is redefined to mean: "The present power situation as we control it."

Space

Various controlling spaces—inside/outside the house, TV space, the west and the eastern city, this planet and Newton's home planet—are integrated, forming a conceptual whole.

Perception

Bryce uses scientific gadgets to expand his vision—the X-ray camera and the second TV remote control device; these are limited and mechanical in comparison to Newton's mysterious ability to cause waves in space to be received on another planet. Peters says that World Enterprises has to "take a wider view," but that is ironic because from the audience's point of view, his perspective is so much narrower than Newton's, and in fact his goal is to *limit* possibilities as he tells his boss that World Enterprises is "technologically overstimulated."

Self-reflexiveness

This event offers a complex comparison of the powers of TV and photography. Though TV is used for secondary functions like sending a private message and facilitating the X-ray camera, it is seen as flexible and having unknown potential; the camera, while having a primary function in the event, gives Bryce the illusion that he has located and fixed Newton's identity. Roeg's use of cinematography undercuts and transcends the limited, scientific view of its functions. The scene between Peters and his boss is highly suggestive of scenes with Harry Flowers, the power boss in *Performance*.

Culture

Power:	As in *The Godfather*, the false distinction between government and crime is exposed. Although Peters' government boss says, "We're not the Mafia—we're not some archaic Italian joke," the actions that will result from this conversation will prove just the opposite.

Sexual coupling:	The function of wives and mistresses is to wait patiently at home while the men shape the world; it's the same old story since Penelope in the *Odyssey*. The family is established explicitly as an important theme, and as a basis of contrast between Newton, the good family man, and Bryce, who is separated from his family and integrates them into his mental life only through incestuous fantasies. Other groupings like the Mafia-type family/syndicate/government or the corporate family begin to be seen as substitutes in a culture where the basic coupling and family group no longer function effectively.
Alcohol:	Both men are drunk; Newton makes his first (and feeble) joke ("You must have put alcohol in my drink"), showing his awareness of the growing problem.
Media:	Their deceptive powers are shown: not only does TV sell products, but it can have "hidden persuaders;" photography has been co-opted for spying like electronic equipment for government bugging. Any kind of technology can be corrupted.
Censorship:	The shot of the American flag and some of the dialogue ("We're dealing with the social-economic ecology! This is modern America, and we're going to keep it that way!") have been cut out of the scene between Peters and his boss, preventing the link between the corrupt power group and the American government from becoming too explicit.

20. The Sexual Revelation

Narrative

Plot:	Newton tells Mary Lou he is leaving; she tries to hold him and they argue. He removes his earth cover and reveals himself to her; she is shocked and terrified. He lies down and she tries to make love with him but is revolted; he thinks back to sex on the home planet. Afterwards, they go outside and talk as Mary Lou is more accepting of the new reality.
Commentary:	This syntagm brings the real separation between Newton and Mary Lou, and confirms the impossibility of their returning to the fusion of syntagm 13.

Adaptation

Adds:	a) The sexual testing function of the unmasking (Culture—sexual coupling).
	b) The revelation of what the alien sexually is like, especially the white fluid (Culture—sexual coupling, Xenophobia).

Montage

Hybrid Parallel Syntagm:	(20-21 = sound bridge, dissolve)
	The syntagm begins as if it were an ordinary sequence with many Inserts. But as the Inserts grow in frequency and inter-relatedness, they form series and the identity of the controlling event—the argument and sexual encounter between Mary Lou and Newton—disintegrates. Further, within that event, Mary Lou and Newton move apart into separate lines of action. At the end, there is both a sound bridge and a visual dissolve to escape from the painful situation into the next syntagm; this kind of double transition

was used only once before in syntagm 10, where Newton and Mary Lou were together in church before he escaped into his revealing subjective images of home. Hence, the montage in this complex syntagm is used to develop the two major themes—Newton's identity (this time in physical and sexual terms) and his separation from Mary Lou. Roeg is highly inventive in using a great variety of means of splintering the identity of any unit:

1) Close-up of Mary Lou and Newton in profile within the diegesis, which evokes the *Persona* shot from syntagm 13, but this time they do not look alike and they are arguing rather than making love; hence, this shot anticipates what is to follow through visual contrast.

2) Cookies flying through the air in slow motion. The disruption of the scene accentuates the fact that this is Newton's first act of violence in the film; it not only deviates from his gentle identity, but also evokes the intercutting between sex and violence from syntagm 4, an association that is strengthened by the oriental motif in Mary Lou's wig and robe. Its movement also anticipates the shots of the lovers from the home planet floating through space.

3) A shift to intercutting between Newton in the bathroom removing his earth cover (he uses two mirrors that further fragment the image—one normal, and the other a small mirror that magnifies his eyes and hence is reminiscent of Oliver's powerful lenses) and Mary Lou polishing her nails. During the revelation, they do not appear in the same frame.

4) Intercutting of Newton's subjective images of making love with his wife, which are introduced by a dissolve and eventually are superimposed onto the images of Mary Lou and Newton unsuccessfully trying to make love. The intercutting reveals the imagination as the true source of power for merging and transformation. After one of the superimpositions, the next shot shows Newton leaving some of the white fluid on Mary Lou as he touches her. His mental power enables him to express his sexuality on the physical plane. Although Mary Lou tries to transcend her physical revulsion, she lacks the mental power for such a transformation. Unlike syntagm 13, he cannot expand her vision. She runs in fear.

5) Return to intercutting between separate actions of Newton and Mary Lou, involving a number of separate shots:

   a) The screen is washed with the sexual fluid from the home planet, marking the end of the union between Mary Lou and Newton both physically and mentally.

   b) A view through a fish-eye lens of Mary Lou crouching in a corner of the kitchen where the argument and syntagm began; she is crying and looks grotesque.

   c) A close-up of Newton alone in his space gear from his home planet, looking beautiful, then looking at his wife and children.

   d) A mirror in which we see the image of Newton restoring his cover.

This physical superimposition is mechanistic and futile in comparison to the ones accomplished mentally and visually in the film, foreshadowing the destructive, limiting function of the fusing of his two physical identities at the hands of the doctors. The disjuncture among the mental, physical, and image planes parallels the disjuncture between the   sight and sound throughout the film, suggesting at the deepest level the complexity of determining and maintaining a true and life-giving identity.

6)   A shift in scene to the dock outside their house where Mary Lou and Newton are temporarily reunited in conversation after their respective safe covers have been restored—the robe that she wore in syntagm 13 before their loving fusion and the hooded coat that he wore when he arrived. The strobic revolving blue light accentuates the tension between them and fragments the scene. She withdraws, leaving him alone with the blue light and his subjective images of his farewell with his real family, which are now associated with the parting from Mary Lou (and possibly with the lyrics from the Rolling Stones' *Love in Vain:* "When the train left the station, it had two lights on behind, the blue light was my baby, and the red light was my mind").

Music

The sex scenes are accompanied by the same futuristic music from the scene in syntagm 11 near the lake when Newton tries to transport himself mentally back home and Mary Lou brings him back down to earth, suggesting that the same pattern is now being repeated on the sexual level.

Hermeneutics

The Alien: We finally see his true form and learn more about his sexuality on the home planet.

Mary Lou: We now learn that she will never substitute for his wife.

Time

Narrative time: Events in this culture are marked by precise signals, telling us when something is ready. An alarm bell signals that cookies are done (like the alarm bell in the pawnshop from the opening syntagm). This bell also signals that Newton is ready to leave Mary Lou and go home. His mental images are ambiguous in time—are they memories, or simultaneous with the action, or fantasies?

Time and motion: The use of slow motion contrasts two kinds of time, showing explicitly that it is relative.

Romantic time: The romance is ending; the possibility of a rebirth lies in Newton's efforts to fuse mental and physical time.

Space

Free floating in space is erotic (as space meant freedom to Oliver).

The fusion of inner and outer space in Newton's sexuality is a model for the possibilities of fusion in lovemaking.

Perception

Shots of mirrors and eyes stress the relativity of perception. What does Newton look like to himself in his earth cover? To us, he appears only *almost* human even with the cover. To the audience and his family, he is beautiful in his own identity; to Mary Lou he is horrifyingly alien. Later, we perceive her as grotesquely ugly through the alien perspective of a fish-eye lens. We have been prepared for Newton's visual transformation, but Mary Lou has not. This is a severe test, but her ability to integrate new perception is very limited. When they talk on the pier, she asks him what his children are like. He replies: "They're like children. They're exactly like children." Like the confusion over the phrase "nice man" in syntagm 13, here the equivocation focuses on whether the term "children" can be applied accurately to a non-human species. How great does the similarity or "likeness" have to be, before the term can be used? As in the earlier syntagm, Mary Lou's question implies she is trying to cling to the similarities while Newton's answer acknowledges the subtle distinctions ("they're exactly like children" implies that, despite the amazing similarities, they belong to a different species). However, his reply could also be interpreted by an ordinary American (like Mary Lou) as meaning, they are typical children.

Self-reflexiveness

His recollection of better sex on the home planet evokes our recollection of better sex between him and Mary Lou. The shot of the cookies falling evokes a similar shot during the mushroom trip in *Performance*. Roeg's casting comments on his theme: like the character he plays, David Bowie the actor is visually alien from the earth creatures around him.

Culture

Biblical myth:

They will not be the founding couple of a new, merged species.

Sexual coupling:
Xenophobia:

These two codes merge in this syntagm and are best treated together. Basically, we learn that Newton and Mary Lou must remain an "odd couple," like all the others we've seen so far. She calls him an alien but means only that he isn't a citizen. Ironically, she doesn't know what she's talking about until she sees—the gap between talking and seeing/understanding, as in the conversation about his children.

His cover involves ears, nails, round irises; hers involves wigs, nail polish, pink nighties. Each is beautiful in his/her context; what turns you on is culturally determined. But the audience's range is (hopefully) expanded. Very far from the conventional appeal of hairy, aggressive masculinity, Newton's sexual appeal is based on "alien" qualities—sensitivity, imaginative power, wetness, a unique angular, delicate aesthetic and other unexperienced species differences. But Mary Lou tries to deny the differences, crying: "I lifted you up once!" She retreats to the American woman's role of maternal love and the illusion of "one flesh." Newton denies this false merger, and tells Mary Lou "You must believe it!"

Water:	The sexual connotations of wetness are made explicit. With the white liquid of his vision, we fully understand Newton's reverential attitude toward water as it is seen to be life-giving in a new way.
Trains:	When he says goodbye to Mary Lou, he thinks of the trains back home and his original leave-taking.
Censorship:	A shot of Mary Lou pissing in fear is removed from the American version of the film. Apparently, the distributors thought that this "natural" reaction to the unnatural was too much for Americans to take. The phrase "pissing in fear" is a cliché, but seeing the literal basis is another matter. Yet, a similar scene is retained in *The Exorcist*, perhaps because the Devil made her do it.

21. Desert Showdown

Narrative

Plot:	Bryce comes to see Newton, who is alone in a shack in the desert. Newton confirms that he is an alien and reveals his goals, his past and future. He asks after Mary Lou and says that he trusts Bryce. Their conversation is interspersed with brief scenes of Mary Lou moaning in her bed, Trevor warning Oliver to get out of WE, and Newton's vision of his family dying at home. He concludes that time is on his side.
Commentary:	This syntagm summarizes the position of all the characters at this point in the narrative and focuses our attention on the future. Newton poignantly pursues the illusions fostered by media clichés, which leave him utterly unprepared for the reality of the next syntagm.

Adaptation

Adds:	Specific references to the Western genre through TV program (Self-reflexiveness; Culture).
Substitutes:	The desert and shack for a Chicago Christmas cocktail party, which Dr. Canutti also attends, as the setting for the conversation (Self-reflexiveness; Culture).

Montage

Ordinary sequence with Inserts:

(21 – 22 = cuts)

The controlling action is the conversation between Bryce and Newton, inside the shack. The syntagm opens with a dissolve to an arid landscape that could be either the home planet or the New Mexico desert. The accompanying sound track of a Western movie—horses and gun shots—makes us choose the latter alternative. Yet, when a truck pulls up from which Nate emerges in Western costume, we notice a disjunction between sound and image, which is explained as the camera pulls back to reveal the view of Nate through the window of the shack, in which Newton is watching a Western on TV.

21A Explanatory Insert: plastic cover gathering water, shows Newton trying to learn how to fulfill his purpose on earth.

21B Displaced Diegetic Insert: Trevor warns Oliver to abandon Newton.

21C   Displaced Diegetic Insert: Mary Lou moaning on her bed.

21D   Subjective or Non-Diagetic Insert: Either Newton sees a solar explosion, or Roeg inserts one; in either case, it suggests why the home planet is dying of drought.

21E   Subjective Insert: Newton's family dying on the home planet; he either sees it or fears it for the future.

21F   Subjective or Non-Diegetic Insert: Flash in the sky.

The conversation, focusing on Newton's self-revelation and placing of trust, is intercut with instances of distrust (Trevor) or the possible sad consequences of placing trust, either correctly (his wife and family) or on the basis of illusion (Mary Lou). Thus the Insert material undermines the main action and increases our sense of Newton's vulnerability; need may have impaired his judgment concerning Bryce. The ambiguity established by the mixed sound track (static, Oriental motif, Western sounds) raises the question: on what kind of reality is this syntagm (and Newton's judgment) based?

Music

The Western soon dominates the music and characterizes Newton's and Bryce's interaction, as semi-classical music signals Trevor and Oliver.

Hermeneutics

The Alien:
Most of the important questions are answered: what planet he comes from; why he came; the fact that he's not the first ("There've always been visitors. I've seen their footsteps and their places," says Newton); the fact that he plans to return.

Nathan Bryce:
Now that Newton has placed trust in Bryce at the same time that new vulnerability is revealed, Bryce's ambiguous moral status is more important.

Oliver Farnsworth and Mary Lou:
They may be in danger; we are unsure of their fates.

Newton's family:
They are in danger of dying of thirst.

All these issues converge on the future: something must be done.

Time

Narrative time:
Time relations and ellipses among syntagm elements are ambiguous. When Bryce asks for evidence, Newton says he only knows that "All things begin and end in eternity," showing his circular, synchronic view of time, in contrast to Bryce's western, scientific desire for linear precision. After Newton looks at the moon and checks Bryce's watch, he concludes that time is on his side. We cannot tell why, so it must be in terms of his time perception.

Space

Again the syntagm merges inner and outer space in perception, in the shack and the desert, in the TV images, and in reality.

Perception

Newton has seen traces of the visitors; Bryce has not, and wants evidence. If Newton is right, Bryce's scientific perspective is limiting rather than illuminating. What is there, and who can see it? Have we in the audience seen them? Are the recent books and films about them correct?

Self-reflexiveness

Roeg's use of the TV Western sounds and images sets the context for the syntagm. The two men meet for a confrontation; Bryce rides up like a cowboy (but in a truck, undercutting the heroics) and probes aggressively for the facts, his directness combining the Western hero and the scientist, and suggesting his potential as gunman. The TV screen frames reality in "art," the shack window frames external reality, and the movie screen frames both of them, suggesting the parallel organization and meaning of all three as in syntagm 7. When Bryce asks Newton: "What are you going to do?" Newton answers: "Oh. You mean what's in my mind." This translated question explains the importance of the Inserts and the dominance of visual over verbal information in Roeg's style by revealing how Newton's mind works—predominantly through images rather than linear verbal constructs.

Culture

Science: Its probing actually limits knowledge and foreshadows the mishandling of Newton's body.

Power: The two buddies of the Western conventionally increase their power through loyalty, forming a rebel group serving pure values through adventure and taming of the unknown. Newton wants and needs this from Bryce, but in his vulnerability he cannot play this buddy role; we suspect that Bryce will not either.

Water: These objects dominate this film, associated with nostalgia,
Guns: power, and survival. Codes concerning all these items and values
Horses: lie at the center of the Western genre.

22. Kidnap and Murder

Narrative

Plot: Newton is at his space launch with much media coverage, about to take off for his home planet. Meanwhile, Oliver is paying off Mary Lou, who cries: "I don't want the money. I want my Tommy." Suddenly, Newton is driven off by Arthur, his chauffeur, who has apparently been bought by the power group. Meanwhile, two killers enter Farnsworth's apartment and murder him and Trevor by throwing them out the window. The fall ends with a cut to Peters diving into the swimming pool; then he embraces his blond wife, they put their children to bed and discuss morality.

| Commentary: | This syntagm marks a total reversal: the fall of Newton and his new group, and the rise of Peters and the group he represents. |

Adaptation

Adds:	a) The murder of Oliver and Trevor (Culture).
	b) Media involvement in the launching (Perception; Culture).
	c) Oliver giving Newton's money to Mary Lou (Culture—sexual coupling).
	d) Peters' inter-racial family (Culture—sexual coupling).

| Substitutes: | The abduction of Newton at a space launch for his arrest by the FBI for illegal entry (Self-reflexiveness; Culture). |

Montage

| Parallel syntagm with Inserts: | (22-23 = music bridge, cut) |

The intercutting moves between what is happening to Newton and to Farnsworth (his partner or alter-ego). Then the syntagm moves into a third event—Peters' domestic scene.

22A Subjective or Non-Diegetic Insert: Oliver and Trevor stand close together by the phonograph as romantic music begins. Is this a treasured moment of Trevor's life passing before his eyes at the moment before death, or is Roeg using it for both Farnsworth and Trevor, suggesting the strength of their bond?

At the beginning of the syntagm, both Newton and Farnsworth are in control for three units each in the parallel series; then in the seventh, trouble begins and the intercutting grows extremely rapid and fragmented. The death plunge is equated with Peters' joyful dive by the matched cut on the action. The extraordinary shot of Trevor's barbell floating through space is almost surreal. The slow motion death fall is romantic, suggesting that Oliver and Trevor are joined in a death ecstasy (reinforced by the Insert), and Peters' dive, in turn, links him with death, perhaps as mastermind of the murders. Then with Peters in control of the action, the syntagm becomes linear and deceptively simple. We become somewhat sympathetic with Peters and realize he's also uncertain, and has probably been manipulated into his role.

Music

| | Romantic music comments on Farnsworth's and Trevor's relationship, and helps link the fall with sexual ecstasy. |

Hermeneutics

| The Alien: | He won't get back home this time. His previously suggested vulnerability is proven here—he's overpowered and in danger. Will he be killed? Will he ever get home? |

| Oliver Farnsworth: | We learn that he remained loyal to the end, and a great deal about his character: he is essentially gentle and passive like Newton: he tells his killers "It had to come," but he did nothing about it; apologizes when the plate glass window doesn't break as they throw him against it the first time; he is loyal to his mate in his last thought. |

| Trevor: | His warnings to Farnsworth prove valid. |

Peters:	He develops a personal identity—a war hero, with a blond wife and two children. He questions his own morality. A co-opted black person controlled by whom?
Nathan Bryce:	Even in his absence, we wonder which side he will be on.
Arthur:	The chauffeur's betrayal is a complete surprise. Was he an agent of the power group from the beginning? If not, what was the price of his loyalty after all these years?

Time

Narrative Time:	After an ellipsis of many months or a year (Bryce said it would take 15 months to perfect the fuel), the action suddenly leaps into frenzied simultaneity of effect, if not diegetic time. Does Oliver leave the office conference with Mary Lou to arrive home in time to be murdered during the exact few minutes of Newton's abduction? And does Peters dive into the pool at the exact moment that Farnsworth/Trevor fall from the building? The editing is structured to suggest exactly this precision—a military operation masterminded by Peters, who, aware of the time schedule, jumps into the pool to celebrate its success. For Roeg, the syntagm is highly rhythmical, elements orchestrated as in a ballet (suggesting the rhythmic cutting of less complex events in *Performance*).
Economic time:	As Farnsworth struggles with his killers, he says, "Listen! I haven't got the time." (This strange remark parallels that made by the father in *Walkabout*. Just before the attempted murder of his children and his successful suicide, he says: "Can't waste time. Got to go now. Can't waste time."). Both comments suggest that the western equation of time and money so influences the businessman that he is unable to experience what is really happening to him and absurdly reverts to his obsession with using time profitably: money robs time of its real content. Again absurdly, the comments are true at another level: both men are now out of time.
Time and motion:	The last moment of life expands time through the memory insert and the slow motion fall.

Space

Flight involves not only freedom but death.
For the first time we get internal space for a character other than Newton—for Farnsworth (and perhaps Trevor).

Perception

As he is being murdered, Farnsworth talks obsessively about his vision: as his glasses are broken, he wails, "Those are my eyes!"; then he pleads, "Let me see you a minute!"; the second before he is thrown, he screams, "Won't you let me see your face?" Like Newton, he depends on his eyes to locate himself in his world. If he could see, he would not be so isolated in death; if Newton's eyes hadn't been co-opted by TV, he could have functioned better in the world. Foreshadows the destruction of Newton's special eyes. His eyes and Newton's are linked with those of the cat in the picture in Farnsworth's office (reminding us of the cat's eyes in syntagm 7, where Newton is watching TV). A cat has nine lives; Newton has lost one of his in losing Oliver, his *doppleganger*.

Self-reflexiveness

The media take over the visuals at the same point that the power group takes over the narrative. Roeg parodies typical coverage of important events—assassinations, space travel, glamourous crimes such as kidnapping—through hand held camera, announcer's clichés, distortion, dense sound track, which make it impossible to see what is really happening.

Culture

Science:
Space technology is co-opted into a media circus.

Icarus myth:
The murder is transformed into a fall and a splash; Farnsworth and Peters make one Icarus, a demonic parody of Newton's fall to earth.

Biblical myth:
The falls are linked with Adam—man is born into sex/violence/death.

Power:
The black man is sent to fight in wars, taught to covet the delicate blonde, rendered uncertain as to his morality—a chain of victimization (harkening back to Louis Armstrong in the opening syntagm) where his reward is a piece of the action that controls him. The hit men for the power group are incompetent clowns in comic costumes like Laurel and Hardy, but they are deadly (reminding us of the plastic clown with the drunk inside in the opening syntagm). They bungle, reminding us of Watergate.

Sexual coupling:
Farnsworth and Trevor die as they lived—in loyal harmony: a successful but doomed odd couple. The interracial couple is introduced: she is part of Peters' "reward." Oliver gives Mary Lou money from Newton, like alimony: another "reward."

Media:
Knowingly or not, they serve the power group in shaping reality through clichés and visual distortion, creating a formula for significant events.

Censorship: The American distributors omit the brief segment where the media report on the launch from the control room, probably to increase linearity in a highly compex intercut syntagm; aesthetically the deletion may be an improvement. They also cut out a stop at a WE gas station during Newton's kidnapping, where Arthur flashes an official I.D. to an attendant who is awed by it. This scene, which links him more closely with the government, and with the hit men who murder Farnsworth, and ultimately with Watergate, was probably omitted for political and economic (oil company) reasons. Also omitted is a brief scene in which Peters and his wife put their brown children to bed. This scene would probably make the film less successful in the southern market.

23. Newton in Captivity

Narrative

Plot:
A waiter wheels a cart through a series of rooms to the one where Newton lies in bed. The waiter gives a martini to Newton, who is watching a TV program where Professor Canutti (Bryce's old boss) is talking about World Enterprises.

| Commentary: | This is the first time Newton has been alone since the opening, before he made his primary alliances. It marks the beginning of a new cycle. |

Adaptation

Adds: The strange variety of decors in the rooms (Space).

Omits: The specific identification of his captors as government agents (Hermeneutics; Culture).

Substitutes: The unknown location of Newton's captivity for a specified location near Washington , D. C. (Hermeneutics).

Montage

Scene:

(23-24 = cut)

After the complexity of the previous syntagms, the continuity of this one signals entrapment; the free play of Newton's identity and imagination has been stopped. The camera moves backward before the waiter who moves forward, pushing the cart, giving the illusion of moving through many frames—an artificial substitute for the editing movement. The TV image functions like an insert, introducing a parallel element of meaning.

Music

The upbeat music suggests Newton's survival after Farnsworth's murder, but the high energy is ironic as the music gets louder when the waiter approaches the inner sanctuary where Newton lies drunk. As he goes through the Oriental room, he hangs up a gong, bringing irony to the continuing theme of Oriental music, which has previously suggested Newton's aesthetic and cultural range.

Hermeneutics

The Alien: Where has he been taken? What will happen to him?

Time

Narrative time: The ellipsis between this and the previous syntagm is ambiguous: is Dr. Canutti's interview a continuation of coverage of the space launch?

Time and motion: The furnishings of the rooms are from different time periods, almost evolutionary, moving from the jungle motif, through a traditional room, to one with ultra modern furnishings; again, an ironic substitute for real freedom of movement through time. The waiter lets in the sun, but Newton ignores it, as if entrapment has made him indifferent to the movement of time: it is no longer on his side.

Economic time: Canutti says that WE "relied too heavily on that two-headed monster innovation. American consumers can tolerate only so many new products and then no more." The pace of progress is controlled by the power structure.

Space

The variety of room decors substitutes for the real variety and freedom that has been attributed to space through the film. Space is distorted through camera work, perspective, and the TV image.

Perception

Newton's is now severely limited; the TV provides his only access to the outside world. Media and government cooperate in telling lies about World Enterprise.

Self-reflexiveness

The bizarre series of rooms are reminiscent of the strange room at the end of *2001: A Space Odyssey*.

Culture

Power:

The power group totally dominates. The implications of Newton's vulnerability are further realized; he is completely helpless.

Sexual coupling:

Newton is served by an effeminate waiter; does he replace Oliver? Is Newton now bisexual?

Alcohol:

Newton has moved on to Martinis, a real drinker's drink.

Howard Hughes myth:

Newton is now completely withdrawn, living (and deteriorating) in a single space.

Censorship:

The waiter's high-pitched, effeminate voice was redubbed to reduce the implications of homosexuality.

24. Peters' Poolside Party

Narrative

Plot:

Seated by his pool, Peters tells his followers, including Arthur and Bryce, how he wants them to help reassure the public about Newton and WE; he implies that they stand to benefit.

Commentary:

This scene parallels the previous one where Newton was served drinks by his new waiter and watched the TV version of the power group's takeover. Now, as Peters is served by Arthur, we see the co-opted Peters co-opting Bryce—the chain continues. Bryce had rebelled against Canutti, but now they serve the same master.

Adaptation

Adds:

The entire poolside scene showing Peters' power (Culture).

Substitutes:

Bryce's complicity in the betrayal for his bafflement and identity as a lesser victim (Narrative; Culture).

Montage

Scene:

(24-25 = cut)

The simple scene suggests the limited mental range of the controlling group.

Music

Its absence suggests their imaginative impoverishment.

Hermeneutics

Nathan Bryce:

We are now certain that he has sold out like Arthur.

Time

Narrative time: Peters is aging, now more so than Bryce.

Perception

The power group shapes the public's knowledge to reassure them.

Culture

Power: Peters subtly bribes Bryce: "I'm not sure you understand how all this might affect you." At this level, the power becomes personalized, suggesting how Peters was probably co-opted, through threats or bribes, positive or negative reinforcement. This suggests the range of the power group; their "flexible" program includes murder, kidnap, bribery etc. as routes to "progress." Canutti, Bryce, and Peters are on one side, with Newton and Farnsworth on the other. Both sides rose in power and wealth, which can be universally corrupting.

Sexual coupling: Peters calls his wife to sit next to him, displaying her to the men he controls, linking his sexual potency to his other powers.

Water and alcohol: As he sits by his pool like a modern Poseidon, Peters explicitly comments on liquor, giving the good advice to avoid it. He knows its corrupting power which parallels that of drugs in the ghetto—which are used to weaken and control the blacks. This is ironically juxtaposed with Newton weakened by martinis in the previous scene; he originally came for water and is now undermined by alcohol.

Clothing: Peters is almost naked in his bathing suit, and sits sprawled, displaying his body. The others are formally dressed and sit erect. This contrast shows Peters' superior position—he doesn't need the conventions.

Media: They are used like liquor to manipulate and pacify the masses.

25. Third Man Theme

Narrative

Plot: Newton is examined by doctors and abandoned by Bryce, whom he calls for help. Bryce meets Mary Lou in a restaurent and persuades her to betray Newton by convincing her to visit him and urge him to make a deal with the power group through Bryce. Meanwhile, Newton watches *The Third Man* on TV and is again probed by the doctors; he assures them that no one saw him arrive on earth, but a flashback contradicts him.

Commentary: Newton's aloneness is intensified by Bryce's explicitly abandoning him. The co-opted Nate now co-opts Mary Lou, taking over Newton's woman and extending the chain of corruption. From this point on, there are frequent flashbacks to an earlier state of innocence.

Adaptation

Adds: a) The *Third Man* film on TV (Self-reflexiveness).
b) The restaurant scene and Nate and Mary Lou's participation in the betrayal of Newton. (Narrative; Hermeneutics).

Montage

Parallel syntagm with Inserts:

(25-26 = cut)

The syntagm intercuts between Newton in captivity being probed and humiliated and the restaurant where Bryce is inducing his woman to betray him. The two lines are linked by *The Third Man* on TV through the sound bridges of the dialogue.

25A Explanatory Insert: *Third Man* on TV, where Valli and Joseph Cotton discuss the betrayal of Orson Welles (Harry Lime).

25B Explanatory Insert: *Third Man* on TV.

25C Displaced Diegetic Insert: The observer watching Newton as he slides down the hill after his arrival. IT is a contradictory message from Roeg, which follows immediately after Newton says: "I came alone, nobody saw me."

Music

The Third Man zither music alludes to another film where music was extremely important in introducing themes, and acts as a sound bridge between Newton's room and the restaurant.

Hermeneutics

The Alien: What will happen to him?

Nathan Bryce: His corruption intensifies and extends to Mary Lou. He will use her, and when she asks if he's seen Newton, he lies.

Mary Lou: Will she also betray Newton?

The Observer: We are reminded of him. Who is he? How did he know to be present when Newton landed?

Time

Narrative time: One syntagm covers important leaps forward (between first examination and restaurant) and backward to the opening, showing that time is lateral in shaping experience. Also, time has increased Bryce's power and diminished Newton's, so it is relative in this regard.

Biological time: Bryce and Mary Lou have aged considerably, and somewhat grotesquely, while Newton has not. Probably the alien's body reflects time differently, but also the effects of aging are used symbolically to reflect moral decline (reminding us of *The Picture of Dorian Grey*).

Space

As in syntagm 9, the TV inserts control inner space, which then shapes outer behavior.

Perception

From this point on, our perception overtakes Newton's, which is on the decline, as suggested by the flashback to the observer; we possess a broader knowledge.

Self-reflexiveness

The use of *The Third Man* suggests that this film incorporates the genre of the British intrigue classic, yet transforms the morality— Roeg's betrayed hero is a positive figure. That film, like this one, handled its hermeneutics very cleverly, witholding important information: who is the third man? The observer? Farnsworth? The real head of the power group, who is never revealed? But Roeg uses the parallel to reveal fully the basic triangle: Newton/ Nathan and Mary Lou or Harry Lime/Joseph Cotton and Valli. Their interactions raise the question of who is really evil and who is the victim. Roeg's insertion of the film implies that it shaped the morality of Mary Lou and Bryce; Roeg must hope that his own film will similarly alter morality, but in the opposite direction.

Culture

Science:

The doctors overestimate their knowledge of Newton's body, but they have the power to reduce him to a child or a prisoner by taking away his rights and forcing him to drop his pants, as if they are raping him. The corrupt medical world is also an important theme in *The Third Man*.

Biblical myth:

The triangular seduction scene evokes Adam, Eve, and Satan.

Xenophobia:

The doctor reassures Newton: "You're perfectly normal," as if that were a good thing to be, but in fact, it ironically foreshadows the negative transformation and limiting of his identity.

Media:

Newton's life on earth has been shaped by media; now it perfectly parallels the situation in the film, except for the moral reversal. His uniqueness has been conditioned away.

26. Reunion with Mary Lou

Narrative

Plot:

Mary Lou comes to visit Tommy. They get drunk; she seduces him; he shoots her with blanks, they make love.

Commentary:

Bryce sent Mary Lou to get Newton to make a deal, but she has her own goal. She has been co-opted, but Newton is corrupted also. Both are drunk; both are into sado/masochistic sex; both adopt qualities of the other sex (which is now seen as decadence resulting from entrapment and an empty life rather than as fluid androgyny). Although he or she recalls the positive sex between them from syntagm 13, their encounter is more reminiscent of Nate's decadent sexual encounter from syntagms 4 and 6, suggesting that she is really Nate's agent.

Adaptation

Adds:

The entire event of the sexual reunion (Culture—sexual coupling; Self-reflexiveness).

Montage

Ordinary Sequence with Inserts:

(26-27 = cut)

In this fairly linear sequence (which has suggested entrapment for Newton in other syntagms) behind locked doors, his imaginative powers weakened, Newton can escape only briefly into a vision of his space wife and a memory of successful lovemaking with Mary Lou (which may be her memory, not his). The fragmentation of the lovemaking (created through strobic lighting, camera work, and cutting) substitutes for the true integration of variety, which marked his earlier sexual experiences.

26A Subjective Insert: Newton's fantasy of a reunion with his family.

26B Subjective or Displaced Diegetic Insert: Mary Lou lighting the candles before the successful lovemaking. Designation depends on whether this is Newton's memory and/or Mary Lou's or Roeg's comparative reminder of the past, which cannot be determined.

26C Subjective or Displaced Diegetic Insert: Flashback to good lovemaking. Designation uncertain as above.

26D Explanatory Insert: Extreme close-up of gun muzzle.

All of the earlier sex scenes are integrated through various kinds of allusions:

a) The playing with the gun (he puts it in his mouth; they "shoot" each other with it; Mary Lou brandishes a banana), the violent sex talk about dominance and fucking, Mary Lou's bra hanging around her back suggest the early, violent lovemaking between Bryce and the eighteen-year-old, which was intercut with the theatrical swordplay in syntagm 4. Mary Lou's motherly behavior toward Newton ("Oh, Tommy! My sweet baby! You look so beautiful to my eyes," says Mary Lou, as she wipes his face and overpowers him) suggests a mother/son kind of incest parallel to Bryce's with his daughter/lovers.

b) Newton's talk of the interchangeability of bodies evokes Bryce's second sex sequence with a number of different young girls in syntagm 6.

c) The Insert of the early sex scene of loving fusion between Newton and Mary Lou is introduced for contrast. The phallic gun and the banana have replaced the microscope and telescope—false cocks rather than expanded eyes; the fragmenting strobic lights have replaced the candlelight—intense sensory input rather than an intimate, romantic environment.

d) The insert also suggests the intercutting structure of the sex scene where he removes his eye covers and the space lovemaking is used for contrast with the present failure. Alcohol now replaces sexual wetness, and the blue strobic light of the dock after their separation here characterizes the decadent reunion.

Music

The gunshots are integrated into the music; they make love to a violent rhythm, as in the sword play rhythm of the Oriental drama.

Hermeneutics

The Alien:

Answers the question of what happens to them: they both become

Mary Lou:	decadent. Reveals the power of the culture, to force two such different creatures into the same behavior.

Time

Narrative time:	Brief returns to two pasts—his home planet (in a vision of a future return?) and his time with Mary Lou—but there is no fusion among them; they serve as sharp contrast to the present and have no transforming power. Newton says: "It's too late. I can't trust you." For what is it too late? An attempt at fusion and the possibility of real coupling? To get home? Time is not on their side.
Biological time:	Again it is unequal; Mary Lou ages, but Newton does not.
Romantic time:	As they make love, Mary Lou looks younger, suggesting that time is relative to emotions, and also that appearance has a symbolic function; the lovemaking takes her back to a better state of being.

Space

In one shot, the camera looks through the rooms with the decors from various time periods, giving visual expression to the idea of multiple pasts.

Perception

Drinking alters both their vision. He looks beautiful to her eyes, but haggard and drunk to ours, as she looks grotesque. The camera takes a drunken point of view. The strobic lighting suggests the need to keep perception incomplete, and fragmented, to avoid seeing.

Self-reflexiveness

When Newton shoots Mary Lou, the action alludes to the key scene in *Performance*, where Chas's shooting of Turner leads to a transforming rebirth; here it is fake, merely decadent play leading to nothing.

Culture

Power:	Ironically, Newton now has great power; he could kill without retribution; he can buy endless bodies for sex. These powers have been given him in compensation for the loss of all his others, and it makes him dangerous (Mary Lou is frightened at one point). This is the dynamics of co-option and probably what has made Peters and those he represents into killers—the substitution (through media and force) of corrupt pleasure/power for the possibilities of imagination, freedom, and growth through trans-formation.
Sexual coupling:	The integration of various sex scenes brings close to completion Roeg's comparative exploration of odd coupling and the in-evitable corrupting influence of contemporary life (especially money, media, and liquor) on all sexuality. Instead of love and rebirth, sex is associated with violence, sensationalistic bi-sexuality, and incest.
Gun:	The key object evoking the pawn shop and TV Western syntagms, and functioning as a phallic symbol for the culture; when he

shoots her with a blank, the sexual pun implies that this coupling can never lead to birth.

Clothing:

His short pants reinforce the incest theme, making him look like Mary Lou's child; his pedal pushers emphasize his bisexuality.

Censorship:

This entire event was cut from the American version, to prevent our seeing Newton's perversion (his burned-out rich man's consumption of male and female bodies) and male nudity, whereas the female nudity was left in the previous scenes, indicating a typical sexism. Ironically, then, the censorship eliminated one of the film's strongest comments on the corrupting effects of the sex/violence stereotyping in the media.

27. Ping Pong

Narrative

Plot:

Mary Lou and Newton play ping pong as she tries to convince him to stay, and then to see Bryce to make a deal to go home. He gives her a wedding ring, which doesn't fit, and she throws it away. They tell each other they don't love each other any more, and he remembers his arrival.

Commentary:

Though what she is trying to do is help in Bryce's betrayal of Newton to the power group (perhaps unknowingly), she actually betrays him more deeply by rejecting the last thing he has to give—the wedding ring.

Adaptation

Adds:

The entire event of the ping pong game and the failed wedding ring gift (Culture—sexual coupling; Space; Self-reflexiveness).

Montage

Scene
with Insert:

(27-28 = cut)

Newton is trapped in linear time.
27A   Subjective or Displaced Diegetic Insert:
The ring glows in the galaxy, then dissolves into the opening syntagm where he examined his many rings. The designation depends on whether it's Newton's memory or Roeg's comparative .comment.

The one Insert is contained, enclosed within the ring and within Newton's visit on earth, suggesting that in the beginning was contained the end—though the rings were the source of his money and power, they also began his inevitable decline.

Hermeneutics

The Alien:

When Mary Lou pulls at his nipples, they don't come off, suggesting that they are no longer part of his earth cover and the doctors have permanently altered his identity.

Mary Lou:

She raises new hopes by suggesting that the power group might let him go home, but she is naive in thinking Bryce could accomplish this, and reveals that she has been corrupted by him, and that he is the true snake in the grass.

Time

Narrative time: The flashback to the opening syntagm contributes a circular element to the film's structure and to Newton's earth experience, suggesting entrapment.

Biological time: Mary Lou looks old again. She tells him it's too late, that his family will be dead when he returns, reversing the previous syntagm where he told her it was too late to get together again (Romantic time); view of time depends on one's point of view.

Romantic time: They no longer love each other; their liaison has been temporary—love is not immortal.

Space

The strange ping pong room, with its woodsy wallpaper and grasslike carpet suggesting the outdoors—the substitution of artificial for real values and experience. Like the money and power over women, it is the power group's substitute for real freedom in space. The artificiality is emphasized by the presence of a crystal chandelier. The ring repeats the circle motif of the space capsule, the Japanese light shade, and the smashed ping pong balls; it acts as a receptor for past images like the space capsule and the alien transparent receiver.

Perception

The doctors want to believe Newton is "perfectly normal;" Mary Lou wants him to show he's an alien, though the evidence is diminishing. She argues that earth has more resources—money, water, grass, alcohol—but the home planet is richer for Newton in terms of emotional survival; value is a matter of point of view, as in the gift of the ring. Only Newton can see its value; he understands its past and its connection with himself. She sees its practical value (it doesn't fit) and its evocation of their failure to fit as a couple, so she throws it away.

Self-reflexiveness

The flashback to the earlier scene unites our memories with Newton's. Ironically, with the previous sex scene cut out of the American version, this scene (with the rings and the mutual declarations "I don't love you any more" doesn't make narrative sense. Mary Lou's rejection of the ring evokes the failed gift scenes in *Walkabout:* the girl rejects the Aborigine's gift of the balloon and the Aborigine rejects the boy's gift of toys.

Culture

Biblical myth: After the sex scene, Mary Lou unwittingly betrays Newton in a fake garden.

Sexual coupling: The game of ping pong functions like surrogate sex that life has been with its mutual timing and smashed balls, suggesting reduced to a game, with deals and moves.

Alcohol: The drinking continues—now champagne.

Clothing: Their tennis outfits and Newton's visor continue the idea of artificial substitutes for real experience.

| The gold ring: | Combines many codes in this scene. Gold is a means of exchange; for Mary Lou it is a ritual sign evoking marriage (is it this for Newton?); it is circular, taking us back to the beginning; it encloses, and hence entraps. it expands experience, by acting as a receiver. |

28. The Maiming

Narrative

| Plot: | The doctors continue to experiment with Newton, taking X-rays of his eyes, which fuse his earth cover eyes to his real ones. He calls for Mary Lou and Bryce, but they have abandoned him. He has images of home. |
| Commentary: | Newton is alone again. The X-ray makes explicit the fore-shadowings and tendencies toward the final exertion of power over Newton—his identity has been steadily altered and limited to a fixed earth identity, completing his decline. The maiming of his eyes links this scene with Oliver's murder. |

Adaptation

| Omits: | a) The fact that it's an election year and its bearing on Newton's being held in captivity (Culture).
b) The specific role of the FBI in his maiming (Culture). |
| Substitutes: | a) The fusing of Newton's eye covers for blinding him (Hermeneutics; Perception; Culture).
b) Syntagms 25 through 28 substitute the refusal to accept alien identity for Newton's removal of his body hair, nipples, eye covers, to prove to them that he's from another planet (Hermeneutics; Perception; Culture). |

Montage

| Scene with Inserts: | (28-29 = dissolve)
The main action involves spinning Newton in a mechanical chair, giving him more liquor to gain greater control over him, and finally, a series of inserts following directly from the altering of his eyes. |

28A Subjective Explanatory Insert: The image looks like explosions on the sun, which may be Newton's memory of or Roeg's explanation of why the home planet is dying of drought.

28B Subjective Insert: Newton's space family greet him as he gets off the train—his wished-for homecoming.

28C Non-Diegetic Insert: The film dissolves to a strange building where a space-launch countdown is apparently in progress.

28D Non-Diegetic Insert: The control room of the launch building where two men discuss the take-off, commenting that it's a waste of money.

28E Subjective or Explanatory Insert: Explosions of the sun, with same ambiguities as 28A.

28F Subjective Insert: Newton's family on the home planet lies dying, covered with dust.

The action in the doctor's office focuses around disorientation (the chair, the liquor) and culminates in trauma (the eyes). The Inserts express the results, moving from his greatest hopes (the reunion) through shots of some other, unknown space effort (which is being substituted for his?) to his worst fear.

Hermeneutics

The Alien: Are his eyes like ours now, or have they been further damaged in some unknown way? His return to the home planet now seems even more unlikely because of the diminishment of his physical and mental powers, and because of the attitude of the American public.

Time

The present is mingled with various versions of the future; we are not sure of the time for any of the Inserts.

Space

Humans are encouraged not to think beyond their own planet— probing space is wasteful.

Perception

Media and the government manipulate point of view, which is relative. They have convinced the people that his space program is a waste of money, altering their attitudes as they altered Newton's identity. From Newton's point of view, the space program is the most valuable way to use money; it is a matter of life and death for his family and for the home planet.

Self-reflexiveness

X-ray probings can be dangerous, like TV, film, photography, science; they can all cause you to "get stuck," the central danger in all of Roeg's films.

Culture

Science: Continues the exploration of medicine, which has done harmful things throughout the ages—out of ignorance or politics. The chart of the cosmos in the office links the doctors with Canutti and Academia. The intellectuals are co-opted and corrupted like the doctors. Both set themselves against the cosmic vision of the charts in ironic contrast to their dangerous limitations.

Alcohol: Explicitly used to make Newton helpless.

Xenophobia: The doctors refuse to accept the fact that Newton is an alien, treating him as if it were an illusion. Either they fear the alien so much that they cannot accept the facts, or they know the truth but must neutralize his uniqueness, which threatens their control.

Censorship: The two brief Inserts of the space launch building and control room have been omitted—perhaps desirable cuts, since they seemed to clutter the syntagm, not expanding but impeding perception of its messages.

29. Recovery and Release

Narrative

Plot: Newton recovers in captivity, is visited by the observer who saw him land at the opening, then leaves his prison.

Commentary: Newton is coming back from the lowest point of his decline, recovering from his maiming and impaired vision. He may have comic resilience, or be capable of many metamorphoses like the butterflies who are associated with him in the syntagm. This recovery begins a new cycle or upswing.

Adaptation

Adds: The second trip in the elevator as he goes down to leave the hotel.

Omits: Upcoming elections as a motive for releasing Newton.

Substitutes: a) The watcher at the foot of the bed for bugging as a way of observing Newton (Perception; Culture).
b) The mysteriously open doors and Newton's casual escape for an official release by a group of guards (Hermeneutics).
c) The silent unidentified observer from the opening for Bowen, the talkative director of the CIA (Culture).

Montage

Episodic Sequence with Inserts: (29-30 = dissolve; music bridge)
The main action is Newton's observed recovery.

29A   Displaced Diegetic Insert: The construction site outside Newton's window.

29B   Displaced Diegetic Insert: The construction site.

The disorientation of the previous syntagm continues here. Frequent use of dissolves, uneven panning, ambiguous time ellipses, close-ups of unexplained details (e.g., raindrops on a window, butterflies in a display case, ice cubes) all make it difficult for the viewer to make connections among the images, a new way of suggesting subjective point of view and Newton's visual impairment. This syntagm contains no dialogue.

Music

As Newton leaves the hotel, we begin to hear "Silent Night," which signals Christmas, telling us the time and suggesting rebirth.

Hermeneutics

The Alien: What will he do now? Will he try to go home?

The observer: Is he the watcher from the opening, now grown a beard? We now feel more sure that he's connected with the power group. Why is he there? Is he there to decide that Newton is now harmless and can be released?

Time

Narrative time: The dissolves mark ellipses of unknown duration, adding to the disorientation of his recovery. The shadow of the observer also anticipates time and change. It is evening when Newton escapes, but of what day? "Silent Night" signals circular time. Sound of clocks in shot as he walks down the corridor toward freedom grows faster and louder, suggesting time is once again on his side.

Economic time:
The images of the construction site are ambiguous; they may be linked with new growth and rebuilding, but they also suggest the wasting and misuse of resources by the power group.

Time and motion:
This time he rides the elevator without fainting, indicating his physical adaptation to earth, whether it be progress or decline; significantly the elevator is descending.

Space

The interior of his prison has become a shambles. Pictures are crooked, furniture is displaced, it's hard to get located in the space. Then Newton is able to abandon the destroyed space and move out into freedom, moving down along the corridor again, suggesting the passage into life (as in the tunnel entry to the space capsule in syntagm 16). That rebirth failed; perhaps this one will too.

Perception

Visual perception is the subject of this syntagm, making explicit the primacy of this sense for survival. Its impairment marked Newton's lowest point; the beginning of its return is used to signal his possible regeneration. The subjective point of view is developed with sophistication through camera work, opticals, cutting. The observer watches Newton, unobserved by him but seen by the audience. This syntagm *tells* us nothing, but *shows* us a great deal.

Culture

Biblical myth:
Newton is identified with Christ, being reborn at Christmas.

Power:
One of the main sources of the power group's control is the successful use of visual perception in the form of observation. There is no real privacy in our culture; the watcher may be anywhere. The image of the butterflies in the case at the beginning of the syntagm suggests Newton as a vulnerable short-lived, exotic creature to be captured and held for observation, (as in *The Collector*). But it also suggests the idea of metamorphosis, an extreme form of change inaccessible to those who control him.

Water and alcohol:
The drinking is somewhat balanced by the rain imagery as Newton looks out his window and by the close-up of the bowl of ice cubes (but this also looks backward, reminding us of Mary Lou, who taught him to drink gin with four ice cubes).

30. Santa Claus and True Love

Narrative

Plot:
Mary Lou buys booze in a liquor store; Bryce, dressed as Santa Claus, waits for her. He is now apparently her lover; they go home, have a drink and she reminisces about Newton.

Commentary:	Bryce and Mary Lou are now united in their betrayal, but they are stuck in liquor and commercial Christmases. They are on the decline, while Newton is possibly on the rise. Mary Lou needs to escape into flashbacks, as Newton did earlier.

Adaptation

Adds:	Bryce's Santa suit (Culture).
Substitutes:	Scenes in liquor store and apartment for Christmas visit to the zoo (Culture).
Omits:	a) How the romance between Mary Lou and Nate began (Hermeneutics). b) The section title: "1990; Icarus drowning" (Narrative).

Montage

Ordinary Sequence with Inserts:	(30-31 = cut) The sequence is controlled by their buying liquor and going home to drink it.

30A   Explanatory Insert: Mary Lou looks at the sky (as she did in syntagm 9 when she spoke of God and heard "Fascination" on TV).

30B   Subjective or Explanatory Insert: Newton and his space wife. Either Mary Lou received this image from Newton and is remembering it, or Roeg inserts the shot to suggest what is really out there, as opposed to Mary Lou's conventional view of heaven.

30C   Subjective Insert: Flashback to the close-up from syntagm 13 where Mary Lou and Newton look alike after their peak fusion. Mary Lou rejected the wedding ring in the previous syntagm, but now her imagination reunites them through reference to two happy pasts, offsetting the influence of media images; yet ironically the shot of their fusion is influenced by media (it suggests shots in *Persona*).

Music

"Silent Night" and Bing Crosby's "True Love" (which we hear in the apartment as Mary Lou and Bryce drink and talk) are both cliché songs used ironically. The commercial Christmas is anything but silent and certainly doesn't suggest the night Christ was born, and "True Love" comments on her present living situation with Bryce in contrast to her memories of Newton.

Hermeneutics

Mary Lou and Bryce:	This syntagm tells us what happens to them. They live together (probably on her money; she pays in the liquor store); they are old, grotesque, unhappy, and cold.

Time

Narrative time:	Mary Lou looks back to the past—to warmth and true love with Tommy.
Economic time:	Bryce tries to pretend that things are getting better, by saying: "You know, I believe Christmas is less commercial this year." He clings to the idea of progress, but Mary Lou answers: "I'd like to go somewhere for Christmas that's real hot—tropical. I guess I'm feeling the cold."
Biological time:	Everyone is old, even the cat with his 9 lives; their visual grotesquery suggests they have lived their time badly.

Space

Mary Lou's imaginative Inserts suggest that her mental space may have expanded. Mary Lou and Bryce occupy a conventional small house or apartment; they lost the spatial imagination from their lives when they parted with Newton.

Perception

Mary Lou and Bryce have different perceptions of the present; they are mentally distant.

Self-reflexiveness

In the apartment, Mary Lou removes her false eyelashes, reminding us of Newton's removal of his earth eyes, and suggesting that her cultural cover is growing uncomfortable for her, too. She counts out four ice cubes into her drink, linking us back to her initiating Newton to alcohol and to the previous syntagm where Newton reached for the ice cubes, but his hand lingered in the bowl, perhaps for the pleasure of the wetness. This syntagm suggests the ending of *Walkabout* where the girl feels mentally distant from her husband after her return from the outback, and imagines an idyllic image of swimming with her brother and the Aborigine in the beautiful lagoon.

Culture

Biblical myth: Bryce is dressed as Santa Claus, the protector of Christ's birth, but in fact he is betrayer; Saint Nick suggests a pun on Old Nick, the Devil, with whom Bryce is actually identified.

Power: The commercial co-option of Christmas is made ludicrous by the fact that as they leave the liquor store, a second Santa Claus holds the door for them. In the apartment, we recognize the Navajo rugs from earlier scenes; they apparently belong to Bryce, and remind us of the Indian jewelry in the opening syntagm. Newton, the Western hero, also exploits the Indians—another link in the co-option chain.

Alcohol: It still dominates their lives.

Clothing: The emphasis on the fakeness of their costumes (he as Santa, she in wig, nail polish, and false lashes as before) contrasts with the music "True Love," and with Bryce's talk about the decommercialization of Christmas. The visuals reveal the truth about their decline and corruption, while the verbal plane lies about morality and values.

Censorship: The scene in the liquor store, including Bryce in a Santa Claus suit, and their later conversation about the decommercialization of Christmas were omitted in the American version. Perhaps the distributors wanted to diminish Roeg's exploration of economic corruption (their motive for making many of the other cuts) as it extends to the holiest ritual of western civilization.

31. A Star is Born

Narrative

Plot: Nate goes to a record store, where he discovers an album called "The Visitor" made by Newton. He finds Newton drinking in a restaurant; they talk about the past and the future.

Commentary:	As earlier in the narrative, Nate tracks Newton down. The story freezes after the lines: WAITER: "I think Mr. Newton has had enough, don't you?" NATE: "I think maybe he has." Apparently, so have we.

Adaptation

Omits:	a) Bryce's request that Newton save the world (Culture). b) Newton's gift to Bryce of a million dollar check (Culture). c) TV interview with Newton where he announces he has decided to abandon his space program because it was too ambitious (Culture).
Substitutes:	a) Breakup of Nate and Mary Lou for the continuation of their relationship (Narrative; Time; Culture—sexual coupling). b) Newton's forgiveness and remaining hope for bitterness and tears of self-pity (Narrative; Hermeneutics; Perception).

Montage

Ordinary sequence:	(30- freeze) The time ellipsis between the two scenes that comprise this sequence is ambiguous. The simplicity is again linked with entrapment; but since it's the last syntagm, this time Newton cannot escape into the next. The final freeze shows what happens to Newton—he gets frozen or stuck in this identity.

Music

The music industry that dominates the airwaves is developed through the record store and Newton's plans for his album—he has made it as a personal message to his wife on the home planet, though it may also have side effects on everyone else who hears it. The song "Stardust" by Artie Shaw takes us back to nostalgic memories of our musical past as Newton reminisces about Mary Lou and his wife on the home planet.

Hermeneutics

The Alien:	This last sequence answers the question—whatever happened to Tommy Newton? He became a rock star. Will he ever get back home? Probably not, but, as he reminds Nate, "there's always a chance." He is still partially decadent—wearing lipstick, steadily drinking; but he still yearns for his wife, he hasn't grown bitter, and he still has money. The question is not fully answered.
Mary Lou:	We don't hear much more about her, except that she is no longer involved with Nate Bryce; another modern liaison has disintegrated.

Time

Narrative time:	Their dialogue is full of reminiscences about various pasts—the previous syntagm where Nate and Mary Lou were together, the more distant past relationships between Mary Lou and Newton and Bryce and Newton, the most distant past between Newton and his wife. They also speculate about the future, leaving these questions open.
Biological time:	While Nate Bryce looks quite old, Newton still looks young, which has ambiguous implications. On the one hand, it may imply that he is infinitely resourceful and has eternal youth; yet, on the other hand, it implies he is stuck—a mask is incapable of change.

Economic time:	Since Newton still has money and time, there is hope.
Romantic time:	All relationships prove temporary.

Space

The sequence moves from Nate Bryce in an enclosd space of a record store, with albums neatly filed and catalogued, to a more open, freer environment of an outdoor restaurant with birds, palm trees, ferns, almost evoking the kind of tropical setting that Mary Lou longed for in the previous syntagm. Newton is still moving in the open spaces, sending home good vibrations.

Perception

Stresses the contrasting perspectives of Newton and Nate. Nate doesn't like the album, but it was made for Newton's wife who will. Nate expects Newton to be bitter, but he can see the other side—"We'd have probably treated you the same if you had come over to our place." Nate assumes there is no chance, but Newton insists: "Of course, there's a chance . . . you're the scientist, you must know there's always a chance." Newton has regained a lot of his earlier breadth of vision. On one point, everyone (Nate, Newton, the waiter, and Roeg) agrees: "Mr. Newton has had enough." The helicopter indicates that the power group is still watching him, suggesting danger if he should rise to power again as a rock star.

Self-reflexiveness

"Stardust" is the name of an earlier Bowie persona—Ziggy Stardust—and the title of an earlier film about the decline of a British rock star named Essex rather than Sussex. "The Visitor" album helps unify Bowie's personae inside and outside the film as Major Tom, Ziggy Stardust, and a protean performer who cultivates the same kind of hermeneutics about his origins, sexual identity, and decadence. We do not actually hear any of Bowie's songs in this film; but we probably have heard them on the radio (Nate: "We hear most everything on the radio these days"). Hence, we are put in a role similar to that of Newton's space wife—having to delay our curiosity until we once again hear the familiar voice of David Bowie.

Culture

Xenophobia:	Newton's statement that his people would have treated earth visitors the same way implies that alienation occurs on all levels. The film ends with a friendly encounter between two characters who represent various polarities: scientist vs. artist, establishment vs. alien, host vs. visitor, straight male vs. bisexual, cynic vs. optimist, sober rationalist vs. drunken visionary. Metaphysically, "the other" is always alien.
Birds:	They fly overhead, still offering some glimmer of hope and freedom.
Alcohol:	He came for water, but he was polluted by alcohol; it remains a serious corrupting force.
Media:	He used it to come to earth, then was corrupted by it, but now has regained control, exploiting it for his own purposes—to send a private message through space, as Roeg is doing in this film. It remains a source of hope because it has the potential to expand sensory perception rather than dulling it like alcohol.

Walkabout

Space does not allow a syntagmatic analysis of *Walkabout*, but a summary of its various codes reveals important similarities with those of *The Man Who Fell to Earth*.

Narrative

As in *The Man Who Fell to Earth*, the narrative encounter between the two cultures peaks when the alien male comes closest to coupling with the woman. Here, too, the scenes of maximum unity and separation focus on vision and verbal communication. After playing in the eucalyptus trees, the girl rubs her sore legs and the Aborigine speaks to her very tenderly. For once understanding his intentions, she assures him she'll be all right. Then they stand face to face in the darkness, and both we and the girl understand his feelings although they are expressed in an alien language. As he turns and walks off, the image dissolves to a silhouette of him standing on one leg on a hilltop, his posture suggesting great confidence. However, when they later reach the house, the Aborigine becomes the outsider, peering at the girl through openings in the structure as she sits inside studying old photographs; her refusal to look at him and understand his feelings helps transform their potential courtship ritual into his death dance.

The white children's co-option of the narrative is dramatized in the sequence where the brother tells an inset story about a boy who broke his neck trying to communicate with his mother, who pretended she could not speak. The sister corrects details, as if fidelity to the original were of prime concern even though she feels it's absurd to tell a story to an alien who doesn't know the language. Yet, ironically, the children don't understand how the story applies to their own situation: the Aborigine will also break his neck trying to communicate with the deceptive girl. The imperialist way in which the story is being used is revealed through the visuals. Recurring images of turning pages are superimposed onto the landscape, as they take over the narrative. Like the house and the mining settlement, the story is an external structure that polarizes people into insiders vs. outsiders and that limits the potential meaning of experience occurring within its boundaries.

Adaptation

The film expands the range of the novel, introducing satiric condemnation of the "advanced" culture by addition of the opening sequence showing the uniformity and desperation of city life, the father's suicide, the intercutting for contrast between the Aborigine's and the white men's kinds of hunting, the interpolated shots of the butcher shop, the bold introduction of radios, automobiles, and weather equipment into the outback. It alters the direction of the original sexist theme; in the novel, the girl is resentful when the Aborigine takes over her motherly leadership role, but the book implies that she is wrong, and that women should not strive for authority. Roeg turns this sexism into an important aspect of failed self-realization. The girl is frightened by the sexual potentiality between herself and the Aborigine; his death dance suggests a failed courtship; her dissatisfaction with her husband upon her return implies that she's made a wrong sexual choice.

Roeg omits much explicit information given in the novel, where the omniscient narrator translates the Aborigine's words for us and makes his thoughts explicit. In the novel, the Aborigine's mysterious death is explained neatly; the narrator tells us it is a "combat" having to do with the Aborigine's cultural fear of death and, in case that is still too mysterious, adds that he has caught the white boy's cold, to which he has no immunity. Roeg retains the mystery of gestures, objects, and events, putting the audience in the position of visitors to an alien culture who must remain open-minded if they are to understand what they see.

As in *The Man Who Fell to Earth*, the moral direction of the whole and of particular characters is radically altered. The Aborigine, like Newton, becomes much more positive; the little brother becomes more sensitive and flexible in relation to the Aborigine, just as Oliver grows more adaptable, courageous and loyal to the alien. The white girl becomes more negative and destructive like Nate Bryce; highly conventional and deceptive, she has been corrupted by her cultural imprinting like Mary Lou. The moral focus of the film as a whole shifts from a sentimental, racist, integrationist adventure story where the black sacrifices himself willingly for the whites to an existential adventure where the white girl's failure to expand her experience contributes directly to the Aborigine's death.

All three of Roeg's adaptations are based on simple, popular literary forms: *Walkabout* on a piece of adolescent literature; *Don't Look Now* on an ironic Gothic tale; *The Man Who Fell to Earth* on a modest, intelligent work of science fiction. The consistent direction of Roeg's adaptation is to complicate and expand these sources, primarily through seven means: adding new social satire; creating a new, fluid structure for reality through montage; heightening mystification and the symbolic significance of details, forcing us to reexamine the familiar and commonplace and creating a rich, dense texture; universalizing limited subjects through a kind of cosmic visual context based on great sweeping camera gestures; fluid movement through inner and outer space; casting that moves out beyond the films; transformation of sentimental or limited moral perspectives. Roeg chooses these simple sources because they embody certain reliably universal themes (entrapment, life and death, alienation from and fear of "the other," the death-dealing qualities of "civilized" life). The literary works act as catalysts for Roeg's unconventional imagination, offering components of potential meaning. Roeg's adaptations exhibit, above all, the desire to create heightened significance out of every aspect of the material he approaches.

Montage

The montage code reinforces Roeg's valuing of complexity and expanded vision, suggesting that the juxtaposition of any two units may simultaneously indicate similarities as well as differences and thereby function as a means of integration rather than opposition. Like *The Man Who Fell to Earth*, *Walkabout* uses a diverse range of syntagms. In the later film, only one of Metz's categories is missing— the bracket syntagm. In *Walkabout*, the repertoire is complete; it opens with a bracket syntagm that powerfully expresses the fragmentation of urban living and contrasts with the integrative structures of the rest of the film. Bits of sound emerge from the city—electronic music, radio static, the humming and strange "bub bub bub" of a singing class, the twangy "wah wah wah" of the digeridoo, and the coldly lucid radio voice of a woman telling us about the preparation of birds marinated in cognac. The fast cutting enhances the sense of separateness, but at the same time, the images emphasize uniformity; people wearing uniforms are clustered in groups. men parade in lines; schoolgirls do breathing exercises in unison; boys are organized into supervised games; people are filed into cubicles, their windows evenly spaced. In the park the trees are properly labelled with their genus as the meat is labelled in the markets.

Once on the outback, the montage tends to obscure boundaries and demonstrates the potential integrative powers of nature. The tension between integration and opposition in the montage is a direct visual expression of the thematic movement between fusion and separation on the narrative level. The integrative power is particularly strong in the hunting sequences that are controlled by the Aborigine's point of view. One opens with a still shot of the Aborigine's black hands on the pale yellow sand, then moves to a montage of still photos of birds, snakes, and kangaroos. As he begins to hunt, the Aborigine's graceful movements are accentuated by the combination of motion and freeze shots that build rhythm and intensity; then suddenly he breaks into a run, the motion becoming entirely continuous and the hand-held camera following as he and his prey move together across the outback as if partners in a dance. When the Aborigine cuts up the carcass of the kangaroo—his reward for skill and grace—Roeg intercuts shots of a white-aproned butcher cutting up meat, which is to be sold in the packages we saw in the opening montage, enabling the consumers to remain oblivious to the real costs in terms of life and death. Although the satirical contrast may seem heavy-handed here and in other sequences (e.g., the intercutting between the children playing in the trees and the Aborigines playing in the abandoned Volkswagen), its obviousness is mitigated by Roeg's larger intention to reveal the basis for *integrating* the two cultures.

Roeg's cutting is most successful when it embodies complexity through expanded vision as in the final hunting sequence. As the Aborigine runs to fetch water, he responds to whatever crosses his path—the wild asses, and the white boy who tags along. When they find the road, the boy is ecstatic, but the Aborigine moves on, encountering a wild boar whom he kills. Without any conventional signal that a change is coming, the film cuts to two white hunters in a jeep, which has a dead animal tied across the front. As the hunter fires his rifle, the sound triggers a montage of fleeing animals and birds, followed by a loop in which, over and over again, the wounded animal falls to the ground, reintegrating the earlier loop of the father falling in front of the burning car and reinforcing the theme of the white man's murderous impulses. After a cut to the Aborigine's tear-stained face, a great variety of visual techniques express his desire to stop what is happening: the wounded beast falls in slow motion; fleeing birds and animals are frozen in stills; then we see a reverse shot of the wounded creature rising to its feet; then the animals, released from the freeze shot, resume their flight. As if to deny the power of this fantasy reversal, the next shot reveals the white hunter slitting the animal's throat. It is as if the Aborigine's cultural perceptions enable him to see traces of destructive aliens (just as Newton could see the pioneers and traces of other visitors) and to visualize the future (as Newton could foresee the death of his family). After this powerful vision of decline and defeat, the Aborigine prepares himself for his death dance.

As in *The Man Who Fell to Earth*, Roeg uses the interplay between sound and image to integrate disparate material. As we see a rising sun dissolve into a larger sun over the desert, we hear a montage of sounds combining radio static, gunshots, city noises, laughter, boys playing in a playground, a man's voice murmuring the word *telescope*, desert sounds, and background choral music. Then we learn the boy is suffering from sunstroke and in his delirium has integrated external stimuli, memories, and imagination as in dreams. In the billabong sequence, the boy responds to a verbal cue from the radio, abruptly asking his sister, "Does drinking give you a big red fat nose?" Then the film quickly cuts to a shot of their father, implying that he had a drinking problem. Then we hear the sound of a crash on the radio and the film cuts to a shot of the father rising in front of his burning car; the soundtrack affirms the association as the boy asks, "Did our car crash?" Roeg uses the radio throughout the film to bring a variety of western sounds into the outback, frequently creating an ironic tension between sound and image. As a group of Aborigines explore the burned-out Volkswagen, one of them turns on the radio, and the loud blast of music frightens them away; then the film cuts to a long shot of the abandoned car while a huckstering radio voice says: "If you've got a clean car you'd like to sell. . . ." In another sequence, while the radio offers a lesson in mathematics, the visuals show the Aborigine working on his hunting tools. After a glorious series of natural images, a dispassionate voice on the radio considers the possible end of the world, observing that man has passed through ten thousand years of pain and suffering so that "there might be a perpetual procession of comfortable shopkeepers." Yet this verbal prophecy of the end of the world is reinforced by the visual image of the two mysterious deaths that frame the film—of the father and of the Aborigine, both hanging in a tree like Christ. The fact that the integrative potential, so powerfully celebrated by Roeg's editing style, is ignored by the white children and their society, leads to a common failure for both cultures—the physical death of one and the spiritual decline of the other as in *The Man Who Fell to Earth.* Roeg's unconventional editing style makes a political statement, rebelling against the imprinted formulae of his medium and his society.

Music

Walkabout incorporates a tremendous range of music, including Italian pop, avant-garde electronic sounds, American and British rock, Aborigine dance music, and sublime choral composition. As in *The Man Who Fell to Earth,* the variety underscores the integration of cultural differences, while insisting on the structural similarity of all music. As a universal language, music is an extremely effective medium for expressing and transmitting feelings; for this reason, it is also capable of manipulating the emotions of the listener. The lyrics make social commentary, but, as in the cutting, this function is sometimes heavy-handed, e.g., Rod Stewart's "Gasoline Alley" puns verbally on the car-burning and suicide which are shortly to follow, and the chorus sings "Who saw him die?" when the children climb the rocks to get a prospect view after their father's death. The music expands film experience by providing another plane of expression for meaning, and integrates visual and structural elements that have separate identities on other planes of expression.

Hermeneutics

As in *The Man Who Fell to Earth,* the central questions involve identity and trust: motives remain unexplained. Though the visual clues tend to be mysterious, they are more trustworthy than the verbal clues, which are often deceptive.

The white girl lies in order to make reality less threatening. Early in the film, she tells her brother that she knows the way and that their father will join them later, creating a false sense of security. When night falls, they act out a polite drama that denies their predicament.

> BOY: Are we going to stay here all night?
> GIRL: If you like.
> BOY: Yes, please.

The boy lies selfishly for his own advantage. Pretending that he cannot walk any farther, he makes his sister carry him on her back. Exploiting his youth, he pretends naivete about his father's death, but later he forces his sister to admit the truth:

BOY: Will Dad be there? Is he dead too? Did he shoot himself?
GIRL: It was an accident.
BOY: No it wasn't. Why did he do it?
GIRL: I don't know. I suppose he thought he was doing the best
thing.
BOY: That's silly.
GIRL: I said I didn't know.

The danger of these "white lies" is exposed when the Aborigine dies.
Having just seen the dead body, the boy asks his sister to explain his
disappearance. Instead of admitting her ignorance, she invents
clichés:

GIRL: He's gone home.
BOY: Why?
GIRL: Well, there was no reason for him to stay. He just wanted
to bring us to the road.
BOY: He didn't say goodbye to us.
GIRL: Yes he did—that's what the dance is about. It's their way
of saying goodbye to people they love.

Then the girl tries to shift their attention to dressing for their return
to civilization; the boy, however, insists on the truth:

GIRL: We want to look nice when they find us.
BOY: I wanted to give him my penknife. . . . He's dead. I tried to
give him my penknife but he wouldn't take it.

The dominant clues to identity are visual, developed through
subtle relations among individuals and groups. As Newton's alien
identity is slowly made clear through a series of partial revelations
and then a full unmasking, the Aborigine is first presented in a long
shot that obscures his individual characteristics; in fact, the white boy
mistakes him for his father. Then, in a series of cuts, the Aborigine
comes closer and we realize he is hunting. When we finally see him in
close-up, he is just spearing the lizard, which he brandishes in front
of the children as his introductory gesture, as if presenting himself
through the animal. As the primary target of his hunt, the lizards
might be seen in a totemic relationship with the Aborigine, for in his
culture identity is controlled by totemism. Although the rite of the
Walkabout has separated him from his group, he is not really isolated
because he has established a relationship with the animals in his
environment. The visiting children, on the other hand, remain
isolated, neither establishing any meaningful relationship with the
animals nor acknowledging common species membership with the
Aborigine. As in *The Man Who Fell to Earth*, their temporary
"family" identification with the host only deepens the tragedy of

their return to separate identities at the end of the film. In the opening montage, they, like their father, are first seen within a group or class that denies individuality; but on the outback, group membership is signalled by isolated telephoto shots of individual animals just as the individual (like Newton) is the source of our knowledge about his society. The individual lizards of the telephoto shots become members of a group as we see several of them, covered with flies, hanging from the Aborigine's waist. Lévi-Strauss quotes Henri Bergson to show how this relationship between individual and group identity is central to totemism.

> "At the same time as the nature of the animal seems to be concentrated into a unique quality, we might say that its individuality is dissolved in a genus. To recognize a man means to distinguish him from other men; but to recognize an animal is normally to decide what species it belongs to . . . . An animal lacks concreteness and individuality, it appears essentially as a quality and thus essentially as a class." It is this direct perception of the class, through the individuals, which characterizes the relation between man and the animal or plant, and it is this also which helps us to understand "this singular thing that is totemism."[29]

The mysteriousness of motives rather than future outcomes is central in *Walkabout*. While Newton's intentions are gradually revealed, and the desire for power clearly motivates the forces who oppose him, in this film we are never certain why the father commits suicide or why he tried to take his "innocent" children with him. Most important, despite the connection with his preceding vision of death while hunting and the rejection by the white girl, the Aborigine's death remains mysterious. Unlike the girl, *we* had recognized his values as a potential lover, brother, father, and teacher. Hence, we recognize his death, whatever its cause, as signifying the loss of what the film has trained us to value.

Time

As one of the main objects of scrutiny in both films, linear time is frequently transformed into what Roeg calls "lateral time." Barthes comments on the purpose and function of this constant rearrangement:

> Generalized distortion . . . is a purely logical phenomenon, and as such, it constantly substitutes meaning for the pure and simple facsimile of narrated events . . . a sort of *logical time* comes to prevail, bearing little resemblance to real time, the

apparent fracturing of units being still closely subordinated to
the logic which binds together the nuclei of the sequence.[30]

Walkabout often moves freely through past, future, and conditional
tenses, showing the simultaneity of times in the experience of a single
event. When the boy sees the three camels, he may be having a vision
of the past (as when Newton sees the pioneers); but the camel
carcasses suggest a vision of the future for the Aborigine, foreshadowing his vision of death in the final hunt. The girl's fantasy
return to the outback at the end of the film suggests the power of the
imagination to transcend time under the pressure of emotional need.

As in *The Man Who Fell to Earth*, *Walkabout* presents a vision of
time as relative. On the outback, Roeg uses the recurring image of the
sun to mark the passing of the days. This technique does not invite
counting how many times the morning sun has dawned in the film.
Instead, days are discrete events, but they happen in the same way
time after time, causing all of experience to flow together. Using
time-lapse photography, Roeg shows a bright gold sun moving
across an orange sky. Later he fades into an image of the white moon
that dissolves into a yellow sun. In contrast, the children mark time
through the sounds of music and words heard on the radio; the
battery allows them precisely 400 hours.

Narrative time is more linear than in *The Man Who Fell to Earth*,
because of the mythic, less urban focus of the location and events.
Economic time is an important element of social commentary in this
film also, as indicated by the built-in obsolescence of the battery, and
the father's desire to hurry up and commit suicide. Even this event is
emptied of its emotion by this obsession with the efficient use of this
resource. Biological time is developed through contrasting reactions
to the natural environment as a source of time information.
Romantic time also provides a basis for contrast between host and
visitors as the Aborigine's entry into manhood suggests his readiness
for sex and love, while the white girl's cultural immobility keeps her
locked into childishness and virginity.

Roeg's recoding of linear time reads something like this: time is
fluid, relative, and uncertain; be prepared for sudden shifts in any
direction. This view involves important issues of freedom. Only
Roeg and his positive figures—the Aborigine, and Newton—can
accept and use polysemous time. The figures who are locked into
linear or public time—the white girl, Peters, Bryce—finally dominate,
as Roeg's film is partially dominated by the distributors who recut it,
rearranging its time structure to conform more closely to their own.

Space

As in *The Man Who Fell to Earth,* the open space in nature is contrasted with the enclosure of the city—the former is linked with freedom, sensuality, mystery, and variety of color and texture, whereas the latter is associated with entrapment, sterility, repetition, and conformity. There are odd juxtapositions which stress both the similarities and the urban diminishment of natural values—a brick wall is frequently intercut with a cliff comprised of rocks of a great variety of shapes and tones, the children swim in a small rectangular pool instead of the adjacent ocean. Whereas in the city everything is neatly categorized and confined within predictable patterns—the streets, the traffic, the fences, the modular office buildings and apartment complexes—the natural environment retains a sense of surprise and obscures the line between appearance and reality: a billabong emerges in the middle of an arid landscape and then just as suddenly dries up; the aborigine teaches the children that water lies hidden below the dry surface.

The camerawork accentuates the animism and transformational power that are dormant in the landscape. Following a shot in which the hazy heat distorts reality as the children climb the rocks, the girl says: "We can see where we are from the top." Suddenly the camera pulls back for a long shot, presenting a romantic interlude of birds soaring and the children on the ridge, as if suggesting from the omniscient point of view an integration with the environment that the children themselves are unable to accomplish. Then the camera pulls back again for an aerial shot, making a dizzying 360° pan of the mountains, which are further distorted by the lens that alters their shape, and by a series of cross-dissolves, which create a sense of lyrical flight. This highly imaginative interlude is ended as the camera moves in for a shot of the children on the ridge; the boy thinks he sees the ocean in the distance, but the sister is forced to admit that she doesn't know whether they are looking at reality or a mirage.

The source of transformational power and expansiveness also lies within inner space. The Aborigine has the imaginative power to transcend external limits in finding water, in hunting, and in rock painting. Impressed with this creativity, the young white boy excitedly tells his sister, "I think he's going to take us to the moon." While he is still reaching out to new experience, the girl is already closed-minded. She seeks the familiar spatial unity—the straight road and the enclosed house. Once they reach the abandoned dwelling, all of her perceptions are shaped by the goal of getting back home, which becomes a "manifest destiny." When her brother discovers the road, she smugly remarks: "I knew we were getting somewhere." The man in the mining town has a similar vision, responding to the unexpected appearance of the children in terms of jurisdiction: "It's all private property. . . . I'm an employee of the company and the mine." His imprisonment within these mental structures is expressed visually as we see him peering out of the house through the slatted windows and twisting sprinklers. The locations of the house and mining town are the principles of organization, giving these sequences their identity. The advanced culture controls experience by imposing external structure rather than discovering the organic structure inherent in experience as the Aborigine does. Thus, the whites find it difficult to improvise and are frequently threatened by the unexpected. Yet, once back in the confinement of her modular kitchen, the girl turns inward and escapes into a lagoon fantasy, indicating that her mind was expanded by her outback experience despite her resistance.

Perception

Like *The Man Who Fell to Earth, Walkabout* develops a contrast between ordinary and expanded perception, in the white children, the Aborigine, and the audience. The frequent shifts between telephoto shots of desert creatures and the sweeping panoramic vistas of the outback constantly remind us that perspective is relative. Roeg's alternation between the two cultural points of view and his interphasing of sound and image force us to adopt an overview which can process the multiple comparisons. The camel sequence, for example, stresses the difference between the perceptions of the brother and sister. When he calls attention to the camels verbally, the camera reveals that her eyes are riveted on the bare skin of the Aborigine. While the boy fantasizes about past cowboys riding the camels through streams of light, she focuses on the smooth flow of the Aborigine's body in the present, and the Aborigine foresees the sad fate of the camels—skeletons swarming with flies. The visuals not only indicate differences in time orientation, but the chief focus of each character: the boy's enthusiasm for adventure, the girl's fear of sex, and the Aborigine's preoccupation with death.

There are repeated instances of men observing women, in the hope of making contact, but being rejected—the Aborigine watches the white girl as she looks at photographs in the house, the boy in the inset story spies on his mother, the meteorologists eye the blond as she crosses her legs. Like the weathermen, the father uses binoculars as he examines his daughter's legs before trying to lure her and his son into joining him in death.

The two cultures differ in the way they allow vision or language to shape perception. As in *The Man Who Fell to Earth*, the Western society is highly verbal whereas the Aborigines and aliens depend more heavily on vision. Although the Aborigine speaks a language we do not understand, his perceptions are effectively communicated through visual images and montage. He sees the physical resemblance between the girl's legs and the white bark of the eucalyptus tree, and between her body in the water and the pale body of a fish. In the context of totemism, he is able to integrate humans and animals, self and other—an assumption expressed vividly in his imitation of the prey he hunts. His totemistic identification of the girl does not reduce her to an object but expresses his animistic sense that her female spirit is powerful and lives in things that look like her. The cross-cutting between her and the fish links his feelings of tenderness and desire for the girl with the respect and identification he feels for his prey. Later, when he sees a white hunter slaughtering game, he uses the same mode of perception to associate the animals' death with his own.

The Aborigine's conception of survival is based on being a *bricoleur,* which Lévi-Strauss associates with a magical mode of thought.

> The "bricoleur" is adept at performing a large number of diverse tasks; but, unlike the engineer, he does not subordinate each of them to the availability of raw material and tools conceived and procured for the purpose of the project. His universe of instruments is closed and the rules of his game are always to make do with "whatever is at hand," that is to say with the set of tools and materials which is always finite and is also heterogeneous because what it contains bears no relation to the current project, or indeed to any particular project, but is the contingent result of all the occasions there have been to renew or enrich the stock or to maintain it with the remains of previous constructions or destructions.[31]

In focusing on event rather than structure, in using and transforming the available rather than waiting for or creating the specialized, the Aborigine reveals the transforming mode of his perception. He creates a dwelling out of the outback, makes a drinking tool out of a reed, paints on stone with natural materials, designs a dancing costume out of bird feathers and other natural substances, transforms

a balloon into a gift for the white girl. The Walkabout ritual forces
him to be a *bricoleur*—to live off the land.

Like Nathan Bryce, the white girl represents the scientific point of
view that values precise definitions and specialized technology. In
preparation for their journey, she gathers cans of food though she is
forced to open them with a rock; she clings to the portable radio, and
preserves her useless nylon stockings. Disinterested in the Aborigine's knowledge of how to survive off the land, she feels more
secure in the abandoned house, which offers little protection.
Nevertheless, she survives by exploiting the Aborigine, an opera-
tional mode she has learned from her culture.

The white children's reliance on conventional verbal structures
(clichés and aphorisms) frequently leads them to deny the emotional
reality of their experience. As their father tries to kill them, he speaks
in a flat monotone, conjugating the verbs of his desperation:

> It's getting late. *I've* got to go now, can't waste time. *We* have got
> to go now. *I* have got to go now. Can't waste time.

Despite their association with this dreadful experience, these same
phrases are adopted by the girl as she later urges her brother not to
give up.

> We've got to get on. It's late. I'm going now.... It's getting late.
> We've got to go now.

When she is finally faced with the Aborigine's dead body, she turns
her back and resorts to moral platitudes, which co-opt the Walkabout
ritual.

> Did you eat your breakfast properly? You always sit down when
> you eat. You shouldn't wander about.

The man in the mining office, though undoubtedly astonished by the
sudden appearance of these two strange children, can only express
conventional admonishment: "Don't touch anything." Western
culture tries to use well-worn phrases to neutralize and demystify new
experiences. The classroom where the students breathe and grunt in
unison provides the proper training ground. The cultivated voices
on the radio speak in well-modulated tones, no matter whether they
are describing table manners or the end of the world.

Even more than her younger brother's, the girl's perception is
seriously restricted by language. Confusing words with things, she
feels sorry for the poor primitive because he has nothing in his

possession which she can classify as a toy. Her rigid categories prevent her from understanding that in his culture work is integrated with play, art with nature. She is unable to recognize the validity of the Aborigine's painting because it is not done with "proper crayons" and hence does not fit into her definition of "proper art." She does not understand that words are arbitrary signs coded by her culture, but assumes they have indexical meanings that are self-evident. Thus, she greets the Aborigine with: "We're English. Do you understand? This is Australia." But her brother is thirsty. He shouts: "Ask him for water." Still trapped in her ethnocentrism and abstraction, she tries to blame him for her failure: "Water, drink. You must understand, anyone can understand that. Water and drink. I can't make it any simpler." The boy simply opens his mouth and points down his throat, creating a sign language with indexical meanings that are immediately accessible to the Aborigine. Ignoring the cultural barrier, the Aborigine simply speaks when he wants to. In this way, he relies on language as gesture, minimizing the importance of semantic meaning. Later, as if to assert her dominance through the verbal mode, the girl teaches the now subservient Aborigine to pronounce the syllables *wa-ter*—the word that caused her failure in their first encounter. When he meekly repeats the word, she doesn't even look up as she replies arrogantly: "Yes, water." Armed with an imperialist vocabulary, she succeeds in subduing the Aborigine, despite his expanded vision and creative repertoire, entrapping him within the narrow game of Master/Slave.

Self-reflexiveness

As in *The Man Who Fell to Earth,* Roeg alludes to media and myths that imprint the white children with cultural models while using his own film *Walkabout* to reprogram his audience. A radio show featuring "superheroes" leads the white boy to consider his own narrative role in the outback adventure.

> BOY: That's the trouble with all heroes. You always know that superheroes are going to get away. . . . Even Bugs Bunny wins all the time. If we were superheroes, would we definitely win?
> GIRL: Yes.
> BOY: Are we superheroes?
> GIRL: I don't know. I hope so.
> BOY: So do I. We're lost, aren't we?

Like the verbal clichés, this self-reflexive use of prefabricated myths allows the children to process new experience as though it were familiar. Although it may help them survive, it prevents them from being transformed by what is new. Each child stars in his or her own movie and casts the Aborigine in a supporting role. Implicit in the structure of star and supporting player is the power relationship that controls their plots; significantly, Roeg's film gives equal narrative time to the three roles, none of which is filled by a star in the ordinary sense of the term.

In his own movie, the boy plays Robinson Crusoe to the Aborigine's Friday. As a myth of self-realization, Defoe's novel stresses the exploration of capabilities and the development of new skills. Like Crusoe, the white boy values the native as a guide who can teach him much about the strange environment in which he finds himself stranded. He learns to gather fruit and use the boomerang; he develops an adequate sign language, and is well on his way to understanding the Aborigine's speech. The boy assumes that the Aborigine likes him and is willing to serve. Like Crusoe, he exploits him in a friendly way, but never doubts that he, not the Aborigine, is the star in this movie, and will reap the rewards of the grand adventure (he secretly pockets the coins he finds, though they are of no immediate value). In pursuing self-realization, Crusoe makes the wilderness his own, but Friday and his people lose their freedom or their life. As Ian Watt points out:

> The new culture-hero's task is done only when he has taken possession of his colony and stocked it with an adequate labor force. . . . Actually Crusoe exemplifies . . . the process of alienation by which capitalism tends to convert man's relationships with his fellows, and even to his own personality, into commodities to be manipulated.[32]

Similarly, the white children treat the Aborigine as an object which, like the radio and mining equipment, becomes obsolete once its purpose is accomplished.

The girl's view of her situation is shaped by captivity narratives—from popular movies like *King Kong* and pulp magazines where the girl is kidnapped by Indians, to romances like Cooper's *Leatherstocking Tales* and sophisticated urban novels like *Clarissa*. In all these versions, a captive girl fights for survival in a threatening environment where she must rely on the power and morality of a "wild man" Most important, she must protect her virginity. The goal is to get back home intact. Her commitment is to the future, which must be made to conform to the past; this attitude destroys the present. Once the girl's outback experience is safely filed among her memories, she can use it as raw material for fantasies about the future. Unlike her brother, she does not see the Aborigine as a valuable guide, but as a necessary evil—a primitive who threatens to contaminate her both sexually and culturally by obscuring the boundaries between black and white, master and slave, primitive and advanced. Indeed, he does capture her imagination. Her movie requires that he be sacrificed for their survival. As he hangs in a tree, he is associated with Christ's martyrdom, which lies deep in the structure of Western mythology. In contrast, the Aborigine's behavior reflects a vision, not of heroes and scapegoats, but of cooperation and cameraderie—a perception which makes him vulnerable like Newton and marks him as a victim in Roeg's movie as well as the children's.

Culture

Walkabout shares most of the same cultural codes as *The Man Who Fell to Earth* because in both films Roeg is exploring very similar social issues. Science: as the father is about to commit suicide, he reads technical material on geology, suggesting that his scientific training is related to the desperation of his life; the meteorologists play silly courtship games as their technology intrudes on the outback, accelerating the destruction of the primitive culture. Biblical myth: the two deaths stress the Crucifixion rather than the Fall, but the entire situation and setting suggest a failure in Eden. Power: the white girl's master/servant relationship with the Aborigine reveals how Imperialist political relations among nations imprint and co-opt individuals. Sexual coupling and Xenophobia again are closely related: they are developed along cultural, class, racial, and species lines, involving some of our deepest taboos; the single blond meteorologist is a scarce and expensive commodity like the equipment; the white girl is afraid of exogamy; she tries to play out the mother role; her "appropriate" marriage is as empty and cold as the relationship between Mary Lou and Bryce. Water and Alcohol: water is a source of survival and subjugation, and is linked with sexuality in the lagoon scenes, while alcohol helps pervert the father. Clothing: its function is symbolic, suggesting cultural allegiances and power relationships. Gun: the white culture has trouble distinguishing between its symbolic power as a toy penis and its realistic destructive potential; it becomes part of the technology that is destroying the balance of nature. Gifts: they are repeatedly misunderstood and rejected. Clichés: they destroy what is exciting and threatening in new experience; they disguise emotional reality. Horses: in the desert outback, the camels function as the horses did in *Man Who Fell to Earth*, suggesting the beauty and freedom of a lost past and a threatened future. Media: The radio replaces television as a source of imprinting that creates illusions and dehumanizes its listeners. Star myth: the little brother's involvement with comic book superheroes replaces the Howard Hughes, Western hero, and rock star myths as self-inflating and potentially self-destructive role models for males in the white culture. The Icarus myth is replaced by the Robinson Crusoe myth at the archetypal center of the film.

In this chapter, we have used three different approaches to reach parallel conclusions: 1) a structuralist analysis of the four narratives in Roeg's canon; 2) a semiological analysis of the intersecting codes within *The Man Who Fell to Earth*, and 3) a summary of the same codes in *Walkabout*. Although the discussion of *Walkabout* is organized by the codes that control *The Man Who Fell to Earth*, the specific insights were reached through an independent formal analysis. While the first two methods undoubtedly lead to greater thoroughness and form a firmer basis for making generalizations, the formalist summary arrives at essentially the same conclusions. These parallels help to indicate the continuity between the first two methods and what we have done in previous chapters, where the practical criticism is always rooted in a basic formalism along with the particular theoretical framework being used. The analysis of the deep structure of Roeg's auteur myth is analogous to our work on Bergman's canon in Chapter 1 and our tracing of the Romance quest through three films in Chapter 5. Yet, in those chapters we derived the structures from external sources—the depth psychology and dreamwork theories of Freud and Jung, and the generic conventions described by Frye—whereas in this chapter we proceeded inductively, discovering the bundles of meaning and deep structure within the films themselves.

Footnotes to Chapter 6

1. Roland Barthes, "The Structuralist Activity," in *The Structuralists from Marx to Lévi-Strauss*, ed. Richard and Fernande DeGeorge (New York: Doubleday & Co., 1972), p. 153.
2. Barthes, pp. 150-152.
3. These cine-structuralists include Geoffrey Nowell Smith, Peter Wollen, Jim Kitses, Alan Lovell, and Ben Brewster. For a controversial discussion of

their value and status as a group, see Charles Eckert, "The English Cine-Structuralists," *Film Comment* (May-June 1973) and Geoffrey Nowell Smith, "I Was a Star Struck Structuralist," *Screen* (Autumn 1973).

4. Claude Lévi-Strauss, "The Structural Study of Myth," *The Structuralists from Marx to Lévi-Strauss*, p. 177.

5. Lévi-Strauss, *The Raw and the Cooked*, trans. John and Dorreen Weightman (New York: Harper and Row, 1969), p. 15.

6. "The Structural Study of Myth," p. 183.

7. "The Structural Study of Myth," p. 193.

8. "The Structural Study of Myth," pp. 192-193.

9. "The Structural Study of Myth," p. 188.

10. Lévi-Strauss, "How Myths Die," *New Literary History*, V. no. 2 (Winter 1974), pp. 269-281.

11. "How Myths Die," p. 281.

12. Ian Watt, "Robinson Crusoe as Myth," in the *Practice of Criticism*, ed. Zitner, Kissane, and Liberman (Chicago: Scott Foresman & Co., 1966), pp. 109, 114.

13. Lévi-Strauss, *The Savage Mind* (Chicago: University of Chicago Press, 1962), p. 13.

14. Lévi-Strauss, *Totemism*, trans. Rodney Neeham (Boston: Beacon Press, 1963), p. 89.

15. Susan Sontag, "The Anthropologist as Hero," *Against Interpretation and Other Essays* (New York: Dell, 1967), pp. 69-70.

16. *The Raw and the Cooked*, p. 12.

17. Sontag, p. 77.

18. "The Structural Study of Myth," p. 174.

19. Christian Metz, *Film Language: A Semiotics of the Cinema* (New York: Oxford University Press, 1974) pp. 123-146.

20. Metz, *Film Language*, p. 42.

21. Metz, *Essais sur la Signification au Cinema, I* (Paris, 1968), p. 79.

22. This summary is based on Stephen Heath, "The Work of Christian Metz," *Screen* (Autumn, 1973), p. 8.

23. For a further discussion of Peirce's system applied to cinema, see Peter Wollen, *Signs and Meanings in the Cinema* (Bloomington: Indiana University Press, 1969), Ch. 3.

24. Jean Piaget, *Structuralism*, trans. and ed. by Chaminah Maschler (New York: Basic Books, 1970), pp. 118-119.

25. See Chapter 9, "The Ultimate Performance," *Close-up: A Critical Perspective on Film* (New York: Harcourt Brace Jovanovich, 1972) and "Seeing is Believing: *The Exorcist* and *Don't Look Now;*" *Cinema* (No. 34, 1974), pp. 23-33.

26. These are the codes primarily affected by the adapted changes.

27. These symbols indicate the kind of transition between syntagms. In this instance, we move from syntagm 1 to syntagm 2 with a cut.

28. Metz, *Film Language*, p. 125.

29. Lévi-Strauss, *Totemism*, p. 93.

30. Barthes, "An Introduction to the Structual Analysis of Narrative," *New Literary History* (Winter 1975), p. 267.

31. Lévi-Strauss, *The Savage Mind*, p. 17.

32. Watt, "Robinson Crusoe as Myth," p. 118.

WALKABOUT. As the Aborigine and white boy communicate by touching and through iconic and indexical signs of manhood, the white girl watches from the background—cautious, condescending, and excluded. Courtesy of 20th Century Fox.

WALKABOUT. The silhouette of the Aborigine standing on one leg powerfully demonstrates his balance and harmony with the outback landscape.

Courtesy of 20th Century Fox.

WALKABOUT. His body decorated with paint and feathers, the Aborigine dances round the house peering at the white girl and making sexual gestures. Extremely sensitive to her emotional response, he reflects her fear in his own facial expression and it ultimately destroys him. Courtesy of 20th Century Fox.

THE MAN WHO FELL TO EARTH. The Alien's first human encounter takes place in a small pawnshop cluttered with objects where he sells a gold ring to a woman, whose jewelry reveals she lives off the Indians. Courtesy of Cinema 5.

THE MAN WHO FELL TO EARTH. At the moment of peak fusion between Mary Lou and the Alien, they stare directly into the camera in a huge close-up, which reveals that, though their features are quite different, they look astonishingly alike. Courtesy of Cinema 5.

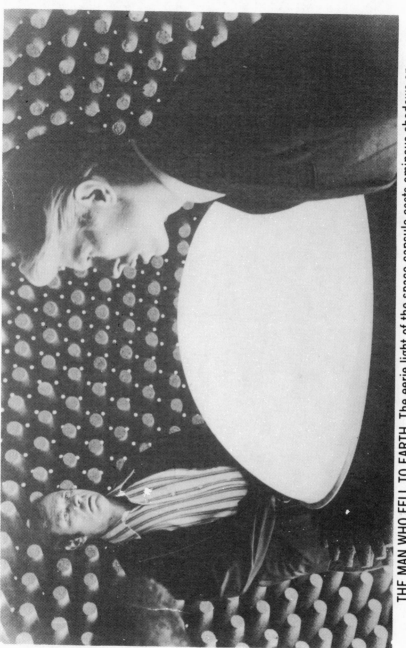

THE MAN WHO FELL TO EARTH. The eerie light of the space capsule casts ominous shadows on the future and faces of the Alien and the Western scientist as they size each other up. Can this vehicle that looks suspiciously like the inside of an egg carton really take the Alien back to his home planet? Courtesy of Cinema 5.

THE MAN WHO FELL TO EARTH. In a vicious mockery of space flight, Newton spins in front of planet photos as doctors perform experiments that ultimately render him earth bound.

Courtesy of Cinema 5.

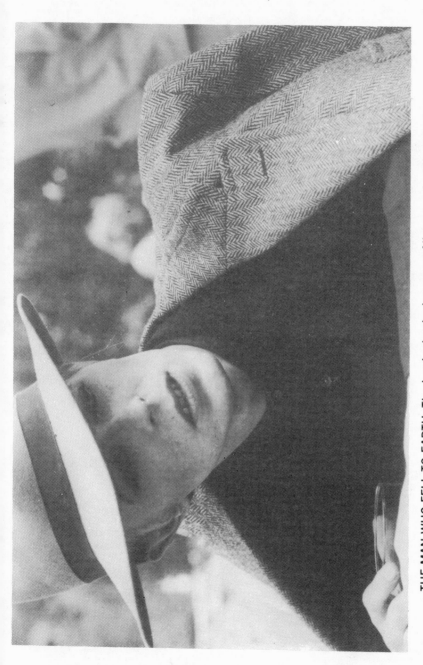

THE MAN WHO FELL TO EARTH. The hard-edged, glamorous Alien as a decadent rock star (Ziggy Stardust?) has clearly had enough! Courtesy of Cinema 5.

INDEX

ABOUT THE AUTHORS

BEVERLE HOUSTON is Professor of English and Film at Pitzer College, Claremont, California, member of the Editorial Executive Committee of Quarterly Review of Film Studies, editor of an issue of QRFS on Feminist and Ideological Criticism, and frequent contributor to film journals.

MARSHA KINDER is Professor of Literature and Film at Occidental College, Los Angeles, California, co-editor of Dreamworks: An Interdisciplinary Quarterly, Editorial Board member and frequent contributor to Film Quarterly and Quarterly Review of Film Studies, editor of an issue of QRFS on the application of semiology and structuralism to practical film criticism.

Co-authors of Close-Up: A Critical Perspective on Film (1972).